£14·95

D0948656

# DIRECTORY OF INTERNATIONAL TERRORISM

mgen
14 R.

# THE
# DIRECTORY OF INTERNATIONAL TERRORISM

GEORGE ROSIE

ADDITIONAL RESEARCH BY PAUL ROSIE

Université d'Ottawa
BIBLIOTHÈQUES
LIBRARIES
University of Ottawa

### MAINSTREAM
### PUBLISHING

8700001038

Copyright © George Rosie, 1986

All rights reserved

First published 1986 by

MAINSTREAM PUBLISHING COMPANY (EDINBURGH) LTD.
7 Albany Street
Edinburgh EH1 3UG

HV
6431
.R67
1986

ISBN 1 85158 021 2

No part of this book may be reproduced, stored in a retrieval system, or transmitted, in any form, or by any means, electronic, mechanical, photocopying, recording or otherwise, without the prior permission of the publishers.

Typeset in 10pt Century Schoolbook by
Pennart Typesetting (Edinburgh) Ltd

Printed by Billing & Son Ltd.

# CONTENTS

DIRECTORY OF INTERNATIONAL TERRORISM

# AUTHOR'S PREFACE

Terrorism is a complex, multi-faceted, and often baffling subject. The organisations involved have a way of emerging, splintering, disappearing and then reappearing which makes it very difficult for the average reader to follow. Individuals come and go, are jailed, die, go underground, or apparently vanish. Counter-terror bureaucracies are formed then reformed, names are changed, and leaders are shuffled around as they are promoted, demoted, forced to resign, or put out to pasture. Incidents proliferate across the world, some of which can trigger off a chain of events which will destabilise a whole region and bring nations to the edge of ruin. At the same time major terrorist actions can shock for a short while, and then be quickly forgotten (except by those affected by the inevitable tragedy). Treatises are written, theories propounded, grievances aired, tactics discussed, occasionally to some effect, usually not. Causes are picked up by the world's media, examined, probed, and then all too often overlooked, until the next bomb explodes, or the next airliner is hijacked.

Finding a way through this labyrinthine political/military phenomenon was difficult. Which is why I have adopted the classic dictionary format of separate entries cross-referenced to one another. It seemed a good way of disentangling the threads in an attempt to understand what was going on. It is, I hope, a useful device, but in this context one with some limitations. Information about many of the individuals involved is often sketchy and hard to come by. Which is why many apparently simple biographical details such as dates of birth, death, home background or education are missing. Even global figures like Yasir Arafat of the Palestine Liberation Organisation (PLO) trail with them a past which still appears open to interpretation. In Arafat's case none of the written sources seem to be entirely sure where (or when) he was born. Similarly the precise date when many of the groups were formed seems to be known only to their members (or possibly the intelligence services which try to keep tabs on them).

I am also painfully aware that many of the incidents, individuals, and organisations which I have circumscribed within a few paragraphs are worthy of an entire book. Many, of course, have been written about at length; the hijackings to Mogadishu and

Entebbe, for example, have been the subject of full-length books, as have the Iranian Embassy siege in London, the American hostage crisis in Iran, the Israeli raid on the Tammuz nuclear reactors in Iraq and the bombing of the Greenpeace ship *Rainbow Warrior.* But other important incidents such as the hijackings to Dawson's Field, Jordan, in 1970, and the attack on the Munich Olympic Games in 1972 have been relatively under-documented, although the general literature on modern terrorism is huge, and is growing all the time.

But much remains to be written. For example, there is not, to the best of my knowledge, a good, popular study of the political and diplomatic impact of terrorism. The way that relatively minor terrorist incidents (such as the bombing of the *La Belle* disco in West Berlin in April 1986) can reverberate around the world, jeopardise alliances and set nation states at one another's throats, is one of the most significant characteristics of the terrorist phenomenon. The role of female terrorists like Ulrike Meinhof and Gudrun Ensslin of the West German Rote Armee Fraktion, Maria Price of the Provisional IRA, and Sophia Petrovskaya of the 19th century Narodnaya Volya is a subject that would bear scrutiny.

Most pressing of all, perhaps, is the need for a careful study of what has been called the "symbiotic relationship" between transnational terrorism and the international media. Many governments (and particularly those of the United States and the United Kingdom) have accused the international press and television of playing into the hands of the terrorists by laying on minute-by-minute, and sometimes live, coverage of terrorist hijackings, hostage taking etc., or by giving air-time and column inches to interviews with terrorist organisers. The media argue that to suppress and censor dramatically important news is a greater threat to Western democracy than terrorism itself.

This book has been compiled exclusively from published sources, mainly newspaper accounts, academic analyses, conference reports, and the many (and varied) books on the subject. In the course of studying the literature on terrorism and counter-terrorism I have often been disturbed, and occasionally appalled, by the *Boy's Own Paper* tone of some accounts of events which are almost always fraught with misery and human suffering. This note I have been at pains to avoid, usually at the expense of detail which could be considered salacious. At the other end of the scale, some of the academic studies in terrorism are so abstruse that they seem to represent a total failure of imagination and empathy. I have tried to steer a way between the two, and in order to avoid producing a mere catalogue of lurid events have endeavoured to select entries which have some kind of wider political or social resonance. The information on weaponry is from sources freely available on the shelves of almost any high-street bookshop.

Given that almost every country on earth has been involved, one way or another, with international terrorism I have adopted an "international" approach. Cash amounts, for example, are given in US dollars, the nearest thing we have to an international currency. Times stated are all local times, and the 24-hour clock has been used. With a few exceptions (such as the Palestine Liberation Organisation) I have used the language of origin for entries, so that the Italian Red Brigades are entered as Brigate Rosse, the West German Red Army Faction is entered as Rote Armee Fraktion, and the French group Direct Action as Action Directe.

Tragically, this book is almost certain to be out of date by the time it is printed. The underlying conflicts and grievances which manifest themselves in political terrorism are so widespread and endemic, that several major incidents are likely to have occurred before this study is published. There are already indications that the French government's new campaign against left-wing terrorism is floundering, and may have succeeded only in provoking the Action Directe into more resourceful bombing activities.

(On the other hand the distinctly chilly relations between France and New Zealand following the bombing of the Greenpeace ship *Rainbow Warrior* in Auckland Harbour appear to have been improved after the intervention of the United Nations; the two French agents convicted of the bombing are to spend the remainder of their sentences in jail in the French Pacific, while France is to formally apologise to New Zealand and offer reparations worth $7 million.)

But there are not many bright spots. What has struck me forcibly in the time it has taken to compile this book is the extent to which terrorism is a weathervane of the political winds which are blowing across the world. The terrorism of the Tamils, for example, is rapidly developing into almost open war with the government of Sri Lanka (which is dominated by Sinhalese) and there is a powerful Tamil lobby within India which would use the crisis as a reason to invade Sri Lanka. The tragedy that began with the storming of the Golden Temple of Amritsar by the Indian Army is now threatening to tear one of the most prosperous parts of India out of the Indian Union.

And the increasingly effective terrorism of Umkonto We Sizwe (the military arm of the African National Congress) in the black townships of South Africa is slackening the white regime's grip on the black communities, and the consequences are likely to be devastating. Umkonto have now taken their bombs and Kalashnikov AK-47 rifles into the city centres of Johannesburg, Durban and Pretoria, while white civilians have been arming themselves to defend their affluent suburbs. The South African regime's response to the growing terrorism of Umkonto (and other groups) has been to step up state repression which in turn has increased South Africa's international isolation, and brought fierce cries for more and stricter economic and diplomatic sanctions.

In Europe the Provisional IRA continues to plague the British and Irish governments while the Anglo-Irish agreement giving the Irish republic a modest say in the running of Northern Ireland has already antagonised the Protestant working class, and threatens to provoke a new round of "loyalist" terrorism from a newly revived group like the Ulster Volunteer Force, or the Ulster Freedom Fighters, or the Red Hand Commandos. Already the Protestants have been carrying out a campaign of low-key terrorism (mainly house burnings) against the predominantly Protestant Royal Ulster Constabulary. It is an attempt to render Ulster ungovernable, and as such bears a chilling resemblance to the terror tactics of Umkonto We Sizwe in the African townships of South Africa.

France is facing a resurgence of terrorism by the Corsican nationalists (who recently killed two people in a holiday camp bombing) and the left-wing Action Directe have made it clear that they are far from finished. In Spain there is little sign that the new democratically-elected government's policies are undermining ETA, who continue with their campaign of assassination against the Spanish military, and their bombings against Spain's economically vital tourist hotels and beaches.

The government of Peru are growing increasingly concerned about the strength and effectiveness of the Sendero Luminoso (Shining Path), the country's Maoist guerrillas, and in Colombia the left-wing activists of the M-19 are still a force to be reckoned with. In the United States the authorities are beginning to confront an odd species of right-wing terrorism from groups like The Order, the Posse Comitatus, the Armies of the Living God, and from a revival of the Ku-Klux Klan. Ironically, some of these (mainly white supremacist) groups have been forging links with the Nation of Islam, the black Muslims of the United States whose leader Louis Farrakhand appears to share their distaste for Jews and liberals.

And while improved airport security appears to have reduced the incidence of aircraft hijackings, and made international air transport safer than it was some years ago, there is growing unease about the security of shipping and seaports. A recent report by the International Chambers of Commerce and the International Maritime Bureau (entitled *Violence at Sea*) calls for the security of ships and shipping to be brought into line with that which surrounds the business of air travel.

But it is the Middle East, with its tangle of Muslim, Socialist, Zionist and Phalangist loyalties, which remains the world's most dangerous flash point. And at the centre of the tangle lies the problem of the Palestinian people, most of whom are still steeped in poverty and misery almost 40 years after they fled from their homes in what was then Palestine.

While the terrorist attacks on the airports at Rome and Vienna in December 1985 were appalling for the damage they did to innocent lives, the fact is they were perpetrated by young men whose future was so bleak that they accepted a suicide mission from Abu Nidal rather than go on living in Sabra and Shatila. If the injustice and misery of the Palestinian refugee camps can produce such nihilism and despair, there will be no shortage of recruits for the terrorist organisers, and the Middle East will continue to be racked by terrorist rage. Which, in a region inhabited by client states of the Superpowers, bodes ill for the future.

The lesson that seeps out of the world's danger points seems obvious to the point of banality; without justice there can be no lasting peace.

*George Rosie.*
July 1986, Edinburgh.

# INTRODUCTION

At around 23.00 on Thursday June 3rd 1982, Shlomo Argov, Israel's 52-year-old ambassador in London, left a diplomatic reception at the Dorchester Hotel in Park Lane. As he was about to step into his car a young Arab gunman walked up to him, shot him in the head at point-blank range and then fled. While Argov lay bleeding on the street, armed police officers from the Diplomatic Protection Squad chased his attacker into nearby South Street where the Arab gunman was shot and captured. Two other Arabs in a getaway car fled from the scene but were quickly picked up by police in the Brixton area of South London. Both Ambassador Argov and his Arab assailant were taken to Westminster hospital suffering from serious gunshot wounds to the head. Both men were gravely injured but both recovered.

Although the attack on Argov was immediately denounced by Yasir Arafat's Palestine Liberation Organisation (PLO) as being "detrimental" to the Palestinian cause, the Israeli government put it down to "Arab terrorists" and within hours Israeli jets raided Palestinian camps in and around Beirut killing at least 50 people and injuring more than 200. Two days later, on June 6th 1982, the Israeli military launched operation "Peace for Galilee", the full-scale invasion of the Lebanon which destabilised that country, drove the PLO into exile in Syria, Tunisia and Iraq, led to the killing of Lebanon's president-elect and to the appalling massacres at Sabra and Shatila and the slaughter of more than 300 American and French marines and soldiers in the suicide bomb attacks in Beirut. The invasion also provoked a political/military crisis within Israel itself.

Whether or not the attack on Shlomo Argov was the genuine cause for the invasion of Lebanon or merely a pretext, it was the spark which caused the Israeli Defence Forces (IDF) to crash across the border to root out the PLO and in the process lay waste to much of Lebanon (and fuel the hatreds of the hitherto quiescent Shi'ite Muslims). Ironically, Argov himself had only bitter words for the invasion. "Only the charlatans can say that the war was worthwhile," he told the *Jewish Chronicle* in July 1983. "Those who initiated the war and led the nation towards it should have thought twice about the cost, especially the cost in human life . . ."

And to compound the irony, on June 8th 1982, two days after the Israeli tanks rolled over the Lebanese border, responsibility for the assassination attempt on Argov was claimed by "Black June", one of the organisations run by Abu Nidal, the sworn enemy of Yasir Arafat and a man who had been sentenced to death by the PLO. One of the three Arabs arrested and jailed in London (for 30 years) was Marwan al-Banna, a 21-year-old nephew of Abu Nidal, who Nidal's men have since tried to release by attacking British diplomats, holidaymakers, and airline offices in, among other places, Greece and India.

The downward spiral of terror and counter-terror precipitated by the attack on Shlomo Argov is one example of how a single act of political terrorism can ramify in many directions unsettling the international order. Similarly, the assassination of Indian Prime Minister Indira Gandhi in October 1984 by two Sikhs of her own bodyguard prompted a wave of anti-Sikh violence throughout India that cost thousands of innocent lives, fuelled the clamour for a separate Sikh homeland of Khalistan and created a political/religious crisis with which the Indian government are still struggling to cope. And Sikh extremists took a terrible revenge in June 1985 when they planted a bomb on an Air-India Boeing 747 which exploded over the Atlantic killing all 329 passengers and crew and causing one of the worst mid-air disasters in aviation history.

It is interesting to compare the calamitous effects of the attack on Shlomo Argov and the assassination of Indira Gandhi with the killing of a much more important world figure, John F. Kennedy, President of the United States. Although Kennedy's murder in Dallas in November 1963 shocked and saddened the American people, power was quickly and smoothly transferred to Vice-President Lyndon B. Johnson. There was no intercommunal strife, no breakdown of law and order, no reprisals on terrified "suspects". Similarly the assassination of Swedish Prime Minister Olof Palme in Stockholm in March 1986 was easily absorbed by Sweden's sophisticated social democracy, with no backlash against the many groups of political exiles which find shelter in Sweden. In a stable polity, acts of terrorism may cause great grief and shock but they usually fail to cause lasting damage.

But the ability of terrorism to ignite a combustible political admixture is one of its most chilling aspects. The assassination of the Austrian Archduke Francis Ferdinand in Sarajevo in 1914 by a little-known Croatian group called "The Black Hand" sent Europe (and the Middle East) lurching towards World War

14

I, a conflagration in which millions were killed and empires were destroyed. Not all acts of terrorism have such grievous effects, but enough of them do to make political terrorism one of the main items on the international agenda, and a problem which more and more governments are being forced to confront.

Transnational terrorism may not subvert stable democracies like Sweden, France, Britain, West Germany, or the USA, but it can make life measurably more unpleasant. Anyone who takes an aeroplane almost anywhere in Europe is made painfully aware of the security measures which hijackers and terrorists have foisted upon the world; baggage screening, x-rays, body searches, metal detecting alarms etc. Most airport employees are now being "vetted" for their political suitability to work as cleaners, porters, cooks, baggage handlers and truck drivers. Huge sums of taxpayers money are spent employing security consultants and security staff, while some British airports (including Heathrow and Manchester) are patrolled by police marksmen carrying Heckler & Koch MP5 submachine-guns.

The lethal schemes of international terrorists have forced the Western world (and probably the Eastern bloc too) to set up a network of anti-terrorist military élites which can be called upon when the terrorists strike; the British Special Air Service (SAS), the American Delta Force, the West German GSG-9, the Dutch Royal Marines, the French GIGN, the Israeli Sayaret Matkal, the Egyptian Sa'aqa, and a number of others. Most of these groups are small, but they are carefully trained, elaborately equipped, and tend to be expensive to maintain. Most have proved effective in a crisis, but military strategists point out that even the best of them can only react to given situations. The initiative is almost always with the terrorist (except in the case of the Israeli Sayaret Matkal which has a record of launching pre-emptive strikes against terrorist groups).

More importantly, perhaps, the self-defensive measures which terrorism imposes on states have a way of eroding civil liberties by giving the police and security services extraordinary powers. Britain's Prevention of Terrorism Act (which was rushed through Parliament in the aftermath of two horrific bombings in Birmingham, England) is a continuing source of concern to British civil libertarians. But so long as the Provisional IRA (PIRA), the Irish National Liberation Army (INLA), the Ulster Volunteer Force (UVF) and all the others continue to fight their battles in the streets of Britain, the British Parliament are likely to go on rubber-stamping the Prevention of Terrorism Act once a year, giving the British police their formidable powers of search and arrest, detention without trial, deportation and internal exile.

Following a wave of bombings in Paris at the beginning of 1986 one of the first acts of the new right-wing government of Jacques Chirac was to announce measures to stiffen France's anti-terrorist laws. Chirac wants to create a "new crime of terrorism", set up special terrorist courts (similar to the jury-less "Diplock" courts of Northern Ireland) and introduce a 30-year prison sentence without remission for terrorist crimes. Chirac also announced plans to establish a "national security council" to co-ordinate the various police and security services trying to combat terrorism. In West Germany the activities of left-wing terror groups like the Rote Armee Fraktion (RAF) prompted the Federal Government to enact a package of laws which has been described as " . . . the most repressive anti-terrorist legislation in existence in a liberal democracy".(1)

In his study of political terrorism the Australian criminologist Grant Wardlaw argues that "The perception of terrorism as a threat to contemporary liberal democracies has already had significant effects on those societies." He says huge amounts of men and resources have been "diverted into internal security functions" and in some states (notably West Germany but also the United Kingdom) laws have been passed which are a real threat to individual freedom. Wardlaw goes on to warn that these changes must be carefully monitored or repressiveness will grow. To avoid that happening, he concludes, Western societies should understand the extent and nature of terrorism ". . . so that they can respond at the minimum effective level with maximum effect". (2)

One way or another the activities of the world's highly mobile terrorist groups touch almost everyone. They may never see a shot fired or hear a bomb go off, but every time they pay a tax bill they are helping to pay for the burgeoning security apparatus (internal and external) which is needed to sustain their government's anti-terrorist measures.

## DEFINITIONS OF TERRORISM

Although modern terrorism has been confronting Europe and America for at least 100 years, a satisfactory definition of terrorism is surprisingly hard to come by. While the British Prevention of Terrorism Act (1976) defines terrorism as the ". . . use of violence for political ends . . ." including ". . . use of violence for the purpose of putting the public or any section of the public in fear . . ." the philosopher Roger Scruton has pointed out that this confuses two distinctly separate ideas, "the use of violence for political ends, and the use of violence in order to put the public in fear". (3) Walter Laqueur of the Centre of Strategic and International Studies in Washington (and a world authority on terrorism) agrees that a "comprehensive" definition of terrorism does not exist "nor will it be found in the foreseeable future . . .". (4) In his study Grant Wardlaw describes this failure to define what is and what is not terrorism as "one of the root causes of both the vacillations in policy which characterise the responses of most individual states to terrorism and of the complete failure of the international community to launch any effective multi-lateral initiatives to combat the problem". (5)

A more recent definition of terrorism comes from Benjamin Netanyahu, Israel's Ambassador to the United Nations (whose brother Jonathan was killed during the Entebbe raid). "Terrorism is the deliberate and systematic murder, maiming and menacing of the innocent to inspire fear for political ends," Netanyahu writes. Like Walter Laqueur he rejects the idea that terrorists are guerrilla fighters whom he describes as "irregular soldiers who wage war on regular military forces". (6) Netanyahu's distinction is interesting, but it ignores the fact that many modern terrorists do both; the Provisional Irish Republican Army (PIRA), for example, regularly attacks the British Army and the Royal Ulster Constabulary (RUC), but PIRA men have also bombed pubs, clubs, shops and buses killing many innocent civilians. The Tamil Tigers of Sri Lanka attack government military convoys with regularity, but do not blanch at killing innocent Sinhalese villagers. Conversely, Fatah, the military arm of the Palestine Liberation Organisation (PLO) mainly confines itself to raids on the Israeli military but its members are inevitably condemned by Netanyahu's own government as "terrorists".

While Netanyahu firmly rejects the now famous idea that "one man's terrorist is another man's freedom fighter" the conundrum is vividly illustrated in Nicaragua where the American government have been enthusiastically supporting the right-wing "Contras" who have been attacking the Sandinista government since the overthrow of Somoza in 1979. To the Sandinistas the Contras are a brutal remnant of Somoza's National Guard who have been killing, raping and terrorising innocent villagers near the border with Honduras; to President Reagan and his administration the Contras are heroic "freedom fighters", the moral equivalent of the 18th-century Americans who shook off the British yoke.

This confusion over who is and who is not a terrorist has persistently plagued efforts by the international community to grapple with the problem. The Soviet and Third World blocs in the United Nations have insisted that, in the final analysis, people who regard themselves as oppressed and/or exploited have the right to resort to insurgency and terror. When the UN were drafting an international convention on hostage-taking in 1977 the Tanzanian delegation insisted on an amendment that the UN should recognise the "... inalienable right of freedom fighters to take up arms to fight their oppressors ..." and that people held "... in perpetual bondage ... could not be stopped from taking their oppressors hostage, if that became inevitable". The fact is, most of the states on the world stage (and particularly the USSR and the USA) seem to regard the insurgent groups with whom they agree as fighters for a just cause, and the others as "terrorists".

Among the many definitions of terrorism being put forward, probably the most comprehensive, if long-winded, comes from Grant Wardlaw who regards terrorism as the threat or use " ... of violence by an individual or a group, whether acting for or in opposition to established authority, when such action is designed to create extreme anxiety and/or fear-inducing effects in a target group larger than the immediate victims with the purpose of coercing that group into acceding to the political demands of the perpetrators".(7) Wardlaw goes on to point out that no matter how repugnant terrorists and their actions may be to civilised people, they should not be written off as acts of witless violence. "Terrorism is not mindless," he warns. "It is a deliberate means to an end. Terrorism has objectives ... ". (8) Walter Laqueur says that once terrorism was " ... the strategy of the poor and the weak used against ruthless tyrants; today its more prominent representatives are no longer poor, and modern technology is giving them powerful weapons. Some present day terrorist groups have quite clearly acquired the characteristics once attributed to tyranny ...".(9)

## THE HISTORY OF MODERN TERRORISM

However much difficulty the academics and lawyers have in defining terrorism there is a general agreement that political terrorism (even transnational political terrorism) is far from being a new phenomenon. In its modern form political terrorism dates back to the latter half of the 19th century. In Walter Laqueur's view probably the most influential terrorist movement of the last 120 years was the "Narodnaya Volya" of Tsarist Russia, a group of mainly upper-class left-wing revolutionaries who saw themselves as tyrannicides rather than regicides, and managed to assassinate Tsar Alexander II in 1881. According to one of the Narodnaya Volya leaders, Emma Goldman, the movement was driven by an "ardent love of others" and historians say the group's morals impressed even their enemies. When President Garfield of the United States was assassinated in 1881 the Russian group published a pamphlet condemning the murder as totally unjustifiable in a democracy such as the USA. After the Narodnaya Volya were virtually wiped out by the Tsarist police in the 1880s, they were succeeded by the Social Revolutionary Party who waged a ferocious campaign of assassination between 1902 and 1910 killing two of the Tsar's interior ministers, a minister of education, provincial governors and the Grand Duke Serge Alexandrovich plus dozens of lesser Russian functionaries and dignitaries.

In the 1890s France and Italy were racked by terrorist attacks by anarchists taking advantage of the spread of mass communications to act out the "propaganda of the deed". At roughly the same time Irish nationalists were trying to bomb the British government into granting independence for Ireland. The British responded by setting up the Special Irish Branch (now the Special Branch) of the Metropolitan Police. While Macedonian, Armenian and Croatian nationalists were attacking the decaying Ottoman Empire (and provoking fearful reprisals) in the United States a species of "blue-collar" terrorism grew up with the Molly Maguires and the Western Union of Mineworkers.

And while the prevailing impression of Indian resistance to British rule is of Gandhian non-violence, in fact British India had been plagued by anti-British terrorism since the 1870s, particularly in Bengal. In 1872 Lord Mayo was assassinated in the Andaman Islands in the Bay of Bengal, in 1897 the Chapekar brothers were executed for killing the British Plague Commissioner in Poona, and in 1906 Bengali Hindus began a campaign of anti-British terror which lasted well into the 1930s (and which found echoes among the Bengali Naxalites of the 1960s and 1970s). The Bengalis were involved in an early terrorist international; in 1905 the Hindu terrorist/intellectual Hem Chandra Das travelled to Paris to learn the arts of bomb-making at a "terrorist salon" run by a Madame Cama, a native of Bombay who had forged links with the European anarchist and socialist groups. Like the Middle Eastern terrorists of the 1980s, the Bengali terrorists of the 1900s preyed upon transport systems (in their case Indian railways) and showed lethal ingenuity in their use of explosives (such as the harmless-looking "coconut bomb" which killed many people).

As early as 1913 the British regime was so worried about Bengali terrorism that one of their senior administrators – R. H. Craddock

– carried out a study of the phenomenon which he ascribed to the explosive growth in the number of over-educated but unemployable youths, and the "excessive influence" of the legal profession, plus a burgeoning "native" press which never failed to badger the British authorities about grievances. Craddock also noted the growth of "neo-Hinduism" and a taste among Bengalis for a largely mythical nationalist/religious popular literature. The result, Craddock concluded, was an explosive mixture which could destabilise Bengal in the years to come (a conclusion which was proved correct by subsequent events).

Similarly, Sikh nationalism and factionalism spilled out into the huge Sikh diaspora during World War I; in 1915 a Sikh militant called Sawath Singh shot dead an American detective in a San Francisco courtroom during the trial of two Sikh militants. The year before that the Canadian government had become so disturbed by Sikh violence that it banned all Sikh immigration. In the period before World War I terrorist groups were active in Poland as well as Tsarist Russia. It was an act of political terrorism by the Croatian "Black Hand" which killed Archduke Francis Ferdinand in Sarajevo in June 1914. The Austrian government refused to believe that the murder had not been instigated by the Serbian government, and issued harsh ultimata which dragged in Serbia's ally Russia and Austria's ally Germany and eventually led to a conflagration which killed millions.

And while the years between World War I and World War II were dominated by the rise of the mass political movements like Communism and Fascism (at least in Europe) political terrorism continued to plague the world. When the Irish terror campaign against the British finally succeeded in 1921, the fledgling Free State was faced by bitter terrorist attacks from the irregulars of the IRA which forced them to take savage counter-measures (including the execution of former comrades-in-arms like Erskine Childers). There were a number of terrorist groups on the fringes of the burgeoning Fascist movements. All through the 1930s the Macedonian IMRO and the Croatian Ustasha waged a nasty little war in the Balkans and late in the decade the IRA began once again bombing the cities and towns on the British mainland in an attempt to "unify" the North and South of Ireland.

It was the assassination of King Alexander of Yugoslavia and the French Foreign Minister, Louis Barthou, in Marseilles in October 1934 that prompted the League of Nations (forerunner of the United Nations) to pass two measures to combat international terrorism. They were the 1937 Convention for the Prevention and

Punishment of Terrorism and the Convention for the Creation of an International Criminal Court. Unfortunately very few nations ever ratified the conventions and the League came to the conclusion that "The rules of international law concerning the repression of terrorist activity are not at present sufficiently precise to guarantee efficient international cooperation on this matter" (a situation which more or less still obtains).

To the German armies occupying most of Europe in World War II the activities of partisans, resistance fighters and guerrillas were, of course, pure terrorism. And in the 1940s and 1950s insurgency and terrorism succeeded in driving the British, French, and Dutch out of their Asian and African colonial empires (although for the most part these were rural rather than urban campaigns, and generally confined to the territories whose independence and/or political transformation was being fought for). But the British in Cyprus, Aden, Kenya and Malaya and the French in Vietnam and Algeria regarded the activities of the various nationalist bombers and gunmen with the same loathing that modern Israel regards the attacks of Fatah or the Popular Front for the Liberation of Palestine.

Most historians of modern terrorism date the current cycle of terrorism back to the early 1960s when the MIR urban guerrillas of Venezuela launched a short and unsuccessful campaign against the democratically elected government of Ramon Betancourt. Similar Latin American terrorist groups sprouted in Uruguay, Brazil, Argentina, Peru, Colombia and Bolivia. They were joined on the world stage in the late 1960s by the Palestinian groups (following the Arab debacle in the Six-Day War) and by the resurgent IRA, and separatist/nationalist movements like the Canadian FLQ and the Basque ETA.

The political failure of the New Left in Europe, America and Japan produced left-wing terrorists like the Rote Armee Fraktion (RAF), the Japanese Red Army, Action Directe, the Brigate Rosse, and minor groups like the Angry Brigade in Britain and the Weather Underground in the USA. Right-wing neo-fascist groups made their appearance all over Europe from Italy and Spain, to Turkey and the Netherlands. By the late 1970s it seemed that every democracy on earth was besieged by a plague of terrorist organisations of every political persuasion, all baying for its downfall.

Since then new mixtures have been added to the cauldron, notably the Sikh extremists of the Indian Punjab, the Tamil groups of Sri Lanka, Kashmiris, Burmese and the Islamic zealots of Iran and Lebanon. And in South Africa the African National Congress (ANC) have abandoned their policy of sabotaging only industrial and military installations, and have taken to planting bombs in the streets and suburbs of Johannesburg, Durban and Pretoria, and running a particularly cruel campaign against black policemen in the African townships like Soweto.

## CATEGORIES OF TERRORISM

Although terrorist groups represent a large and often bewildering variety of causes, both well known and obscure, one commentator (T. P. Thornton) suggests there are two large categories of terrorism within which most terrorist acts can be slotted; enforcement terror and agitational terror. (10) The first is used by those in power to sustain their authority, the second is the terror used by those wishing to usurp that authority. A similar distinction is put forward by W. F. May who categorises terror into the "regime of terror" (i.e. incumbent terror) and the "siege of terror" (i.e. insurgent terror).(11) Grant Wardlaw finds it puzzling (and by inference reprehensible) that the world's academic community tend to study insurgent terror while totally ignoring the often appalling terrorism wrought by the world's more unsavoury states.

Paul Wilkinson of Aberdeen University in Scotland refines this slightly into three main categories; revolutionary terrorism, sub-revolutionary terrorism, and repressive terrorism. Revolutionary terrorism he sees as terror to overthrow a state while repressive terrorism is the terror used by the state to defend (or sustain) itself. Sub-revolutionary terrorism, Wilkinson argues, is terror deployed to achieve limited goals like forcing a change in government policy, or reacting to government policy or "punishing" repressive or hostile individuals. (12)

Revolutionary and sub-revolutionary terrorism seems to divide itself into four main categories;

1: Nationalist/separatist groups like the Provisional and Official IRA, the Basque ETA, the French-Canadian FLQ, the Tamil groups and the Sikh extremists all of whom have fought to wrest an independent homeland from a larger power. The Palestine Liberation Organisation (PLO) and its many splinter groups and offshoots also fall into this category. Many of these groups (such as the Sikhs, the Palestinians and to some extent the Provisional IRA) have a religious or sectarian overlay, but the main thrust of their campaign is nationalist/separatist. They may, however, have very different ideas of what kind of country they wish to inherit;

the Provisional IRA, for example, appears to be seeking a fairly conventional form of united Ireland, while the Official IRA, and the Irish National Liberation Army want some kind of socialist republic.

2: "Revolutionary" left-wing groups who are fighting to overthrow a society they see as unjust and repressive. The various Latin-American groups of the 1960s and 1970s such as the Uruguayan Tupamaros, the Argentine Montoneros, and the Maoist Sendero Luminoso of Peru all fall into this category. In Latin America, where the hold of democracy is very tenuous, these terrorist organisations have tended to be self-defeating. The Tupamaros' campaigns of the early 1970s succeeded only in subverting the democracy of Uruguay and replacing it with a repressive right-wing regime. The activities of the Monotoneros and the ELP in the Argentine created the military coup and the "dirty war" which followed. The communist-led New People's Army (NPA) now confronting the new government of Cory Aquino in the Philippines falls into this category.

The various West European terrorist organisations which grew out of the New Left in the late 1960s, such as the Rote Armee Fraktion (Germany), Action Directe (France) and the Brigate Rosse (Italy) are revolutionary left-wing groups struggling against what they see as the materialism and repression of Western society. Some of these groups – particularly the Rote Armee Fraktion – have occasionally made common cause with left-wing Palestinian organisations such as the Popular Front for the Liberation of Palestine (PFLP). A sub-category is formed by the radical/revolutionary Islamic groups of the Middle East who are trying to replace the established religious order in Muslim countries with a more extreme version of Islam. The Beirut-based Islamic Jihad are waging a holy war to set up an Iranian-style theocracy in Lebanon, as well as the overthrow of the State of Israel.

3: Right-wing, reactionary terrorist groups who are acting either in defence of an established order, or reacting to the success of revolutionary groups. This is sometimes known as "Black Terrorism". Spain, Italy, Turkey and Latin America have produced a number of these organisations; the Turkish Grey Wolves fall into this category, as do the Japanese Shield Society, and the Italian Avanguardia Nazionale (who perpetrated Europe's worst-ever terrorist incident when they bombed the railway station at Bologna in 1980). The American Ku-Klux Klan also belong to this group. Although the various Ulster "Loyalist" groups like the Ulster Volunteer Force or the Ulster Freedom Fighters cannot be regarded as "fascist" in the European sense of the word, they are defending the British status quo which the Republicans are struggling to overthrow.

4: Individual terrorists, usually assassins, some of whom later claim to have been acting on behalf of a cause and in concert with other people (although this is hardly ever proved). Normally they turn out to be deranged individuals with odd obsessions some of which are pseudo-political. Mehmet Ali Agca, the young Turk who tried to assassinate Pope John Paul II in Rome in 1981, did have connections with the Grey Wolves, but during his interrogation and trial claimed to be the living embodiment of Jesus Christ. Lee Harvey Oswald who (apparently) shot President Kennedy in 1963 was an erratic supporter of left-wing causes who had defected to Russia and then returned. Sirhan Sirhan the young Arab who killed Senator Robert Kennedy in 1968 was upset by Kennedy's apparent hostility to the Arab cause. James Earl Ray who assassinated Martin Luther King in 1968 was an extreme version of the southern racist. Hendrick Verwoerd, the architect of South African apartheid was knifed to death, not by an outraged black African, but by a crazed half-Greek parliamentary messenger. Security consultants say that the "crazy with the gun" is the most unpredictable and possibly most dangerous threat to world leaders.

## INTERNATIONAL TERRORISM AND THE INTERNATIONAL MEDIA

International terrorism in its now familiar modern form coincided in the 1960s with the maturing of two technologies; mass air travel and mass communications, particularly satellite television communications. From the mid-1960s on it became possible for a terrorist group to hijack an aircraft (or a ship) anywhere in the world and have news of the event flashed round the globe within hours. A bomb placed in a Tel Aviv street, a burst of gunfire in a crowded airport terminal in Athens or a car bomb in the streets of London will guarantee world-wide coverage for the name (and possibly the grievances) of the bombers or shooters. A passenger liner hijacked in the Mediterranean or the Atlantic can be shuttled from port to port with the world's press and television in hot pursuit, leaving a clutch of governments perplexed, embarrassed, and at odds with one another.

Similarly the storming of a foreign embassy and the capture of foreign diplomats can be developed into a tense, dramatic siege which the world's media will watch with rapt attention. A major terror/counter-terror incident (such as the hijackings to Entebbe or

Mogadishu or the capture of the Iranian Embassy in London) can be guaranteed to produce a wave of world-wide publicity followed by a series of instant books, documentary films or even Hollywood feature films (as in the case of the Entebbe operation).

Political terrorists like Illich Sanchez ("Carlos the Jackal") began to assume a kind of lurid glamour in the Western societies in which they operated. The idea of the "propaganda of the deed" elaborated by the Italian and French anarchists of the late 19th century (when mass communications were beginning to spread rapidly through the world) came to fruition in the bombings, shootings, kidnappings and hijackings of the late 20th century. Some commentators argue that the Western media have now developed an almost "symbiotic" relationship with the terrorist international.

Walter Laqueur is one of those who argues that the relationship between the Western media and terrorism is distinctly unhealthy. He points out that proximity to the media was the main reason that the Latin American groups abandoned the countryside in the early 1960s and moved into the cities. "The media, with their inbuilt tendency towards sensationalism have always magnified terrorist exploits quite irrespective of their intrinsic importance," Laqueur writes. "Terrorist groups numbering perhaps a dozen members have been described as 'armies', their 'official communiqués' have been discussed in countless television shows, radio broadcasts, articles and editorials. In a few cases even non-existent groups have been given a great deal of publicity."(13)

Increasingly Western governments (and particularly those of Britain and the USA) are arguing that terrorism cannot be defeated until the Western media stop playing into the hands of the terrorists by providing saturation coverage of every major incident. The media (and particularly the American media) respond by saying that what is happening must be reported, and the better the reportage the more likely Western societies are to understand the phenomenon with which they are confronted. These arguments were vigorously aired during and after the hijacking of a TWA jet to Beirut in June 1985 when the American TV crews were given access to the hostages, and relayed day-by-day, often live coverage of the events home to the United States. In Britain, the BBC fell foul of the British government in 1985 for planning to broadcast television interviews with two Ulster extremists, one of whom had been a leading light in the Provisional IRA.

In his analysis of terrorism, Benjamin Netanyahu argues that the Western media should be enlisted in the war against the terrorists. "Terrorism's reliance on the press and television of the democracies gives the media tremendous power not only to amplify terrorism's message but also to snuff it out," Netanyahu contends. "They can and should refuse to broadcast indiscriminately interviews with terrorists. They can and should expose the sham of terrorists' claims. They can and should expose their grisly acts for what they are ... A thoughtful press can turn terrorism's greatest weapon against the terrorists themselves."(14)

At the same time, Western governments are not always distressed by media coverage of terrorist incidents. The dramatic television coverage of a British Special Air Service (SAS) counter-revolutionary warfare unit storming the Iranian Embassy in London in 1980 and releasing the hostages worked wonders for that regiment's image. It also boosted the British government's credibility. Prime Minister Margaret Thatcher, it seems, was delighted with the operation and watched video replays of the events at the SAS depot in London, while the regiment itself was almost embarrassed by the amount of support they received from the British public. Similarly the West German government basked in the glow of the success of their GSG-9 unit's operation against the hijackers of a Lufthansa jet at Mogadishu airport as did the Israeli government in 1976 when the rescue mission to Entebbe airport in Uganda went according to plan.

## TERRORISM AND WEAPONS TECHNOLOGY

Just as the advent of satellite-relayed television pictures from hand-held "minicams" (miniature TV cameras) and press interviews "faxed" or telexed from all round the world can transform obscure terrorists into world figures overnight, so modern weapons technology has made terrorist groups much more effective (or at least destructive). The development of small, easily concealed, rapid-fire machine pistols and hand-held grenade launchers has increased the terrorists' potential for destruction by leaps and bounds. One young man armed with, say, a Czech-made "Scorpion" machine pistol with a rate of fire of more than 800 rounds a minute can wreak bloody havoc in a crowded airport terminal within seconds. Many terrorist groups would have been helpless without a regular supply (from Eastern-bloc countries) of cheap, robust, mass-produced Kalashnikov AK-47 assault rifles (probably the most widely-used firearm ever made). The light, plastic and aluminium high-velocity Armalite AR-15 rifle has now replaced the Thompson machine-gun in the affections of the PIRA.

The current military drive to make the individual infantryman an even more formidable figure has produced a generation of high-powered weapons which are beginning to find their way into the hands of terrorists. An Arab group armed with a Soviet-made SA-7 surface-to-air heat-seeking missile was picked up in Rome in 1973, while in 1975 Black September attacked an El Al aircraft at Orly Airport in Paris with a hand-held RPG-7 (Rocket Propelled Grenade). Soviet-built RPG-7s have also been used occasionally by the PIRA in Northern Ireland (as have American M-60 heavy machine-guns).

Similarly, modern explosives pack enormous destructive power into very little bulk. A minute charge of Czech-made high explosive placed under the seat of a TWA jet in March 1986 killed four people and almost brought down the airliner. No 19th-century French or Italian anarchist fired by the "philosophy of the bomb" and "propaganda of the deed" could even have dreamed of the kind of lethal destructive power so easily obtained by modern terrorists.

The ultimate nightmare, of course, is that somehow one of the groups will lay their hands on a nuclear weapon and use it against the world. There are a number of ways that terrorists could acquire such a weapon; they could be given (or sold) one by an irresponsible government, they could steal one from a military stockpile (in the way that a US rocket was once smuggled out of West Germany) or they could hire the expertise to build their own. Ever since a 20-year-old student at the Massachusetts Institute of Technology (MIT) produced a paper (complete with diagrams) showing how to build a small-scale nuclear device, this prospect has haunted the world's intelligence and security services. Knowing how to build an atomic device and being able to do it are two different things, but some nuclear experts say that if enough plutonium oxide could be acquired (say 10 kilos) then a workable fission device could be assembled by terrorists from easily-obtained materials. Others disagree and claim that, to date, the process of building an atomic bomb is beyond the technical expertise of even the best-funded terrorist groups.

## TERROR STATES AND THE RULE OF LAW

One major problem which vexes Western governments in their confrontation with terrorism is how to cope with the nation states which overtly and covertly support the transnational terrorist groups. Although Libya, Syria, Iran and Iraq are considered by the West to be particularly guilty in this respect, they are not the only states within whose boundaries terrorists lurk. The long fight against the PIRA has frequently irritated relations between the United Kingdom and the Republic of Ireland (where PIRA find refuge) and the United States (where PIRA find much of their cash and arms). At the same time the Indian government has regularly accused Britain of refusing to take stern enough measures against the many radical Sikhs who form part of Britain's Indian community.

Similarly the readiness of the Basques of south-west France to give shelter and support to ETA terrorists from across the Spanish border has generated occasional tensions between Spain and France, and the Soviet Union takes a very dim view of Pakistan's habit of providing a base and support for "mujahadin" fighters from Afghanistan. The USA waxes indignant about left-wing and Islamic regimes who fund terrorists, but for many years the USA sheltered (and encouraged) a variety of lethal groups of right-wing Cuban exiles, who planted the bomb which destroyed a Cuban airliner in October 1976 and were involved in the assassination of Chilean exile Orlando Letelier (and his American research assistant) in Washington in September 1976.

But while there is little or no prospect of a British government sending warplanes to bomb Dundalk or Dublin, or the Spanish sending an armoured column into south-west France to round up ETA terrorists, some states have paid a price for giving sanctuary to terrorist groups. Moderate, pro-Western Tunisia, for example, was raided by Israeli warplanes and more than 60 people killed in September 1985 after three men from Yasir Arafat's Force 17 killed three Israelis at Larnaca in Cyprus. America's belief that Libya was behind most of the attacks against US citizens in the Mediterranean area sent the powerful US Sixth Fleet south into a confrontation with Colonel Qaddafi's gunboats in the Bay of Sirte in which three or four Libyan boats were destroyed and up to 100 men killed. And the Israeli army's chase into the Lebanon after the Palestine Liberation Organisation (PLO) pushed that fractured country over the edge into chaos.

It could be that the greatest danger terrorism poses to the world is that, someday, it will force the superpowers into a shooting war with one another. Syria and Libya, for example, are both client states of the Soviet Union; they are also the most persistent and enthusiastic supporters of Arab terrorists. Commentators and diplomats close to the US administration have been insisting for some time that the Soviet Union is the ultimate terrorist paymaster. Jeanne Kirkpatrick, former US ambassador to the UN told a conference in Washington in 1974 that "The most powerful totalitarian state of our time (the Soviet Union) is also the principal supporter and sponsor of international terrorism". Author Jean-

Francois Revel told the same conference that terrorism is not an "isolated phenomenon" but an integral part of "the Soviet Union's programme of global domination . . .". Whether or not this is true, the fact is that powerful and influential Americans believe it to be so.

The Soviet Union may or may not be at the heart of the so-called "terror international" but there is little doubt that the terrorist network relies on the support of sympathetic nation states. Western intelligence claim that Colonel Qaddafi's Libya has trained and financed terrorist groups from all over the world. The Palestine Liberation Organisation (and therefore its military wing Fatah) receives massive funding from the oil-rich states of Saudi Arabia, Kuwait and Dubai. The fanatical Shi'ite Muslims of Lebanon (who gave the world the suicide car bomb) look to Ayatollah Khomenei's Iran for their inspiration and training. There is now strong evidence that radical Arab governments have provided arms and training to European terrorist groups like the PIRA, ETA, the Rote Armee Fraktion (RAF) and the Brigate Rosse. In 1984 an Italian judge investigating the Brigate Rosse issued an arrest warrant for Abu Iyad, the PLO's head of military intelligence. The Italian courts believe they have strong evidence of gun-running between the PLO and the Brigate Rosse.

Western governments are firmly convinced that terrorist groups operating in Europe would find life a lot more difficult without the network of safe houses, diplomatic pouches, cash transfers, etc., provided by the embassies and consulates of sympathetic countries, usually, but not always Arab nations. Benjamin Netanyahu believes that terrorism is overwhelmingly "an extension of warfare sustained and supported by the states built on the foundations of Marxism and radical Islam".(14)

But while direct military action by individual states such as Israel or the USA is always possible (and is beginning to appear increasingly inevitable) the West appears to face enormous problems in bringing political, diplomatic and commercial pressure on the "terror states" (as they have been dubbed). After the attacks on Rome and Vienna airports at the end of 1985 President Reagan sent American envoys around Europe to try to stitch together a coordinated campaign of sanctions against the Qaddafi regime in Libya. The effort failed, partly because the Europeans were not convinced that Qaddafi had been behind the attacks (all the evidence pointed to the Syrians) but also because countries like Italy, West Germany and Britain had large and extremely profitable investments in Libya.

While France, Britain and West Germany have been prepared to purge their countries of Libyan diplomats who they know (or suspect) to have been dabbling in terrorist or quasi-terrorist activities (and in Britain's case break off all formal relations with Libya) they have not been prepared to impose sanctions. And while President Reagan has issued an "executive order" to all American citizens living in Libya to leave the country, hundreds have remained. The US State Department regards them as potential hostages should Qaddafi decide to retaliate against the USA.

## HIJACKING AND ATTACKS ON AIR TRANSPORT

Nothing has proved more vulnerable to the ravages of terrorism than the international airline system. Although the kind of spectacular hijackings which were common in the late 1960s and 1970s (Dawson's Field, Entebbe, Mogadishu etc.) appear to be decreasing, the tragic result of the hijacking to Luqa Airport in Malta in November 1985 demonstrated that airport security is far from perfect, as did the bombs which were planted aboard the Air-India Boeing 747 in June 1985 (killing 329 people) and on the TWA 727 in March 1986 (killing four people). The hijacking of a TWA jetliner to Beirut airport by a small group of Shi'ite Muslims in June 1985 and the protracted negotiations which followed showed that the terrorists are still able to stage a publicity coup by striking at the airlines.

But Western governments are now under growing pressure to isolate and quarantine terrorist-supporting states such as Libya, Syria, Iraq and Iran. In April 1986, a week after a TWA flight from Rome to Athens was almost wrecked by a small charge placed under a passenger seat (the passenger and three others were killed) the International Federation of Airline Pilots Associations (IFAPA) meeting in London resolved to boycott all countries giving sanctuary or encouragement to hijackers. They are also pressing their governments to deny the aircraft of the "terror states" access to Western airports. The pilots argue that a comprehensive boycott would do so much damage to the economies of these countries that they would be forced to rein in the hijackers and terrorists. The IFAPA resolution is the kind of action which Benjamin Netanyahu deems essential if terrorism is to be thwarted. Netanyahu describes the cutting off of air services as a "potent sanction that can be readily applied" and suggests that it should also be extended to shipping.(15)

In fact, the international community has been trying – without much success – to grapple with the problem of aerial hijacking since the 1960s (although the practice began in 1930 when Peruvian bandits took over a Fokker F-7 and forced the pilot to fly to a jungle airstrip). In the 50 years between 1930 and 1981 at least 647 aircraft were hijacked by political terrorists or criminals; 236 in the USA, 150 in South America, 142 in Europe, 86 in Asia, 28 in Africa and five in Australasia. In the same period 488 people were killed; 349 passengers, 88 hijackers, 41 airline staff, seven law officers and three others.

Three important international conventions on hijacking have formed the basis of many laws: the Tokyo Convention of 1963, the Hague Convention of 1970 and the Montreal Convention of 1971. According to international legal expert D. J. Harris the Tokyo Convention was largely concerned with "the long standing problem of jurisdiction over all crimes aboard aircraft" (16) and languished for some years until an upsurge of hijacking in the late 1960s brought it into force. The Hague and Montreal Conventions of 1970 and 1971 tightened up the rules considerably, but Harris says that problems of jurisdiction and extradition of offenders (particularly the latter) remain.

In 1978 at an economic summit in Bonn the leaders of seven leading Western states issued a declaration to the effect that ". . . in cases where a country refuses extradition or prosecution of those who have hijacked an aircraft and/or do not return such aircraft, the heads of state and government are jointly resolved that their governments should take immediate action to cease all flights to that country".(17) The leaders also pledged themselves to halt all incoming flights from the guilty countries and urged other governments "to join them in this commitment". While the Bonn Declaration does not have the weight of an international treaty, it is regarded as a step in the right direction (although the resolution of the countries involved is still to be tested).

In 1970, after the hijacking and destruction of four airliners at Dawson's Field in Jordan, the United Nations passed Resolution 2645 condemning "without exception" all acts of "aerial hijacking" and called on member states to "take all measures appropriate" to prevent and deter hijacking and punish the hijackers. The resolution also called for the "extradition of such persons for the purpose of their prosecution and punishment . . .". But like many UN Resolutions, 2645 has been largely ignored by many of the countries sympathetic to the hijackers.

In Britain the resolutions of the international conventions have been translated into the Tokyo Convention Act of 1967, the Hijacking Act of 1971 (which imposes a life sentence on convicted hijackers), the Protection of Aircraft Act of 1973 and the Policing of Airports Act of 1974. In the United States the relevant laws are the Anti-Hijacking Act of 1974 (which carries a death sentence for hijackers 'where someone is killed, and a 20-year sentence otherwise) and the Air Transportation Security Act of 1974. Many other countries have passed similar laws and regulations.

But general statements of law and declarations of good intentions have not been enough to stop many hijackers and their weapons slipping through airport security measures. The Greek government has been a signatory to all the international conventions, but according to the American officials, security at Athens airport has long been a disgrace. The international airport at Cairo is also described as a "major problem" and security officers from the International Air Transport Association believe that the small bomb which killed four people on the TWA flight from Rome to Athens in March 1986 was planted by an airport worker at Cairo (although Egyptian security officials dispute this).

The drive is now on to install virtually terrorist-proof security systems at as many of the world's major airports as possible. One British-designed security system visualises a system of bullet-proof sealed cubicles through which every passenger (and airport worker) would pass before entering the airport terminal. If firearms or explosives were sensed by the automatic sensors, the potential offender would be automatically sealed into a bullet-proof cubicle where he/she could be dealt with by armed security men. Some experts are advocating the system of elaborate security checks carried out by the Israeli state airline El Al, which causes inevitable delays and inconvenience to passengers, but which makes El Al one of the world's safest airlines with which to fly.

Security officials are also worried about the spread of firearms made largely from plastic like the Austrian-built Glock 17 handgun which can be taken apart in minutes and hidden in luggage. In 1985 Noel Koch, one of the Pentagon's anti-terrorist experts twice smuggled a dismantled Glock-17 through the strict security checks at Washington airport and is now urging the US government to take measures against such weapons. Congressman Mario Biaggi has introduced a bill banning such weapons after one of his staff carried a Glock-17 handgun through the sophisticated security check-point on Capitol Hill. American intelligence reports that the Qaddafi regime has been trying to buy up to 300 Glock-17 handguns through Austrian middlemen.

Most international airlines now carry one or two armed security men, or "Skymarshalls", at least on flights to and from parts of the world where terrorism has been a problem. A number of these officials have been involved in in-flight gun battles with hijackers, and in one such incident in November 1985 an Egyptair jet was forced to land after the skin of the aircraft was pierced by a bullet. Israeli Skymarshalls normally carry special low-velocity firearms which will kill or injure a terrorist without passing through his body or puncturing the aircraft fuselage.

One of the extraordinary results of international terrorism has been the growth of privately owned security and anti-terrorist firms set up to protect diplomats, businessmen, celebrities etc., from possible kidnap or assassination. In Britain a number of these firms are operated by men who learned their trade in the Special Air Service (SAS) or other élite military units. A study in the US by J. A. Nathan revealed around 40 firms offering "an impressive panoply" of anti-terrorist services, including bodyguards, chauffeur training etc. But according to Nathan most of these private operators were also prepared to negotiate with terrorists to free kidnapped executives, supply information on specific terrorists, and even involve themselves in "paramilitary operations to release kidnap victims, and ferreting out terrorists in pre-emptive missions". (18).

The terrorist threat has obliged the US government to find $4.4 billion to beef up security at American embassies around the world, while the spate of hijackings and attacks on aircraft and airports in 1985/86 caused a slump in Europe's tourist industry. By 1986 tourist authorities and hoteliers from all over Europe – from Greece to Scotland – were reporting that business was down by as much as 30% as Americans cancelled their European holidays for fear of running across one of the terrorist gangs prowling Europe. Tourist-industry arguments that American tourists were statistically safer in the airports of Europe than they were in the streets of Manhattan or Detroit were to no avail.

## CONCLUSIONS

Given the confusion and irresolution of the international community, the growth of ever-more powerful (and easily concealed) weapons and explosives, and the number of political and social grievances which suppurate in many corners of the world it seems unlikely that the next few decades will see any marked decline in international terrorism. Fashions may change, however. Rigorous airport security may make aerial hijacking a much more difficult option than it has been in the past, although it is unlikely to eradicate it altogether. Attacks on shipping – as the *Achille Lauro* hijacking of 1985 proved – may become a better option for the terrorists, ports and harbours being much easier to penetrate than airports. There has yet to be a serious attack on any of the hundreds of offshore oil and gas production platforms which now festoon the North Sea, the Gulf of Mexico, the Mediterranean and the Atlantic coast of Brazil. Oil refineries, gas processing plants, pipelines and pumping stations are all tempting targets for the world's terrorist groups (and have been attacked in locations as diverse as Iraq, South Africa and Scotland).

Against that, the world's various anti-terrorist forces and intelligence-gathering operations are growing in expertise as well as number and are beginning to co-ordinate their information. They may prove formidable enough to at least "contain" the international terrorists until political settlements emerge and are accepted. The so-called Anglo-Irish agreement over the future of Northern Ireland, while it has outraged the Ulster Protestants, is seen by most Irish and Britons as a gleam of light in what has been a very long, dark tunnel. The Basques of northern Spain (or at least some of them) are reported to be impressed by the package of devolution measures worked out by the newly democratic Spanish government in Madrid. The criminal Mafia are now a greater problem to the Italian government than the left-wing activists of the Brigate Rosse, and the activities of Action Directe in France and the Rote Armee Fraktion in West Germany are now at a low level.

On the other hand the Sikh terrorism now rampant in the Punjab (and which has spilled into Britain, Canada and Europe) threatens to erupt into open warfare, while casualties in the Tamil insurgency in Sri Lanka (which is being supported by Tamils of southern India) are growing steadily worse with no resolution in sight. Many Kashmiris are also pressing the Indian government for independence. The African National Congress (ANC) have stepped up their terror campaign in South Africa and the bombs of Umkonto We Sizwe (the ANC's military wing) have been exploding in the plush white suburbs of Durban and elsewhere. And so long as Israelis and Palestinians, Jews and Arabs, are locked in a lethal conflict over the same small patch of the Eastern Mediterranean, the focus of world terrorism will remain the Middle East.

In his recent study of terrorism Benjamin Netanyahu, Israel's Ambassador to the United Nations avers that "international terrorism is not a sporadic phenomenon born of social misery and frustration" but something "rooted in the political ambitions and designs of expansionist states and the groups that serve them".

Netanyahu claims that without the support of such states (Libya, Syria, Iran, Iraq ) "international terrorism would be impossible".(19) Netanyahu also claims that the conjunction of Marxism and Islamic fundamentalism has produced a political situation in which terrorism will continue regardless of whether justice is done to the Palestinians. Other commentators regard this as an over-simplification and insist that the sheer squalor and hopelessness of the Palestinian refugee camps is a fertile breeding ground for Arab terrorism, and are bitterly critical of the hugely prosperous Arab governments of the Middle East for allowing the misery to continue.

After spending three months in 1985/86 criss-crossing the Middle East talking to Arab terrorists (and their leaders) in the camps of the Middle East, Rod Norland and Ray Wilkinson of the US magazine *Newsweek* reported that "Terrorists are not born, they're made, and nobody makes them better than the star-crossed Palestinian refugee camps in Lebanon". After dozens of interviews Norland and Wilkinson concluded that they had found " ... a cycle of reprisal and retaliation that will not easily come to an end. Libya may provide most of the funds, Syria most of the guns, Lebanon many of the recruits. But it is the Palestinian cause, the lack of a homeland and the moribund peace process that provides the motive driving these men to put themselves outside the pale of civilized conduct." (20)

## NOTES TO THE TEXT

1. Grant Wardlaw. *Political Terrorism. Theory, tactics and counter-measures*. Cambridge University Press, 1985.
2. Ibid.
3. Roger Scruton. *A Dictionary of Political Thought*. Pan Books, 1982.
4. Walter Laqueur. *Terrorism*. Abacus, 1978.
5. Wardlaw. *Political Terrorism*.
6. Benjamin Netanyahu. *Terrorism: How the West Can Win*. Farrar, Straus & Giroux. 1986.
7. Wardlaw. *Political Terrorism*.
8. Ibid.
9. Laqueur. *Terrorism*.
10. T. P. Thornton. *Terror as a weapon of political agitation* in C. Eckstein (ed) *Internal War*. Collier-Macmillan. 1964.
11. W. F. May. *Terrorism as strategy and ecstasy* in *Social Research*, 41, 1978.
12. Paul Wilkinson. *Terrorism and the Liberal State*. Macmillan. 1978.
13. Laqueur. *Terrorism*.

14. Netanyahu. *Terrorism: How the West Can Win.*
15. Ibid.
16. J. D. Harris. *Cases and Materials on International Law.* Sweet & Maxwell, 1979.
17. The Bonn Declaration was issued by Canada, France, West Germany, Italy, Japan, United Kingdom and the United States.
18. J. A. Nathan. *The new feudalism* in *Foreign Policy*, No 42, 1981.
19. Netanyahu. *Terrorism: How the West Can Win.*
20. *Newsweek*. April 7, 1986.

# A

**ABBAS, ABU (born 1948).** Also known as Abul Abbas, Abu Khaled. Left-wing Palestinian and leader of the PALESTINE LIBERATION FRONT (PLF), accused by the US and Israeli governments of planning the *ACHILLE LAURO* HIJACKING in October 1985 in the course of which an American citizen was shot. Although intercepted by American warplanes and held by the Italian authorities following the hijacking , Abbas was released on October 12th 1985 and allowed to fly to Yugoslavia. The refusal of the Italian government to extradite Abbas to the USA infuriated the American government and put some strain on US-Italian relations. The US government say they are determined that Abbas shall be brought to justice.

A close associate of YASIR ARAFAT, Chairman of the PALESTINE LIBERATION ORGANISATION (PLO), Abbas became one of the world's most sought after terrorist leaders after the *Achille Lauro* debacle. Although Abbas was responsible for persuading the hijackers to surrender to the Egyptian authorities at Port Said on October 10th 1985 the US and Israeli governments believe that he planned the hijack and hold him ultimately responsible for the death of the elderly American passenger LEON KLINGHOFFER.

Born in refugee camp in Syria, and a life-long devotee of the Palestine cause, Abbas studied at Damascus University and was recruited into the radical POPULAR FRONT FOR THE LIBERATION OF PALESTINE – GENERAL COMMAND (PFLP-GC) in 1968. After guerrilla training in the Soviet Union Abbas split with the PFLP-GC and joined the recently formed PLF as its operations chief. He was involved in the bitter inter-Palestinian fighting in Lebanon. Abbas is attributed with a number of daring (if unsuccessful) military/terrorist exploits, including the famous hang glider raid on an oil refinery in Haifa, Israel in 1981. Politically ambitious, Abbas has remained loyal to Yasir Arafat, and when the PLO was exiled to Tunisia in 1982, Abbas, with Arafat's backing, was elected to the PLO's powerful Executive Committee.

After negotiating the surrender of the four *Achille Lauro* hijackers Abbas joined them on the flight to Tunisia where they were to be disciplined by the PLO. When US warplanes intercepted the Egyptair flight and forced it to land in Sicily, Abbas was held by the Italian authorities and taken to Rome. The Americans immediately issued a warrant for his arrest but the Italian government refused to extradite the Palestinian. On October 12th 1985, dressed as an Egyptian airforce officer, Abbas was allowed to leave Rome on a flight to Belgrade, from where he flew to Aden in South Yemen, and then to Baghdad in Syria.

**ABDULLAH,HAMMID ALI**. One of the four young Palestinians of the PALESTINE LIBERATION FRONT (PLF) who hijacked the Italian cruise liner *ACHILLE LAURO* in October 1985. Abdullah Hammid (23) and his three co-conspirators were tried in Genoa in December 1985 on charges of illegal possession of weapons and explosives (the least of the charges against them). All were found guilty, and sentenced to terms of imprisonment ranging from eight years to four years. But they still have to stand trial on charges of hijacking and murder.

**ABERCORN RESTAURANT BOMBING. (March 4th 1972.)** Attack on a crowded restaurant in the centre of Belfast which killed two women and injured more than 130 other people. Many of the casualties suffered appalling mutilation. The attack horrified and scandalised public opinion in both Britain and the Irish Republic as the restaurant was crowded with Saturday afternoon shoppers, mainly women and children. Significantly no group, either Republican or Protestant ever claimed responsibility for the bombing.

**ACAO LIBERTADORA NACIONAL (ALN)**. Left-wing Brazilian group which emerged in the late 1960s and was led (for a few years) by the Latin American theorist CARLOS MARIGHELLA author of the *Minimanual of the Urban Guerrilla*. Under the influence of the hard-line Marighella the ALN waged a particularly ruthless urban terror campaign (mainly in Rio de Janeiro and São Paulo) which produced an even more ruthless response from Brazil's security forces which destroyed the ALN by the mid-1970s. After Marighella's death (in a police ambush near São Paulo in October 1969) the ALN was led by Camara Fereira, who was shot dead in November 1970. In terms of numbers the ALN was a small group, but their skilful manipulation of the Brazilian (and world) media gave them an importance beyond their achievements. They were, however, roundly denounced by other left-wing organisations in Latin America as "military adventurers".

**ACCION NACIONAL ESPANOLA (ANE).** (Spanish National Action). Right-wing Spanish terrorist/assassination organisation which emerged in the 1970s in the Basque country of northern Spain in reaction to the activities of the Basque separatist group EUSKADI TA ASKATASUNA (ETA). The ANE have been responsible for a number of killings of alleged ETA members in Spain and in France, and bomb attacks in Bilbao and San Sebastian.

*ACHILLE LAURO* **HIJACKING. (October 7th-11th 1985).** The hijacking of the Italian-owned cruise liner *Achille Lauro* by four members of the PALESTINE LIBERATION FRONT (PLF). The liner was held hostage for three days while the hijackers demanded the release of 50 Palestinians held in Israel. One American passenger was killed before the hijackers surrendered to PLF leader ABU ABBAS and the Egyptian authorities. When the Egyptian aircraft carrying the hijackers to Tunisia was intercepted by US aircraft and forced to land in Sicily, the Egyptian president denounced the US action as "piracy".The *Achille Lauro* affair put a considerable strain on relations between the USA and Egypt and Italy.

The hijacking began at 08.45 on October 7th 1985 when four Palestinians, HALLAH AL-HASSAN (17), MAJED YOUSEF AL-MOLKY (23), ABDEL ATIF IBRAHIM (20), HAMMID ALI ABDULLAH (23), burst into the liner's dining room firing submachine-guns and wounding two of the passengers. The four men then took over the ship (which had 427 passengers and 80 crew aboard) and demanded the release of 50 Palestinians being held in Israel. When the hijack negotiations began to turn sour on October 8th 1985 the gunmen killed LEON KLINGHOFFER (69), an elderly American invalid, and forced two of the ship's crew to throw his body overboard. After being refused permission to dock at Tartus in Syria the ship sailed back to Port Said where Abu Abbas, head of the PLF and a senior member of the PALESTINE LIBERATION ORGANISATION (PLO) executive, persuaded the hijackers to surrender to the Egyptian authorities.

But when an Egyptian Boeing 737 jet carrying the four hijackers and Abu Abbas left Egypt for Tunisia late in the evening of Thursday 10th October it was intercepted over the Mediterranean by four American F-14 warplanes from the US aircraft carrier *Saratoga*, and forced to land at Sigonella NATO base on Sicily. The hijackers were then arrested by the Italian authorities but not before an extraordinary confrontation between American troops of the DELTA FORCE and the Italian police. The face-off was resolved when President Reagan personally ordered the Delta Force commander to stand down.

It was later revealed by Abbas that the terrorists had been planning a suicide raid on the Israeli port of Ashdod when they were discovered on the *Achille Lauro* cleaning their weapons. They then took over the ship. Although the US government promptly asked the Italians to extradite the four men to the USA, and also issued an arrest warrant for Abbas, the Italians insisted that the four Arab hijackers stand trial in Italy. They also angered the Americans by allowing Abbas and his aide to fly to Yugoslavia.

Although President Reagan's swift action to impound the terrorists was widely popular within the USA, it was denounced by President Hosni Mubarak of Egypt as "piracy" and there were riots outside the American and Israeli embassies. In Italy, the Minister of Defence resigned because the Italian government failed to hold Abu Abbas, and his resignation led to the collapse of Prime Minister Bettino Craxi's coalition government. And the PLO warned that the American intervention would only serve to exacerbate the situation in the Middle East and possibly generate even more terrorism.

**ACTION DIRECTE (AD)**. (Direct Action). Left-wing French group which first appeared in the late 1970s with a series of attacks in and around Paris, Toulouse and Marseilles. The AD are one of a number of West European left-wing groups which are still active and maintain contact with one another. In January 1985 the AD announced the formation of a "political military front" with the West German ROTE ARMEE FRAKTION (RAF) to attack US and NATO bases throughout Europe. In April 1986 the AD confessed to an assassination attempt on Guy Brana, the Vice-President of the French employers' association. Brana was unhurt, but after the attack five people, allegedly AD activists, were arrested and charged with firearms and explosives offences. The police also recovered more than $2 million dollars which had been stolen in a Paris bank raid.

The AD are thought to have been built on two earlier organisations and were led by Jean-Marc Rouillan and Nathalie Merugnon (both of whom were captured and then later released by the French authorities). In the early 1980s AD launched bomb attacks on police stations, magistrates courts, computer companies and the Ecole Militaire in Paris. They also issued "communiqués" denouncing French activities in Africa. Raids by French police on AD "safe" houses produced large quantities of cash, and quantities of lethal equipment including anti-tank weapons and plastic explosives. The rash of AD bombings in Paris in 1981 forced the French to make sweeping changes in their internal security forces.

**ADAMS, GERRY (born 1949).** Influential left-wing Irish Republican politician and Vice-President of the Provisional Sinn Fein who was elected to the British Parliament as MP for Belfast West in 1983 but has never taken his seat. Although he has always denied membership of the PROVISIONAL IRISH REPUBLICAN ARMY (PIRA) Adams is widely believed to be one of the three men who ran the PIRA in Ulster in the 1970s following the arrest of SEAN MACSTIOFAIN, the PIRA's Chief of Staff.

An active Republican, Adams was interned in Belfast in 1971, released in 1972 to take part in secret talks with the British government, jailed again in 1973, and then given an extra 18 months for trying to escape from the Maze Prison in Belfast. Adams was charged in 1978 with being a member of the IRA, held in jail for seven months, and then released because of lack of evidence. Since then Adams has become increasingly political and has been struggling to give the Republican movement a more Socialist cast. Adams has sought to forge links with left-wing politicians in Britain, and in late 1982 was invited to address Labour MPs and councillors in London, a visit which was banned under the Prevention of Terrorism Act by the British government. The ban on Adams was lifted when he won the Parliamentary constituency of West Belfast in the British general election of 1983.

**AFRICAN NATIONAL CONGRESS (ANC).** The most important of the black South African organisations opposing the South African government, and led by OLIVER TAMBO, the African lawyer who once shared a legal practice with the jailed NELSON MANDELA. Now based in Zambia, through their military wing UMKONTO WE SIZWE (Spear of the Nation) the ANC have become increasingly militant and revolutionary and are believed to have around 6,000 guerrillas in Zambia, Mozambique and Angola. The ANC leaders are seen by most (although not all) Africans as the black "government in exile" and the heirs-apparent to the white regime of South Africa. Although not a communist organisation, the ANC has close links with the illegal South African Communist Party, and the ANC's central policy document, the "Manifesto of the Azanian People", describes the ANC's goal as the destruction of the system of "racial capitalism" in South Africa.

In January 1986 ANC president Oliver Tambo pledged to escalate the campaign of unrest and guerrilla warfare inside South Africa. Tambo denounced the white regime as "the heirs of Hitler" and called for a "real people's war" which would render South Africa "ungovernable and apartheid unworkable". Tambo went on to urge the guerrillas of Umkonto We Sizwe to inflict "bigger blows at every stage" against the government. In May 1986 the South African government responded to the growing threat from the ANC by striking at alleged ANC targets in Zimbabwe, Zambia and Lesotho, killing three people, and damaging ANC property.

The ANC began life in 1912 as the South African Native National Congress in response to the growing injustice of the white regime. Heavily influenced in its early days by the philosophy of MAHATMA GANDHI (then a South African lawyer) the ANC organised passive (and largely futile) resistance to white power and the occasional short-lived strike. For many years the ANC was led by Chief Albert Luthuli (who was awarded a Nobel Peace Prize in 1960).

But when the ANC was finally banned by the South African government in 1961, the ANC's new young leaders, Nelson Mandela and Oliver Tambo formed Umkonto We Sizwe to carry out a campaign of industrial and economic sabotage in an attempt to bring the South African economy to its knees. Umkonto's strategy has not proved particularly successful, and in recent years the ANC has taken to assassination and terrorism, particularly against those Africans such as police officers and suspected police informers who they see as propping up the white state. The poet Benjamin Moloise, hanged in October 1985 for the murder of a black policeman, was a member of the ANC.

Although the ANC is a modestly-funded organisation (compared to the PLO) it manages to maintain small offices around the world, including the USA, East and West Germany, India, Italy, Australia, Cuba, Egypt and Canada. Their headquarters are in Lusaka, Zambia. Through its "Radio Freedom" radio stations, the ANC broadcasts regularly in Angola, Zambia, Malagasay, Ethiopia and Tanzania.

**AGCA, MEHMET ALI (born 1956).** Right-wing Turkish gunman and convicted murderer who tried to assassinate Pope John Paul II in St Peter's Square, Rome, on May 13th 1981. Quickly captured by the Italian police, Agca claimed that he was a member of a right-wing Turkish terror group known as the GREY WOLVES. Initially Agca claimed to have been acting alone, but he then changed his story and said he had been working on behalf of the Bulgarian Secret Service and the KGB. Agca was jailed for life for his attempt to murder the Pope.

In his testimony to the Italian authorities Agca implicated three Bulgarians and two Turks in the plot to assassinate the Pope. Only one of the men, a Bulgarian airline official SERGEI ANTONOV, was arrested by the Italian police to stand trial. The other four men lived in Bulgaria, Switzerland and West Germany respectively, but their trials went ahead because under Italian law an accused person can be tried in absentia. In March 1986 Antonov, the two Bulgarians and the two Turks were acquitted as "innocent for lack of sufficient proof of guilt" and Antonov was allowed to leave the country. Agca himself was given an extra year in jail for smuggling a firearm into Italy.

The protracted trial in Rome (which lasted 10 months and cost an estimated $600,000) was bizarre. Agca persistently claimed to be the reincarnation of Jesus Christ, while accusing the Vatican and the US White House of a "secret accord" to "dominate the world with lies and slander". He also claimed that the Bulgarian secret police played a key role in the plot to kill the Pope and that he and his two Turkish co-defendants were offered more than a million German marks by the Bulgarians. The Bulgarian authorities have consistently and vehemently denied Agca's accusations.

## AIR FRANCE HIJACKING TO ENTEBBE AIRPORT, UGANDA. (June 27th-July 4th 1976).

An aerial hijacking by the POPULAR FRONT FOR THE LIBERATION OF PALESTINE (PFLP) which was ended by a raid by the Israeli Defence Forces to release 106 Jewish hostages being held at Entebbe Airport in Uganda. The successful military operation demonstrated the long arm of the Israelis, and did much to discredit the brutal regime of Idi Amin. Codenamed Operation "JONATHAN", the raid also boosted Israeli prestige at a time when it was flagging and when the Palestine case was being argued with renewed vigour. The Israeli action received massive world-wide publicity, and the events were made into two full-length feature films.

The sequence of events which led to the Entebbe raid began on June 27th 1976 when Air France flight 139 from Tel Aviv to Paris with over 250 passengers and crew aboard was taken over by a group of eight Arab and German PFLP terrorists soon after it left Athens. The hijackers were led by a young German called Wilfred Boese, one-time member of the ROTE ARMEE FRAKTION (RAF) and described themselves as the "Che Guevara Force of the Commando of the Palestine Liberation Forces". They ordered the aircraft to Benghazi in Libya and then to Entebbe in Uganda where the jet landed in the early hours of June 28th 1976.

After some negotiation with Western diplomats, 146 of the passengers and crew were released by their Arab, German and Ugandan captors. But another 106 people, mainly Jewish, were kept as hostage. The PFLP were demanding the release of 53 Arab terrorists being held in various Western (and Arab) countries. When an Israeli officer pleaded with Idi Amin to intervene he was told by the Ugandan dictator that his hands were tied, that the terrorists were very determined, and would ". . . begin with blowing up the plane, and then they'll kill everyone at once with explosives". But the Israelis had no doubt that the Ugandan government were conniving with the hijackers. Amin himself visited the hostages after throwing a strong cordon of soldiers around the airport.

With no hope of a negotiated settlement, and after days of intense planning and intelligence-gathering the Israeli government launched Operation "Jonathan" (called after Lieutenant Colonel JONATHAN NETANYAHU who led the raid). On July 3rd 1976 a force of élite Israeli paratroops took off from Israel in three Hercules transports, flew the 3,000 or so miles to Uganda, and landed at Entebbe airport in complete darkness a few minutes after midnight on July 4th 1976. Taking the Ugandans and the hijackers completely by surprise, the Israeli paratroops stormed the airport buildings and released the Jewish hostages. In the course of a half-hour battle, the Israeli forces killed 20 Ugandan soldiers, seven of the hijackers, and destroyed 11 Soviet-built MIG pursuit jets on the runway. Only one Israeli soldier (the force commander Jonathan Netanyahu) was killed, together with three of the hostages. The entire operation on the ground at Entebbe took just under one hour. After refuelling their three Hercules aircraft at Nairobi in Kenya, the Israeli paratroops and the rescued civilians flew back to Israel where they were given an emotional welcome.

Shimon Peres, Israel's Minister of Defence said, "The mission in Uganda, in one short hour, strengthened the backbone of the Jewish people and of the whole free world." But in an act of cruel and petty revenge the Ugandans killed an elderly British woman, Dora Bloch, who had been taken to a Ugandan hospital after falling ill during her hijacking ordeal. The terrorist who escaped from the Israelis has never been properly identified. One theory is that he was the Peruvian anarchist Antonio Bouvier. But another, more widely-held, belief is that he was ILLICH RAMIREZ SANCHEZ, also known as "Carlos The Jackal".

**AIR-INDIA BOMBING, NORTH ATLANTIC. (June 23rd 1985).** One of the worst disasters in aviation history, and believed to be due to a bombing attack when an Air-India Boeing 747 crashed into the sea off the west coast of Ireland killing 329 passengers and crew. Most of the people killed were Canadian citizens of Indian descent. Although no group ever admitted responsibility for the bombing, the authorities believe it was the work of Sikh extremists aggrieved by the Indian government's action at the GOLDEN TEMPLE OF AMRITSAR. The Air-India disaster is linked to an explosion that same day at TOKYO AIRPORT in Japan when luggage from a flight from Vancouver blew up, killing two Japanese baggage-handlers. The Air-India bombing forced the Canadian government to drastically tighten up airport security, and rethink its strategy for dealing with Sikh (and other) radicals.

Air-India Flight 182 from Montreal to Delhi was destroyed at 07.14 on June 22nd 1985 while flying at 30,000 feet over the Atlantic about 180 miles west of the Irish coast. There were 329 people aboard, 22 crew and 307 passengers (including eight Air-India employees). There were no survivors, although 131 bodies were recovered from the Atlantic by British and Irish search and rescue vessels. Examination by Irish pathologists showed that at least four of the casualties had been alive when they hit the water, but died from drowning. And while the wreckage of the Boeing 747 was strewn over miles of ocean bed at depths up to 7,000 feet, large portions of it were recovered for examination by the Indian authorities (including the "black box" flight recorders).

Close examination of the wreckage of Flight 182 at the Bhabha Atomic Research Centre in Bombay revealed that a large piece from the aircraft's forward cargo hold contained at least 13 holes probably caused by shrapnel from an explosion. Also the flight recorders and tapes from the Shannon Airport control-tower revealed what were described as a "series of rumbles and a human cry". But some independent experts say there is no conclusive proof that the Air-India Boeing 747 was downed by a bomb.

Investigations by the Royal Canadian Mounted Police (RCMP) revealed that two Sikhs, calling themselves M. Singh and L. Singh, had checked in bags at Vancouver to be transferred to Air-India Flight 182 at Montreal. But neither man joined the flight, and they are now suspected of being the terrorists who contrived to have the bomb loaded into the baggage hold of Air-India Flight 182. But the Sikh community in Canada strenuously deny that Sikhs bombed the aircraft and many blame the Indian government for the disaster as part of a long-standing plot to discredit the Sikh independence movement. In 1986 it was revealed that the Indian government had been running a sub-rosa operation in Canada designed to embarrass Canadian Sikhs. One Indian diplomat in Toronto asked for political asylum in Canada after being ordered to infiltrate a Sikh group. The disclosure caused some diplomatic tension between the Canadian and Indian governments.

**AIR LANKA BOMBING, COLOMBIA. (May 3rd 1986).** The bombing of an Air Lanka Lockheed Tristar on the ground at Colombo's Katunayake Airport on May 3rd 1986 which killed 15 people and injured 41 others. The Sri Lanka government blamed the attack on Tamil separatists of the LIBERATION TIGERS OF TAMIL EELAM (The Tamil Tigers), an accusation which the Tamil Tigers hotly denied. Suspicion also fell on a group known as the Eelam Revolutionary Students Organisation (EROS). The Sri Lankans believe that the bombing was timed to coincide with the presence in Sri Lanka of an Indian delegation trying to arrange peace talks between the separatists and the Sri Lankan government. The Air Lanka Tristar was blown apart at 09.10 on May 3rd 1986 when an estimated 112lbs of explosive ignited in the aircraft's cargo-hold while passengers were boarding the flight. Most of those killed were European and Japanese holidaymakers bound for the Maldive Islands. The flight had started at Gatwick Airport, London, and stopped at Zurich and Dubai on its way to Colombo. Sri Lankan security forces believe that the explosives were put into the cargo hold in a consignment of meat being airlifted to hotels in the Maldive Islands.

**AKACHE, ZOHAIR YOUSIF (1954-1977).** Also known as "Captain Martyr Mahmoud". Leader of the four-man terrorist group who mounted the LUFTHANSA HIJACKING TO MOGADISHU AIRPORT, SOMALIA who was killed on October 18th, when German anti-terrorist police from the GRENZSCHUTZGRUPPE 9 (GSG-9) stormed the aircraft. Born in a Palestinian refugee camp in Beirut, Akache joined the POPULAR FRONT FOR THE LIBERATION OF PALESTINE (PFLP), and later studied engineering in England between 1973 and 1976. During his time in London Akache was in constant trouble with the British police, and after a short jail sentence was finally deported to Beirut in March 1976. He returned to London under false passports in 1977. Akache was attributed with the killing of ABDULLAH AL-HAJARI, the former Prime Minister of North Yemen on April 10th 1977, outside the Royal Lancaster Hotel, London.

**ALEXANDER I, KING OF YUGOSLAVIA (1888-1934).**
Yugoslavian monarch assassinated along with French foreign
minister Louis Barthou in Marseilles on October 9th 1934. The
killings caused an international outrage and prompted the League
of Nations to try (unsuccessfully) to grapple with the problem
of international political terrorism. Alexander and Barthou were
attacked at 16.10 when a young Croatian nationalist called Petrus
Kalemen jumped onto the running board of their open car and fired
a hail of bullets from an automatic rifle. Kalemen died soon after
from the mauling he received at the hands of the police bodyguard.
Another 40 people were injured when the mounted guards charged
into the crowd lining the route. While King Alexander I died
instantly, Barthou survived for an hour. Later the French Sûreté
decided that the assassination had been the result of a conspiracy
of Croatian nationalists.

The Croatian assassins of King Alexander and Louis Barthou
were among the first of the "modern" terrorist groups. They were
well funded and highly mobile, equipped with false passports,
efficient firearms and assisted by a well-placed "back-up"
organisation. The killing of Alexander and Barthou provoked
the League of Nations (forerunner of the United Nations) into
establishing two international conventions designed to combat
political terrorism; the 1937 Convention for the Prevention and
Punishment of Terrorism, and the 1937 Convention for the Creation
of an International Criminal Court. The former "criminalised"
attacks on heads of state and other such "internationally protected
persons" while the latter was one of the early efforts to impose
international law on the terrorist networks. While the League's
intentions were good, few nations could be persuaded to ratify the
conventions, and the measures fell by the wayside.

**ALEXANDER II, TSAR OF RUSSIA (1818-1881).** Tsar of Russia
between 1855 and 1881 who was assassinated by members of the
radical group NARODNAYA VOLYA in a St Petersburg street on
March 1st 1881. Alexander was mortally wounded by a primitive
bomb thrown by Ivan Grinevetsky (who also died from the
explosion). The Tsar had got out of his carriage to see the results
of another bomb thrown by Grinevetsky's fellow conspirators when
the young radical struck. Alexander never regained consciousness
and died two hours later. Grinevetsky died within eight hours.
The rest of the conspirators, including the leader SOPHIA
PETROVSKAYA, were quickly rounded up by the police. All were
tried, found guilty, and brutally and inefficiently hanged.

Ironically, Alexander II was succeeded by his son Alexander III who was even more of an autocrat than his father, and who virtually turned the Russian Empire into one of the first of the modern police states. In 1887 an abortive attempt was made by another radical group to assassinate Alexander III. It failed miserably, and one of the conspirators who was hanged was Alexander Ilyich Ulyanov, elder brother of Vladimir Ilyich Ulyanov who became known as Lenin.

**ALGIERS, BATTLE OF. (January-March 1957).** A crucial and particularly bitter episode in the war between the Algerian nationalists led by SAADI YACEF of the FRONT DE LIBERATION NATIONALE (FLN) and the French colonial authorities led by JACQUES MASSU and his 10th Parachute Division. Although ruthless action by the French military and police, including the extensive use of torture, temporarily halted the FLN's bombing campaign in the city, it alienated so many Arabs in the process that their "victory" probably helped to lose the war for France. It is estimated that in the course of the battle almost 40% of the male population of the Algiers Casbah (Arab quarter) were arrested or detained. French historians have claimed that the viciousness with which the Algiers counter-insurgency was waged, particularly the use of "la torture" infected the French body politic for many years.

**ALIANZA APOSTOLICA ANTICOMMUNISTA (AAA).** (The Anti-Communist Apostolic Alliance). A quasi-Fascist group with high Catholic overtones which waged a campaign of terror against Basque and Catalan separatists and left-wing labour leaders in Spain in the 1970s and early 1980s. The AAA's most notorious action was the assassination of four liberal lawyers in broad daylight on January 24th 1977 in Madrid. In September 1977 the AAA killed two people when they bombed a left-wing newspaper office. Like many traditionalist Spaniards, the members of the AAA were dismayed by the liberalisation of Spain after the death of Franco, and saw themselves as defenders of Spain's unity, and as a bastion of Christian civilisation.

**ALON, YOSEF.** Israeli diplomat and military hero assassinated in Washington in December 1975. Alon was one of Israel's most famous military pilots, and was air attaché at the Israeli Embassy in Washington when he was shot to death outside his home in a city suburb. Although the American police never solved the crime, the Israelis believe that Alon was killed by American "Black Power" gunmen acting on an assassination contract from BLACK SEPTEMBER. After Alon's killing a Palestinian newspaper published in Beirut warned "nothing will stop the Palestinian people from expanding the scope of the war against its enemies".

**AMAL.** The militia of the minority Shi'ite Muslims of Lebanon led by Nabbih Berri. Drawn mainly from the poorest part of Lebanon's Muslim population, the Amal have proved to be particularly bitter enemies of Israel but have also turned their guns against the Palestinians (whom they blame for bringing down the wrath of Israel on the Shi'ite communities). During the Israeli invasion of the Lebanon in 1982 the Amal fought the Israelis with more determination than most, particularly in the operations around Beirut airport. In the summer of 1983 an attempt by the Lebanese government's forces to destroy the Amal militia by taking the organisation's headquarters at Borj al-Barajneh failed. In the first six months of 1986 Amal were engaged in open warfare with the various Palestinian groups which were struggling to re-establish themselves in the south of Lebanon after being driven out by the Israelis in 1982.

**AMERICAN AIR FORCE BASE ATTACK, RHEIN-MAIN. (August 8th 1985).** Car bomb attack by the ROTE ARMEE FRAKTION (RAF) and ACTION DIRECTE (AD) on one of the largest US Air Force bases in West Germany. The attack, timed for 07.15, killed one US airman, the wife of another, and injured 30 people. West German security believe that the attackers used the military identity card of American soldier Edward Pimental, 20, to gain access to the base. Pimental was found shot dead in nearby Wiesbaden on the morning of the bombing. He was last seen leaving a local nightclub with a man and a woman. The woman is believed to have been Andrea Martina Klump (28), suspected member of the RAF.

**AMERICAN EMBASSY BOMBINGS, BEIRUT. (April 18th 1983).** Bombing attack by Shi'ite Muslim fundamentalists on the American Embassy in Beirut which destroyed the building, killed 63 people and injured more than 100. At 13.00 a dark-coloured delivery van drove into the Embassy car park where the driver exploded a huge quantity of explosive. The suicide bomb virtually destroyed the seven-storey sea-front building. And the attack was a serious blow to US policy in the Lebanon because it killed eight senior agents of the CENTRAL INTELLIGENCE AGENCY (CIA) including the CIA's Middle East analyst Robert Ames.

More than a year later, on September 20th 1984, Shi'ite extremists launched another suicide attack on the American Embassy annexe in East Beirut, killing 14 people and injuring more than 30 with 2,000lbs of explosive packed into a Chevrolet van.

**AMERICAN EMBASSY BOMBING, KUWAIT. (December 12th 1983).** Suicide bombing attack on the US Embassy building in Kuwait which killed five people. The explosives were packed into a truck which crashed through the Embassy gates and rammed a three-storey annexe. All that remained of the driver was his thumb, which was enough to identify him as Raad Muftin Ajeel, a 25-year-old Iraqi Shi'ite Muslim. If Ajeel had succeeded in reaching the chancellory building the casualties would have been much heavier. The bomb at the US Embassy was one of six bombing attacks in Kuwait that day. All were perpetrated by Shi'ite fundamentalists.

**AMERICAN EMBASSY HOSTAGE CRISIS, TEHERAN. (November 4th 1979 – January 20th 1981).** The 444-day-long diplomatic/political crisis began on November 4th 1979 when Iranian students took over the huge American Embassy complex in the centre of Teheran and held the staff of 53 hostage. In return for their safety and/or release the Iranians demanded the return of the deposed Shah to stand trial in Iran. An attempt by the US military to rescue the hostages failed, and the crisis ran on for 15 months until their release was negotiated by the intervention of the Algerian government. The American Embassy hostage crisis badly damaged President Jimmy Carter's re-election prospects. President Carter's response to the takeover of the Embassy was to deport large numbers of Iranians, halt oil imports from Iran, freeze Iranian assets in the USA, impose economic sanctions and break off diplomatic relations. American credibility was weakened considerably when "EAGLE CLAW", the military operation to free the hostages ended in disaster on April 24th 1980. In July 1981 the deposed Shah died of cancer in Cairo.

Following the abortive US rescue attempt the hostages were dispersed around Iran and were threatened with a "trial" by the Iranian authorities. The Iranians also demanded the return of the late Shah's vast wealth, the unfreezing of Iranian assets in the USA, and a guarantee of "no interference" in Iranian affairs. In November 1980 Vice-President Edmund Muskie accepted the Iranian demands "in principle", and on January 19th 1981 the

Americans signed an agreement in Algeria. On January 20th 1981 (the day that newly elected President Ronald Reagan was sworn in) the 52 American hostages were released. They were flown to Wiesbaden in West Germany where they were met by ex-President Jimmy Carter.

**AMERICAN MARINE HQ ATTACK, BEIRUT. (October 23rd 1983).** A suicide bombing attack by Shi'ite Muslims of the ISLAMIC JIHAD on the headquarters of the US Marines near Beirut International Airport which killed 241 marines and sailors. It was the worst attack on American forces since the end of the Vietnam war, and a forensic study by the FEDERAL BUREAU OF INVESTIGATION (FBI) decided that the explosion had been caused by six tons of dynamite. A simultaneous suicide attack destroyed the FRENCH ARMY HQ, BEIRUT a few miles away. In February 1984 the US Marines of the Multi National Force (MNF) withdrew from Lebanon. A commission of inquiry into the incident by the US Marine Corps blamed the local commanders for slack security.

The Marine HQ was attacked at 06.20 on October 23rd 1983 when a yellow-painted Mercedes truck loaded with 12,000lbs of explosive crashed through the gate in the Marine compound, and drove straight into the four-storey building. In the huge explosion that followed the reinforced concrete building collapsed on itself, killing 241 marines and sailors. Marine Eddie DiFranco, who survived the blast, said that the driver of the truck was smiling as he drove at full speed into the headquarters building. A few hours after the bombings a telephone call was made to the Agence France Press in Beirut claiming the attack for Islamic Jihad.

**ANAND MARG.** (The Path of Eternal Bliss). Mystical, quasi-Hindu cult banned by the Indian government in 1975 following a series of assassinations and bombings. The Anand Marg's most important victim was Narayan Mishra, India's railways minister who was assassinated by a bomb on January 2nd 1975 in Bihar. Two other people were killed in the bombing (one a railway employee and the other a member of the Bihar state legislature) and 25 people were injured. The Anand Marg were also blamed for an attempt on the life of Ajit Nath Ray, Chief Justice of India on March 20th 1975. When they banned the Anand Marg on July 4th 1975 the Indian government claimed that the organisation had drawn up a political "hit list" and were "bent on creating conditions of violence and chaos" throughout India, and were resorting to political murder "to suppress dissent and terrorise the government". The Anand Marg were based in Bihar and claimed to be supporters of Jaya Prakesh Narayan's socialist party, although Narayan denied any connection with the group.

**ANGRY BRIGADE.** British left-wing anarchist group who tried to import the ideas of the West German ROTE ARMEE FRAKTION into Britain in the early 1970s. Eight of the group were jailed in 1972 when they became known as the STOKE NEWINGTON EIGHT. The Angry Brigade were responsible for a series of bombings in and around London in 1971, including attacks on the homes of British Home Secretary Robert Carr, the Commissioner of the Metropolitan Police, the Attorney General, the Miss World Competition in the Albert Hall, and the Metropolitan Police computer at Tintagel House in South London.

**ANIMAL RIGHTS MILITIA (ARM).** Shadowy British animal-welfare group which has conducted a series of raids on breeding and research establishments which experiment on animals. In January 1986 ARM activists planted crude bombs under the cars of Peter Savage, sales director of an animal importing and breeding firm, and Brian Meldrum, head of a psychiatric research team. Other bombs were planted at the homes of Alan Armitage, director of a research laboratory and Professor Ted Evans, head of a university neuro-science unit. Warnings were given, and none of the bombs exploded. Most British animal welfare groups condemned the ARM attacks, but a spokesman for the Animal Liberation Front (ALF) from which the ARM is a splinter, said, "I wouldn't be at all concerned if a vivisector was killed compared with the death and suffering they cause to millions of animals." A British government minister described the bomb planting as a "serious crime" and promised "vigorous" investigation.

**ANTI-ABORTION TERRORISM.** A phenonomenon which has emerged in the United States in the 1980s. Since March 1982 there have been more than 40 bombings, and 150 "acts of vandalism" on abortion clinics all over the USA, from California to New York City and Washington DC. The anti-abortion terror groups have been operating under a number of names including The Army of God, God's Army and The Armies of the Living God. Almost all the dozen or so people who have been arrested in connection with the attacks have been fundamentalist Christians incensed by the failure of conventional lobbying to halt abortion. Although the

FEDERAL BUREAU OF INVESTIGATION (FBI) has declared that there is little or no evidence of serious organisation, the American authorities are concerned that the anti-abortion campaign has been attracting support from far right groups such as the Posse Comitatus, which has stated that abortion is part of a conspiracy "masterminded by the Jews". Another right-wing group declares that "Almost all abortion doctors are Jews. Abortion makes money for Jews. Almost all abortion nurses are Lesbians." So far, no one has been seriously injured, and most clinics have been attacked when they were empty. But in December 1985 one New York abortion clinic was bombed minutes after the staff and patients had been evacuated, and another in Portland, Oregon received a lethal parcel bomb that was designed to explode when opened.

**ANTI-JEWISH TERRORISM.** The Institute of Jewish Affairs in London has been monitoring attacks on Jewish and Israeli individuals and institutions in Western Europe since 1980 and say that of the 845 "terrorist-type attacks" logged 139 of them have been serious, many involving fatalities. While some of these incidents have included Palestinian and other Arab terrorist attacks on Israeli airlines, offices, diplomats etc., a large number have been attacks on Jewish (not Israeli) restaurants, synagogues, clubs, homes and individuals. Terrorist groups and individuals of both left and right have been involved in attacks on European Jews, in locations as far apart as Athens in Greece to Glasgow in Scotland. Most of the fatalities and serious injuries have been inflicted on Jews in France and Italy, but less serious violence appears to be most common in Britain.

The most notorious incidents were the attacks on GOLDENBERG'S RESTAURANT in Paris in August 1982 (which killed six and injured 22) and the RUE COPERNIC SYNAGOGUE BOMBING in Paris in October 1980 (which killed four and injured 15). There have also been serious attacks on Jewish synagogues in Antwerp (1981), Vienna (1981) and Rome (1982), and minor ones in Leeds, London, Marseilles, Edinburgh, Glasgow, Cork, Rome, Dusseldorf, Manchester and Copenhagen. There have also been attacks on Jewish community centres, museums, Kosher food stores, travel agencies, shops, graveyards, cafés, banks and individuals (including the Nazi-hunter Simon Weisenthal). The Institute of Jewish Affairs describes the attacks on Jewish synagogues and graveyards as " . . . a particularly pernicious form of anti-semitic vandalism, uniquely painful . . .".

**ANTONOV, SERGEI.** The 37-year-old Bulgarian implicated in the assassination attempt on Pope John Paul II in May 1981 by the Turk MEHMET ALI AGCA. Agca claimed that Antonov was a member of the Bulgarian Secret Service which had organised the plot to kill the Pope, and that Antonov's job with the Bulgarian state airline was a "cover" for his sub rosa activities. But after a lengthy trial in Rome, Antonov was found "innocent for lack of sufficient proof of guilt" at the end of March 1986 and released. Two other Bulgarians and two Turks who had been accused along with Antonov were also acquitted on the same basis. The accusations against the three Bulgarians led Bulgaria to withdraw its Ambassador to Italy in 1982, while the Italian defence minister described the attack on the Pope as "an act of war" by Bulgaria.

**"ANVIL", OPERATION. (November 1981).** The abortive coup d'état on the government of the Seychelles organised and led by mercenary leader MICHAEL ("MAD MIKE") HOARE. The attempted coup was carried out on behalf of exiled Seychellois in Paris and London, and according to most accounts had the tacit support of the governments of both Kenya and South Africa. But when the operation went badly wrong and Hoare and some of the mercenaries fled back to South Africa, they were arrested, tried and jailed by the South African authorities.

The attempted coup went disastrously wrong on the 22nd November 1981 when Hoare tried to infiltrate 47 mercenaries through Mahé airport disguised as a South African beer-drinking society called "The Ancient Order of Frothblowers". Their concealed weapons (mainly KALASHNIKOV AK-47 assault rifles) were discovered by the Seychelles customs officers, and in the ensuing gun battle one of the mercenaries was shot dead (probably by his own side). After the battle with the Seychellois army and police, Hoare and 45 of his mercenaries made good their escape by hijacking an Air-India Boeing 727 which they flew to Durban in South Africa. They were arrested on arrival by the South African authorities. The seven mercenaries who had been left behind in the Seychelles were quickly rounded up by the Seychelloise army.

In July 1982, 45 of the mercenaries were tried in South Africa on hijacking and arms-smuggling charges. Hoare was sentenced to 20 years in jail (remitted to 10 years because of his age) while the others were given sentences ranging from five years to four months. Hoare was released in May 1985, having served less than one third of his sentence. The six men and one woman captured in the Seychelles were tried in June 1982 and the men sentenced to death. But the sentence was never carried out, and the mercenaries were set free in the summer of 1983.

**AQUINO, BENIGNO (1932-1983).** Philippine opposition leader assassinated on 21st August 1983 at Manila airport on his return to the Philippines after three years of political exile in the USA. Initially Aquino's death was blamed on lone assassin ROLANDO GALMAN who was immediately shot dead by security forces. But investigations suggested a conspiracy within the corrupt and demoralised Philippines army. Eventually, 25 senior army officers, including Chief of Staff General Fabian Ver, stood trial for Aquino's murder, but were acquitted on December 2nd 1985. A few weeks previously Aquino's widow Corazon announced her intention to stand against Ferdinand Marcos for the Presidency of the Philippines. After a bitter election battle during which the Marcos regime was accused of trying to rig the electoral process, the Philippines military threw their weight behind Aquino. In February 1986 Ferdinand Marcos was forced to stand down and go into exile in Hawaii, while the new regime launched a campaign to locate and recover the estimated $3 billion Marcos had salted away throughout the western world. The new regime also announced its intention to set up a new investigation into the death of Benigno Aquino.

**ARAFAT, YASIR (born 1929).** Also known as Abu Ammar. Real name Abdel-Rahman Abdel-Raouf Arafat al-Qudwa al-Husseini. Chairman of the PALESTINE LIBERATION ORGANIZATION (PLO) since 1969, and head of FATAH since the early 1960s, Arafat has become one of the most important leaders of the Arab world. While beset with external and internal enemies he remains the main spokesman for the dispossessed Palestinian people.

Born either in Cairo or Jerusalem into a middle-class Sunni Muslim family Arafat studied engineering at Cairo University in the late 1940s and early 1950s. While a student in Cairo Arafat met young Palestinian activists like SALAH KHALAF and KHALIL WAZIR with whom he was to found the guerrilla/terrorist movement FATAH in October 1959. According to Palestinian sources, Arafat fought with the Egyptians in the war of 1956 and then joined the Ministry of Public Works in Kuwait in 1957. It was among the Palestine community of Kuwait that Arafat was able to lay the groundwork for the Fatah movement (which carried out sporadic guerrilla operations in the mid-1960s).

In 1969, following the humiliation of the Arab nations by the Israelis in the Six-Day War of 1967, Arafat and his Fatah colleagues were able to take over the structures of the PALESTINE LIBERATION ORGANISATION (PLO) which had been set up by the Arab states in 1964. Arafat has been chairman of the PLO (and of Fatah) ever since.

**ARAMBURA, PEDRO EUGENIO**. One-time President of Argentina who was kidnapped and then killed by the Argentine MONTONEROS in May 1970. Arambura's assassination was the opening shot in the Montoneros' campaign of terror against Argentine society. The activities of the Montoneros and similar groups led directly to the military coup of 1976 and the notorious "dirty war" which followed.

**ARGOV, SHLOMO**. Israeli ambassador to Britain who was shot and badly injured in a London street on June 3rd 1982. Although Argov survived the attack, it set in motion a chain of events which are still reverberating round the world. Argov's assailants were quickly arrested, and found to be members of BLACK JUNE, an organisation run by the terrorist leader ABU NIDAL. Nidal's men have since launched terrorist attacks on British diplomats and institutions in an attempt to force the release of the Black June men from British jails. The assassination attempt on Argov was one of the factors which prompted the Israeli government to launch Operation "Peace for Galilee", the invasion of Lebanon in June 1982 which drove the PALESTINE LIBERATION ORGANISATION (PLO) out of Lebanon and into exile in Tunisia and Syria.

Shlomo Argov, then 52, was shot in the head and seriously injured while getting into his car outside the Dorchester Hotel, London, on the evening of June 3rd 1982. His assailant was himself promptly shot and injured by an armed policemen, and the two other members of the assassination squad were arrested by London police in South London shortly after. While the PLO immediately denied any responsibility for the attack on Argov, claiming it would be "detrimental" to their cause, on the 6th of June the Israeli Defence Forces launched their massive invasion of the Lebanon which drove the PLO out of the country. Two days later, on June 8th, Palestinian Abu Nidal announced that his men had carried out the assassination attempt on Argov.

On March 5th 1983 three Arabs – Marwan Al-Banna, Navoft Rosan and Hussein Said – were convicted of the attempted murder of Shlomo Argov. Rosan was sentenced to 35 years in jail, while Al-Banna and Said received sentences of 30 years. Rosan was said to have been the leader of the assassination squad, and Al-Banna a nephew of Abu Nidal. Since the trial and conviction of the Black June squad, Abu Nidal's men have attacked British diplomats in India and Greece, and bombed British airline offices and holidaymakers around Europe.

**ARMALITE AR-15 (M-16).** Light, portable, American-designed assault rifle, much favoured by some terrorist groups, particularly the PROVISIONAL IRISH REPUBLICAN ARMY (PIRA) who smuggle the weapons in from the USA. Designed by Eugene Stoner, and manufactured by the Colt Company, the Armalite came into service with the US forces in 1959 since when millions have been produced. Made from plastic and aluminium, the Armalite measures 39 inches, weighs 6.35lbs, has a 30-round magazine, and an automatic rate of fire of 800 rounds per minute (compared to the KALASHNIKOV AK-47's 650 rounds per minute). A smaller (but slightly heavier) version of the Armalite called the "Colt Commando" was developed for the use of US Special Forces. The weapon has also been used by the British Army's SPECIAL AIR SERVICE (SAS).

**ARMENIAN SECRET ARMY FOR THE LIBERATION OF ARMENIA (ASALA).** Left-wing pro-Soviet Armenian organisation whose long-term aim is the establishment of an independent Armenian Republic, but which is trying to pressure the Turkish government to halt "discrimination" against the Armenian language, and Armenian culture. ASALA also seek to revenge the estimated 1.5 million Armenians killed by the Turks in 1915-16. Over the past 10 years ASALA have operated throughout Europe, the Middle East and North America attacking Turkish individuals and institutions.

Since their inception in Beirut in 1975 ASALA have specialised in attacking Turkish diplomats throughout the world. In 1981 ASALA probably carried out more terrorist attacks than any other organisation; 40 attacks in 11 countries including the seizure of the Turkish consulate in Paris, and the murder of Turkish diplomats in Switzerland, Denmark and France. The organisation also waged a clandestine war against the French and Swiss authorities for arresting Armenians travelling on bogus passports. In fact the Swiss bowed to ASALA pressure in 1981 and released two arrested Armenians after ASALA bombed and attacked Swiss targets in Beirut, London, Paris, Milan, Rome, Berne and Los Angeles in late 1980 and early 1981.

ASALA model themselves on the more extreme Palestinian groups (from whom they receive support). The organisation is pro-Soviet, regard Soviet Armenia as a "free country" and are probably being promoted by the Soviet intelligence services to harass the pro-NATO Turkish government.

**ARMY OF THE PROVISIONAL GOVERNMENT (APG).** One of a number of Scottish separatist groups which emerged in the 1970s during the upsurge of Scottish nationalist/separatist political feeling which saw 11 Scottish National Party (SNP) members elected to the British Parliament. Most of the group were jailed in 1975 on bank robbery and conspiracy charges, and were roundly denounced by the SNP for their "comic opera military activities" which could only embarrass the SNP's "constitutional campaign" for an independent Scotland. The APG hoped to finance their activities by a series of bank raids in Scotland and England and when caught were planning to break into military arsenals and disrupt power supplies. Some of the APG men had served in the British Army, and one had been a major with experience of guerrilla and counter-insurgency warfare. Another had served 11 years with the Royal Engineers and had considerable experience of explosives.

**ARYAN NATIONS.** A right-wing American "umbrella" organisation which sustains links between like-minded groups such as the Christian Identity Movement, THE ORDER, The Covenant, the Sword and the Arm of the Lord (CSA), the KU-KLUX KLAN and Posse Comitatus. Based at Hayden Lake, Idaho, the Aryan Nations were founded in 1974 by a Christian fundamentalist called Richard Girnt Butler who preaches the creed that Christ was not a Jew, that the White Anglo-Saxons are the true "chosen race" and that the United States is the "promised land" of the Bible. Through a computerised "bulletin board" known as the Aryan Liberty Net the Aryan Nations have forged contacts with most of the right-wing extremist groups in the USA and Canada, and also have links with the Neo-Nazis of West Germany. They regard modern America as hopelessly degenerate and overrun by inferior races, and have threatened white-supremacist violence.

The growth of right-wing violence in the USA is beginning to worry the Federal authorities, and in December 1984 Federal attornies (prosecutors) from California, Oregon, Idaho, Alabama and Colorado met in Seattle to work out a "common strategy" to thwart the illegal activities of the American right. One of the

Rand Corporation's studies on right-wing terrorists and potential terrorists warns they are not "mentally unstable alarmists" or intemperate hotheads. "They are well trained in the use of arms and explosives, are skilled armorers and bomb-makers, and are adept at guerrilla warfare techniques and outdoor survival."

The American authorities are also watching with some care (and some astonishment) the growing links between white right-wing extremists and the Black Muslims who also seem to dislike Jews and Liberals. In October 1985 a "white nationalist delegation" attended a NATION OF ISLAM rally as guests of the Black Muslim leader Louis Farrakhan. Tom Metzger of the White People's Political Association told a convention of right-wing groups that America was like a "rotting carcass" off which the Jews were living "like the parasites they are. Farrakhan understands this."

**ASSAD, RIFAAT**. Head of the Syrian security and intelligence forces and brother of the Syrian president Hafez el Assad. Described as one of the most powerful men in Syria (and therefore the Middle East) Rifaat Assad has used his power mercilessly to guard his brother's regime against its opponents, particularly the Islamic fundamentalists of the MUSLIM BROTHERHOOD.

**ASSASSINATION**. The killing of political leaders, statesmen, politicans, or royalty, usually, but not always, for political reasons. Since the 1880s a surprisingly large number of world leaders have been killed by assassins, some acting as part of a conspiracy, others acting completely alone, and often for motives that are obscure. Probably the most notorious were the assassinations of Tsar ALEXANDER II of Russia (1881), Archduke FRANCIS FERDINAND of Austria (1914), King ALEXANDER I of Yugoslavia (1934), MAHATMA GANDHI of India (1948) and JAMES GARFIELD (1881), WILLIAM McKINLEY (1901) and JOHN F. KENNEDY (1963), all Presidents of the United States of America. But political assassins have also claimed the lives of hundreds of ambassadors, diplomats, police officials, United Nations negotiators, military officers, political exiles, and other terrorist leaders and political agitators. Unsuccessful attempts have been made on the lives of President Charles de Gaulle of France, Presidents Gerald Ford and Ronald Reagan of the USA, and the entire British cabinet (in Brighton in 1984).

Assassination is, of course, an ancient political strategy. Well organised bands of political/religious assassins existed among the Jewish "zealots" of the first century AD. Called the "siccari" (after the short swords which were their favourite weapons) they were an austere, fanatically anti-Roman sect who specialised in attacking religious leaders, Roman dignitaries, and burning the houses of "corrupt" Jewish priests. The word "assassin" is a European corruption of "hashashin" (the hashish eaters), a small but violent sect of Ismaili Muslims who flourished in the Middle East in the 11th and 12th centuries. For more than 100 years the hashashin waged a murderous campaign against Muslim and Christian leaders, even trying to kill the great Muslim statesman Saladin. Because killing was a quasi-mystical experience to them, the hashashin always used a dagger on their victims. They were finally rooted out in the 12th century by the Mogul emperor Halaku. A similar kind of religiosity informed the activities of the Indian "thuggee" (from which the word "thug" is derived) which was stamped out by the British Raj in the middle of the 19th century.

But the lists of royalty, heads of state and political leaders (and ex-leaders) who have been assassinated over the past 100 years are very long. Among them are Irish secretary Lord Frederick Cavendish (1882); President François Carnot of France (1894); the Shah of Persia (1896); Antonio Canovos, Prime Minister of Spain (1897); Elizabeth Empress of Austria (1898); King Umberto of Italy (1900); the Royal Family of Serbia (1903); Grand Duke Serge Alexandrovich (1905); King Carlos of Portugal (1908); King George of the Hellenes (1913); MICHAEL COLLINS (1922); Austrian Chancellor ENGELBERT DOLLFUSS (1934); Foreign Minister Louis Barthou of France (1934); Lord Moyne (1944); UN mediator Count Bernadotte (1948); King Faisal of Iraq (1958); Patrice Lumumba (1961); General Trujillo (1961); Dag Hammerskjold (1961); Ngo Dinh Diem (1963); MALCOLM X (1965); HENDRICK VERWOERD (1966); Prime Minister Mossadeq of Iran (1965); MARTIN LUTHER KING (1968) and ROBERT KENNEDY (1968).

More recently, assassination victims have included German ambassador Count KARL VON SPRETI (1970); PIERRE LAPORTE (1970); Prime Minister CARRERO BLANCO (1972); Indian cabinet minister V.M. Mishra (1975); Herbert Chitepo (1975); King Faisal of Saudi Arabia (1975); Murtala Mohammed of Nigeria (1976); British ambassador CHRISTOPHER EWART-BIGGS (1976); SAID HAMMAMI of the PLO (1978); ALDO MORO (1978); British ambassador Sir Richard Sykes (1979); AIREY NEAVE (1979); Lord MOUNTBATTEN OF BURMA (1979); Archbishop OSCAR ROMERO (1980); ex-dictator ANASTASIO SOMOZA (1980); General Zia ur Rahman of Bangladesh (1981);

President of Egypt ANWAR SADAT (1981); President-elect BASHIR GEMAYEL (1982); Prime Minister INDIRA GANDHI (1984) and Prime Minister OLOF PALME (1986).

**ASSEN TRAIN SIEGE, HOLLAND. (May 23rd-June 11th 1977).** The hijacking by South Moluccan terrorists of a Dutch commuter train near the small town of Assen in Holland. After more than two weeks of futile negotiations the siege ended when the anti-terrorist unit of the Royal Netherlands Marine Corps stormed the train, killing off the hijackers. Two of the 80 hostages died in the crossfire. After the siege the Dutch prime minister said, "That violence proved necessary to put an end to the seizure of the hostages is something that we feel as a defeat." The South Moluccans had also taken over a primary school at Bovinsmilde, but surrendered after four days when most of the schoolchildren became ill with a stomach virus.

The commuter train with 85 passengers aboard was seized near Assen on May 23rd 1977 by 13 South Moluccans armed with handguns and grenades. After 19 days of siege and negotiation, and with both hijackers and hostages showing signs of cracking under the strain, the psychologist in charge of the hostage negotiations advised the government that further negotations were useless and probably dangerous. On June 11th 1977 the Dutch ordered the marine anti-terrorist unit to storm the train. Although the British Army's SPECIAL AIR SERVICE (SAS) were on hand with "flash-bang" stun grenades, the Dutch decided to create a diversion by using a flight of "Starfighter" jets to swoop low over the train with their afterburners switched on. In the noise and confusion created by the aircraft the marines burst into the coaches killing six of the hijackers (including the leader who called himself "Max"). During the attack two of the hostage passengers leapt to their feet and were killed in the cross fire.

**ATHENS AIRPORT ATTACK. (December 26th 1968).** An armed attack by Arab gunmen from the POPULAR FRONT FOR THE LIBERATION OF PALESTINE (PFLP) on an Israeli airliner about to take off from Athens airport. One passenger was killed, an Israeli stewardess was badly injured, and the aircraft caught fire. The two PFLP men were quickly arrested by Greek police and put on trial in Athens at the end of December. The PFLP admitted responsibility for the attack and said it had been ordered because El Al (the Israeli state airline) was used to ferry Israeli air force pilots to and from training programmes in the United States.

The El Al Boeing 707 with 51 passengers and crew aboard was attacked on December 26th 1968 as it was about to take off on a scheduled flight from Athens to Paris. The two young gunmen – later named as Mahmoud Muhammad (25) and Maher Suleiman (19) – drew a submachine-gun and incendiary grenades from a holdall, and attacked the airliner. One passenger was killed outright, a stewardess was badly injured trying to jump from the aircraft, and the incendiary grenades ignited one of the aircraft's engines (although the fire was promptly extinguished by the airport fire brigade). The two PFLP men were tried by the Greek authorities on a number of serious charges (including murder and illegal possession of weapons) and at the end of March 1969 given long prison sentences. The two young Arabs argued – unsuccessfully – that they were "combatants" in a war against Israel, acting under orders, and should be treated by the rules of the Geneva Convention. They said they were under instructions to destroy the aircraft but not to harm any of the passengers or crew.

**ATHENS AIRPORT SIEGE. (August 5th 1973).** Killing of five airline passengers in the terminal of Athens airport by two members of BLACK SEPTEMBER intent on revenging the assassination of ABU YOUSSEF in Beirut by members of the Israeli MOSSAD. The gunmen tried to hold the Greek police at bay by taking 35 passengers hostage but surrendered to the authorities. At their trial the two men, Shafik El-Arida (22) and Tallal Khaled Kaddourah (21) said that they had attacked the TWA passengers because the flight was carrying Jewish immigrants to Israel. The men were later identified as belonging to a group of FATAH dissidents. After a one-day trial in Athens, both men were sentenced to death on January 23rd 1974. The release of the two men was demanded by the Muslims who mounted the "VORI" HIJACKING, KARACHI, on February 2nd 1974. To avoid more harassment from Arab terrorists, the Greek government commuted the death sentences to life imprisonment and then released the two men on May 5th 1974 and deported them to Libya. The Greeks' decision caused an international furore and charges of "softness" on terrorist demands.

**AUSTRALIAN SECURITY AND INTELLIGENCE ORGAN-ISATION (ASIO).** The Australian government's intelligence-gathering and counter-intelligence operation which was founded in the 1950s after the Soviet defector Vladimir Petrov revealed extensive KGB activities in the Antipodes, particularly among recent immigrants to Australia. In 1983 the ASIO were investigated by a Royal Commission after it was revealed they had been tapping the telephones of politicians and cabinet ministers. The ASIO were grievously embarrassed at the end of 1983 when some of their agents (the worse for drink) staged a mock hostage-rescue operation at the Melbourne Sheraton Hotel terrifying guests and staff by their behaviour. The ASIO was described by the Australian press as a "bunch of stumblebums" and John Ryan, head of the ASIO's secret intelligence division was forced to resign. In 1984 the Australian government tightened its control of the ASIO.

**AVANGUARDIA NAZIONALE.** (National Vanguard). Right-wing Italian terrorist group blamed for the BOLOGNA RAILWAY STATION BOMBING in August 1980 in which more than 80 people died. The founder of the group was the notorious right-wing terrorist organiser STEFANO DELLE CHIAIE now thought to be living in South America. The group are also believed to be responsible for the murder of Italian magistrate Vittorio Occorsio in Rome in July 1976 after the jurist had been denounced by Delle Chiaie as "an enemy of Fascism".

The Avanguardia Nazionale was formed by Delle Chiaie in 1959 and in the 1960s became one of the most feared "Black Terror" (right-wing/fascist) groups in Europe with a reputation as particularly vicious street fighters. The Avanguardia Nazionale forged links with right-wing groups in Greece, Spain, Portugal and France out of which a right-wing terror international known as the "Black Orchestra" grew up. On December 7th 1970 the Avanguardia Nazionale were involved in an abortive coup d'état against the Italian government when they forced their way into the Ministry of the Interior and seized 200 machine-guns. But for reasons which have never been satisfactorily explained the coup was called off by its leader Prince Valerio Borghese, and Delle Chiaie and some of the Avanguarde Nazionale leaders went into exile in Spain.

**AZANIAN AFRICAN PEOPLE'S ORGANISATION (AZAPO).** A radical blacks-only offshoot of the AFRICAN NATIONAL CONGRESS (ANC) which has played an increasingly important role in the turbulent black townships of South Africa. Launched in May 1978, AZAPO is a "black consciousness" movement which allows no whites, "coloureds" or Asians in its ranks, and nurses a bitter contempt for white liberals whom it sees as a force for confusing the issue. AZAPO's initial aim was to organise black workers in industrial struggle against the white regime and the organisation has tried to establish close links with South Africa's increasingly powerful black trade unions. AZAPO have been accused by other black groups of acting as agents provocateurs in the black townships, inciting black youngsters to futile and often fatal assaults on the country's powerful security forces.

# B

**BAADER, ANDREAS (1943-1977).** Left-wing West German terrorist leader of the eponymous BAADER-MEINHOF GANG (also known as the ROTE ARMEE FRAKTION). Baader and his colleagues ran a bombing, assassination and armed robbery campaign which terrorised West Germany in the early 1970s before being caught, and sentenced to long prison terms. Baader and two of his colleagues committed suicide in Stammheim prison after two attempts to release them – the kidnapping of HANNS MARTIN SCHLYER and the LUFTHANSA HIJACKING TO MOGADISHU – failed.

A handsome, articulate product of a middle-class family (his father was a historian) Baader became involved in radical student politics in the late 1960s, and began his violent career in 1968 by planting an incendiary bomb in a department store in Frankfurt. Although promptly arrested by the police, Baader was released on appeal in June 1969, became something of a hero to the international left, went underground when his appeal failed, but was quickly captured. Thanks to Berlin's liberal prison regime, Baader's colleagues were able to engineer his escape from a Berlin library in which he was "researching" a book.

Baader then fled to Jordan where he and his colleagues were trained by the POPULAR FRONT FOR THE LIBERATION OF PALESTINE (PFLP) in the arts of terrorism. When the radical lawyer Horst Mahler was jailed in October 1970, Baader and his colleague ULRIKE MEINHOF (a TV reporter turned terrorist) took control of the organisation, and launched a campaign of bombings, bank robberies and kidnappings which killed at least 20 people, and which plagued West Germany throughout the early 1970s.

Although extremely violent, Baader's career as a terrorist was short. He was arrested in Frankfurt in 1972, and spent the rest of his life in prison. He committed suicide in Stammheim Prison on October 18th 1977 after the failure of the hijacking to Mogadishu. But the terrorist group which Baader helped to found, the Rote Armee Fraktion (RAF), still operates in West Germany.

**BAADER-MEINHOF GANG.** See ROTE ARMEE FRAKTION (RAF).

**"BABYLON", OPERATION**. Military codename for the Israeli bombing raid which destroyed the TAMMUZ nuclear reactors near Baghdad in Syria on June 7th 1981.

**BALCOMBE STREET SEIGE, LONDON. (December 6th-12th 1975)**. A four-man "active service unit" of the PROVISIONAL IRISH REPUBLICAN ARMY (PIRA) were trapped in a flat at Balcombe Street in West London after a police chase. The men held the occupants, John and Sheila Matthews, hostage for seven days. The gunmen eventually surrendered when they heard that the police had called in the SPECIAL AIR SERVICE (SAS). Their two middle-aged hostages were released unharmed. The incident raised, for the first time, the constitutional problem of who the SAS were responsible to in hostage-taking situations. It was decided that, on mainland Britain at least, the army were answerable to the civil police.

The siege began on the evening of December 6th 1975 after the four PIRA men (three Irishmen and a Scot) shot up Scott's Restaurant in Mayfair, London, and were chased into Balcombe Street where they took over the flat at number 22b. In return for the safety of the residents, Mr and Mrs Matthews, the gunmen demanded an aircraft to take them to Dublin, but they were told by the Metropolitan Police that there could be "no deals". After seven days of constant negotiation the men surrendered in the afternoon of December 12th 1975 after hearing on the radio that the police had asked the SAS to intervene.

In February 1976 the men – Martin O'Connell, Edward Butler, Harry Duggan and Hugh Doherty – were found guilty of six murders in the London area, including that of ROSS McWHIRTER and sentenced to life imprisonment. The judge recommended that the PIRA men serve at least 30 years in jail. A year later, in February 1977, two of their accomplices, James Murphy and Anthony Cunningham, were jailed for 10 years each.

**BANCA DEL AGRICULTURA BOMBING, MILAN. (December 12th 1969)**. Bombing attack by right-wing terrorists on a city-centre bank in the Piazza Fontana which killed 16 people and injured many others. Although the attack was the work of right-wingers from the AVANGUARDIA NAZIONALE, the Italian police blamed left-wing anarchists and jailed anarchist leader PIETRO VALPREDA. On the same day the Avanguardia Nazionale exploded two more bombs in Rome (which did relatively little damage). The Milan and Rome bombs were part of the

Avanguardia Nazionale's strategy of causing destruction which would be blamed on the militant left who would then be repressed by the military, thus setting up the conditions for a fascist state.

**BANNA, HASAN AL (1903-1949).** Egyptian-born Muslim fundamentalist who founded the MAJALLAT AL IKHWAN AL MUSLIMIN (The MUSLIM BROTHERHOOD) in 1925. The militant Muslim Brotherhood has now spread to most Muslim countries in the world, and has been particularly troublesome to the governments of Egypt and Syria. Hasan al Banna himself was shot dead in Cairo in January 1949 by Egyptian government agents after a Muslim Brotherhood assassination squad had killed Egypt's prime minister Nokrashi Pasha. But the Muslim Brotherhood which Banna founded in 1925 continues to flourish and is one of the mainsprings of the current upsurge of Muslim fundamentalism which has rocked the Middle East and North Africa.

An ascetic, deeply religious man who was appalled by the "pollution" of Islamic life and religion by Western influences, Banna founded the Muslim Brotherhood in Ismailia when only 22 years old. A government primary schoolteacher by profession, he built up the brotherhood organisation in the Canal Zone of Egypt, building schools, mosques, Islamic clubs, and even encouraging a variety of small (religiously approved) industries. In 1939 Banna moved to Cairo where he cast his net wider, and in 1941 he was arrested for organising demonstrations against the British authorities.

Through the 1940s the Muslim Brotherhood grew steadily more militant, and in the 1948 war against the new state of Israel armed members of the Brotherhood fought in the Egyptian Army. As early as 1942 or 1943 Banna had set up a specially-selected "secret apparatus" of armed men. When this group was discovered by the Egyptian government, the Muslim Brotherhood was proscribed in December 1948. Shortly after the banning a squad from the "secret apparatus" shot dead the Egyptian prime minister, and within weeks Banna himself was killed by government agents.

**BARRIL, PAUL.** One of the four French secret service officers arrested and indicted in September 1985 for leaking information to the French press about the plans by the DIRECTION GENERALE DE LA SECURITE EXTERIEURE (DGSE) to sink the Greenpeace ship *RAINBOW WARRIOR*. Previously head of the French anti-terrorist group GROUPE D'INTERVENTION DE LA GENDARMERIE NATIONALE (GIGN) and an expert marksman, combat diver and parachutist, Barril is one of the France's best-known anti-terrorist officials. A supporter of the hard-line methods of the French "action service" teams, Barril resigned from GIGN in 1983 after he was refused permission to blow up a houseboat in the Seine suspected of being a hideout of the left-wing terrorist group ACTION DIRECTE (AD). Although not directly involved in the DGSE operation against the *Rainbow Warrior*, Barril apparently felt that the DGSE were being forced to take the blame for an essentially political decision.

**BECKWITH, CHARLES A**. American special forces colonel who set up the American anti-terrorist DELTA FORCE which was closely modelled on the British Army's SPECIAL AIR SERVICE (SAS). Beckwith served on detachment with the SAS from 1962 to 1963, and was involved in a number of SAS counter insurgency (COIN) operations in Malaya. Impressed by the flexibility and expertise of the SAS, Beckwith spent many years trying to persuade the United States Army to set up a similar specialised force. Eventually, after the LUFTHANSA HIJACKING TO MOGADISHU in 1977 the Pentagon agreed, and "activated" 1st Special Forces Operational Detachment Delta with Beckwith in command. But Delta Force's first major assignment was the "EAGLE CLAW" OPERATION, the abortive attempt to solve the AMERICAN EMBASSY HOSTAGE CRISIS, TEHERAN. Beckwith retired from the US Army in 1981 and now runs a private security consultancy in Austin, Texas. He was hired by the American government to prepare a report on the planning of the security operations for the 1984 Olympics in Los Angeles.

**BEGIN, MENACHEM (born 1913)**. One-time leader of the IRGUN ZVAI LEUMI (IRGUN) terrorist group who became prime minister of Israel. A Russian Jew from Brest-Litovsk, Begin emigrated to British-controlled Palestine during the early years of World War II. Regarded by the British authorities as one of the most dangerous of the Jewish extremists, it was Begin's Irgun which blew up the KING DAVID HOTEL in July 1946. In April 1948 Irgun and the smaller group Lehi were responsible for DEIR YASSIN MASSACRE. Begin was elected to the Knesset (parliament) in 1948, became leader of the right-wing Likud (Unity) Party in 1973, and became prime minister of Israel in 1977. Begin presided over Operation "Peace for Galilee", the invasion of Beirut in June 1982, and his standing was undermined by the SABRA AND SHATILA MASSACRES. He resigned for reasons of ill health in September 1983.

**BEILEN TRAIN SEIGE, HOLLAND. (December 2nd-14th 1975).** A 12-day-long siege of a hijacked passenger train at Beilen in Holland during which three people, including the driver of the train, were shot dead. The train had been taken over by a group of armed South Moluccan terrorists, agitating for the independence of South Molucca from the state of Indonesia. After 12 days during which the train was surrounded by more than 1,000 marines and police, the gunmen finally surrendered to the authorities on December 14th 1975. The Moluccan "government in exile" (to whose youth wing the hijackers belonged) played an important part in talking the gunmen out of the situation. While the train siege was going on another group of South Moluccans occupied the INDONESIAN CONSULATE, AMSTERDAM. Both incidents were organised by Eddie Appono, leader of the Free South Moluccan Organisation. South Moluccans staged another, much bloodier, train siege at ASSEN in May 1976 during which nine people were killed.

**BEIRUT AIRPORT RAID. (December 28th 1968).** A reprisal raid by the Israeli SAYARET MATKAL on Arab-owned aircraft at Beirut airport for the ATHENS AIRPORT ATTACK on an Israeli airliner two days previously. The 40-strong Israeli team swept in from the sea in helicopters, and in full view of hundreds of people destroyed 13 parked Lebanese airliners. The Israeli raid cost Lloyd's of London more than $16 million in insurance compensation. Although popular with the Israeli public, the Beirut airport raid was used by France as a reason to cut off all military supplies to Israel at a time when Israel relied heavily on French equipment.

The Beirut airport raid began at 21.30 on December 28th 1968 and was led by Brigadier General Rafael Eytan. While Eytan's men were clearing the aircraft of passengers, laying their explosive charges and discouraging the Lebanese police from intervening, Eytan spent an hour sipping Arabic coffee in the main terminal, paying for it with an Israeli note. At 22.30 Eytan and the Sayaret Matkal group climbed back into their helicopters and flew off, leaving behind them the wreckage of a Boeing 707, a VC-10, three Comets, two Caravelles and a Viscount plus an assortment of smaller aircraft. Eight of the aircraft belonged to the Lebanese state company Middle East Airlines (MEA) while the other five were owned by Lebanese International Airlines and Trans-Mediterranean Airlines.

The Sayaret Matkal attack on the Lebanese airliners was judged an audacious success by the Israeli public already growing weary of assaults on their airline. But the United States announced their displeasure, the French Government used it as a reason for cutting off all arms and equipment supplies to Israel (as part of France's policy of moving closer to the Arabs) and the world-wide media attention gave enormous publicity to the Palestinian cause.

**BEIRUT RAID. (April 9th-10th 1973).** An attack by the Israeli SAYARET MATKAL teams on the BLACK SEPTEMBER command structure in Beirut which killed three leading Palestinians and destroyed a Black September ordnance depot and removed a large quantity of Black September files and intelligence material. Initially the Israeli government were reluctant to admit responsibility for the raid (which involved civilian deaths) but eventually did so and claimed they had "killed the murderers who were planning to murder again". But the speed and brutality with which it was carried out created a wave of sympathy for the Palestinians throughout the Middle East, with huge pro-Palestinian demonstrations in Beirut and Cairo.

After careful planning and intelligence gathering by the Israeli MOSSAD on the night of April 9th 1973, 30 or so Israelis slipped ashore in rubber dinghies from Israeli patrol boats. All were dressed in civilian clothes. The men split into three groups of 10, climbed into hire cars which were waiting for them near the beach, and drove to their assigned targets around Beirut.

One group led by JONATHAN NETANYAHU attacked an apartment block on Rue 68 where they shot to death Black September leader ABU YOUSSEF, his deputy Kemel Adwan, and the PLO's chief spokesman in Beirut (and an accomplished poet) Kammal Nasser. The wives of Nasser and Adwan also died in the attack, as did an innocent 70-year-old Italian woman who opened her door at the wrong moment and was killed by gunfire. Another Israeli group attacked an apartment block in the south of Beirut which was the headquarters of the DEMOCRATIC FRONT FOR THE LIBERATION OF PALESTINE (DFLP). This building was heavily guarded, and a protracted gun battle ensued in which two Israelis died and two were wounded. After 30 minutes of close-quarters shooting the Israelis laid their charges, blew up the building, and fled in their hire cars, leaving heavy Arab casualties behind them. The third attack group blew up three other terrorist offices in Beirut, plus a Black September "bomb-factory", in the town of Sidon. This group met little or no resistance, did their work swiftly, and drove off.

Covered by Israeli helicopters dropping spikes on the road behind them to delay any pursuing vehicles, all three attack groups converged on the beach where they had come ashore, parked their hire cars, and were taken out of Beirut by sea. The eight Mossad agents who had been "planted" in Beirut to prepare the raid were taken off with the Sayaret Matkal soldiers. The killings in Beirut were bitterly condemned by Arab governments and by Palestinian organisations who pledged vengeance. More than half a million people marched in the funeral procession for Youssef, Adwan and Nasser in Beirut, while in Cairo a large memorial service for the three men was held at the Omar Makram mosque. Israeli General David Elazar told newsmen that "Israel will not play by the rules of limited warfare".

**BHINDRANWALE, SANT JARNAIL SINGH (1947-1984).** Sikh religious extremist and terrorist leader who was killed when the Indian Army attacked the GOLDEN TEMPLE OF AMRITSAR in June 1984. The Government claimed that Bhindranwale and his followers had taken over the Sikh holy place to use as a base for subversive and terrorist activities. The storming of the Sikh holy shrines and the death of Bhindranwale (and 500 other Sikhs) was bitterly resented by the Sikh community and led directly to the assassination of Prime Minister INDIRA GANDHI by two Sikh policemen in October 1984.

An impressive hawk-faced man over six foot tall, Bhindranwale was born into a deeply religious Sikh family in the Punjab in 1947 (the year of India's independence). Bhindranwale became a preacher and religious teacher at an early age and a Sikh "sant" (saint) at the age of 26. Although Bhindranwale always disavowed politics, he became associated with the Dal Khalsa, the movement for an independent Sikh homeland of Khalistan (The Land of the Pure). Ironically in the light of subsequent events the ruling Congress Party promoted and encouraged Bhindranwale and the Dal Khalsa in an attempt to undermine the main Sikh party, the Akali Dal.

But Bhindranwale proved to be no political stooge, and became increasingly militant and outspoken. After the murder of Baba Gurbichan Singh, the Guru of a Sikh minority sect, Bhindranwale announced that the killer deserved the highest of honours, and should be given his weight in gold. Similar remarks following the murder of a prominent newspaper editor forced the Indian government to issue a warrant for Bhindranwale's arrest. He was duly picked up in September 1980 and spent a short time in jail. Undeterred, Bhindranwale became steadily more radical and outspoken and after a rash of murders by Sikh fanatics (including the killing of Deputy Police Inspector General A. S. Atwal and one of his agents) Prime Minister Gandhi declared "President's Rule" (central government rule) in the Punjab in an attempt to loosen the grip of Bhindranwale on the province.

But the initiative failed, forcing Mrs Gandhi to take even more draconian measures against the violence of the radical Sikhs. According to some sources, in March and April 1983 at least 80 people were killed and 107 injured in attacks by Bhindranwale's zealous young Sikhs. There was strong evidence that Bhindranwale was operating a long "hit list" of people he regarded as being hostile to his cause.

With Bhindranwale's grip on the Punjab growing stronger by the day, and with the Golden Temple being expertly fortified by the experienced Sikh soldier SHAHBEG SINGH, the Indian government felt they had to strike before the situation got out of hand. Bhindranwale's career came to an end on June 5th 1984 when Indira Gandhi launched "BLUE STAR" OPERATION to clear the huge Golden Temple complex of the Sant and his many followers. The Sant's body (badly mutilated in the violence) was cremated on the evening of June 7th 1984 watched by a crowd of 10,000 people held back by the police and army.

**BIRMINGHAM PUB BOMBINGS. (November 21st 1974).** Twenty-one people, mainly teenagers, were killed and 120 were injured when two crowded city-centre pubs in Birmingham, England, were bombed by the PROVISIONAL IRISH REPUBLICAN ARMY (PIRA). The high casualties, and the appalling nature of many of the injuries provoked one of the few incidents of backlash against Irish people living in England. The Birmingham bombings also prompted the Labour Government of Harold Wilson to rush through the Prevention of Terrorism Act (1974) which gave the British authorities draconian powers against suspected terrorists. Two days after the bombings six Irishmen were charged with murder and at their trial in 1975 were given long sentences, although in recent years there has been some doubt about their guilt.

The bombs exploded at 20.20 on November 21st 1974 in "The Mulberry Bush" and "The Tavern In the Town" pubs. Both pubs were within 50 yards of one another. A warning was given to a Birmingham newspaper at 20.11, but the bombs exploded before the police could clear the area. Seventeen people were killed instantly, another four died later, and more than 120 were injured, some gravely. Fleets of taxis, private cars and ambulances from all over the West Midlands were used to ferry the injured and shocked teenagers to city hospitals. In the wake of the explosions there were anti-Irish demonstrations in Birmingham, attacks were made on some of the Irish people living in the city, a Roman Catholic church was firebombed, and an Irish community centre was set alight. Strikes and walkouts were called at Midlands car factories, and demands were made for the restoration of hanging for terrorist murders.

On November 24th, three days after the bombings, six men from Northern Ireland were charged with the murder of 17-year-old Jane Davis, the youngest of the 21 victims. They were Hugh Callaghan (44), Patrick Hill (30), Robert Hunter (29), Richard McIlkenny (31), William Power (29) and John Walker (39). In August 1975 all six were jailed for life at Lancaster Crown Court for the murder of the 21 bomb victims and for conspiracy to cause explosions. The trial was one of the biggest for mass murder in British legal history.

On November 30th, less than two weeks after the Birmingham pub bombings, the British government passed the Prevention of Terrorism Act (PTA) under which the IRA became an illegal organisation in mainland Britain (it had already been proscribed in Northern Ireland and the Irish Republic). The PTA gave the British police the right to arrest suspected terrorists without warrant, and to detain them without trial. The 1974 Act was superseded two years later by the Prevention of Terrorism Act (1976) which has to be renewed annually by Parliament because of its civil liberties implications.

**"BLACK AND TANS".** Name given to the hastily-assembled British paramilitary force which was sent to Ireland in 1920 to try to suppress the IRISH REPUBLICAN ARMY (IRA), and which acquired a reputation for brutality and incompetence. Composed mainly of World War I veterans (and not the sweepings of British prisons as Republican mythology contends) the Black and Tans were recruited for a "rough and dangerous task" which proved beyond their political and military capacity. Their undisciplined behaviour did much to alienate the Irish, scandalise British public opinion, and eventually force the British government to the conference table with the Republican leaders.

Officially part of the Royal Irish Constabulary (RIC), the Black and Tans were inexperienced (except in trench warfare), largely undisciplined, and totally untrained for the police work they were asked to do. On September 20th 1920 the Black and Tans badly damaged the village of Balbriggan north of Dublin, an outrage which they followed the next day by burning the villages of Milltown Malbay, Ennistymon, Lahinch and Trim. The behaviour of the unit provoked a storm of disgust in mainland Britain, and demands that it should be disbanded as it was producing "a peculiarly revolting form of guerrilla warfare in which the chief sufferers are women and children".

By the beginning of 1921 the Black and Tans numbered almost 7,000. And although they were roundly detested by Sinn Fein and the IRA they were not regarded as being so dangerous as the so-called RIC "Auxiliaries" who were a crack unit of ex-British officers. Recruiting for the Black and Tans (and the Auxiliaries) ceased on July 1921, and in October the men were withdrawn from Ireland and returned to mainland Britain (where many of them joined the ranks of the unemployed). Some ex-Black and Tans became members of the British Palestine Police, and one became that organisation's commanding officer.

**BLACK JUNE**. One of the many names used by the ABU NIDAL organisation of Arab terrorists.

**BLACK PANTHER PARTY (BPP)**. (The Black Panthers.) Highly militant US black-power organisation founded in October 1966 in Oakland, California, by HUEY NEWTON and BOBBY SEALE, and once described by the FEDERAL BUREAU OF INVESTIGATION (FBI) as "the greatest threat to the internal security of the country". Originally called the Afro-American Party, the BPP hoped to politicise the violence which was then erupting in the black ghettoes of many American cities. With their military-style discipline and anti-white rhetoric the BPP became internationally notorious in 1967 for entering the California State Legislature in Sacramento, heavily armed. The BPP grew increasingly violent after the assassination in 1968 of the black leader MARTIN LUTHER KING and in 1969 21 BPP members were indicted in New York on charges of conspiring to bomb shops and offices in New York City. Other BPP leaders included ELDRIDGE CLEAVER, Stokely Carmichael, David Hilliard and Rap Brown.

**BLACK SEPTEMBER**. Palestinian terrorist organisation named after the bloody events in Jordan in September 1970 when King Hussein of Jordan turned his British-trained army against the

Palestinian organisations driving them into exile in Lebanon, Syria and Iraq. Black September appears to have been a clandestine organisation of FATAH, the military arm of the PALESTINE LIBERATION ORGANISATION (PLO), and is thought to have been devised by two senior Fatah security officers. Black September were responsible for the MUNICH OLYMPICS ATTACK in 1972 which forced the European countries to reorganise and co-ordinate their anti-terrorist and counter-revolutionary warfare (CRW) forces.

The two Fatah officers credited with creating Black September were ABU DAOUD and ALI HASSAN SALAMEH. Abu Daoud said in a TV interview in Jordan in 1973 that "There is no such thing as Black September. Fatah announced its operations under this name so that Fatah would not appear as the direct executors of the operations." Another senior Fatah man described Black September as a "spontaneous reaction" to the events of September 1970 by rank-and-file guerrillas from a variety of Palestinian groups including Fatah. A number of Palestinians believed by the Israelis to be Black September leaders were hunted down and killed by the MOSSAD in 1973 all over Europe and the Middle East.

**"BLOODY FRIDAY", BELFAST, NORTHERN IRELAND. (July 21st 1972).** One of the worst days in the violent history of Northern Ireland when the PROVISIONAL IRISH REPUBLICAN ARMY (PIRA) engineered 26 explosions throughout the city of Belfast, killing 11 people (including two British soldiers) and injuring more than 100. One bomb in the crowded Oxford Street bus station killed seven people. The slaughter of innocent civilians, and the terrible mutilations caused to the injured, went some way to discredit the PIRA.

**"BLOODY SUNDAY", DUBLIN, IRELAND. (November 21st 1920).** An assassination operation in Dublin by the IRISH REPUBLICAN ARMY (IRA) during which 11 British intelligence officers were killed, and another three badly wounded. The attack was sanctioned by IRA leader MICHAEL COLLINS and took place at 09.00 on a Sunday in lodging houses all round Dublin. It was carried out by a carefully-selected team of gunmen known as "The Squad". Collins' aim was to cripple the intelligence-gathering capacity of the British regime in Dublin. To a large extent he succeeded.

**"BLOODY SUNDAY", LONDONDERRY, NORTHERN IRE-LAND. (January 30th 1972).** A tragic incident in the Catholic

Bogside area of Londonderry, when 13 people were shot to death by soldiers of the 1st Battallion the Parachute Regiment, one of the British Army's élite units. The shootings occurred after a civil rights march organised by the Derry Civil Rights Association had gone ahead despite having been banned. The tragedy generated great bitterness in the Republican community, was denounced by foreign governments, and led to the British Embassy in Dublin being burned to the ground. The political instability created by "Bloody Sunday" led to the suspension of the Protestant-dominated Stormont Parliament and the imposition of "direct rule" of Northern Ireland from London.

An inquiry into the shootings by Lord Widgery, the Lord Chief Justice of England (published in April 1972) decided that the march should not have taken place and had created a "dangerous situation", but that the army should have been less aggressive in trying to round up the transgressors. And while Widgery accepted that the army had been fired upon first, none of the dead civilians were found to have been in the possession of weapons or explosives. The Widgery Report did little to assuage the bitterness of the province's Catholic population, and the events of "Bloody Sunday" passed into the mythology of Irish Republicanism.

**"BLUE STAR", OPERATION.** Military code name for the GOLDEN TEMPLE OF AMRITSAR ASSAULT by the Indian Army in June 1984. The temple buildings had been taken over by heavily-armed Sikh extremists led by SANT JARNAIL SINGH BHINDRANWALE who was killed in the army attack. Operation "Blue Star" outraged Sikh sensibilities, sparked off widespread inter-communal violence, and led to the assassination of Prime Minister INDIRA GANDHI.

**BOGOTA PALACE OF JUSTICE SIEGE. (November 13th-14th 1985).** Takeover of the Palace of Justice in Bogota, Colombia, by 24 members of the left-wing M-19 guerrilla group. In the siege that followed at least 100 people died including Bogota's Chief Justice Alfonso Reyes Echandia, and 10 other judges. All the M-19 guerrillas, including their leader LUIS OTERO died when the Colombian army retook the building. The Colombian authorities were later criticised for their handling of the crisis, and for paying too high a price for their stand against the M-19 terrorists.

The siege of Bogota's five-storey Palace of Justice began on the morning of Wednesday the 13th November when the M-19 guerrillas burst into the building through the underground garage.

They quickly took over the building trapping hundreds of people inside and took a dozen Supreme Court judges hostage. The M-19 accused the Colombian authorities of having betrayed a 1984 truce. The government of President Betancur refused to negotiate with the M-19 and called in armoured vehicles to smash their way into the building. Most of the 500 or so people who had been trapped in the Palace of Justice escaped at that point.

Explosive charges were then used killing many of the remaining hostages, forcing the guerrillas to retreat to the fourth floor. Early in the morning of Thursday 14th 1985 the M-19 released one judge, Reinaldo Arcienagas, with a truce/cease-fire plan. But the government refused to negotiate, and early in the afternoon of the 14th November the terrorists killed their hostages. At around 15.00 government troops launched their final assault inside the Palace of Justice, killing all the M-19 guerrillas.

**BOLOGNA RAILWAY STATION BOMBING. (August 2nd 1980)**. Europe's worst single terrorist attack. At least 84 people were killed and more than 250 were injured when right-wing Italian extremists planted a massive bomb in the main railway station at Bologna in the north of Italy. Investigations into the finances of the P-2 masonic order revealed that an international right-wing group called AVANGUARDIA NAZIONALE had been responsible for the bombing, although members of that organisation are still to be tried by the Italian courts.

The 100lb bomb at Bologna station went off at 10.25 on August 2nd 1980 when the railway station was crowded with holidaymakers. The devastation was enormous; the station roof collapsed, a waiting-room and restaurant were destroyed, and four coaches of a waiting express train were crushed. The immediate death toll was 76, and another eight people died of their injuries later in the month. More than 200 people were injured, many of them under the rubble of the station. Responsibility for the attack was immediately claimed by a little known right-wing group called Armed Revolutionary Nucleii, who withdrew their claim as soon as the death and injury toll became known. More than 20 right-wing extremists were quickly rounded up by the Italian police, but evidence against them was slight. But in 1982 nine right-wing Italian extremists were extradited from London, five of them on charges connected with the Bologna Station bombing.

**BRIGATE ROSSE**. (The Red Brigades). Notorious left-wing Italian terrorist group similar in social background to the West

German ROTE ARMEE FRAKTION (RAF). One of the largest of the European left-wing groups which grew out of the failure of the New Left in the late 1960s, the Brigate Rosse also had roots in the old-established Communist Party of Italy. The Brigate Rosse had contacts with most of the main European and Middle Eastern terrorist groups, and specialised in the kidnapping and murder of Italian judges, politicians and businessmen. Among their victims were ex-Prime Minister ALDO MORO (1978) and the American general JAMES DOZIER (1981). The police operation to rescue Dozier resulted in the arrest and conviction of dozens of Brigate Rosse members. Although Brigate Rosse leader RENATO CURCIO was captured in 1976, the organisation remained active well into the 1980s.

The Brigate Rosse began their operations in 1974 under the intellectual leadership of Renato Curcio and his wife Margherita Cagol (who was killed in a shooting in 1975). Although deprived of Curcio's leadership at an early stage (1976) and fiercely persecuted by the Italian police after the killing of Aldo Moro in 1978, the Brigate Rosse persisted in their campaign of assassination and bombing. By 1982 it was estimated that the Brigate Rosse had killed 50 people, kidnapped another 50, and cost the Italian state around $90 million worth of damage. The police hunt for the kidnapped American general James Dozier uncovered a Brigate Rosse plan to launch an armed attack on the annual (1981) conference of the right-wing Christian Democratic Party.

Some historians have claimed that the Brigate Rosse had close contacts with the Soviet and Bulgarian intelligence services, and received large and regular supplies of arms and ammunition from the PALESTINE LIBERATION ORGANISATION (PLO). There has been considerable speculation about the connections (philosophical and otherwise) between the Brigate Rosse and the established Communist Party of Italy. The Italian Communists have consistently denounced the terrorists as "small clandestine groups mainly composed of intellectuals with desperate utopian ideals far removed from the realities of the day".

**BRIGHTON BOMBING. (October 12th 1984).** The bombing of the Grand Hotel in Brighton, England, during the final stages of the ruling Conservative Party's annual conference. The hotel was HQ for most of the British government during the conference, including Margaret Thatcher and her husband Denis. Five people died as a result of the blast including Conservative MP Sir Anthony Berry. Industry minister Norman Tebbit and his wife were badly injured when the hotel collapsed under them. Mrs Thatcher was unhurt. Responsibility for the attack was claimed by the PROVISIONAL IRISH REPUBLICAN ARMY (PIRA), and in April 1986 a Belfast man called Patrick Joseph Magee was put on trial in London convicted of the bombing.

The bomb which wrecked the Grand Hotel, Brighton, was concealed in a sixth-floor bathroom, and was detonated at 02.54. Prime Minister Thatcher had been working on her Conference Speech when the bomb went off above her. She was rushed out of the hotel to safety, but Norman Tebbit and his wife Margaret were trapped in the collapse of the hotel. John Wakeham MP, the government Chief Whip was also badly injured and his wife Roberta was killed. Others who died were Eric Taylor, Jeanne Shattock and Mrs Muriel McLean, wife of the party's Scottish President.

At the trial of Patrick Magee in May 1986 the police alleged that the bomb which caused the damage had been planted in the bathroom of Room 629 on the sixth floor of the Edwardian building. One of the previous occupants of the room, one "Roy Walsh", could not be traced. The police allege that the fingerprints on the hotel registration card made out to "Walsh" were those of Joseph Magee. Magee was also charged (along with others) of conspiring to plant bombs in 16 other hotels throughout England.

The PIRA attempt to kill or injure most of the British government at one stroke almost succeeded. "Today we were unlucky," a PIRA spokesman told the British government. "But remember, we have only to be lucky once; you will have to be lucky always." Margaret Thatcher described the bombing as " an indiscriminate attempt to massacre innocent and unsuspecting men and women . . . to cripple Her Majesty's democratically elected government".

# C

**CABINDA RAID. (May 1985).** An abortive raid by members of the South African Defence Forces (SADF) on oilfield installations in Cabinda Province in the north of Angola. Although the South African government described the operation as "reconnaissance", the Angolans say it was an attempt to cripple Cabinda Province's offshore oil industry which produces 170,000 to 180,000 barrels of crude oil per day. The raiding party of 12 commandos was led by Captain Wynand Petrus Di Toit. Two of the soldiers were killed, and one captured. Large quantities of explosives, machine-guns (silenced), Makarov pistols and short-wave radio transmitters were seized by the Angolan authorities.

**CAHILL, JOE (born 1920).** One-time Belfast commander of the PROVISIONAL IRISH REPUBLICAN ARMY (PIRA) and now an executive member of the Provisional Sinn Fein (generally regarded as PIRA's political wing). Cahill narrowly escaped the death sentence in Northern Ireland in 1942 for the shooting of a Belfast policeman, and in 1973 was jailed for three years in the Irish Republic for his role in the *CLAUDIA* AFFAIR, a gun-running operation which he is said to have masterminded. After his release Cahill (whose health is not good) devoted most of his time and energy to the political work of Provisional Sinn Fein and organising aid for Republican prisoners and their families.

**CAPPUCI, HILARION.** The pro-Arab Greek Catholic Archbishop of Jerusalem who was jailed by the Israelis for his part in a plot to run guns into Israel. Capucci was given a 12-year jail sentence on December 9th 1974.

**CARGESE HOLIDAY CAMP ATTACK, CORSICA. (May 1st 1986).** The first fatal attack by the FRONT DU LIBERATION NATIONALE CORSE (FLNC) in their 10-year bombing campaign to separate Corsica from France. Two people were killed and three injured when 15 hooded men from the FLNC raided a holiday camp at Cargese, 40 miles north of the island's capital of Ajaccio. After tying up the camp owners and 30 tourists, the terrorists left.

Jacques Rosselet, the owner of the holiday camp managed to untie himself and his wife, who immediately went to fetch the police. Rosselet was trying to defuse the bomb when the police arrived, but it exploded killing him, a policeman, and injuring three others. The Cargese attack was immediately denounced as "unjustifiable" by France's interior minister Charles Pasqua (himself a Corsican). "We are not dealing with nationalists," Pasqua said, "but with gangsters. We live in a democratic country where nothing can justify violence."

**"CARLOS THE JACKAL". See SANCHEZ, ILICH RAMIREZ.**

**CARRERO BLANCO, LUIS.** Spanish prime minister and heir to Generalissimo Franco who was assassinated by terrorists from the Basque organisation EUSKADI TA ASKATASUNA (ETA) on December 20th 1973. The killing of Carrero Blanco by the ETA terrorists was seen by the Spanish government as a brutal challenge to their authority and provoked a wave of police repression throughout the Basque region of northern Spain. It was reported that the explosives which were used to kill Carrero Blanco were supplied by the PROVISIONAL IRISH REPUBLICAN ARMY (PIRA) with whom ETA were known to have contacts.

The killing of Admiral Luis Carrero Blanco was a savage blow to the Franco regime. Carrero Blanco had been vice-president of Spain since 1967 and was appointed Prime Minister when General Franco stood down in June 1973. Franco's idea was that the formidable right-wing admiral might dampen the liberal enthusiasms of King Juan Carlos whom he had nominated in 1969 to succeed him as head of state. The adroit and influential Carrero Blanco was succeeded by Carlo Arias Navarro, a cautious and inexperienced lawyer who gave the young King Juan Carlos room to manoeuvre.

Carrero Blanco was killed by a huge bomb which exploded under his car at 09.30 on December 20th 1973 as he was being driven away from the church of San Francisco de Borja near the centre of Madrid. So much explosive was used that the prime minister's car was thrown more than 60 feet into the air over the roof of the church to land on the other side of the building. Carrero Blanco's bodyguard was killed instantly, his driver died later in hospital, and although the prime minister was alive when taken from the car, he died before reaching hospital. The huge charge of explosive which killed Carrero Blanco had been placed in a tunnel under the road and detonated by remote control. Three men posing as "sculptors" had hired a room in a nearby house from which they had painstakingly dug a tunnel under the road. When Carrero Blanco's car passed over the tunnel the explosives were detonated. While ETA promptly claimed responsibility for the killings, the Basque "Government in Exile" issued a statement "doubting" whether it had been the work of Basques. But an ETA press conference held in south-west France produced so many details of the assassination that ETA were held responsible.

The Canadian Embassy (which is near the scene of the explosion) had heard that a "major" terrorist act was about to take place and informed the Spanish police, but the police were unable to trace the explosives. Another 24lbs of plastic explosive were found in a car parked near the scene of the assassination. The killing of Carrero Blanco strained relations between Spain and France which the Franco regime accused of turning a blind eye to the activities of Basque terrorists who found sanctuary and support in the Basque country of south-west France.

**CELLS COMBATANTE COMMUNISTE (CCC).** (Fighting Communist Cells.) Belgian left-wing terrorist group connected with the French organisation ACTION DIRECTE. In December 1985 four of the group's leaders – Pierre Carette, Bertrand Sisoye, Didier Chevolet and Pascal Vandegeerde were arrested at the town of Namur. Belgian authorities say that the CCC were responsible for almost 30 bombings in the country between October 1984 and December 1985, including a number of attacks on NATO pipelines and other installations. On December 6th 1985 the CCC planted a bomb in a courthouse in Liege in an attempt to kill Jean Gol, Belgium's Justice Minister. Gol was in Brussels at the time but a young law student died in the attack. Belgian police say that the explosives used by the CCC are from a stolen cache also used by Action Directe and the West German group ROTE ARMEE FRAKTION (RAF).

**CENTRAL INTELLIGENCE AGENCY (CIA).** The principle foreign intelligence-gathering organisation of the United States of America. Based at Langley in Virginia, but with "stations" and outposts throughout the world, the CIA is one of the biggest intelligence bureaucracies in the world. Racked by crisis and scandal in the 1970s, the CIA is now being restored to its original power and influence. Although criticised for its excesses, the CIA is one of the more democratically accountable intelligence agencies, and its leaders occasionally appear before Congressional committees to answer difficult (and often dangerous) questions. Formed under the National Security Act of 1947 the CIA grew in power and influence along with the global confrontation between the USA and the Soviet Union.

Now organised into four "directorates" (Intelligence, Operations, Support and Science & Technology) the CIA is believed to employ around 20,000 staff full-time with a large number of "contract" employees round the world. One of the first priorities of the current Director of Central Intelligence (DCI), William Casey, was to improve the agency's analysis of intelligence, the failures of which had led the USA into a number of strategic blunders (such as believing that the Shah of Iran had overwhelming support in his country, and that the Viet Cong had little or no support in theirs). The CIA's clandestine activities are the responsibility of the Operations directorate, most of whose staff are employed overseas in the "Area Divisions" (Far East, Western Europe, Western Hemisphere, Middle East, Soviet Bloc and Africa). What used to be called "covert operations" are now known as "special activities" and are the responsibility of the "International Affairs Division". Most of the CIA Operations Directorate staff work from US Embassies around the world.

In the 1950s CIA chief Allan Dulles used the agency ruthlessly to promote American policy, and great effort was put into subverting governments the CIA regarded as "hostile" (Iran, Guatemala, Egypt, Indonesia, the Congo etc.). The CIA were behind the abortive "Bay of Pigs" invasion of Cuba in 1961 after which débâcle President JOHN F. KENNEDY sacked Dulles.

During the Vietnam war the CIA were heavily involved in clandestine and counter-insurgency operations (in Vietnam itself, but also in Laos and Cambodia), and the agency's "PHOENIX" operation became a byword for American iniquity to the international Left. The CIA's operations inside the USA (mainly spying on anti-war groups) led the agency into a political mire. Domestic operations were specifically against the CIA's charter and the Senate inquiry into these operations, led by the late Senator Frank Church, did much to discredit the CIA, and temporarily emasculate the organisation.

The current DCI, William Casey, told the *New York Times* that following the Church Committee's investigations the CIA was cut back almost by half, and that the number of CIA personnel involved in clandestine operations dropped from 2,000 to 200. The Reagan administration, however, has been reconstructing the CIA as an instrument of US policy, and in recent years CIA agents are known to have been operating inside Afghanistan, Nicaragua, Guatemala, El Salvador and Iran. President Reagan has passed an order permitting the CIA to operate legally within the borders of the USA.

**CHARTOUNY, HABIB TANIOS**. Twenty-six-year-old Lebanese Christian who laid and detonated the bomb which killed Lebanon's President-elect BASHIR GEMAYEL in Beirut on September 14th 1982. Chartouny – a known member of the Christian but anti-Phalangist Syrian People's Party (SPP) – was quickly captured after warning his sister to leave the building which also housed Gemayel's HQ. He told his interrogators that he had not intended to kill Gemayel, only to scare him into realising that he was as vulnerable as everyone else in Lebanon. Chartouny's assassination of Gemayel further destabilised the Lebanon and led directly to the massacres of Palestinians at the SABRA AND SHATILA camps in Beirut a few days later. Chartouny said that he had been recruited into the SPP when a student in Paris, and that the explosives and detonator which killed Gemayel had been supplied by an officer of the SPP who later disappeared into Syria.

**CHIN PENG**. Chinese leader of the MALAYAN RACES LIBERATION ARMY (MRLA) and Malayan Communist Party (MCP) during the guerrilla war against the British colonial regime in the MALAYA EMERGENCY of 1948 to 1960. Chin Peng – who had been awarded an OBE by the British for his war-time resistance to the Japanese – proved to be an elusive and skilled terrorist leader, but was ultimately out-gunned and politically out-manoeuvred by the British. Probably Chin Peng's biggest failure was to confuse the popular demand for an independent Malaya with clamour for a Communist revolution. After the defeat of the MRLA insurgency and the independence of Malaya in 1957, the remnant of Chin Peng's force retreated into southern Thailand, and renamed themselves the Malayan National Liberation Army (MNLA). Since the late 1960s the handful of communist guerrilla/terrorists have made sporadic raids into Malaya which have been easily contained by the Malayan government's security forces.

**"CHOPIN EXPRESS" HIJACKING, AUSTRIA. (September 28th-29th 1973)**. The hijacking by Arab terrorists of a Moscow to Vienna express train carrying Soviet Jews emigrating to Israel. The hijackers took three of the Jews and an Austrian customs official hostage, and demanded that the Austrian government close down the Schonau transit camp which was being used by the Jewish Agency to receive Soviet Jews on their way to the West (normally

Israel). When the Austrian government agreed to the terrorists demands to shut down Schonau, they were roundly denounced by the US and Israel whose prime minister, Golda Meir, described the Austrian decision as "a great victory for terrorist organisations".

Despite the scorn heaped on Austria for allowing a handful of Arabs to dictate government policy, Chancellor Kreisky said that his country "would not become a secondary theatre of the Middle East conflict". The Arab gunmen who staged the coup said they had done it "because the immigration of Soviet Union Jews forms a great danger to our cause". There was some suspicion in the West that the Soviet and Czech authorities had connived at the hijacking in order to rid themselves of a source of embarrassment.

The two armed Arabs took over the so-called "Chopin Express" (which up until then had carried more than 70,000 Jews to the West) on September 28th 1973 at the small town of Marchegg on the Austria-Czechoslovakia border. They had apparently boarded the train at Bratislava in Czechoslovakia. Armed with automatic weapons and grenades they seized six Jews and two Austrian customs officials. Three of the Jews and one of the customs men managed to escape leaving the Arabs with four hostages. They immediately demanded transport to take them to Vienna International Airport and an aircraft to fly them to an Arab country. They called themselves the "Eagles of the Palestinian Revolution", but were members of the POPULAR FRONT FOR THE LIBERATION OF PALESTINE (PFLP).

After their demand for transport was met they declared that the four hostages would be killed unless the Austrian government agreed to close down the Schonau Castle transit camp which was being used by the Jewish Agency to welcome Soviet Jews into the West. Although the Austrian government of Bruno Kreisky was in constant touch with the Israelis (who were urging a hard line with the terrorists) the Austrians eventually gave in to the two Arab gunmen. In the early hours of September 29th 1973 the four hostages were released unharmed, the Arabs were flown out of Vienna to Libya, and the Schonau transit camp was duly closed down by the Austrian authorities. On September 30th 1973, at a press conference in Tripoli the two hijackers (calling themselves Abu Ali and Abu Salim) said that their object had been "to attack Zionist targets outside Israel – not merely to kidnap people".

On October 1st 1973 Golda Meir accused the Austrians of giving "the greatest encouragement to terror throughout the world" and described the closure of Schonau as "a great victory for terrorist organisations. This is the first time a Government has come to an agreement of this kind." Pressure was also exerted by the USA; on October 3rd 1973 President Richard Nixon pleaded with Chancellor Kreisky to change his mind about the Schonau transit camp on the grounds that "we simply cannot have governments, however small, giving in to blackmail by terrorist organisations". The Austrians, however, refused to budge and Kreisky said they would not be influenced by "telegrams, threats, pressures and insults".

The Arab world was predictably pleased at the outcome. The Cairo-based "Voice of Palestine" radio station said that Jewish immigration to Israel from the Soviet Union was "one of the greatest dangers to the rights of Palestinians in their homeland" and congratulated the Austrians for withstanding the pressures from abroad. The Palestinian propaganda machinery in Beirut, however, warned the Austrians that any backsliding on Schonau would "not serve Austria's interests, stability or security".

**CLAUDIA AFFAIR.** An abortive attempt by the PROVISIONAL IRISH REPUBLICAN ARMY (PIRA) to run arms and ammunition from Libya into Ireland for use against the British in Northern Ireland. The attempt failed when the ship *Claudia* was seized by the Irish authorities in Waterford Bay off the coast of Ireland on March 29th 1973 and all the weapons impounded. The cargo consisted of five tons of arms and ammunition, including 250 KALASHNIKOV AK-47 assault rifles, 247 Webley revolvers, 20,000 rounds of ammunition, 100 anti-tank mines, 600lbs of TNT, 500lbs of gelignite, 300 hand grenades, and 100 cases of anti-personnel mines. The ship itself was registered in Cyprus, and owned by a West German company one of whose principals had been convicted in 1967 of smuggling arms to the PESH MERGA guerrillas in Iraq. Four men, including JOE CAHILL, the PIRA's one-time commander in Belfast, were later convicted of gun-running. When accused of being the organiser of the operation, Cahill told the Irish judge, "You do me an honour". The interception of the *Claudia* was regarded as the result of painstaking intelligence work by the Irish police and the British SECRET INTELLIGENCE SERVICE (SIS).

**CLEAVER, ELDRIDGE (born 1934).** American "Black Power" leader of the late 1960s and early 1970s whose books *Soul on Ice* and *Post Prison Writings* were highly regarded by the American New Left and black consciousness movement. Cleaver was one of the early members of the BLACK PANTHER PARTY (BPP) and an influential voice in black radical politics. In 1968 he jumped bail and fled the USA, first to Cuba and then to Algeria where he set up a BPP office (and from where he led a BPP delegation to North Korea). But over the years Cleaver gradually abandoned revolutionary politics, returned to the USA, and by May 1986 was running for the California Senate as a conservative Republican candidate. Still an effective orator, Cleaver delighted his conservative audiences by telling them that he was a man "with the courage to change, to grow" and that he is now determined to defeat that brand of Democratic politics which has "made black people dependent on the Federal budget".

**COLLINS, MICHAEL (1890-1922).** First prime minister of the Irish Free State and a guerrilla leader of great ability who led the fight against the British between 1917 and 1921 as Director of Organization of the Irish Volunteers. Collins was one of the chief negotiators of the controversial treaty with the British which gave Ireland independence but as part of the British empire. More radical Republicans regarded the treaty as a "sell out" and turned their guns against the new Irish Free State in a bitter civil war in which Michael Collins was killed in August 1922.

After the British government had banned the self-appointed Dail (Parliament) of Ireland in 1919 Collins was able to use his military talents to great effect. Having been involved in the EASTER RISING in Dublin of 1916, Collins knew that the troubles would continue, and between 1916 and 1919 cultivated contacts within the Irish civil service and the Royal Irish Constabulary (RIC) and the Dublin Metropolitan Police (DMP). These contacts were to form the basis of a superb intelligence network which Collins turned against the British to great effect in 1920 and 1921.

Collins was capable of operating with great ruthlessness. In 1920 he set up a carefully selected 12-man execution team known as The Squad or The Twelve Apostles whose job was to eliminate troublesome DMP detectives or British military intelligence officers. Collins' Twelve Apostles were responsible for the killings in Dublin on November 21st 1920, an event which became known as "BLOODY SUNDAY". For most of the rebellion against the British regime Collins was a hunted man with a price on his head who cycled daily around Dublin on his old Raleigh bicycle cultivating his intelligence/terror network.

In 1921 Collins was involved in the negotiations in London with the British government of David Lloyd George over a peace treaty to settle the war in Ireland. Eventually, after weeks of negotiation, the Irish leaders agreed to "Dominion status" within the British Commonwealth for an Irish Free State in the South of Ireland.

But hard-line Republicans regarded the treaty which accepted the division of Ireland into North and South as an act of gross betrayal of everything they had fought for, and launched a bitter campaign against the pro-treaty forces of Michael Collins. In the civil war that followed, Michael Collins was shot dead when his car was ambushed by IRA men in Cork on August 22nd 1922.

**COMACCHIO COMPANY**. A specially-trained unit of British Royal Marines assigned to protect Britain's offshore oil and gas platforms against terrorist attack or hijacking. The marines train regularly in the "clearing" of oil rigs, platforms and pipe-laying barges of terrorists by helicopter and sea-borne assaults. Their special skills include using magnetic pads to climb the huge steel structures. A detachment of Comacchio marines are also based permanently at the Royal Navy's nuclear submarine base at Faslane on the west coast of Scotland. Called after a World War II battle at Lake Comacchio in Italy (where the Royal Marines won their only Victoria Cross of the war), the unit is based at Arbroath on the east coast of Scotland.

**CONNOLLY, JAMES (1868-1916)**. Scots-born radical Socialist who became one of the most influential Irish Republican theorists and who was executed by the British for his role in the EASTER RISING in Dublin in 1916. Connolly was the leader of the Citizens Army which, along with the Irish Volunteers of Padraig Pearse, took over the General Post Office in Dublin and declared an Irish Republic. Connolly is seen by many left-wing Republicans as the founding father of the IRISH REPUBLICAN ARMY (IRA). A fierce egalitarian and brilliant left-wing polemicist, Connolly despised the religious sectarianism which has continued to plague Ireland throughout the 20th century.

Although deeply committed to the Irish cause, Connolly was born in Edinburgh in Scotland of Irish parents. After a spell on an Edinburgh newspaper, he served with the Royal Scots (the oldest regiment in the British Army) then returned to work for the Edinburgh Corporation. He joined the Scottish Socialist Federation and began writing articles for left-wing magazines such as *Justice* and *Labour Leader*. In 1896 Connolly was offered the job as full time organiser of the Dublin Socialist Club, a job he accepted with alacrity.

Within days of landing in Ireland the young Scot had set up the Irish Socialist Republican Party and was agitating for the creation of an "Irish Socialist Republic based upon the public ownership by the Irish people of the land, and instruments of production, distribution and exchange". Connolly spent a few years in the United States (where he set up a Newark New Jersey Branch of the Industrial Workers of the World).

In 1910 Connolly returned to Ireland, and became the Belfast-based organiser of the Irish Transport & General Workers Union (ITGWU) and became involved in the famous Dublin lock-out of 1913. In October 1913 he founded the Irish Citizens Army, described as Europe's "first Red Guard" (although it was basically a semi-armed force designed to protect ITGWU workers against thugs hired by managements). Connolly did, however, recognise the potential of his little Citizens Army to form the nucleus of something much more formidable which might shake the British hold on Ireland.

A proficient military student and a man with experience of the British Army, it was Connolly who led the arguments for an armed uprising against the British as the Irish Home Rule Act foundered in World War I. In April 1916 he made common cause with Padraig Pearse's Irish Volunteers (most of whom were politically to the right of Connolly's men) and helped plot the fateful Easter Rising of 1916 which led to his death and subsequent martyrdom.

**"CONTRA" GUERRILLAS**. The right-wing guerrillas of Nicaragua who are fighting the left-wing SANDINISTA regime which ousted the dictator ANASTASIO SOMOZA in 1979. Based mainly in Honduras, and supported by cash, arms and "advisers" from the United States, the Contras have proved no real military threat to the better-trained and better-equipped Sandinista Army. They have, however, been troublesome and have forced the Sandinista government to spend more money defending itself than the cash-strapped economy of Nicaragua can afford. In March 1986 Contra operations in the border areas provoked the Sandinista Army into a cross-border "hot pursuit" foray which fuelled American arguments that the Sandinistas are an aggressive Communist regime who are a threat to Central America.

The Contras are far from being a unified force, and are split into a number of separate (and often mutually hostile) groups. The largest is the FDN which is thought to number around 12,000 and which operates in the southern part of Honduras. The FDN is led by Adolfo Calero and Enrique Bermudez (once Somoza's military attaché in Washington). The FDN receives most of the aid the US government gives to the Contras, and is also backed by right-wing Nicaraguan exiles and assorted US "anti-communist" organisations.

Also operating in the north of the country are Misura and Misurata groups, mostly Miskito Indians alienated by the heavy-handed treatment of their tribes by the Sandinista government.

The Contra force operating in the south (and based over the border in Costa Rica) is known as Arde. This group is an estimated 1,000-2,000 strong and until recently was led by the charismatic Eden Pastora also known as Commander Zero. Once a leading Sandinista (he was deputy Defence Minister) Pastora fell out with the Marxist government and turned his military talents against it. But Pastora refuses to have anything to do with the other Contra groups, particularly the FDN which, he says, is made up of the men who killed his father.

The initial strategy of the Contras was to occupy a large portion of Nicaragua's thinly populated north-eastern area and declare it a "free territory" from which they would gradually extend into the rest of Nicaragua with help from the USA. The Sandinista response to the Contra incursions was to "militarise" the whole area and forcibly resettle the Miskito Indians who lived along the Coco River. Many of the Miskitos became bitter at this treatment and fled across the border to join the Contras, or to set up their own anti-Sandinista groups.

A large number of the Contras are ex-members of Anastasio Somoza's National Guard which was used to prop up a particularly corrupt and vicious regime. The Sandinistas, and many foreign observers, claim that the Contras (especially the FDN) have been waging a brutal campaign of terror, extortion and rape among the harmless villagers of the border areas in an attempt to undermine support for the Sandinista government. Contra methods have been widely denounced by the international aid agencies operating in Nicaragua.

President Ronald Reagan's support for the Contras – who the President regards as "freedom fighters" – has provoked a political crisis in Washington between the Administration and both Houses of Congress. Both Congress and the Senate have proved reluctant to give the Contras a "blank cheque" and are fearful that American forces will eventually get sucked into a situation in which they will suffer heavy casualties and cannot win. Many senators and congressmen are unimpressed by the Contras' democratic credentials and fear the restoration of a corrupt right-wing dictatorship which the USA will be obliged to support.

**CUBANA AIRLINES BOMBING. (October 6th 1976).** The bombing of a Cubana Airlines passenger jet by American-based

Cuban exiles in which 73 people were killed. The attack sparked off a major diplomatic row, not only between the US and Cuban governments (who immediately suspended all flights to the USA) but also between the USA and British Guyana. There were 11 Guyanese citizens aboard the jet, and Guyanese prime minister Forbes Burnham accused the USA of complicity in their deaths. President Ford of the USA renounced the US-Cuban hijacking agreement. An American government inquiry revealed that the attack was the work of exiled Cubans living in Florida and Venezuela and that no US agency was involved.

The Cubana DC-8 jet of the Cuban state airline exploded and crashed into the sea shortly after taking off from Seawell Airport, Barbados, on October 6th 1976 en route from Guyana to Cuba. All 73 passengers and crew lost their lives including 57 Cubans, 11 Guyanese and five North Koreans. On October 7th 1976 a telephone caller to the *Miami Herald* newspaper in Florida USA claimed that the bomb had been planted by the "El Condor" group of Cuban exiles. But at a rally in Havana on October 15th 1976 Fidel Castro blamed the CENTRAL INTELLIGENCE AGENCY (CIA) for downing the jet as a reprisal for Cuba's role in the war in the West African state of Angola. President Gerald Ford reacted by abrogating the US-Cuba hijacking agreement of February 15th 1973.

Although both Cuba and Guyana insisted that the United States government had a hand in the tragedy, on October 7th 1976 the police in Trinidad arrested two Cubans (naturalised Venezuelans) who had disembarked from the doomed aircraft without their luggage. Within the next two weeks the Venezuelan police arrested 14 Cuban exiles suspected of being involved in the Cubana airliner crash and the assassination in Washington of Chilean exile ORLANDO LETELIER.

**CURCIO, RENATO**. Founder-member and one-time leader of the Italian left-wing terrorist group BRIGATE ROSSE (Red Brigades). One of the most dangerous of the European terrorist organisers, Curcio is now serving a life sentence in an Italian jail. Curcio and the Brigate Rosse relied heavily on the support of the Czechoslovakian intelligence bureaucracy, and Curcio was a regular visitor to the Czech intelligence base at Karlova Vary. On Curcio's first arrest in 1974 the Italian police discovered a quantity of fake passports in his possession all of which contained Czech entry visas. When Curcio was arrested a second time – in January 1976 – the Brigate Rosse tried to force the Italian government to release him by mounting a campaign of murder and intimidation against Italian judges, magistrates and jurors. But Curcio was eventually brought to justice in 1978 and after a lengthy and much-publicised trial was jailed for life along with a number of his Brigate Rosse colleagues.

**CURIEL, HENRI (1914-1978)**. Egyptian-born Jew and left-wing activist who set up the Paris-based organisation SOLIDARITÉ in 1963 which is believed to have provided support for a variety of West European and Middle Eastern terrorist groups. Curiel was closely associated with the PALESTINE LIBERATION ORGANISATION (PLO) in Paris in the 1970s. He was assassinated outside his Paris home in May 1978 by unknown gunmen. Two years after his death the French police uncovered an organisation known as "Les Amis d'Henri Curiel" which appeared to be carrying on the work of providing support and logistics for terrorist groups.

An ardent Communist, Henri Curiel was expelled from Egypt in 1950, lived for a time in Rome, and after a clandestine entry into France was jailed for assisting the FRONT DE LIBERATION NATIONALE (FLN) in Algeria. On his release from jail in 1962 Curiel set up Solidarité and established strong contacts with a number of Third World liberation movements as well as terrorist groups like the Argentinian MONTONEROS and the BLACK PANTHER PARTY (BPP) of the USA. After being exposed as a terrorist supporter by the French press in 1976, Curiel disbanded Solidarité and replaced it with a group called "Aide et Amitié". In October 1977 Aide et Amitié was accused by the German magazine *Der Spiegel* of supporting European terror groups such as the ROTE ARMEE FRAKTION (RAF).

Curiel was on the point of suing *Der Spiegel* for libel when he was shot dead on the stairway of his apartment block in Rue Rollin, Paris, on May 31st 1978. His killers were never traced, but there was speculation that Curiel had been murdered by one of the Israeli MOSSAD's execution teams. But he could equally well have been killed by one of the anti-PLO Palestinian groups, or by right-wingers.

**CZOLGOSZ, LEON**. Polish-American anarchist who assassinated President WILLIAM MCKINLEY in Buffalo, New York, in September 1901.

# D

**DAOUD, ABU**. Mohammed Daoud Awdah. Reputedly a high-ranking officer of the BLACK SEPTEMBER Palestinian group, and believed by the Israelis to have been one of the planners of the MUNICH OLYMPICS ATTACK in September 1972. Daoud was arrested in Amman in February 1973 while plotting against the Jordanian regime, and told his interrogators that the shadowy Black September was, in fact, an arm of FATAH the military wing of the PALESTINE LIBERATION ORGANISATION (PLO) (something the PLO had always denied). He was jailed by the Jordanians, but released in September 1973. In January 1977 Daoud was at the centre of a high-level diplomatic storm when he was released by the French authorities after being arrested in Paris where he had been sent to attend the funeral of an assassinated PLO representative.

Daoud was one of 17 Arab infiltrators picked up by the Jordanian police in February 1973, tried, sentenced to death for subversion, but then jailed for life. He was released in September 1973 on the demand of Black September terrorists who attacked the SAUDI ARABIAN EMBASSY, KHARTOUM. He became internationally notorious in January 1977 when he was arrested in Paris while attending the funeral of murdered PLO executive MAHMOUD SALEH. Abu Daoud was picked up on January 7th by the French secret service who were acting on information from the West German and Israeli police. After a series of noisy protests from Arab countries (and particularly from Syria) the French authorities released the Palestinian. Strenuous efforts by both the Israeli and West German governments to have Daoud extradited to stand trial for the Munich Olympics attack failed, and the French allowed him to leave the country.

The Israeli government denounced the French action as "a shameful capitulation to the pressure of Arab states and threats from terrorist organisations" and accused France of violating its extradition treaty with Israel and failing to honour its obligations under the European Convention on the Suppression of Terrorism. The West German government and the Bavarian State government objected to the French decision, while Secretary of State Henry

Kissinger of the USA declared his "dismay" at Abu Daoud's release. In Algiers Abu Daoud blamed his arrest on "certain elements of the French police" who were trying to disrupt the friendly relations of France and the Arab countries.

**DAVISON, IAN (born 1958).** British-born PLO terrorist, and one of the trio of gunmen who killed three Israelis at the LARNACA MARINA, Cyprus, on September 26th 1985 and then surrendered to the Cyprus police. Davison gave his name to the police as "George Hannah". Although Davison and his two comrades claimed to be on assignment for FORCE 17 (an élite unit of FATAH) both Force 17 and the PALESTINE LIBERATION ORGANISATION (PLO) claimed the men were not acting under orders. Davison who comes from a working-class family in the north-east of England and had no obvious political motivation, left England in April 1983 and was not heard from again until he appeared in Tripoli, Lebanon, fighting in the ranks of the PLO. In May 1985 his parents received a letter from Tunisia suggesting that Davison was undergoing PLO training in that country. It is possible that Davison was recruited to the PLO cause by Palestinian activists operating in the colleges and universities of north-east England.

**DAWSON'S FIELD HIJACKINGS, JORDAN. (Sept 6th-10th 1970).** One of the most significant terrorist events in postwar history. Three Western airliners were hijacked by gunmen from the POPULAR FRONT FOR THE LIBERATION OF PALESTINE (PFLP) and flown to an airstrip near Amman in Jordan called Dawson's Field from where the PFLP demanded the release of PFLP members jailed in Switzerland, Britain and West Germany. With the terrorists threatening the death of more than 300 passengers and crew, King Hussein's army were helpless to act. As part of the same operation another aircraft was hijacked to Beirut and flown to Cairo where it was blown up on the runway after the passengers and crew had been freed. After 24 days of negotiation the PFLP men were released and the hostages freed. But the three jetliners were spectacularly destroyed at Dawson's Field in front of the world's press and television.

But King Hussein of Jordan saw the PFLP operation as a direct threat to his authority and he turned his troops against the Palestinians, destroying their military command and forcing them into exile in Lebanon where their presence did much to destabilise that country and eventually brought down the wrath of the Israelis. The BLACK SEPTEMBER Palestinian groups (who staged the

MUNICH OLYMPICS ATTACK in 1972) were so-called after the events in Jordan of September 1970. Black September took an early revenge on Hussein by killing his prime minister WASFI TELL in Cairo on November 28th 1971.

The Dawson's Field crisis began on September 6th 1970 when a TWA Boeing 707 with 155 passengers and crew aboard was hijacked over Belgium and flown to Jordan where it was joined the same day by a Swissair DC-8 carrying 155 passengers and crew which had been hijacked over France. On the same day an attempt to take over an El Al Boeing 707 was thwarted by an Israeli SKYMARSHALL who shot dead one of the Arabs, and captured the other, LEILA KHALED. Late in the afternoon of September 6th the PFLP struck against a Pan American jet over Holland and forced it to fly to Beirut where it was refuelled and flown to Cairo on September 7th 1970. Shortly after it arrived at Cairo the passengers were told to "get out fast" and the aircraft was blown up on the runway.

With more than 300 hostages and two aircraft in their possession, the PFLP demanded the release of three of their members jailed in Switzerland for the ZURICH AIRPORT ATTACK of February 1969, three PFLP members being held in West Germany for attacking El Al passengers at Munich airport, and Leila Khaled being held in Britain for the attempted hijack of an El Al airliner over England. On September 9th 1970 the PFLP added the 125 passengers and crew of a British VC-10 to their hostage list by hijacking the aircraft over the Persian Gulf and flying it to Dawson's Field.

The International Committee of the Red Cross (ICRC) were called in to negotiate with the PFLP hijackers. The ICRC persuaded the PFLP to release some of the passengers and to allow in supplies of water, food, medical supplies and sanitary equipment for the hundreds of men, women and children trapped in fearsome temperatures on the desert airfield. After heavy diplomatic pressure the Iraqi government prevailed upon the PALESTINE LIBERATION ORGANISATION (PLO) to persuade the PFLP to allow the hostages to be moved to the relative comfort of Amman. This was done by a fleet of vehicles on September 11th 1970.

Half an hour after the hostages left Dawson's Field the British, Swiss and American jet liners were destroyed by a series of explosions. The PFLP claimed that the aircraft had been blown up because of the "militant and irresponsible actions" of the British, US, Swiss and West German governments (who had refused to release the PFLP terrorists unless all the hostages were freed regardless of race or nationality). On September 12th 1970 the PFLP set free another 250 hostages, leaving 54 Israelis, Israeli-Americans, and airline crew members being held in groups scattered around Amman.

On September 25th 1970 the Jordanian army discovered 16 of the hostages (six Swiss, two West Germans and eight Britons) at the Wahdat refugee camp near Amman. Another 32 hostages (all Americans) were released by the PFLP on September 26th 1970. The hostages were all unharmed and said they had been kept in small groups and moved around Jordan constantly by their captors. On September 29th the last six hostages (all Americans, four of them Jews) were released and flown out of Jordan on September 30th 1970. That same day a Comet of the Royal Air Force (RAF) flew Leila Khaled out of Britain to Cairo, via Munich and Zurich where it picked up the other PFLP members set free by the Swiss and German governments.

The exchange of Leila Khaled and six convicted terrorists for the Western hostages was widely regarded (particularly by the Israelis) as a climb-down on the part of the three governments, and one which the British government has never repeated. The Secretary General of the United Nations, U Thant, called for the setting up of an international tribunal which would try hijackers who should be prosecuted "in the name of the peoples of the world". After the Dawson's Field hijackings President Nixon of the USA ordered the setting up of a force of government SKYMARSHALLS to "ride shotgun" in American-owned aircraft and announced measures to tighten up security at American airports. And the huge wave of critical publicity about Dawson's Field forced the expulsion of the PFLP from the Central Committee of the PLO for causing "great harm to the Palestinian revolution".

**DEBRAY, REGIS**. French-born "revolutionary" philosopher who was an intellectual companion to ERNESTO "CHE" GUEVARA on his ill-fated expedition to promote revolution in Bolivia in 1967. After Guevara's death, Debray was arrested and tried by the Bolivian authorities and sentenced to 30 years in jail. He was released early, and returned to France (eventually becoming a minor member of the government of François Mitterrand). In 1972 Debray was involved in a plot to kidnap the wanted Nazi Klaus Barbie from his shelter in Bolivia and take him back to France to stand trial.

Debray was influential in left-wing circles in the late 1960s and early 1970s and his most important work was probably *Revolution In The Revolution* which identified the "strategic value" of terrorism so long as it was "subordinate to the fundamental struggle" of the revolutionary movement. Like his Cuban mentors Fidel Castro and Ernesto "Che" Guevara, Debray believed that urban terrorism was less decisive and less likely to spark off revolution than rural insurgency.

**DEGUELDRE, ROGER.** French Army deserter who led the feared "Delta" teams of the right-wing ORGANISATION ARMEE SECRETE (OAS) in Algeria between 1961 and 1962. Degueldre's "Delta" squads were the cutting edge of the OAS terrorist operation (both in Algeria and in France) and were responsible for the deaths of hundreds of French and Algerian men, women and children. After the collapse of the OAS in June 1962 Degueldre was tried by a military court, sentenced to death, and executed by firing squad at the beginning of July 1962.

A lieutenant in the Foreign Legion Degueldre was a much-decorated hero of France's colonial war in Indo-China and a fanatical French patriot. Described as "the real chief of action of the OAS" by the beginning of 1961 Degueldre had put together a force of around 500 seasoned gunmen (mostly embittered deserters from the French army) which he called the "Delta Commando". By the end of 1961 Degueldre's "Delta" squads were killing dozens of people every month, and robbing banks to finance their operations. In January 1962 Degueldre's men virtually wiped out "Les Barbouzes", the special anti-terrorist squad which had been set up by the French government to track down the OAS.

Degueldre's terrorist career came to an end at the beginning of April 1961 when he was arrested by the French army after a tip-off from a disaffected member of the OAS. While the lives of the high-ranking generals who had led the OAS were spared, the military court which tried Degueldre in June 1962 condemned him to death. A plot was laid by Degueldre's mistress and a band of OAS faithfuls to release him, but it failed. Degueldre was shot by firing squad on July 6th 1962 at the Fort D'Ivry near Paris. The execution was botched, took several minutes, and five "coups de grâce" were needed before the wretched OAS leader died.

**DEIR YASSIN MASSACRE. (April 9th 1948).** A massacre by Jewish terrorists of the Arab village of Deir Yassin on the outskirts of Jerusalem in which an estimated 200 Arab men, women and children lost their lives. The killings were carried out by the IRGUN ZVAI LEUMI (IRGUN) which was then led by MENACHEM BEGIN, later to become prime minister of Israel. The smaller terrorist group Lehi (also known as The Stern Gang) were also involved. Irgun justified the massacre on the grounds that Deir Yassin was a centre of Arab resistance, although recent evidence suggests that the Arab villagers had signed a peace agreement with the Jews a few months before. The brutal killings at Deir Yassin was one of the incidents that led to the exodus of almost 600,000 Palestinians from the region of what is now Israel.

**DELLE CHIAIE, STEFANO**. Ruthless right-wing Italian terrorist and founder of a neo-Fascist group called AVANGUARDIA NAZIONALE, believed by the Italian authorities to have been behind a number of serious terrorist attacks including the BOLOGNA RAILWAY STATION BOMBING on August 3rd 1980. Delle Chiaie fled to Spain in 1970 and then to Latin America where he built a formidable sub rosa counter-insurgency career, and where he is still at large despite efforts by the Italian and Bolivian police to capture him.

Delle Chiaie and his neo-Fascist colleagues developed what they called a "strategy of tension", i.e. to carry out serious terrorist acts, blame them on the Left, and hope to create the kind of political chaos and instability which only a military coup d'état could resolve. After which, it was hoped, a new version of European Fascism could be developed. Delle Chiaie and the Avanguardia Nazionale developed close links with other European neo-Fascist groups, particularly in Spain, Greece, Portugal, and France. A small, insignificant-looking man, Delle Chiaie became one of the most wanted terrorist leaders in Europe in the 1970s and 1980s. His career as a political terrorist began in Rome in the 1950s when he abandoned the Italian Fascist Party as hopelessly moderate and set up the Avanguardia Nazionale which throughout the 1960s waged a bitter campaign against left-wing organisations at street level. He organised a number of serious attacks in Italy including the bombing of the BANCA DEL AGRICULTURA in Milan on December 12th 1969 which killed 16 people. A left-wing group was blamed for the Milan bombing. Delle Chiaie was also involved in the abortive coup d'état in Italy in 1970 organised by Count Valerio Borghese.

After the failure of the coup d'état Delle Chiaie fled to Spain where he opened a restaurant in Madrid, and with the connivance of Franco's police ran an assassination campaign against the Basque separatist movement ETA (both in Spain and France). At the same time he developed contacts with right-wing groups in Argentina and Chile and Bolivia, and in 1976, after the death of Franco, Delle Chiaie went to Chile to work for the Chilean security police. Following the assassination of the Chilean ex-Ambassador ORLANDO LETELIER in Washington DC in 1978, Delle Chiaie travelled Latin America (El Salvador, Nicaragua, Argentina) advising right-wing regimes on how to cope with "anarchists and terrorists" and then moved to Bolivia where he became involved in the coup d'état of July 17th 1980. One of Delle Chiaie's co-conspirators was ex-Nazi Klaus Barbie, now waiting trial in France for his war-time activities. This coup had the backing of the Argentine military regime with whom Delle Chiaie had worked.

In October 1982 a joint Italian-Bolivian police operation failed to capture Delle Chiaie, although his colleague PIERLUIGI PAGLIAI was shot and wounded in the police operation, and deported from Bolivia to Italy. Delle Chiaie, however, was warned in advance of the police raid, and slipped over the border into Argentina (where he is thought to be still hiding).

**DELTA FORCE.** 1st Special Forces Operational Detachment-Delta (SFOD-D). The anti-terrorist unit of the United States Army which was "activated" in December 1981 and was involved in the abortive "EAGLE CLAW" OPERATION to rescue the American diplomats being held hostage in the AMERICAN EMBASSY, TEHERAN. Closely modelled on the British Army's SPECIAL AIR SERVICE (SAS) regiment, Delta Force was conceived and brought into being by Colonel CHARLES BECKWITH. In 1985 the unit were part of the joint-services operation which intercepted the aircraft carrying the hijackers of the *ACHILLE LAURO* cruise liner. Recently the reputation of Delta Force has been sullied by a series of fraud charges laid against the unit's officers and men.

Beckwith became convinced that the American Army needed a specially trained unit like Delta Force after serving on detachment with the British SAS on manoeuvres all over Europe, and on counter-insurgency operations in Malaya. After years of advocacy and pleading the Pentagon gave Beckwith the go-ahead in 1977 (spurred on by the successful West German police operation after the LUFTHANSA HIJACKING TO MOGADISHU AIRPORT, SOMALIA). Since being set up Delta Force have been involved in operations in Teheran, Grenada, the Mediterranean and, according to some sources, in support of the Nicaraguan CONTRA guerrillas on the Nicaragua/Honduras border. Some military critics say the unit has been badly used by the US authorities for "shock" work better handled by Rangers or Paratroops.

In the operation in October 1985 to capture the four Arabs who hijacked the *Achille Lauro* cruise liner Delta Force were almost involved in a shoot-out with the Italian Carabinieri. When the Boeing 737 carrying the hijackers was forced by US fighters to land at Sigonella airport in Sicily the aircraft was surrounded by both Italian police and 50 men from Delta Force who had just landed in C-141 transports. Delta Force commander Carl W. Stiner had orders to take the terrorists back to the USA while the Italians were determined the men should not leave Italian soil. After a face-to-face argument during which, according to one witness, Delta Force "were pulling back the bolts on their rifles" the White House ordered Stiner to back down and leave the hijackers to Italian justice.

Like the SAS, Delta Force is built on four-man patrols each member of which, as well as being a well-trained soldier, has a speciality (communications expert, medic, linguist, marksman, mechanic, explosives expert etc.). Like the SAS, Delta Force specialises in Close Quarter Battle (CQB) training, the solving of hostage-taking situations, and resolving the hijacking of aircraft, trains, ships and buildings. Delta Force is based at Fort Bragg in North Carolina, but is on constant standby for operations anywhere in the world.

In November 1985 the unit's credibility was badly damaged when a Delta Force lieutenant-colonel was indicted on seven charges of fraud totalling more than $65,000. Army and Justice Department investigators suspect Delta Force troops of "diverting" as much as $500,000 for their personal use, and at least 80 members of the unit have been reprimanded or court-martialled for cheating on their expense accounts. Their critics within the Pentagon say this is the inevitable consequence of setting up a semi-clandestine force "answerable only to God".

**DEMOCRATIC FRONT FOR THE LIBERATION OF ARABISTAN**. The name adopted by the five-man team of Iranian Arabs involved in the IRANIAN EMBASSY SIEGE, LONDON, in May-June 1980. The Iraqi-trained group claimed to be struggling for a "free Khuzestan". Only one man survived the storming of the Embassy by the SPECIAL AIR SERVICE (SAS).

**DEMOCRATIC FRONT FOR THE LIBERATION OF PALESTINE (DFLP)**. Left-wing Palestinian group which split from the POPULAR FRONT FOR THE LIBERATION OF PALESTINE (PFLP) in 1969 after a series of bitter internal disputes. Led by Nayef Hawatma, a Christian-born Jordanian, the DFLP were dedicated to "politicising" the "peasants and workers" of the region and tried to set up a system of "soviets" throughout

Jordan. The DFLP opposed the PFLP's policy of staging terrorist attacks outside the "occupied territories" and argued that the Palestine movement should work for a "Democratic Palestine State" within which Jews and Arabs would have equal rights, and both cultures would be equally respected.

Although some Israelis were encouraged by what they saw as the DFLP's "moderation" any support for Hawatma's group vanished when the DFLP staged the MA'ALOT MASSACRE on May 15th 1974 during which 22 Israeli children were killed. Although perpetually critical of the FATAH leadership of the the the PALESTINE LIBERATION ORGANISATION (PLO) the DFLP have remained members of the PLO's ruling Executive Committee.

**DIRECTION GENERALE DE LA SECURITE EXTERIEURE (DGSE).** General Directorate for External Security. The French government's foreign intelligence-gathering apparatus which became notorious in 1985 for the *RAINBOW WARRIOR* ATTACK in Auckland Harbour, New Zealand. After two DGSE agents were arrested and convicted of a conspiracy to destroy the *Rainbow Warrior* the head of the DGSE, Vice-Admiral PIERRE LACOSTE was forced to resign.

**DOLLFUSS, ENGELBERT (1892-1934).** Right-wing Chancellor of Austria who was assassinated by German Nazis in Vienna on July 25th 1934 as part of Hitler's strategy to destabilise and then take over Austria. Dollfuss was shot when 154 members of the German SS dressed as Austrian soldiers burst into the Federal Chancellory and shot Dollfuss in the throat. He was attacked at noon and died of his wounds six hours later. Simultaneously Austrian Nazis took over the radio station and broadcast that Dollfuss had resigned, and that they were taking power. The German-backed Nazi putsch was quickly put down by the Austrian authorities. Thirteen of the Nazi group who murdered Dolfuss were tried and hanged.

**DOZIER, JAMES (born 1931).** American Brigadier-General and senior NATO officer who was kidnapped in Verona, Italy, in December 1981 by left-wing terrorists from the BRIGATE ROSSE. After being held captive for 42 days Dozier was traced to an apartment in Padua and released on January 28th 1981 by the Italian government's anti-terrorist squad. The massive police/army manhunt for Dozier resulted in the extensive penetration of the Brigate Rosse network, and the arrest and jailing of many of the group's leaders and members. The five Brigate Rosse members who kidnapped Dozier were given long jail sentences.

A veteran (and hero) of the Vietnam war and a senior officer in Nato's south European command, Dozier was snatched from his apartment in Verona on December 17th 1981. Held for 42 days in a small tent on the floor of an apartment in Padua, Dozier did everything he could to confuse and mislead his five captors (two of whom were women). Eventually Italian police tracked Dozier down to Padua, and on January 28th 1982, the Italian government's anti-terrorist unit (nicknamed "The Leatherheads") stormed the apartment in a 90-second operation. A bulldozer was used to create a diversion in the street outside. No shots were fired and no one was injured. The intensive police hunt for Dozier almost certainly thwarted a serious terrorist attack on the annual conference of the Italian Christian Democratic Party on January 22nd 1981. Police uncovered a plan by the Brigate Rosse for a grenade and machine-gun attack on the conference during a live TV broadcast. The police were able to arrest the 15 Brigate Rosse members who had been assigned to the assault.

**"DROPPIN' WELL" BOMBING, NORTHERN IRELAND. (December 6th 1982).** One of the worst single terrorist incidents in the recent Irish troubles. Seventeen people were killed and 66 injured when the IRISH NATIONAL LIBERATION ARMY (INLA) bombed the "Droppin' Well" pub and disco at Ballykelly in Northern Ireland. The INLA justified their attack on the grounds that the "Droppin' Well" was frequented by off-duty British soldiers and their Irish girl friends. Around 5lbs of explosive were left under a table in the disco which was crowded with more than 100 people, and when it exploded most of the building collapsed on the inhabitants. Eleven of the dead were soldiers from the 1st Battalion the Cheshire Regiment, and six of the other victims were young women. Only three people were killed by the blast, the others died in the falling masonry. In June 1986 five people (four of them from one family) were charged with the murders, and put on trial at Belfast Crown Court. All were alleged to have been members of the INLA.

**DZERZHINSKY, FELIKS EDMUNDOVICH.** Polish-born nobleman turned revolutionary who founded the Soviet secret police security apparatus which evolved into the modern KOMITET GOSUDARSTVENNOI BEZOPASTNOSTI (KGB), the largest intelligence gathering and security organisation in the world. Described as a brilliant but austere and humourless man (who had suffered at the hands of the Tsar's state police OKHRANA) Dzerzhinsky was a fanatical revolutionary, and a firm believer in the use of terror to sustain the Bolshevik revolution. In June 1918 Dzerzhinsky is reported as saying, "We stand for organised terror", although later in the same year he is said to have wandered the Kremlin weeping bitterly and crying, "I have spilt so much blood that I no longer have any right to live." It has been argued that Dzerzhinsky's use of terror as an instrument of policy between 1917 and 1926 is the ideological basis of the modern KGB's support for international terrorism.

Some historians claim that if Lenin had lived he would have "purged" the party of Dzerzhinsky. But after suffering his third stroke Lenin died in 1924 and in the fierce struggle for power between Stalin and Trotsky that followed Lenin's death, Dzerzhinsky threw in his lot with Stalin. Until his death in 1926 Dzerzhinsky was one of Stalin's most powerful and astute supporters, first against Trotsky, and later against the Politburo "rightists" led by Nikolai Bukharin (who believed that Stalin was planning to set up a Moscow-based dictatorship). When Stalin's body was removed from the Lenin Mausoleum in disgrace, the dictator was buried at the Kremlin Wall next to Feliks Dzerzhinsky. A statue of Dzerzhinsky now overlooks the KGB's headquarters in Dzerzhinsky Square, Moscow.

# E

**"EAGLE CLAW" OPERATION. (April 24th-25th 1980).** The ill-fated rescue attempt by the US military to release the 52 American diplomats and staff being held in the AMERICAN EMBASSY HOSTAGE CRISIS in Teheran, Iran. The operation was led by Colonel CHARLES BECKWITH, commander of the US Army's élite counter-terrorist unit DELTA FORCE. Operation "Eagle Claw" came to grief in the Iranian desert on the night of April 24th-25th 1980 when three of the naval helicopters assigned to the mission broke down, and another collided with a fuel-carrying cargo aircraft. Eight US servicemen died in the incident. The mission was then abandoned.

Planning for a hostage-rescue mission began within days of the American Embassy in Teheran being taken over by militant students on November 4th 1979. The plan worked out by a joint task-force was to fly the Delta Force men into Iran from the island of Masirah off the coast of Oman to a point 200 miles south-east of Teheran dubbed "Desert One". There they would rendezvous with eight helicopters from the US aircraft carrier *Nimitz*. The helicopters were to be refuelled from EC-130 tanker aircraft. Once inside Teheran the 118-strong Delta Force would storm the Embassy complex, free the hostages, shepherd them to a nearby soccer stadium from which they and the Delta Force men would be plucked by helicopters. From there they would be flown to the airport at Manzariyeh near Qom, and flown back to Masirah Island on a C-141 "Starlifter".

It was an audacious, but complex and hazardous plan which began at 18.00 on April 24th 1980 and which got no further than "Desert One", the rendezvous point 200 miles south-east of Teheran. No sooner had the first C-130 landed than a civilian bus crowded with passengers appeared on the scene, and a petrol tanker had to be blown up. Only six of the eight RH-53D naval helicopters arrived at the rendezvous point, and all were more than an hour late, having flown through a fierce sandstorm. One of them broke down after landing. With only five helicopters at his disposal (three short of the number required) Colonel Beckwith aborted the operation, and ordered the C-130s and the RH-53Ds back to their bases.

But at 02.40 on April 25th 1980, one of the helicopters collided with a tanker aircraft killing five airmen and three marines. The remaining four helicopters were abandoned at "Desert One" and were captured by the Iranians (who made much of the aborted US mission). Later Beckwith told the US Senate's Armed Forces Committee that Operation "Eagle Claw" had been dogged by bad luck from the beginning, but recommended that the US should set up a permanent joint-forces team to cope with such situations as the Teheran rescue attempt.

**EASTER RISING, DUBLIN. (April 24th-29th 1916).** A rebellion in Dublin by Irish Republicans demanding the setting up of an Irish state independent from Britain. The action was led by militias organised by Padraig Pearse of the Irish Republican Brotherhood and Scots-born JAMES CONNOLLY of Sinn Fein. Pearse declared a "Provisional Government" of the Irish Republic from the General Post Office (GPO) which served as the rebels' headquarters. After five days of fighting, during which more than 1300 people were killed and wounded, the rebellion was put down by the British Army. But the British government made the calamitous political mistake of transforming the unpopular rebel leadership into Irish martyrs by executing 14 of them at Kilmainham jail. The 1916 Easter Rising now has a central role in modern Irish history, and in Republican mythology.

Although the British government had passed an Irish Home Rule Bill in 1914 it was suspended partly due to the opposition of Ulster Protestants (who had raised the ULSTER VOLUNTEER FORCE to fight the measure) and partly to the crisis brought on by World War I. Frustrated, the Irish nationalists led by Pearse, Connolly, Plunkett and Clarke planned an insurrection. On the morning of Easter Monday 1916, men of the Irish Volunteers (led by Pearse) and the Citizens Army (led by Connolly) took over key points of Dublin, including the General Post Office, the Four Courts, Jacobs Biscuit Factory, Kingsbridge Station, St Stephens Green and the Imperial Hotel. "From the moment the first shot is fired," Connolly declared, "there will be no longer Volunteers or Citizen Army but only the Army of the Irish Republic." Connolly's declaration of Easter 1916 is regarded by many Republicans as the birth of the IRISH REPUBLICAN ARMY (IRA).

The British response to the Republican putsch was savage; large numbers of troops and artillery were rushed into Dublin. On April 27th 1916 British artillery was brought into play against the GPO, and a British gunboat sailed up the Liffey to bombard the Four Courts buildings. After evacuating the burning GPO buildings and setting up new HQ in nearby Moore Street, Pearse and Connolly agreed to an unconditional surrender on April 30th 1916 to save any further civilian casualties. In the next few days 90 of the rebels, including all the leaders, were tried by military courts-martial and sentenced to death. Thousands more (including MICHAEL COLLINS who was to prove a terrorist/guerrilla leader of genius) were shipped off to prison camps in Britain.

Although the Easter Rising was regarded at the time by many Irish as a "stab in the back" when more than 100,000 Irishmen were fighting in the British Army, the decision by General Sir John Maxwell to "teach the Irish a lesson" transformed the situation utterly. The executions began on May 3rd 1916 when Pearse, MacDonagh and Clarke were shot, and lasted until May 12th 1916 when the crippled Sean MacDiarmada and the grievously injured James Connolly were executed. Connolly was taken from a stretcher and strapped to a chair for his execution.

Although the other insurgents under sentence of death were later reprieved (including Eamonn De Valera, later President of Ireland) the hasty and brutal executions of the leaders of the Easter Rising stoked the fires of Irish Republican nationalism which have been burning ever since, and continue to plague the British authorities in Northern Ireland.

## EGYPTAIR HIJACKING TO LUQA AIRPORT, MALTA.

**(November 23rd-24th 1985)**. The bloodiest hijack in aviation history in which 57 people died at Luqa Airport in Malta, most of them when Egyptian commandos stormed a hijacked Egyptair jet. The aircraft had been taken over by four young Arabs claiming to be members of the EGYPTIAN LIBERATION ORGANISATION (ELO) thought to have the backing of the Palestinian terrorist leader ABU NIDAL. Following the heavy death toll, the Egyptian authorities were severely criticised for the way their SA'AQA ("Thunderbolt") unit carried out the operation to rescue the passengers and crew. And the incident exacerbated the already bad relations between Egypt and Libya; the Egyptians openly accused the Libyans of supporting the hijacking in which many Egyptians died.

The Egyptair Boeing 737 on a flight from Athens to Cairo with 98 passengers and crew aboard was hijacked over the Mediterranean in the evening of November 23rd 1985. Following a brief gun-battle between the hijackers and Egyptian SKYMARSHALLS the fuselage of the aircraft was punctured and the Boeing was forced to make an emergency landing at Luqa Airport near Malta's capital Valetta. After releasing 11 women passengers and two female crew members, the hijackers threatened to kill hostages every hour on the hour until the Maltese allowed the jet to be refuelled. They did, in fact, shoot five people – two Israelis and three Americans. One of the Israelis, 23-year-old Nitzan Mendelson, died.

Fearing that the hijackers planned to systematically kill all the passengers, at 21.15 on November 24th 1985 six members of the Egyptian commando unit stormed the aircraft. To create a diversion two Egyptians entered the aircraft's rear baggage hold and blew a hole in the floor, while other soldiers blew in the over-wing escape hatches. But the operation failed to take the hijackers by surprise; grenades were thrown, a gun-battle ensued, and the rear of the aircraft caught fire. Of the 57 people who died, eight were killed by grenade fragments, seven by bullet wounds, and the rest from the effects of the fire. Only one of the terrorists, a 22-year-old Palestinian called OMAR MOHAMMED ALI REZAQ, survived the attack. Despite criticism of the way the rescue attempt was planned and executed, the Egyptian government said, "We had to fight terrorism and fight it hard."

## EGYPTIAN LIBERATION ORGANISATION (ELO). Name
adopted by the Muslim terrorists involved in the bloody EGYPTAIR HIJACKING TO LUQA AIRPORT, MALTA in November 1985. The ELO is thought to be one of the many *noms de guerre* of the ABU NIDAL organisation.

## EJERCITO REVOLUCIONARIO DEL PUEBLO (ERP).
Argentine's most active left-wing terrorist group set up in July 1970 as the military arm of the Trotskyist Partido Revolucionario de los Trabajadores (PRT), an affiliate of the Fourth International. The ERP carried out a long string of assassinations in Argentina including policemen, army officers and moderate trade union leaders. In 1972 they kidnapped and then killed Dr Oberdan Sallustro, Fiat's general manager in Argentina, and in 1976 blew up the Chief of Police of Buenos Aires.

With an estimated 5,000 members and supporters, the ERP were smaller than the Peronist MONTONEROS, but better armed, better organised, and a greater threat to the Argentine government. Politically, however, the ERP were confused. Raised as the fighting arm of a Trotskyist organisation connected to the Fourth International, the ERP soon found Trotskyist ideology too constricting. In 1973 the ERP formally severed their links with the PRT and the Fourth International. But the ERP were founder members (and the paymasters) of the JUNTA OF REVOLUTIONARY CO-ORDINATION (JRC).

Mainly middle-class in origin, the ERP were led by the Cuban-trained MARIO SANTUCHO who was killed by the police in July 1976. In 1973 the ERP attacked a nuclear power station near Buenos Aires. ERP terrorism reached its peak in 1975 and 1976, and their activities did much to provoke Argentine's military coup of 1976, and the notorious "dirty war" of repression.

**EL AL HIJACKING TO ALGERIA. (July 23rd 1968)**. The first aerial hijacking by an Arab terrorist group, and one which revealed the helplessness of the international community to deal with the phenomenon. The POPULAR FRONT FOR THE LIBERATION OF PALESTINE (PFLP) took over an Israeli-owned airliner bound from Rome to Athens and forced it to fly to Algeria where the aircraft, the crew, and some of the Israeli passengers were held prisoner by the Algerian government while the PFLP demanded the release of 1,000 Arabs held by Israel. Intense diplomatic pressure was brought to bear on the recently independent Algerian state and eventually all the passengers and crew were released unharmed. But the International Federation of Airline Pilots Association's (IFAPA) vote to block all flights by Western airlines to Algeria came to nothing, while the International Air Transport Association's plea for all governments to ratify the Tokyo Convention of 1963 which outlawed hijacking was ignored.

The hijacking began on July 23rd 1968 shortly after the El Al Boeing 707 with 45 passengers and crew on board left Rome on a scheduled flight to Athens. Five Arabs armed with handguns and grenades took over the flight, announced that the aircraft had been renamed "Liberation of Palestine" and forced the crew to fly to Dar-el-Beida airport near Algiers where the aircraft landed. The 23 non-Israeli passengers on the flight were immediately released, and flown by Air Algérie to Paris, but the 22 Israelis (12 passengers and 10 crew) were detained by the Algerians who told them that Algeria was "opposed to the State of Israel".

On the same day, July 23rd 1968, a statement was issued in Beirut by the PFLP admitting responsibility for the hijacking, and claiming that while the Algerian government had no advance knowledge of the incident they had been asked to hold the aircraft and its Israeli passengers hostage. On July 29th 1968 a six-man delegation from the PFLP, the PALESTINE LIBERATION

ORGANISATION (PLO) and FATAH flew to Algiers to try to persuade the Algerian government to hang onto the aircraft and the Israelis until the Israeli government released 1,000 Arabs held in Israel.

Two days previously, on July 27th 1968, 10 of the Israelis (four women passengers, three children and three El Al stewardesses) were flown out of Algeria to Switzerland leaving only 12 male Israelis (five passengers and seven aircrew) held by the Algerians. After being refused access to the 12 passengers and crew, the pilots' organisation IFAPA voted to boycott all flights by Western airlines into Algeria. Alarmed at the prospect of isolation, the Algerians allowed IFAPA to satisfy itself that the 12 Israelis were safe and well, and on August 17th 1968 the IFAPA boycott was called off. The affair was resolved when the Israeli government agreed to release 16 Arab prisoners, the first time that the Israelis gave into the demands of a terrorist group.

**ENSSLIN, GUDRUN**. West German terrorist and member of the notorious left-wing ROTE ARMEE FRAKTION (RAF) who committed suicide in prison in 1976 after the West German GRENZSCHUTZGRUPPE 9 (GSG-9) thwarted the LUFTHANSA HIJACKING TO MOGADISHU AIRPORT, SOMALIA. Ensslin hanged herself on the same night as her one-time lover ANDREAS BAADER shot himself to death in the same prison. Another leading RAF member, JAN-CARL RASPE also killed himself.

Like most of the RAF (also known as the BAADER-MEINHOF gang) Gudrun Ensslin was an educated product of the West German middle class. The daughter of an Evangelical pastor, Ensslin read philosophy at the University of Tubingen, and studied for a doctorate at the Free University of Berlin where she became involved in radical politics. In 1968 Ensslin and Andreas Baader were jailed for planting a firebomb in a Frankfurt store but were released on bail in 1969. When Baader was rearrested, Ensslin was involved in the plot to release him from jail in Berlin, after which she and the others fled to the Middle East where they trained as guerrillas in Palestinian camps. Ensslin's brief career as an urban terrorist came to an end in 1972 when she was arrested along with Baader, Meinhof and most of the RAF. During a lengthy trial at Stammheim near Stuttgart various attempts were made by other terrorist groups to force the release of the RAF leadership. They all failed, and in the early hours of October 18th 1977 Ensslin, Baader and Raspe killed themselves in the high-security jail at Stammheim.

**ENTEBBE RESCUE.** See AIR FRANCE HIJACKING TO ENTEBBE AIRPORT, UGANDA.

**ETHNIKI ORGANOSIS KYPRION AGONISTON (EOKA).** (National Organisation of Cypriot Fighters). Greek Cypriot underground terrorist/guerrilla army which fought the British for the independence of Cyprus between 1955 and 1958, under the leadership of General GEORGE GRIVAS. The military campaign began on March 31st 1955 with a wave of bombings throughout the island, and ended in 1958, with more than 40,000 British troops trying, unsuccessfully, to crush EOKA. Eventually the Republic of Cyprus was set up under a constitution drafted in London, Athens, and Ankara. EOKA were successful in their goal of an independent Cyprus, but failed to achieve "Enosis", i.e. union with Greece. But the British strategy of deploying the Turkish minority against the Greeks generated bitter inter-communal strife, and led eventually to the invasion of Cyprus by the Turks in 1974 and the north-south partition of the island.

**EUSKADI TA ASKATASUNA (ETA).** (Euskadi and Freedom). The much-fragmented guerrilla/terrorist organisation of the Basques of northern Spain and southern France who have been fighting for more than 25 years for an independent Basque homeland. Now seasoned and skilled urban terrorists, ETA have specialised in attacking senior officers of the Spanish military. In December 1973 they assassinated Prime Minister Admiral LUIS CARRERO BLANCO, and in January 1984 killed General Miguel Quintana. Since December 1973 ETA have assassinated 54 senior Spanish military officers, the most recent being retired General Juan Atares (shot in December 1985) and Vice-Admiral Cristobal Colon (killed in Madrid in February 1986). Like the IRISH REPUBLICAN ARMY (IRA) with whom they have contacts, ETA has been riven by left/right, Marxist/Roman Catholic disputes. In 1985 ETA bombers tried to cripple Spain's vital tourist industry by setting off 19 bombs in tourist resorts, a campaign they repeated in 1986 with a series of small-scale bombing attacks on Spanish tourist hotels.

In April 1986 the French police arrested Domingo Iturbe Abasalo, also known as Txomin, who is believed to be the military head of ETA, and architect of the Carrero Blanco killing. Txomin was arrested near Biarritz and charged with breach of his French "residence order" which confined him to Tours. The Spanish government immediately asked for his extradition in the belief

110

that the right-wing regime of Jacques Chirac was more inclined to turn Basque terrorists over to the Spanish police than the French socialists were. On April 25th, a few days before Txomin was arrested, a car bomb killed five members of the Civil Guard in the centre of Madrid.

The war between ETA and the Spanish authorities has been one of the most vicious in Europe (500 people have been killed in 17 years) but a security report commissioned by the Basque regional government and published in April 1986 decided that the problems of the Basque country were susceptible to political solutions. The report described ETA as "an unfortunate child of the Franco dictatorship" and called for imaginitive steps to accommodate Basque nationalism within the framework of Spain and the European Economic Community (EEC). The report recommended that ETA terrorists should be tried in Basque courts and not, as currently happens, in special courts in Madrid. It also recommended that anti-terrorist duties should be assumed by the Basque police from Spain's National Police.

Although a resourceful clandestine organisation, the history of ETA is one of schism and dissension. Formed in 1959, ETA split in 1966 into ETA-Zarra (Old ETA) and ETA-Berri (Young ETA). Four years later ETA-Zarra subdivided into ETA-5 and ETA-6 with the latter abandoning the armed struggle. A few years later ETA-5 split into ETA-Military and ETA-Politico Military which in 1981 split again into ETA-7 and ETA-8. Of all the ETA sub-groups, ETA-Military (known as "The Milis") are the most seasoned and effective, and operate under the slogan "Actions Unite. Words Divide."

ETA's carefully contrived "cell" structure has made the organisation difficult (but not impossible) to infiltrate. Usually an ETA "irurko" or commando consists of three people who may know very few (if any) other ETA members. In the late 1970s ETA-Military's commander Miguel Angel Apalategui instigated a system of "sleeping commandos", individuals or groups who lead respectable normal lives but who are asked to perform one particular action, and one only. Once the action – sabotage, a shooting, a bombing – has been carried out they revert to their normal lives, and are never asked to perform again. ETA's first action in 1961 (an abortive attempt to derail a train carrying Fascist veterans to a rally in San Sebastian) sparked off a cycle of brutal police repression and ETA terrorism which has continued ever since. ETA's most spectacular attack on the Spanish regime was in December 1973 when they blew up Prime Minister Admiral Luis Carrero Blanco with a huge bomb, the explosives for which are believed to have been supplied by the PROVISIONAL IRISH REPUBLICAN ARMY (PIRA).

Like the PIRA, ETA terrorists benefit from a long border over which support can be gained and refuge sought. Many of the Basques of south-west France are sympathetic to ETA's aims, and France has long been a source of arms, explosives, cash and support for the ETA militants. This situation galls and frustrates the Spanish security forces (as it does the British in Northern Ireland) and in 1980 there was a grave diplomatic incident when members of a Spanish anti-terrorist force crossed the border and shot dead two Basque terrorists in a bar in France.

Politically, however, ETA have been undermined to some extent by the new Spanish regime's plans for the devolution of power from the central government in Madrid to the Spanish regions, including the Basque country. This policy has given weight to the Basque majority who are willing to try out the new constitutional arrangements. But it is unlikely that the Basque zealots of ETA-Military (and some of the other groups) will ever be satisfied with less than a completely independent Basque homeland, and they are expected to go on fighting.

**EWART-BIGGS, CHRISTOPHER**. British ambassador to the Republic of Ireland who was assassinated by the PROVISIONAL IRISH REPUBLICAN ARMY (PIRA) on July 21st 1976, only two weeks after he had taken office. The ambassador was killed by a landmine concealed in the drive of his official residence at Sandyford, County Dublin. A young civil servant from the Northern Ireland Office, Judith Cook, was killed in the car with him. In the wake of the Ewart-Biggs killing the Dublin government declared a state of emergency, and passed tough new anti-terrorist legislation in an attempt to curb the PIRA and other extremist groups. Ewart-Biggs' widow, Jane, was made a Life Peer in 1978 and has since worked for peace and reconciliation in Ireland. She also instigated a literary prize for authors whose work is thought to have added to the peace process.

# F

**FANON, FRANTZ (1925-1961).** French-speaking revolutionary philosopher whose work was influential among the radical movements of the Third World and the New Left of Europe and North America. His book *The Wretched of the Earth* which describes the impact of European colonialism on the colonial peoples and rationalises anti-colonial violence is probably his most important work. Fanon regarded revolutionary and anti-colonial violence as liberating and purifying and essential to the psychological well-being of the colonial people. As a philosopher Fanon was described by Jean-Paul Sartre as "the first since Engels to bring the processes of history into the clear light of day".

Born in the French colony of Martinique, Fanon studied medicine and psychiatry in France, and worked in an Algerian hospital during the BATTLE OF ALGIERS. The bitterness and repression which marked the Algerian war against Metropolitan France is reflected in much of Fanon's writing. Fanon warned colonial people against emulating Europe. "Two centuries ago," he wrote, "a former European colony decided to catch up with Europe. It succeeded so well that the United States of America became a monster in which the taints, the sickness and inhumanity of Europe have grown to appalling dimensions." Fanon died of leukaemia in Washington in December 1961 at the age of 36. Another important Fanon work is *Black Skins, White Masks.*

**FARABUNDO MARTI LIBERATION NACIONALE (FMLN).** Left-wing guerrilla group operating in El Salvador responsible for the kidnapping of Ines Duarte Duran, 35, eldest (and favourite) daughter of Jose Napoleon Duarte, President of El Salvador. Ines Duarte Duran was kidnapped in September 1985 near the University of San Salvador where she was a student. Both her bodyguards were killed in the attack. The US government offered President Duarte "all appropriate assets" to help recover his daughter, but she was later released in exchange for FMLN members being held in El Salvador jails. Three months earlier, in June 1985, the FMLN attacked sidewalk cafés in the affluent Zona Rosa district of San Salvadore killing 13 people, four of them US marines.

**FATAH**. The military wing and largest single component of the PALESTINE LIBERATION ORGANISATION (PLO). Founded in 1956 as a hit-and-run guerrilla force to fight the Israeli Defence Forces (IDF), Fatah has been led since 1964 by YASIR ARAFAT now also Chairman of the PLO. In a key document ("The Seven Points", January 1969) Fatah describes itself as "the expression of the Palestinian people and of its will to free its land from Zionist colonisation in order to recover its national identity". As part of the PLO, Fatah is funded mainly from Palestinian investments and by oil-rich Arab governments and is estimated to keep 10,000 to 15,000 men under arms. Although by far the biggest of the Palestinian groups, Fatah is regularly denounced by other organisations for its ineffectiveness, and for the gap between its rhetoric and deeds.

Fatah, a "palindromic syndrome" for Harakat al-Tahrir al-Filastiniyya (Palestinian Liberation Movement), was set up in the late 1950s and predates the PLO by about six years. In 1968, following the crushing defeat of the Arab armies by Israel in the "Six-Day War" of June 1967, Fatah led a coalition of guerrilla groups which took over the political apparatus of the PLO. Fatah's leader and co-founder, Yasir Arafat, became Chairman of the PLO, a position he has held ever since. Since then Fatah and the guerrillas have dominated the PLO Executive Committee with eight of the 14 seats (at the elections in 1983).

Although Fatah is a well-funded and fairly well-equipped military machine, it has rarely proved a match for the Israelis, even in the "occupied" territories such as the Gaza and the West Bank of the Jordan. In September 1970 Fatah and the other Palestinian organisations were hounded out of Jordan by King Hussein's army (an action some Fatah members commemorated by setting up BLACK SEPTEMBER). And in 1982 the Fatah troops were unable to prevent the PLO and its cadres being driven out of Lebanon and into exile in Syria, Iraq, Algeria, Tunisia and Yemen.

The limitations of Fatah's guerrilla/terrorist strategy were set out in the 1960s by Palestinian critic Naji Alush who pointed to the profound differences between the struggle of the Palestinian and that of other Arabs (such as the Algerians) against European colonialism. Fatah were faced, Alush wrote, not with a straightforward war against a frightened colonial regime but with "...a battle for the uprooting of a state recognised by the United Nations, supported by world public opinion and the principal capitalist states". While the great powers might be ready to accept the independence of Algeria from France, Alush argued, "...they are not ready to accept the liquidation of the Zionist's state".

When the Fatah fighters were driven out of Lebanon in August 1982 by the Israelis and scattered throughout the Arab world the defeat caused a number of splits in the Fatah ranks. One group, led by ABU MOUSSA, broke away from Yasir Arafat's PLO in 1983 and found sanctuary in Syria (which also supports the anti-Arafat POPULAR FRONT FOR THE LIBERATION OF PALESTINE-GENERAL COMMAND). Another Fatah splinter-group is the FATAH REVOLUTIONARY COUNCIL (FRC), the organisation of ABU NIDAL.

**FATAH REVOLUTIONARY COUNCIL (FRC).** The Syrian-backed "umbrella" organisation of the terrorist network run by ABU NIDAL. The FRC emerged in the early 1970s when Abu Nidal and other Palestinians grew frustrated with the ineffectiveness of the mainstream FATAH organisation and the leadership of YASIR ARAFAT. Shortly after the FRC split from Fatah in 1974 Abu Nidal's men tried to kill Arafat, who in turn issued a "death sentence" on the FRC and its leadership. Originally backed by the Iraqis, FRC terrorists have operated under the names BLACK JUNE, the Arab Revolutionary Brigades and the REVOLUTIONARY ORGANISATION OF SOCIALIST MUSLIMS (ROSM). The FRC is thought to consist of around 200-500 dedicated Arab terrorists who have carried out operations in London, Kuwait, Paris, Portugal, Yugoslavia, Rumania and Poland. The FRC now appear to be based in the Syrian capital of Damascus, with training camps in the Bekaa valley in Lebanon.

**FEDERAL BUREAU OF INVESTIGATION (FBI).** The main internal security arm of the United States government. A Federal agency set up in 1908, the FBI now employs 6,000 agents backed by 8,000 support staff. It is based in Washington DC with "field offices" around the country. The modern FBI is the creation of J. Edgar Hoover who ran the bureau from 1924 until his death in 1972. In the 1930s the FBI spent most of their resources fighting organised crime but during World War II were given an anti-espionage and internal-security role by President Roosevelt. While reasonably successful in winkling out Nazi activists and spies, Hoover became obsessed with the threat to the USA posed by Soviet Communism, and in the post-war period did much to fuel America's paranoia about the Communist menace.

As the main Federal agency responsible for combating internal terrorism, the FBI has developed Special Weapons and Tactics

(SWAT) teams which operate through a special command-and-control centre at FBI headquarters in Washington. FBI anti-terrorist teams have been used in a number of internal terrorist incidents, such as the one in 1976 when a group of Serbian nationalists hijacked an American Airlines jet in an attempt to force the release of one of their colleagues jailed in Chicago. The attempt failed. The FBI now has a strong force of agents with experience of hijacking, kidnapping, hostage-taking, and other forms of terrorism, and FBI teams have aircraft and helicopters at their disposal to airlift them to incidents in any part of the USA.

But the Church Committee report into the activities of the FBI in 1976 showed that for many years the Bureau had been indulging in totally illegal activities. Between 1942 and 1968 the FBI had carried out more than 200 "black-bag jobs" (i.e. burglaries) against legal but left-wing or liberal organisations. The Church Committee also accused the FBI of carrying out a campaign of character assassination against MARTIN LUTHER KING, the black civil rights leader who was assassinated in Memphis in 1968.

After Hoover's death in 1972 the FBI passed briefly into the hands of Patrick Grey, and then to Clarence Kelley (a professional agent) and finally to Federal judge William Webster. The FBI is almost unique in combining internal-security and counter-espionage work with investigation into crimes against federal law (such as kidnapping, transgression of civil rights etc.).

**FELTRINELLI, GIANGIACOMO (1926-1972).** Wealthy and eccentric Italian publisher and financier of extreme left-wing causes, once dubbed "the father of European terrorism" who was killed on March 15th 1972 when a bomb he was laying exploded prematurely. Through his publishing house and bookshops, Feltrinelli published many terrorist tracts, including the Brazilian CARLOS MARIGHELLA's notorious terrorist handbook *MINIMANUAL OF THE URBAN GUERRILLA*. Historians of terrorism have never decided whether Feltrinelli was a rich buffoon with a taste for left-wing causes, or whether his apparent ineptitude was a cover for a dangerous terrorist organiser who may have been an officer of the Soviet intelligence service.

What is known is that the eccentric Feltrinelli had a wide range of contacts with other European and Palestinian terrorist groups such as the BRIGATE ROSSE, the ROTE ARMEE FRAKTION (RAF), and the POPULAR FRONT FOR THE LIBERATION OF PALESTINE (PFLP). One account suggests that it was Feltrinelli who suggested to PFLP leader GEORGE HABASH that the PFLP should "go international" with its terror campaign. After Feltrinelli's death in 1972 the Italian police discovered that the millionaire/terrorist had set up a network of "safe" houses well stocked with Soviet-made weapons, maps, false passports etc.

Although he was born into an extremely wealthy north Italian family, Feltrinelli seems to have been attracted to the revolutionary left for most of his life. In the 1940s he joined the Communist Party of Italy, and in the 1960s he spent at least two training sessions in Czechoslovakia. He entertained the German terrorist ULRIKE MEINHOF, travelled to Cuba to meet Fidel Castro, agreed to publish *Tricontinental*, the journal of the TRICONTINENTAL CONFERENCE, assisted in the defence of REGIS DEBRAY in Bolivia, took part in the Paris riots in 1968, and that same year published *Italy 1968: Political Guerrilla Warfare*.

Feltrinelli went underground in 1969, although he managed to organise a terrorist summit at a Jesuit college in Florence which was attended by delegates from 14 of the world's terrorist organisations. Ironically, one of Feltrinelli's financial holdings was a large shareholding in the Vatican's Banca Unione, which Feltrinelli sold to Mafia financier Michel Sindona (who was murdered in an Italian prison in March 1986) and used the cash to promote his left-wing subversive activities.

Some writers argue that far from being a driving force in European terrorism, he was simply exploited by the terror groups for his huge reserves of cash. He has been described as a rich fantasist who "adored the concept of Third World revolution" and who liked nothing more than to strut in the uniform of Uruguayan TUPAMAROS. Reputed to be technically inept and physically clumsy, Feltrinelli finally blew himself up on May 14th 1972 while trying to set a bomb to an electricity pylon outside Florence. But in 1979 Brigate Rosse leader Augusto Viel eulogized Feltrinelli as "a revolutionary who had fallen in battle", and claimed that the wealthy publisher had "developed a continental strategy of long-lasting and decisive importance".

**FENIAN BROTHERHOOD**. Loose organisation of various 19th Century Irish republican movements, including the Irish Republican Brotherhood, Clann na Gael, The Triangle and The Invincibles. The activities of Fenian "dynamiters" in late 19th century England led the Metropolitan Police to set up the "Special Irish Branch" (now the Special Branch). Fenians were responsible for the murder of Lord Frederick Cavendish, the newly appointed

Chief Secretary for Ireland in Pheonix Park, Dublin, in May 1882 (a killing which probably set back the Irish cause many years). Much of the Fenians' support came from the Irish community in the United States of America.

**FIRMENICH, MARIO**. Leader of the MONTONEROS of Argentina, the large terrorist/guerrilla movement which grew from the left-wing of the Peronist movement.

**FORCE 17.** One of the élite units of FATAH, the military wing of the PALESTINE LIBERATION ORGANISATION (PLO). Raised as a special bodyguard for YASIR ARAFAT and originally consisting of 10 members, Force 17 became a commando unit of the PLO during the civil war in Lebanon when it numbered 1,000. Better trained and equipped than PLO regulars, Force 17 so impressed Arafat with its efficiency that he increased its numbers to 1500. Although Force 17 and the PLO deny it, the Israelis believe it was behind the LARNACA MARINA ATTACK in Cyprus in September 1985. In August 1985 Israeli patrol vessels intercepted two launches carrying Force 17 guerrillas from Cyprus to the Lebanon. Some Force 17 detachments are believed to be specially trained in mine-laying, shore landings, and underwater sabotage. Western intelligence believe there are Force 17 groups or cells all over Western Europe, including Britain, France and West Germany.

**FRANZ FERDINAND (1863-1914)**. Archduke of Austria and heir to the throne of Austria-Hungary whose assassination in Sarajevo in Bosnia on June 28th 1914 precipitated World War I. Franz Ferdinand and his wife Sophie were on a state visit to Bosnia when they were killed by a young student called GAVRILO PRINCIP. Princip was part of a terrorist conspiracy by two groups of Serbian nationalists, Young Bosnia and The Black Hand (which supplied the weapons). Although the conspiracy to kill Franz Ferdinand had no approval from the Serbian government, it was supported by elements in Serbian military intelligence.

The assassination of Archduke Franz Ferdinand was probably the most momentous act of political terrorism in 20th century history. The Austrian government were convinced that the Serbian authorities were behind the killing of Franz Ferdinand, and delivered a harsh ultimatum to Serbia on July 23rd. The Austrians demanded the suppression of all Pan-Slavic propaganda, the dismissal of Serbian officials named by the Austrians, and a rigorous joint Austrian/Serbian inquiry into the assassination. While the Serbs did what they could to comply, the demands were seen as an affront to growing Serbian (and Slavic) nationalism, and war broke out five days later. It spread to the great powers of Europe when Austria-Hungary invoked the alliance with Germany, and the Serbs called on the Russian Empire for help. By the end of the year Britain, France and Belgium had been drawn into the conflagration in which millions died and which changed the shape of Europe.

**FRENCH ARMY HQ BOMBING, BEIRUT. (October 23rd 1983).** A suicide bomb attack on the French Army headquarters in Beirut which killed 58 French paratroopers. The bomb outrage in Beirut was France's worst single military loss since the end of the Algerian war. Responsibility for the attack, and for the AMERICAN MARINE HQ BOMBING, was claimed by an organisation called ISLAMIC JIHAD. The French struck back with air attacks on pro-Iranian Shia Muslim camps in the Bekaa valley although there was little evidence that the Beirut attack had been carried out by anyone from the camps.

The bombing of the eight-storey French-occupied building a few miles south of Beirut Airport happened at 06.20 on October 23rd 1983. A truck loaded with explosives was driven through the gates, past the French sentries, and into the side of the building and then exploded. The entire eight-storey building collapsed on its side killing 58 of the men inside, most of whom were in bed at the time. As almost all the evidence (including the perpetrator) was blown to pieces in the explosion, French investigators were never able to determine who inflicted the massive blow on their troops. In February 1984, three months after the attacks on the French and American military HQ the Multi National Force (MNF) pulled out of Lebanon.

**FRENCH EMBASSY ATTACK, THE HAGUE, HOLLAND. (September 13th 1974).** Attack on the French Embassy in the Hague, Holland, by three members of the UNITED RED ARMY OF JAPAN (URAJ) to force the release of URAJ courier YOSHIAKA YAMADA who had been jailed in France. After the seizure of their Embassy and the taking of their Ambassador hostage, the French asked the Dutch government for permission to storm the Embassy with French special forces. The Dutch refused. Eventually, after five days of siege, the French released Yamada, paid him

$300,000 and provided him with a safe passage to the Middle East. The operation to release Yamada was organised by the terrorist organiser ILLICH RAMIREZ SANCHEZ ("Carlos the Jackal") then operating in France.

**FRENTE SANDINISTA DE LIBERACION NACIONAL (FSLN).** Better known as The Sandinistas. The left-wing Nicaraguan insurgents who toppled the dictatorship of ANASTASIO SOMOZA in July 1979. Named after AUGUSTO CESAR SANDINO, the Nicaraguan revolutionary who was killed in 1934, the FSLN consisted of a number of guerrilla/terrorist groups some of whom had been fighting the corrupt Somoza dictatorship since the early 1960s. The FSLN campaign combined both rural insurgency and urban terror, and before the Somoza regime collapsed in the summer of 1979 the insurgents had control of 20 of Nicaragua's cities and towns. Since taking power the FSLN government have been plagued by a guerrilla/terror campaign waged by right-wing CONTRAS heavily supported by the USA. Many of the Contras are former members of Somoza's notorious National Guard.

**FRENTE REVOLUCIONARIO ANTI-FASCISTA Y PATRIOTICO (FRAP).** Left-wing (Maoist) Spanish group active in the 1970s. When a number of FRAP terrorists were sentenced to death on September 12th 1975 for killing a policeman in Madrid a few months previously, the sentences raised an international furore. Pope Paul VI pleaded for their lives, most Western countries withdrew their ambassadors from Spain for "consultation", while Mexico demanded Spain's expulsion from the United Nations. In Lisbon a crowd (probably led by FRAP members) looted the Spanish Embassy. But the protests were in vain, and on September 27th 1975 the FRAP men were executed by firing squads.

**FROMME, LYNETTE.** The 26-year-old American woman who tried to assassinate President Gerald Ford in Sacramento on September 5th 1975 while the President was walking to the State Capitol building. Ford's life was probably saved by one of his Secret Service agents who deflected Fromme's aim. Fromme was a follower of the convicted murderer, Charles Manson, who had been jailed in 1969. She attempted to kill the President to publicise Manson's case. Although her defence argued that Fromme was deranged, she was found fit to plead and sentenced to life imprisonment.

Three weeks after Fromme tried to kill Ford another attempt on the president's life was made by 45-year-old SARA JANE MOORE.

## FRONT DE LIBERATION NATIONALE (FLN). (National
Liberation Front). Algerian nationalist guerrilla/terrorist force which fought the French colonial regime in Algeria between the end of 1954 and 1962. The FLN fought an effective two-pronged campaign against the French; a guerrilla war in the cities and countryside of Algeria, and a diplomatic campaign in the capitals of Europe and Africa. Eventually, in 1962, the French agreed to hold an "independence" plebiscite at which 99% of the votes were cast in favour of Algerian independence. The FLN's political leader throughout the war, Ahmed Ben Bella, became the first President of independent Algeria.

The FLN's war against the French was launched on November 1st 1954 when 300 or so FLN fighters armed with weapons left over from World War II attacked French targets all over Algeria. Although the attacks were ineptly carried out and no great success, they began a cycle of terror followed by repression followed by more terror which was to last for many years and cost thousands of French and Arab lives. On August 20th 1955, for example, the FLN butchered French men, women and children in the Philipeville area, an atrocity which was followed by the killing of thousands of innocent Muslims by the French colonialists. These massacres drove many hitherto apolitical Muslims into the arms of the FLN.

In 1956 the FLN took their war into the streets of Algiers where they had built up a formidable terror network. Operating out of the Algiers Casbah (Arab quarter) the FLN's campaign of assassination, bombing and sabotage threatened to create anarchy in the city. The French responded by turning Algiers over to the 10th Colonial Parachute Division led by General JACQUES MASSU. Massu's "paras" waged a ferocious counter-insurgency (COIN) campaign against the FLN which more or less smashed the FLN operation in and around Algiers. This bitter battle between the French Army and the FLN was known as the BATTLE OF ALGIERS.

Although the FLN were militarily no match for the French, and were heavily infiltrated by French agents who were able to exploit the FLN's chronic right-left, Arab-Berber splits, their provisional government (Gouvernement Provisoire de la Republique Algerienne) set up in 1958 was recognised by a growing number of Third World countries as well as the Soviet Union and Red

China. And Metropolitan France was becoming increasingly tired of the carnage in Algeria, and the recurring scandals provoked by the colonial regime's use of torture and repression. By the early 1960s the FLN campaign had undermined the will of the French to continue the war and in March 1962 talks were held at Evian between Georges Pompidou and Ben Bella on ways to end the war. An immediate ceasefire was agreed, and after some haggling, the withdrawal of French troops from Algeria.

Although the FLN lost the military battle they won the political war. Their final victory came in July 1962 when the French and Algerian people voted to accept the Evian Agreements, the terms of which were dictated by the FLN. After the French withdrawal the FLN admitted that their victory while complete had been costly; the Arab population of Algeria had been reduced by more than 1,000,000. Almost 17,500 French troops were killed by the FLN in the eight-year long war.

## FRONT DU LIBERATION NATIONAL CORSE (FLNC).

(National Liberation Front of Corsica). An illegal separatist organisation which has been agitating for the independence of the island of Corsica from France. Since the mid-1970s the FLNC have exploded several hundred bombs in Corsica and in mainland France. Their targets have ranged from French military bases to the homes of French "immigrants" to Corsica. The FLNC are also bitterly opposed to Corsica's tourist industry arguing that mass tourism undermines the island's culture and way of life, while benefiting only the French owners of the big tourist centres.

In 1981 the FLNC called a short-lived "truce" in their war against the French authorities after President Mitterrand promised a "new deal" for Corsica and the Corsicans, but soon resumed their violent activities. On March 28th and 29th 1986 the FLNC stepped up their bombing campaign when they set off 13 explosions in airline offices, banks and public buildings in Nice, Marseilles, and Aix-en-Provence in the south of France. A few days previously FLNC bombers struck at the holiday village of Ajaccio on Corsica itself causing extensive damage. The most serious incident by Corsican separatists was the CARGESE HOLIDAY CAMP ATTACK in May 1986.

## FRONT DU LIBERATION DE QUEBEC (FLQ). (Front for the Liberation of Quebec). Militant mainly left-wing French-Canadian group which wanted to separate Quebec from the rest of English-speaking Canada. The FLQ were active in the late 1960s and early

1970s and forced the Canadian government of Pierre Trudeau to impose a harsh (if temporary) regime on Quebec under the War Measures Act. FLQ terrorism reached its peak in October 1970 when they kidnapped Richard Cross, the UK trade commissioner in Montreal, and a few days later PIERRE LAPORTE, Quebec's minister of labour and immigration. Cross was discovered unharmed, but Laporte was killed by the terrorists.

The long-standing grievances of the French Canadians of Quebec (who are among the poorest of Canada's population) became a political force in the 1960s. Many French Canadians resented the dominance of both Anglophone Canada and the United States over their economy and culture and began to seriously argue the case for an independent, French-speaking Quebec. The pro-independence Parti Québécois (led by ex-Liberal René Lévesque) was given an unexpected boost in July 1967 when President Charles de Gaulle, on a visit to Montreal, ended his speech with "Vive le Québec Libre" (long live Free Quebec). By the late 1960s the political tide appeared to be running strongly in favour of the Quebec separatists.

The FLQ was founded in 1963 by a Belgian immigrant called George Schoeters and was supported by young French Canadians impatient with the constitutional route to independence. They launched a propaganda campaign to "radicalise" the Québécois, and in the mid-1960s took to bombing industrial premises (and the political meetings of the ruling Liberal Party). The crisis came to a head in October 1970 when, after the kidnapping of Cross and Laporte, the government of Pierre Trudeau implemented the War Measures Act which gave sweeping powers to the Canadian police and military. Although the Trudeau government were accused by the opposition of using a sledgehammer to crack a nut, the government defended their action by citing the long list of bombings, killings, kidnappings, and robberies to which Canada had been subjected by the FLQ.

On October 17th 1970 the Trudeau government's hand was strengthened when the murdered body of Pierre Laporte was found in the boot of a car in Montreal. The killing of Laporte outraged French Canadian opinion, damaged support for the FLQ, and turned the political tide against the separatists. On December 3rd 1970 Richard Cross was located by the Royal Canadian Mounted Police (RCMP) in a Montreal suburb and after hours of negotiation his kidnappers were allowed out of Canada to Cuba. Originally they had demanded the release of 25 FLQ activists, transport to Cuba or Algeria, publication of the FLQ manifesto and $500,000 in gold bullion.

**FUERZAS ARMADAS DE LIBERACION NACIONAL (FALN)**. (Armed Forces of National Liberation). Organisation of American-based Puerto Rican separatists which emerged in 1974, and operated mainly in New York City and Chicago. In the course of their campaign the FALN exploded almost 200 bombs, killing four people and injuring more than 50. They attacked the offices of the FEDERAL BUREAU OF INVESTIGATION (FBI), Gulf Oil, the Chrysler Corporation, various banks and also the famous Fraunces Tavern in Manhattan. Between 1977 and 1984 the FALN carried out more than 160 bombings, shootings and fire-raising attacks, but only one in 1985. The FBI estimated that the FALN contained no more than 50 members, 10 of whom were jailed in 1980. The FALN's most expert bomb-maker, William Morales, was jailed in 1983 along with four of his colleagues, and another 13 members of FALN were picked up in September 1985 (in Boston, Mexico, Puerto Rico and Dallas).

**FUERZAS ARMADAS DE REVOLUCION (FAR)**. (Armed Forces of the Revolution). One of the left-wing terror groups active in Guatemala in the 1960s and early 1970s. FAR were responsible for the killings of a number of high-ranking Americans in Guatemala, including military advisors John D. Webber, Ernest A. Munro and Ambassador John Gordon Mein (in 1968). The group also kidnapped and killed the West German ambassador Count KARL VON SPRETI in 1970. FAR's bloody campaign of kidnapping and assassination provoked a wave of right-wing counter-violence in which thousands of people died.

# G

**GADDAFI, MUAMMAR.** See QADDAFI, MUAMMAR.

**GALMAN, ROLANDO.** Young Philippino airport worker who was shot dead immediately after BENITO AQUINO was assassinated in August 1983. Galman was killed by the military in an attempt to shift the blame for Aquino's murder. But the government were forced to admit that Galman was not the assassin and eventually 25 senior military men were tried, but acquitted, of Aquino's killing.

**GANDHI, INDIRA (1917-1984).** Prime Minister of India who was assassinated by Sikh members of her own bodyguard in October 1984 in revenge for the Indian Army's attack on the GOLDEN TEMPLE OF AMRITSAR in June 1984. Mrs Gandhi's assassination led to a wave of severe anti-Sikh violence throughout India during which more than 2,000 Sikhs were killed by enraged Hindus. The massacres fuelled Sikh demands for their own independent state of "Khalistan". Mrs Gandhi was succeeded as Prime Minister by her son, Rajid Gandhi

Mrs Gandhi was shot to death in the grounds of her official residence at Number One, Safdarjang Road, Delhi, at 09.15 on October 31st 1984. The Prime Minister was on her way to a television interview with the British actor Peter Ustinov when she was shot down by two members of her own bodyguard, Sub-Inspector BEANT SINGH and Constable SATWANT SINGH. While Mrs Gandhi was rushed by private car to the India Institute of Medical Sciences (where she was declared dead at 14.30) her two assailants were marched into a police post where Beant Singh was shot dead and Satwant Singh was wounded by ill-disciplined members of the Indo-Tibetan Border Police. Mrs Gandhi was found to have more than 20 bullet wounds in her body which led to claims (unproven) that more than two assassins had been involved.

Ironically, Sub-Inspector Beant Singh had been removed from Mrs Gandhi's bodyguard when it was learned that he had been meeting with Sikh extremists in Delhi but Mrs Gandhi had insisted that he should be reinstated. Ex-Constable Satwant Singh is currently standing trial in India for his part in Mrs Gandhi's assassination.

**GANDHI, MAHATMA (1869-1948).** Real name Mohandas Karamchand. The spiritual leader of the Indian independence movement who was assassinated in Delhi by a fanatical young Hindu in January 1948 less than six months after India became independent of British rule. Ten days earlier Gandhi had survived another attempt on his life when a Hindu youth tried to kill him with a crude bomb.

Born in Porbandar, and an English barrister by training, Gandhi first practised the techniques of passive resistance in South Africa between 1907 and 1914 (against the Transvaal Government's anti-Indian legislation). Gandhi returned to India in 1915, became leader of the Congress Movement, preached passive resistance and civil disobedience against the British Raj, and was jailed four times. He consistently denounced terrorism and violence, and was regarded by many Hindus as "Mahatma" or "great soul". But Gandhi's acceptance of the post-independence partition of the subcontinent into India and Pakistan infuriated many Hindu militants, one of whom, NATHURAM VINAYAK GODSE shot Gandhi to death on January 30th 1948. Godse fired three shots at point-blank range into Gandhi's body, and the old man died with an invocation to God on his lips.

**GARFIELD, JAMES ABRAM (1831-1881).** Republican President of the USA who was assassinated in the summer of 1881 after less than a year in office. Born in Ohio, Garfield was a lawyer by profession, and was elected first to the Ohio state senate and then to the House of Representatives. After a distinguished career in the American Civil War he was elected President (against W. S. Hancock) in 1880. Garfield was shot in the back at point-blank range on July 2nd 1881 at the railway station in Washington DC. Although grievously wounded, the President survived until September 19th 1881 when he died at Elberon, New Jersey. After the shooting Garfield never left his sick bed, but his aides never revealed whether he was "incapacitated" in the constitutional sense. Garfield's assassin was an unbalanced Chicago lawyer called Charles J. Guiteau who resented the fact that he had been turned down for the job of American consul general in Marseilles. A lawyer turned religious journalist, Guiteau announced that he had received a vision from God to rid the country of Garfield, and replace him with Chester Arthur. (Arthur did, in fact, replace Garfield.)

**GAZA BUS HIJACKING, ISRAEL. (April 12th 1984).** A relatively minor armed hijacking which blew into a major political crisis within the Israeli government, damaged the reputation of the SHIN BET anti-terrorist force, and led to the resignation of Attorney General Yitzhak Zamir. The row generated accusations of government "cover up" in the Israeli press, but Israeli public opinion proved to be firmly on the side of the Shin Bet.

The crisis began when four Palestinian Arabs hijacked a bus travelling from Tel Aviv to Ashkelon, and forced the driver to drive to the Gaza Strip. The hijacking came to an end when an Israeli army unit led by Brigadier General Yitzhak Mordechai stormed the coach, killing two of the hijackers. In the exchange of fire a young woman soldier travelling on the bus was killed. The operation went sour when the soldiers handed the two surviving hijackers over to Shin Bet agents who, apparently, beat the two Arabs to death. The post-mortem examinations showed that the two Palestinians had been killed by repeated blows to the head from a blunt instrument.

At first the Shin Bet claimed that the two Arabs had died in the course of the army assault, a story which was accepted by the authorities until the Israeli newspaper *Hadashot* ran a front-page picture showing one of the hijackers, apparently uninjured, being led away from the coach. The military investigation into the deaths cleared Brigadier Mordechai, but revealed that the Shin Bet had been lying to the authorities. Attorney General Zamir, determined that Shin Bet should not be above the law, demanded that the intelligence agents face legal prosecution. The Israeli cabinet was convinced that any such prosecution would cause grave damage to the sensitive anti-terrorist operations of Shin Bet, and refused. In May 1986, Attorney General Zamir was sacked. The Israeli press used the issue to accuse the government of "cover up", but public opinion proved to be firmly on the side of the Shin Bet anti-terrorist squad who were seen as protecting Israeli society from Arab killers.

**GEMAYEL, BASHIR.** Christian militia leader and President-elect of Lebanon who was killed by a car bomb on September 14th 1982 before he could take office. Gemayel's death inflamed the Christian forces in the country and led directly to the SABRA AND SHATILA MASSACRES of October 1982 in Beirut in which 800 to 2,000 Palestinian and other Arab men, women and children were killed. Gemayel was succeeded by his older (more moderate) brother Amin Gemayel. Since his death Bashir Gemayel has become a cult figure to the Christians of East Beirut which is frequently decked out with portraits of the "martyr-president".

The youngest of the six children of Sheik Pierre Gemayel, founder of the Christian "Phalange" movement, Bashir Gemayel studied law at the Université St Joseph in Beirut, did postgraduate research at Dallas in Texas, and worked in a Washington law firm for a short period before returning to the Lebanon. Ruthless and ambitious (if impulsive) Gemayel founded the Lebanese Forces in 1976, a well-equipped force of right-wing Christians which he used to devastating effect against fellow-Christians Tony Franjieh (in April 1978) and Dany Chamoun (in July 1980).

Having secured power in the Lebanese Christian community, Gemayel forged powerful links with the Israelis and after the Israeli Defence Forces (IDF) had driven the PALESTINE LIBERATION ORGANISATION (PLO) out of Lebanon, Gemayel was selected as President of Lebanon by 62 Deputies on August 23rd 1982. But on September 14th, three weeks after his election, Gemayel was killed when an electrically-detonated bomb demolished the Phalange HQ in East Beirut. Along with Bashir 25 party workers were killed.

The Christians immediately blamed Palestinian agents for Gemayel's death, and two days later hundreds (and possibly thousands) of Palestinian and other Arabs were slaughtered at the Sabra and Shatila refugee camps by Christian militia men. The massacres both discredited the Christian forces and rocked the Israeli government who were backing them. But Gemayel's assassin was, in fact, a Lebanese Christian called HABIB TANIOS CHARTOUNY who had been recruited by a Syrian organisation known as the Syrian People's Party (SPP).

**GEORGIOU, COSTAS (1951-1976).** Also known as "Colonel Callan". Ex-British Army paratrooper who led a small British mercenary force in northern Angola on behalf of the Frente National por el Liberacao de Angola (FLNA) of Holden Roberto against the Marxist government of Angola. A brave but cruel and probably psychopathic soldier, Georgiou ordered the MAQUELA MASSACRE of February 1976. He was later tried by the Angolan authorities for his mercenary activities, and executed in June 1976.

A Greek Cypriot by birth, Georgiou's family emigrated to North London in the early 1960s. Georgiou joined the 1st Battalion the Parachute Regiment where he became a skilled machine-gunner and one of the battalion's best riflemen. But after a post office raid in Northern Ireland, Georgiou was dishonourably discharged from the British Army after a five year prison sentence. His short career as a British mercenary began in December 1975 when he flew to northern Angola to fight the FLNA. Georgiou adopted the name

"Callan" and commanded a small band of British mercenaries who were harassing the government forces.

Shortly after the Maquela Massacre Georgiou was captured by the Angolan government which staged a show trial of Georgiou and 12 other British and American mercenaries in Luanda in June 1976. The Angolan "Popular Revolutionary Tribunal" found all the mercenaries guilty of spreading "fear, shame and outrage" through northern Angola. Nine of them were given long prison sentences, but Georgiou and three others were condemned to death and executed on July 10th 1976, despite pleas for clemency from the British and American governments.

**GLAVNOYE RAZVEDYVATELNOYE UPRAVLENIYE (GRU).** Soviet military intelligence. The Soviet General Staff's equivalent of the KOMITET GOSUDARSTVENNOI BEZO-PASTNOSTI (KGB). Although smaller and constitutionally subordinate to its civilian counterpart the KGB, the GRU is nevertheless an efficient and well-funded intelligence-gathering organisation with a headquarters staff estimated at 5,000 or so, plus another 100,000 within the Soviet Union and abroad. One of the GRU's operating arms are the so-called SPETNAZ troops, the Soviet Union's special forces who are trained in subversion, infiltration, sabotage and assassination. The GRU's Spetnaz groups have recently been active in Afghanistan against the Afghan guerrillas. And GRU are reputedly responsible for the training of foreign terrorists mainly at the Sanprobal Military Academy in the Crimea, and the Higher Infantry School in Odessa.

Founded in 1920 and based at 19 Znamensky Street in Moscow, the GRU concentrates on gathering military intelligence for the Soviet General Staff through four divisions (Training, Information, Auxiliary and Operations). In the Stalin period the GRU and the civilian agencies were played off against one another and, according to GRU defector Oleg Penkovsky, GRU officers remain bitter and suspicious of the KGB. The GRU's reputation and credibility suffered a serious blow after Penkovsky's well publicised defection to the West. The GRU operates its own global network of agents independent of the KGB although there is an area of overlap between the two agencies at the higher levels of the Soviet bureaucracy. The GRU's present Director is Peter Ivanovich Ivashutin, one-time Deputy Chairman of the KGB.

**GODARD, YVES**. French soldier, intelligence specialist and counter-insurgency expert who was Chief of Staff to General

JACQUES MASSU during the Algerian insurrection of 1957-1960 and who later became a leading member of the right-wing ORGANISATION ARMEE SECRETE (OAS). After the abortive OAS putsch against the government of General de Gaulle, Godard was tried and sentenced to death in absentia.

Godard fought with the French "maquis" against the Germans at the end of World War II, rejoined the regular army in 1948, and for five years commanded the 11th Shock Battalion which had been set up as a special "dirty tricks" unit by the French parachute regiment and the Service de Documentation Extérieure et de Contre-Espionnage (SDECE). As Massu's right-hand man Godard was known for his ruthlessness and subtlety in the campaign against the Algerian nationalists of the FLN. Godard became involved with the OAS campaign after being purged by General de Gaulle in 1960. After the abortive coup d'état against de Gaulle in 1962 Godard went underground, but was tried and sentenced to death. Unlike most of his colleagues Godard did not return to France after the "amnesty" of 1968, and died in exile in Belgium in 1975.

**GODSE, NATHURAM VINAYAK**. The 37-year-old Hindu extremist who shot and killed MAHATMA GANDHI on January 30th 1948. Godse was editor of a small Hindu nationalist journal and a member of the radical Hindu organisations RASHTRIYA SWAYAMSEVAK SANGH (RSS) who believed that Gandhi and the Congress leadership had sold out to the Muslims. After the killing, Godse and eight fellow conspirators were tried by a special court in New Delhi from May to December 1948. In February 1949 Godse was convicted of Gandhi's murder, sentenced to be hanged, and after his appeals failed, executed on November 15th 1949.

**GOLDEN TEMPLE ASSAULT, AMRITSAR. (June 5th-6th 1984)**. Attack by the Indian army on The Golden Temple of Amritsar in the Punjab to clear the temple of Sikh extremists and terrorists led by JARNAIL SINGH BHINDRANWALE. While the attack on the Sikh religion's holiest place killed Bhindranwale and almost 500 of his followers, it infuriated Sikh opinion throughout the world, and was followed by widespread rioting in India and the assassination of the Indian Prime Pinister INDIRA GANDHI in October 1984.

The operation to clear the Golden Temple (codenamed "BLUE STAR") began at 19.00 on June 5th 1985, and was supervised by a Sikh officer, Major-General Kuldip Singh Brar. Brar had instructions to do as little damage as possible to the temple itself, and had hoped to take the temple by using small groups of élite commandos from the Parachute and Guards regiments. But stubborn and well-organised resistance by the Sikhs (orchestrated by Major-General SHAHBEG SINGH) led to increasingly heavier weapons being used which caused many casualties and serious damage to the Golden Temple.

After more than 12 hours of fanatical resistance, Bhindranwale and his followers were driven out of their holy shrine the Akal Takht by the 105mm guns of General Brar's tanks. In the course of the fighting the Akal Takht was reduced to rubble. The bodies of Bhindranwale and his military adviser Shahbeg Singh were found in the ruins of the temple, along with almost 500 of their followers. Official figures for army casualties were 83 men killed and 251 wounded, but unofficial figures have put the army's casualties at more than 700 dead, and 2,000 wounded. Civilian casualties were 493 people killed and 86 injured, but unofficial estimates are much higher.

A fresh round of violence in the Punjab was set in train in April 30th 1986 when the Punjab police and paramilitary forces moved into the Golden Temple for a second time to arrest and drive out Sikh radicals who had, once again, taken over the complex of buildings. The police operation lasted 13 hours, and was carried out by officers in bare feet (out of deference to Sikh religious custom) and using small arms and "stun grenades". One man was killed, and 300 people were arrested.

**GOLDENBERG'S RESTAURANT ATTACK, PARIS. (August 9th 1982).** An attack by six gunmen on a famous Jewish restaurant in the Rue des Rosiers in Paris, which killed six people and injured another 22. The gunmen opened fire on the crowded restaurant with automatic weapons, and hurled hand grenades. The attack was initially claimed by the left-wing group ACTION DIRECTE (AD) but it has been suggested that the killings may have been the work of a right-wing group out to discredit the left. The attack on Goldenberg's Restaurant was the worst attack on a Jewish (as opposed to Israeli) target in Western Europe in recent years.

**GOULDING, CATHAL (born 1922).** Left-wing Irish Republican, and one-time Chief of Staff of the OFFICIAL IRISH REPUBLICAN ARMY (OIRA). In recent years Goulding has been a bitter critic of the PROVISIONAL IRISH REPUBLICAN ARMY's bombing campaign which he has described as "inhuman". Goulding was behind the OIRA's decision to suspend their military operations and concentrate on left-wing political work.

Born in Dublin into a family with powerful Republican views, Goulding was interned in the Irish Republic during the war, and became involved in the IRA's post-war revival. Together with SEAN MACSTIOFAIN (later to be one of the leaders of the PIRA) he was sentenced to eight years in prison in England after an arms raid in Felstead, Essex in 1953. By the late 1960s Goulding was one of the most influential members of the IRA, and became the organisation's Chief of Staff in 1969. When the IRA split into "Official" and "Provisional" factions in 1972, Goulding became leader of the Marxist-inclined OIRA. Goulding was instrumental in calling the OIRA cease-fire in 1972, since when he has supported the Republican Workers Party (once known as Official Sinn Fein).

**GRAND MOSQUE ATTACK, MECCA. (November 20th-29th 1979).** An attack by Muslim fundamentalists on Islam's holiest shrine which stunned and outraged the Muslim world. The siege was ended on November 29th 1979 when two thousand Saudi Arabian troops and police retook the mosque after nine days of heavy fighting. While much of the Muslim world blamed the USA for the attack on the Grand Mosque, the incident was perpetrated by Sunni Muslim extremists bent on "cleansing" Islam before the end of the world. In January 1980, after a series of remarkably speedy trials before Saudi Arabian religious courts, 63 people were executed for their part in the attack on the Grand Mosque.

The attack began in the early morning of November 20th 1979 when the Mosque was packed with around 40,000 Muslim pilgrims from all over the world. Around 200 heavily-armed and well-equipped men entered the Mosque, shot dead one of the Chief Imam's acolytes, and took up positions all round the huge building. The outraged Saudi Arabian authorities immediately cut all links with the outside world, and after failing to persuade the occupiers of the Mosque to surrender, ordered the National Guard and the police to take the building. The use of firearms had to be sanctioned by the Ulama, a council of religious judges. Advised by five French military specialists, the counter-attack began on November 25th 1979. But it took four days of stiff fighting before the Saudi Arabian forces winkled the Sunni fanatics out of the labyrinthine building. The fundamentalists had come well prepared with gas-masks, food, and huge quantities of ammunition. In the course of the operation at least 255 people – troops, fundamentalists and pilgrims – were killed, and almost 600 injured.

After the Ayatollah Ruhollah Khomeini of Iran blamed the takeover of the Grand Mosque on "criminal American imperialism" the region was racked by a wave of anti-American demonstrations and riots. In the Pakistani city of Islamabad two American marines were killed when an irate crowd attacked the American Embassy. The Islamic world appears to have misinterpreted a speech by a Saudi spokesman who blamed the attack on "renegades" which was translated as "non-believers" (Muslim shorthand for Westerners).

The culprits were, however, followers of the fanatical Sunni fundamentalist Juhaiman Saif al Otaiba, a former member of the Saudi National Guard who believed (and preached) that the Saudi regime was corrupt and ungodly, and had to be purged. The affair came to an end on January 9th 1980 when 41 Saudis, 10 Egyptians, six South Yemenis, three Kuwaitis, a North Yemeni, a Sudanese and an Iraqi were executed in eight cities and towns throughout Saudi Arabia.

**GRENZSCHUTZGRUPPE 9 (GSG-9).** (Border Protection Group 9). West Germany's élite anti-terrorist federal police squad, formed in 1972 following the police débâcle of the MUNICH OLYMPICS ATTACK in which 11 Israeli athletes died. Based at Hangelaar near Cologne, GSG-9 are exceptionally well funded and equipped with their own fleet of Mercedes limousines, armoured cars, specially equipped motorcycles and helicopters. Their commander ULRICH WEGENER was partly trained by the Israelis who have described GSG-9 as "the best anti-terrorist group in the world". GSG-9 achieved world-wide fame following the LUFTHANSA HIJACKING TO MOGADISHU AIRPORT, SOMALIA in October 1977 when GSG-9 officers aided by two members of the British SPECIAL AIR SERVICE (SAS), stormed the airliner, releasing the passengers and crew. The GSG-9 operation went a long way to restoring West German credibility.

Like the British SAS, GSG-9 personnel are trained to use a wide variety of weapons and explosives and communications systems. An important part of their training involves assaults on "dummy" aircraft of all kinds, including, apparently, Soviet civil airliners. All GSG-9 members are volunteers from the border guard, must have an IQ of at least 110, and are accepted only after a battery of psychological and physical tests. Nine out of 10 volunteers are then eliminated in the six-month training course. GSG-9 officers spend at least four hours a day on training on a range of weapons from Smith & Wesson 0.38 calibre revolvers and HECKLER & KOCH MP5 submachine guns, to the expensive Mauser 66 sniper rifle.

GSG-9 is organised into six units of approximately 30 men each. There is a "command" group, four "action" groups and a "backup" group. All four "action" groups have identical capabilities. The officers are trained to use the minimum of force necessary in any situation.

**GREY WOLVES**. Neo-fascist Turkish terrorist group active in Turkey and Western Europe in the 1970s. Drawn from the youth wing of the fascist National Action Party (NAP) led by Colonel Alparslan Turkes, the Grey Wolves were accused by the Turkish authorities in 1981 of carrying out 694 murders in the years 1974 to 1980. Most of their victims were prominent Turkish left-wingers such as labour leaders, liberal journalists, academics and politicians. One of the Grey Wolves assassins was MEHMET ALI AGCA, the young Turk who tried to assassinate Pope John Paul II in May 1981. The Grey Wolves are thought to have an extensive European network among the Turkish community in West Germany. Some intelligence experts estimate their numbers at 26,000 in more than 80 branches, with organisations throughout Europe. They are described by one authority as "a particularly dangerous example of an exile fascist movement with a built-in propensity for terrorism".

**GREY'S SCOUTS**. A small, lightly armed counter-insurgency force used by the illegal Rhodesian regime in their protracted war against African insurgents in the 1960s and 1970s. The mixed (black and white) unit dated back to the 19th century and comprised around 300 skilled horsemen and trackers who patrolled the borders between Rhodesia and her African neighbours looking for signs of terrorist incursion. Other Rhodesian counter-insurgency forces were the RHODESIAN SPECIAL AIR SERVICE (RSAS) and the SELOUS SCOUTS.

**GRIVAS, GEORGE THEODOROS (1898-1974)**. Also known as "Dighenis". Greek Cypriot soldier who led EOKA guerrillas against the British between 1955 and 1959. Grivas was a zealot for "Enosis", the union of Cyprus with Greece, and when President Makarios accepted independence rather than Enosis, Grivas led EOKA against the Cypriot government in the early 1970s. Born in Cyprus, Grivas served as an officer in the Greek Army between 1941 and 1953, then returned to Cyprus to wage a guerrilla/terrorist campaign against the British. Operating under the nom-de-guerre of "Dighenis", he launched his terrorist assault on April 1st 1955, and despite strenuous British efforts was never captured. When

Cyprus became independent in August 1960 Grivas was made a general, and given charge of the Cyprus National Guard. Bitter at President Makarios for refusing to pursue union with Greece, in 1971 Grivas went "underground" again to put pressure on the Cyprus government. He died of cancer in 1974.

**GROUPE D'INTERVENTION DE LA GENDARMERIE NATIONALE (GIGN).** The anti-terrorist force of the French Gendarmerie Nationale. A small force of 54 men (four officers and 50 NCO's) the GIGN are divided into three squads, one of which is always on duty. Well equipped with sophisticated electronics, GIGN officers are expert marksmen, parachutists, climbers and skilled with explosives. Like the West German GRENZSCHUTZGRUPPE-9 (GSG-9) and the British Army's SPECIAL AIR SERVICE (SAS) the GIGN constantly practise ways of storming buildings, trains, ships and aircraft to release hostages and deal with terrorists and/or criminals.

**GRU.** See GLAVNOYE RAZVEDYVATELNOYE UPRAV-LENIYE.

**GRUPA DE RESISTENCIA ANTIFASCISTA PRIMO OCTOBRE (GRAPO).** (The Antifascist Resistance Group of October First). Left-wing Spanish group who take their name from the killing of four Spanish police officers on October 1st 1975 in response to the execution of five left-wing terrorists. Like many terror groups GRAPO financed their activities by extortion and bank robberies, and are thought to have been behind at least one attempt to kill King Juan Carlos. In 1978 they were penetrated by the Spanish police and 20 of their hierarchy were arrested and jailed. In 1979 GRAPO's 29-year-old leader Juan Carlos Delgado de Codex was shot dead trying to escape arrest.

**GRUPO ESPECIALE PARA LOS OPERACIONES (GEO).** (Special Operations Group). The Spanish government's recently-formed police anti-terrorist unit. Carefully selected to screen out extreme right and left wingers, most GEO officers come from the Spanish security service and the civil guard. The GEO undergo the now common counter-revolutionary warfare (CRW) training routines largely pioneered by the British Army's SPECIAL AIR SERVICE (SAS). GEO officers train with HECKLER & KOCH MP5 and UZI submachine-guns, and with sniper rifles. In May 1981 the GEO were severely tested when they stormed the Banco

Central in the centre of Barcelona which had been taken over by 24 right-wing gunmen. Despite the fact that the terrorists were heavily armed and held more than 200 hostages only one person was killed in the GEO assault (although some of the terrorists escaped in the confusion).

**GUEVARA, ERNESTO "CHE" (1928-1967).** Latin American guerrilla leader and revolutionary theorist who helped Fidel Castro to power in Cuba. Guevara served as a member of the Cuban government between 1960 and 1965, and was killed trying to organise an insurrection in Bolivia in 1967. Born in Argentina to a middle-class family, Guevara qualified as a doctor in 1953, joined Castro in Mexico in 1956, and fought in the campaign to topple BATISTA. Guevara became President of the Cuban National Bank, then Minister for Industries. After a dispute with Castro he resigned in 1965 to pursue the revolution elsewhere in Latin America. He travelled to Bolivia, tried to raise a rebellion among the tin-miners but was captured and executed by the Bolivian security forces in October 1967. Guevara's death coincided with left-wing student unrest in the USA and Western Europe, and consequently he became something of a martyr-hero to the student radicals of the day.

# H

**HABASH, GEORGE**. Founder and Secretary General of the militant POPULAR FRONT FOR THE LIBERATION OF PALESTINE (PFLP) which has carried out some of the most dramatic terrorist raids and hijackings of the last two decades, including the hijackings to DAWSON'S FIELD in 1970 and the LUFTHANSA HIJACKING TO ENTEBBE AIRPORT, UGANDA in 1976. Regarded as one of the most radical and extreme of the Palestinian leaders, Habash is a dedicated Marxist who sees the Soviet Union as one of the main allies of the Palestinian movement, and has admitted that the movement receives weapons and training from Soviet-bloc countries. A handsome articulate man, Habash is second only to YASIR ARAFAT in charisma and influence within the Palestinian movement.

Born in 1925 as a Palestinian Christian, Habash and his family were driven from their home in Lod in 1948 by the advance of the Jewish forces. He qualified as a medical doctor at the American University of Beirut where he made extensive contacts with other embittered young Palestinians eager to pluck something from the wreckage of the Palestine state. Together with a Syrian called Hani al-Hindi, Habash founded the secret Arab Nationalists Movement (ALN) which by the 1960s was widely spread throughout the Arab world, and which in 1967 spawned the PFLP over which Habash has presided ever since as the PFLP's secretary-general.

As the leader of the most powerful Palestinian group outside of FATAH George Habash has often been seen as a challenger for the leadership of the Palestinian movement. In 1968 Habash was jailed by the Syrians for a PFLP attack on the Trans-Arabia Pipeline, but managed to escape in November 1968. After the PFLP hijacking of an El Al aircraft in 1968 Habash is quoted as saying, "To kill a Jew far from the battlefield has more effect than killing hundreds of Jews in battle." Habash was a member of the central committee of the PALESTINE LIBERATION ORGANISATION (PLO) from 1970 to 1974 when he led the "Rejection Front" out of the PLO in disgust at the PLO's "surrenderist" policies.

Ever since the late 1940s Habash had been a "Pan-Arabist" and believed that the co-ordinated support of the entire Arab world was needed to reinstate Palestine. In 1974 Habash told a Beirut newspaper that "it is the Palestinian, Jordanian, Syrian, Egyptian, Iraqi and Lebanese masses who are able to guarantee the victory of our Palestinian people's struggle". But in recent years Habash appears to have patched up his quarrels with Arafat, and has made a number of key public appearances at Arafat's side (particularly in 1982 in Lebanon). Habash is now regarded as one of the elder statesmen of the Palestinian movement, although there is no evidence that his radical view of the Middle East situation has changed.

**HAGANAH**. (Defence). The main self-defence force of the Jewish community in pre-war Palestine which was founded in the 1920s to protect Jewish settlers and settlements against Arab attacks. In the late 1940s the "Haganah Army" absorbed the other Jewish groups such as IRGUN, Palmach and the Lehi which had fought the British and Arabs. In the Arab insurgency of 1936-1939 the Haganah Army were trained (quite illegally) by ORDE WINGATE, a British officer of exceptional military talent. The Haganah Army was the foundation upon which the formidable Israeli Defence Force (IDF) was built.

**HAIFA RAID, ISRAEL. (March 11th 1978)**. An attack by 11 FATAH terrorists on the coastal area around the Israeli port of Haifa in which 35 people died (including nine of the Fatah gunmen) and more than 70 were injured. The attackers landed by dinghy on a beach near Haifa, killed an American woman, hijacked a bus and ordered the driver to take them to Tel Aviv. They were stopped by Israeli troops and police at a roadblock near Tel Aviv, and in the exchange of fire the crowded bus caught fire and 25 passengers and nine Fatah men were killed. The two Fatah gunmen who survived said they had planned to take over a holiday hotel and try to force the release of five terrorists held by the Israelis including KOZO OKAMOTO. The Israeli response to the Haifa raid was to launch sea and air strikes against Palestinian positions in southern Lebanon.

**HAJARI, ABDULLAH AL**. Prime Minister of North Yemen assassinated in London in 1977 by Arab gunmen.

**HAMIEH, HAMZA AKL (born 1954)**. Also known as Hamza. Shi'ite zealot and military commander of the AMAL militia. Hamza has been responsible for at least six aircraft hijackings including the takeover of a Kuwait Airways Boeing 707 at Beirut airport on

February 24th 1982. A charismatic figure, Hamza is lionised by the young Shi'ites of the Lebanon. He led a number of attacks on the Western multinational force (MNF) in Beirut before the MNF finally withdrew.

Born into a poor family in the Shi'ite stronghold of Baalbeck in the Bekaa Valley, Hamza has been involved in the Lebanon's sporadic civil war since 1975 when he joined the left-wing Muslims against the right-wing Christians. Heavily influenced by the militant Shi'ite imam, MUSA AL SADR, Hamza fought against the brief Israeli invasion of southern Lebanon in 1978, and spent a year (1981-1982) training in Iran. Hamza's career as a hijacker began in 1979 a few months after Imam Musa Al Sadr disappeared in September 1978 during a trip to Libya. All Hamza's subsequent hijackings were attempts to publicise the mysterious disappearance of Imam Sadr, and to force the Libyan government to explain the circumstances. Hamza's hijacking groups were usually known as "The Sons of Musa Al Sadr".

**HAMMAMI, SAID**. The representative of the PALESTINE LIBERATION ORGANISATION (PLO) in London who was shot to death on January 5th 1978 by an Arab gunman opposed to the policies of PLO leader YASIR ARAFAT. At first the PLO blamed Israeli intelligence for the killing, but later accused the ABU NIDAL organisation. It was suggested that Hammami had made tentative contacts with the Israelis and was advocating some accommodation between the PLO and Israel. Five days after Hammami's death the PLO named a new guerrilla unit after him.

Hammami, aged 36, was killed at 15.30 on January 5th 1978 in the PLO's office in central London (a basement of the building occupied by the Arab League). He was shot once in the head and twice in the body by a young Arab wielding a 0.32 calibre pistol. The killer was chased into the street by Arab students who had been in the office at the time of the murder, but the gunman escaped. The PLO immediately despatched four senior officials to London to investigate the killings, and while their initial reaction was to blame Israeli intelligence for the murder, at Hammami's funeral in Beirut on January 8th 1978 a senior PLO man accused Abu Nidal's BLACK JUNE organisation. On January 9th 1978 a London-based Arab newspaper was told that Hammami's killing had been the work of Black June.

**HAREL, ISSER**. ("Little Isser"). Legendary Israeli spymaster who ran the Israeli MOSSAD between 1952 and 1963. Born Isser

Halperin in Central Russia in 1912, the diminutive Harel emigrated to Palestine in the 1930s. A fanatical Zionist and a veteran of HAGANAH, in 1952 Harel was given the job of reorganising Israel's intelligence services. Despite his harmless appearance, Harel was an implaccable intelligence chief and organised many of Israel's most daring operations including the kidnapping of the Nazi Adolf Eichmann, who was later tried in Israel and hanged.

When Harel discovered that the Egyptians were using ex-Nazi scientists to develop two long-range rockets ("Al Kafir" and "Al Zair") the Mossad instigated a terror campaign against scientists and engineers in Egypt, Germany and Switzerland. Letter-bombs were despatched, aircraft were sabotaged, threats were made, and people were injured and killed. At a time when the Israeli government were trying to forge new links with the West Germans (and to persuade the West German government to get their citizens out of Egypt by diplomatic means), Harel's strong-arm methods in Europe alarmed the Israeli cabinet.

And when two Mossad agents were arrested and tried in Switzerland in 1962, Prime Minister David Ben Gurion demanded Harel's resignation. Harel resigned, claiming that while he had the support of most of the cabinet he could not stay on without the confidence of the prime minister. In 1965 he was brought back to act as a government "adviser" on intelligence matters. Harel made no apology for his war on ex-Nazi scientists working for Egypt to destroy the state of Israel. He described them as men "marked to die".

**HARRODS BOMBING. (December 17th 1983).** A bombing raid on the famous Harrods department store in Knightsbridge, London, by the PROVISIONAL IRISH REPUBLICAN ARMY (PIRA). Two London police officers and three shoppers were killed and 91 people were injured when a car bomb exploded in the street outside the crowded store. The attack was a public relations disaster for the PIRA which later issued a statement claiming that the bombing had not been authorised by the ruling "Army Council" and promising that there would be "no repetition of this type of operation".

The car bomb exploded at 13.20 on Saturday December 17th 1983 when Harrods and the streets around the store were thronged with pre-Christmas shoppers. Forty minutes earlier a man had warned the Telephone Samaritans about a "car bomb outside Harrods" but as the police, including "sniffer dog" teams, were closing in to clear the store and the streets around, the car bomb exploded. Five people were killed and 91 injured (including 13 police officers). After the outrage there was pressure on the British and Irish governments to ban Sinn Fein (which was resisted) and renewed demands in Britain for the restoration of the death penalty for terrorist killings. The British government appealed to Irish-Americans not to support the kind of organisation which would place bombs in the street at Christmas time.

**HASSAN, HALLAH AL**. One of the four young Arabs who mounted the *ACHILLE LAURO* HIJACKING.

**HEARST, PATRICIA (born 1954)**. American heiress and member of the newspaper-owning Hearst family who was kidnapped in Los Angeles on February 4th 1974 by six members of the SYMBIONESE LIBERATION ARMY (SLA), a local group of Marxist revolutionaries. Hearst spent more than 18 months with the SLA in the course of which she was "turned" by the organisation (by a process of sexual abuse and incessant indoctrination) and became an active member. Hearst was involved in an armed robbery on the Hibernia Bank in San Francisco on April 15th 1974, for which she was arrested by the FEDERAL BUREAU OF INVESTIGATION (FBI) in San Francisco in August 1975. She was tried and convicted of armed robbery, and in September 1976 sentenced to seven years in jail. But there was a powerful feeling in the United States that Hearst was more of a victim than a terrorist, and after a well-publicised campaign for her release, she was freed by President Carter. She left prison on February 1st 1979, five years after being kidnapped. She later wrote a book about her experiences called *Every Secret Thing*.

**HEBRON GANG**. Small group of young Palestinian Arabs who waged a brief terrorist campaign against Israeli settlers around the West Bank town of Hebron in 1985. Before they were cornered and killed by the Israeli Defence Forces (IDF) in October 1985 the Hebron Gang had killed five Israelis and wounded many more. The group had no connection with the PALESTINE LIBERATION ORGANISATION (PLO) or any of its splinter movements, a fact which was seen as a sign of the growing frustration of Palestine Arabs in the Israeli-occupied territories.

**HECKLER & KOCH MP5**. Efficient, lightweight 9mm submachine-gun much favoured by counter-terror squads such as the British SPECIAL AIR SERVICE (SAS), the West German GRENZSCHUTZGRUPPE-9 (GSG-9), and by police forces in Switzerland and Holland. Made by Heckler & Koch GmbH in

Oberndorf, West Germany, the MP5 weighs only 4.5 lbs, has a barrel length of 8.8 inches, and can fire 650 rounds per minute. The magazine holds 15 or 30 rounds, and parts of the MP5 are interchangeable with the H&K G3 assault rifle. A specially shortened version of the weapon – the MP5K – has been developed for concealment by anti-terrorist units and bodyguard details. One "bodyguard" version can be fitted into a special briefcase and fired from concealment. Following the attacks on ROME and VIENNA airports in December 1985 the British police were armed with H&K MP5's for airport security duty, a decision heavily criticised by some firearms experts who argued that the H&K MP5's high-velocity 9mm bullet was likely to penetrate the target and strike innocent bystanders.

**HERRON, TOMMY (1937-1973).** One-time vice-chairman of the ULSTER DEFENCE ASSOCIATION (UDA) and one of the Protestant organisation's chief spokesmen who was found shot dead at Lisburn near Belfast on September 16th 1973. The UDA leadership dismissed the idea that Herron had been killed by either the PROVISIONAL IRISH REPUBLICAN ARMY (PIRA) or Protestant extremists and ascribed his murder to "cranks" who had taken exception to his style of leadership.

**HIJACKING.** The taking over of public-service vehicles usually, but not always, for political reasons. Some hijackings are calculated to draw world attention to a political cause, others to hold passengers hostage in exchange for achieving a political objective (such as the release of "political" prisoners). Occasionally vehicles are hijacked for use as transport to a part of the world normally out of bounds politically; e.g. Cuba to North Americans, or Western Europe to Soviet citizens. Air transport is the system most heavily preyed upon by hijackers, but ships and railway trains have also been taken over for political ends. Hijacking reached a peak in the late 1960s and early 1970s when a remarkable number of hijacks were successful. Since then the resolve of most Western governments has been stiffened, and airport security has been tightened.

Although aerial hijacking dates back to 1930 when Peruvian bandits took over a Fokker aircraft and held it to ransom in a jungle airstrip, politically-inspired hijacking began in earnest in the 1960s with a rash of North American aircraft being hijacked to socialist Cuba. Both the Cuban and American governments found the activity embarrassing and signed an anti-hijack pact which lasted until the CUBANA AIRLINES BOMBING by right-wing Cuban exiles in 1976. Fidel Castro accused the US government of being involved in the outrage and the anti-hijack treaty was abrogated. In the late 1960s hijacking was taken up by various Palestinian groups (BLACK SEPTEMBER, the POPULAR FRONT FOR THE LIBERATION OF PALESTINE, FATAH) as part of their campaign against Israel. In 1974, however, YASIR ARAFAT of the PALESTINE LIBERATION ORGANISATION (PLO) and commander of Fatah condemned hijacking as counterproductive, and the incidence dropped off (at least among those Palestinian groups under the influence of the PLO).

In the 50 years between 1931 and 1981, 647 aircraft were hijacked, most (although not all) for political reasons. Of the total, 236 took place in North America, 150 in South America, 142 in Europe, 86 in Asia, 28 in Africa and 5 in Australasia. In these incidents a total of 488 people were killed; 349 passengers, 88 hijackers, 41 airline staff, seven law enforcement officers and three others. The 1986 hijack total stands at around 700, and the casualty list has been added to considerably, particularly by the EGYPTAIR HIJACKING TO LUQA AIRPORT, MALTA, in October 1985 in the course of which 57 people died.

The international community has been struggling for years to grapple with the problem of aerial hijacking. Following the destruction of three Western airliners on the ground at DAWSON'S FIELD in Jordan in September 1970 by the PFLP, U Thant, then Secretary-General of the United Nations called for the setting up of a special international tribunal to try hijackers. U Thant regarded it as a crime which should be prosecuted "in the name of the peoples of the world". In the wake of Dawson's Field the UN passed Resolution 2645 calling on all member states to take "all measures appropriate" to prevent hijacking and punish the hijackers, but Resolution 2645 has been largely ignored.

Three international conventions form the basis of such anti-hijack laws as have been passed; the Tokyo Convention of 1963, the Hague Convention of 1970, and the Montreal Convention of 1971. There was also an important "declaration" produced at the Bonn Economic Summit in 1978 and signed by Canada, France, West Germany, Italy, Japan, the UK and the USA. While lacking the weight of an international convention the Bonn Declaration of 1978 pledged the signatories to ban flights to and from those countries which connive at or sanction hijacking. They also urged other governments to "join them in this commitment". This action has been advocated for years by the International Federation of Airline

Pilots Associations (IFAPA). The IFAPA have placed an embargo on Beirut Airport, and after their annual conference in London in April 1986 they promised to press their members to extend the ban to other countries which promote, or turn a blind eye to hijacking.

In the USA the international conventions on hijacking have been translated into the Anti-Hijacking Act of 1974 (which carries a death penalty if anyone is killed in the incident) and the Air Transportation Security Act of 1974. In Britain the relevant laws are the Tokyo Convention Act of 1967, the Hijacking Act of 1971, the Protection of Aircraft Act of 1973, and the Policing of Airports Act of 1974. Other Western countries have passed similar measures.

And as the hijacking of the cruise liner *ACHILLE LAURO* in October 1985 demonstrates, hijackers have not confined their activities to aircraft. In January 1961 Portuguese dissidents took over the liner *SANTA MARIA* and sailed it to refuge in Brazil; the US freighter *Columbia Eagle* was hijacked in March 1970 by men protesting against the Vietnam war; in 1972 the police in Cyprus thwarted a plan by Palestinians to hijack an Italian cruise liner plying between Cyprus and Israel; in February 1974 the Greek ship *VORI* was hijacked at anchor in Karachi by Pakistani muslims sympathetic to the Arab cause; in September 1975 the Moro National Liberation Front captured a Japanese ship in the waters of the Philippines, and then repeated the ploy four years later in October 1979 by taking over a Malaysian ship (and killing three of the passengers).

The most notorious railway train hijacking in recent years took place in May-June 1977 when a group of embittered Asians fighting for the independence of South Molucca (part of what is now Indonesia) took over an express train at ASSEN in Holland. The South Moluccans held the train for almost three weeks, and succumbed only when Dutch marines stormed the train. Five of the hijackers and two passengers were killed in the assault. In 1975 another group of South Moluccans hijacked an express train at BEILEN in Holland, and held it for 12 days. In the GAZA BUS HIJACKING in April 1984 four young Arabs took over an Israeli coach and held the passengers hostage.

**HINDAWI, NEZAR**. The Jordanian Arab charged by the British police of trying to use his Irish-born girlfriend to plant a bomb aboard an El Al flight from London to Israel in April 1986.

**HIZBULLAH**. (The Party Of God). The militant Shi'ite Muslim political/religious sect whose military arm ISLAMIC JIHAD is thought to have been responsible for many of the terrorist attacks in the LEBANON including the AMERICAN MARINE HQ BOMBING, BEIRUT, in October 1983. The Hizbullah is believed to be led by Sheik Ibrahim al Amin, a mullah (priest) trained in Iran.

**HOARE, THOMAS MICHAEL**. Also known as "Mad Mike". Irish-born mercenary leader who formed the notorious "Five Commando" in the Congo in 1964, and who organised Operation "ANVIL", the abortive coup d'état against the Seychelles government in November 1981. Although he was never a regular soldier, Hoare's declared (but unfulfilled) ambition was to transform the ill-disciplined, often brutal white mercenaries under his command into a disciplined fighting force modelled on the British Army. Hoare was jailed for life in South Africa after hijacking an Air India jet after the failed coup in the Seychelles, but was released in May 1985 having served less than a third of his sentence. Hoare published his own account of the Congo events in a book called *Mercenary* first published in 1967.

**HUKBALAHAP (HUK)**. The Communist-led insurgents who threatened the government of the Philippines in the late 1940s and early 1950s. The Huks were led by LOUIS TAROC who had formed the Huk army in 1942 and fought brilliantly against the Japanese occupation. The Huks were eventually outmanoeuvred by RAMON MAGSASAY who cleaned up the corrupt Philippines army, and pushed through a series of political and social reforms which blunted the political edge of the Huk offensive. Taroc disbanded the Huks and surrendered in 1953.

**HYDE PARK BOMBING, LONDON. (July 20th 1982)**. A bomb attack by the PROVISIONAL IRISH REPUBLICAN ARMY (PIRA) on a 16-strong cavalry detachment of the British Army's Household Cavalry as they were passing through Hyde Park in the centre of London. Four cavalrymen died in the attack, and two policemen, and seven civilians were injured. Seven cavalry horses were also killed in the bombing, and the television and newspaper pictures of dead and dying horses caused a wave of revulsion throughout Europe. The Irish prime minister Charles Haughey said the bombing "did irreparable damage to the good name of Ireland and the cause of Irish unity".

The bombing happened at 10.43 on July 20th 1982 when the cavalry detachment were on their way to ceremonial duties. The bombers used 5-10 lbs of high explosive around which they wrapped hundreds of large steel nails, crude but effective shrapnel which did terrible injury to the men and horses. A few hours later another bomb was exploded in the REGENT'S PARK bandstand killing and injuring bandsmen of the Royal Green Jackets. The bombers were described by the British prime minister as "evil and brutal men who know nothing of democracy", but the PIRA claimed their right to self-defence under Article 51 of the United Nations Charter. "Sefton", one of the injured cavalry horses, later became a favourite with the British public. A fund for the victims was set up in Dublin and administered by the Royal Dublin Society.

# I

**IBRAHIM, ATIF ABDEL**. One of the four Arab gunmen involved in the *ACHILLE LAURO* HIJACKING.

**INDONESIAN CONSULATE SIEGE, AMSTERDAM. (December 4th-19th 1975)**. A two-week-long siege of the Indonesian Consulate in Amsterdam by six armed South Moluccans demanding that the Dutch government keep their promise to mediate on behalf of Molucca for independence from Indonesia. Several consular officials escaped but one Indonesian who jumped from an upper floor died of his injuries. The takeover of the consulate was timed to coincide with the BEILEN TRAIN SIEGE. After 15 days of negotiations during which many of the consulate hostages were released, the Moluccans finally surrendered on the promise that the Dutch government would have discussions with the Moluccan "government in exile". In April 1976 the six gunmen were jailed for six years each. Terrorism expert Walter Laqueur cites the South Moluccans as one of international terrorism's "proletarian" groups who failed to obtain arms or cash from East or West "because their objectives did not coincide with the interests of foreign governments".

**INNER MACEDONIAN REVOLUTIONARY ORGANISATION (IMRO)**. Right-wing Macedonian separatist/nationalist group founded at the turn of the century, but which flourished between World War I and World War II. IMRO acquired a reputation as one of the most ruthless terrorist bands in Europe. Led by Damian Gruev, IMRO's original battle was with the Turkish Ottoman Empire, but when Macedonia was split between Greece, Bulgaria and Serbia in 1912, IMRO continued to fight for a Macedonian homeland. The organisation was covertly aided, and then later suppressed by the Bulgarian government. Eventually IMRO degenerated into a semi-criminal organisation, dealing in drugs, and carrying out assassination "contracts" for cash. IMRO benefited from pre-war state-supported terrorism, and received funds from Fascist Italy, Hungary and Bulgaria.

**IRANIAN EMBASSY SIEGE, LONDON. (April 30th-May 5th 1980).** The takeover of the Iranian Embassy in Princes Gate, London, by five Iranian Arabs who held the Embassy staff and British citizens hostage for six days. The siege ended when a Counter Revolutionary Warfare (CRW) unit from the British Army's SPECIAL AIR SERVICE (SAS) stormed the building, killing five of the six hostage-takers and capturing one. Two of the hostages were killed by the Iranians. At the trial of the surviving terrorist it emerged that the men had been trained by the Iraqi government anxious to embarrass the regime of Ayatollah Khomeinei.

The six-day-long siege and its dramatic finale was watched by the world's press and television, and the success of the SAS rescue operation was widely seen as evidence of a Western democracy's determination to thwart transnational terrorism. The success of the SAS rescue operation probably helped to defuse the anti-Western feeling which was building up in Iran over British and American "complicity" in the takeover of the London Embassy by anti-Khomeini forces.

The siege began at 11.30 on April 30th 1980 when the five terrorists – belonging to an organisation called the DEMOCRATIC REVOLUTIONARY FRONT FOR THE LIBERATION OF ARABISTAN – burst into the Embassy through the front door, overpowered the British police officer on duty (Police Constable Trevor Lock), and took over the building which had 26 hostages inside. The terrorists were led by 27-year-old SALIM TOWFIGH (also known as Oan). The purpose of the Embassy takeover was to publicise the plight of Iranian Arabs, and the five gunmen demanded a flight to take themselves, their hostages and an Arab ambassador to an unnamed Arab country. The British authorities refused to negotiate. Five of the 26 hostages were released before the SAS attack, and two were shot to death; Abbas Lavasani, the Embassy press attaché and his assistant Ali-Akbar Samadzadeh.

The siege of the Iranian Embassy ended at 19.26 on May 5th 1980 when a CRW unit from B Squadron of the SAS burst in through the windows at the front and rear of the building, threw "flash bang" grenades to stun and blind the terrorists, and quickly shot the five gunmen calling themselves Hassan, Makki, Shai, Faisal and Oan. The only surviving terrorist was the young man who called himself Ali, whose real name was FOWZI NEJAD. The SAS were later criticised for the ruthlessness of their operation, but their supporters pointed out that innocent lives were at stake, and that the gunmen had pledged to fight to the death. The terrorists had also claimed that they had booby-trapped the building. The surviving gunman was later tried in London and jailed for life.

**IRGUN ZVAI LEUMI (IRGUN).** Aggresssive Jewish guerrilla/terrorist group set up in the 1930s to defend Jewish settlers in Palestine against Arab attacks, and who, in the latter years of World War II, turned their guns against "the British conqueror". Irgun was the military arm of the New Zionist Organisation, and for some years was commanded by MENACHEM BEGIN later Prime Minister of Israel. Welded by Jewish intellectual David Raziel into an effective clandestine military force Irgun's war against the British was helped by the "benign neglect" of the French who allowed Irgun to operate in Europe with impunity.

Irgun's terror campaign against the British (which horrified many Jews inside and outside Palestine) was cruel but carefully controlled. Irgun were responsible for the assassination of the anti-Semitic British Minister for the Middle East, Lord Moyne (in November 1944), the KING DAVID HOTEL BOMBING (in July 1946) and the audacious destruction of 27 RAF aircraft on the ground at Kastina Airport. Under Begin's leadership the Irgun were probably the most effective of the Jewish groups fighting to set up the state of Israel, and were rivalled in ruthlessness only by the smaller Lohamei Heruth Israel (LEHI).

Although attacked in the British media for their "barbarism", the Irgun prided themselves on their carefully controlled policy of "an eye for an eye". When a Jewish youth was sentenced by the British to 18 lashes for carrying arms, the Irgun captured two British officers and gave them 18 lashes each before releasing them. And when the British executed four convicted Jewish terrorists in July 1947, the Irgun responded by capturing and hanging two British Army sergeants, Clifford Martin and Mervyn Paice, leaving their booby-trapped bodies hanging in an orchard.

But by the late 1940s Irgun had grown too powerful for Israel's fledgling government, and after the massacre of 250 Arab civilians at DEIR YASSIN near Jerusalem in April 1948, Prime Minister David Ben Gurion acted against the Irgun. In September 1948 he issued an order to Irgun (and other Jewish terror groups) to disband and be absorbed into the mainstream Haganah Army (the predecessor of the Israeli Defence Forces).

**IRISH NATIONAL LIBERATION ARMY (INLA).** Small but very violent left-wing Irish Republican group who are effectively the military arm of the Irish Republican Socialist Party (IRSP) and who are regarded as "wild men" by the larger PROVISIONAL IRISH REPUBLICAN ARMY (PIRA). The INLA emerged in 1975 after the Marxist-inclined OFFICIAL IRISH REPUBLICAN ARMY (OIRA) declared a ceasefire in 1972. It was INLA who killed the Conservative Northern Ireland spokesman, AIREY NEAVE, in London in 1979, who assassinated Protestant leader JOHN McKEAGUE in Belfast in 1981, and who blew up the "DROPPIN' WELL" DISCO in County Londonderry in 1982. Three INLA men died in the MAZE PRISON HUNGER STRIKES in 1981.

The British believe that INLA was formed by disaffected members of the OIRA disgusted at the ceasefire of 1972 but too left-wing to join cause with traditionalist/Catholic PIRA. In the mid-1970s INLA was involved in a bloody feud with the OIRA in the course of which it is said INLA killed OIRA commander Billy McMillen. INLA were declared illegal in Britain in 1979 when it was claimed in Parliament that they had been receiving arms from terrorist groups in the Middle East.

**IRISH REPUBLICAN ARMY (IRA).** The 60-year-old armed-force wing of the Irish Republican movement which in modern times has fragmented into the PROVISIONAL IRISH REPUBLICAN ARMY (PIRA) the OFFICIAL IRISH REPUBLICAN ARMY (OIRA) and the small IRISH NATIONAL LIBERATION ARMY (INLA). The various manifestations of the IRA continue to harass and attack the British province of Northern Ireland and embarrass the government of the Irish Republic. The declared policy of the IRA is to force the withdrawal of the British from Northern Ireland, and create a united Ireland even against the wishes of the Protestant majority in the north. The IRA (and particularly the PIRA) is well supported by the powerful Irish-American community of the United States, although most of their money for arms and explosives is raised inside Ireland.

The almost defunct IRA were given a new lease of life in the late 1960s when the largely Roman Catholic civil rights campaign in Northern Ireland flared into open warfare, and Protestant hard-liners tried to stage pogroms against Catholics in Belfast and Londonderry. The IRA men did what they could to defend the Catholic communities, and the new round of "troubles" which began in 1968 provided the IRA with a rush of recruits from the Catholic/Republican parts of Northern Ireland. In 1970, however, there was a falling out among the IRA which led to the setting up of the Marxist-inclined "Official" IRA and the traditionalist "Provisional" IRA (much the larger of the two groups).

Created (or at least named) in 1916, the IRA are descendents of earlier Irish Republican armed-force organisatison such as the FENIAN BROTHERHOOD, and the Irish Republican Brotherhood. The IRA were first "named" by JAMES CONNOLLY during the abortive EASTER RISING in Dublin in 1916 and fought the British during the "troubles" which led up to the setting up of an independent Ireland in 1921. When the nascent Irish republic split into pro-treaty and anti-treaty forces in the Irish Civil War of the early 1920s, the IRA formed the anti-treaty army and was eventually defeated by the Free State Army of MICHAEL COLLINS.

In the 1930s the IRA resumed their campaign to create a united Ireland by driving the British out of Northern Ireland, and in the late 1930s launched a bombing campaign on the British mainland. Bombing attacks were made in Manchester, London, Glasgow and Coventry (where five people were killed, 50 injured, and two young IRA men hanged). The IRA bombing campaign obliged the Irish government to proscribe the organisation in June 1939, after which the IRA was hounded by police and security forces on both sides of the Irish border. During World War II there were a few links between the IRA and the German Nazis, but nothing came of them; both sides are reported to have found the other incomprehensible.

Between 1956 and 1962 the IRA waged a strenuous campaign along the border between the Republic and Northern Ireland which involved more than 100 IRA men, cost the lives of six RUC policemen and 11 Republicans, and faced the British taxpayer with a bill for $1.5 million in damages, and $15 million in extra policing. But in the face of public apathy (on both sides of the border) the IRA command abandoned the "border campaign" in February 1962. Throughout most of the 1960s the IRA was dormant, apart from staging a few spectacular incidents such as the felling of Nelson's Pillar in Dublin in 1966. Support for Irish Republicanism, however, continued to grow, fuelled by the 50th anniversary celebrations of the Easter Rising.

In 1967 CATHAL GOULDING, then commander of the IRA, agreed that the IRA should become involved in the Northern Ireland Civil Rights Association (NICRA) and its policy of passive confrontation with the ROYAL ULSTER CONSTABULARY (RUC). The non-violent strategy worked well, and attracted world-wide sympathy and publicity without the IRA firing a shot. Cathal Goulding later said that his plan was to "get Protestants involved, and get away from the old divisions. Our objectives were civil rights reform for Catholic and Protestant working class, and the splitting of the Unionist Party."

But the non-violent civil rights movement gradually broke down in anarchy, the Protestant para-military groups began to re-emerge, and in August 1969 the traditional Apprentice Boys march in Londonderry collapsed in bloodshed which almost led to civil war. Within months British troops were back on the streets of Northern Ireland (to protect the Roman Catholics from the enraged Protestants) and the "physical force" advocates within the IRA were in the ascendancy. In January 1970 the IRA split into "Official" and "Provisional" wings, a rupture which Goulding described as "inevitable" because "the Provisionals did not like our socialist policies". After Goulding and the OIRA called a ceasefire in 1972, the hard-liners left OIRA and formed INLA. Goulding and the OIRA continue to insist that PIRA's bombing and shooting campaigns against the British and the Protestants are counter-productive.

**IRON GUARD**. Fascist terrorist group which emerged in Rumania in the 1920s and 1930s and which developed into one of the most feared organisations in eastern Europe. The Iron Guard were responsible for the assassination of two of Rumania's prime ministers (Duca in 1933 and Calinescu in 1939).

**ISLAMIC JIHAD**. (Islamic Holy War). Shadowy pro-Iranian Lebanese fundamentalist group first heard of when it claimed responsibility for the AMERICAN MARINE HQ and FRENCH ARMY HQ attacks in Beirut in October 1983. Describing themselves as "Soldiers of God" the Islamic Jihad have waged a particularly ruthless campaign of bombing, assassination and kidnapping against Western interests and individuals in Lebanon. Although Islamic Jihad operate mainly inside Lebanon, they also carried out the KUWAIT BOMBINGS in December 1983.

It is believed that the loosely organised Islamic Jihad is a Shi'ite Muslim organisation which grew up in the Baalbek Valley in Lebanon in 1982-83. Although probably trained in terrorist techniques by Iranian zealots in Baalbeck Valley camps, it is unlikely that Islamic Jihad take their orders from Iran. It may be the name given to the active arm of the HIZBULLAH (Party of God) movement. Islamic Jihad were described by the Shi'ite religious leader Sheikh Mohammed Fadlallah as "a cover not for one group, but different groups". Islamic Jihad were also responsible for the assassination of Dr Malcolm Kerr, the US-born President of the American University in Beirut in January 1984, and for the kidnapping of a number of Western journalists, diplomats and clergymen (most of whom were released unharmed).

## ISRAELI ARMY HQ BOMBING, TYRE. (November 4th 1984).

A suicide car-bomb attack on the Israeli Army's headquarters in the south Lebanese town of Tyre in which 61 people died. Although responsibility for the bombing was claimed by Shi'ite Muslim extremists of the ISLAMIC JIHAD, the Israelis responded to it by carrying out air strikes against Syrian, Palestinian and Druse targets throughout Lebanon. These attacks provoked a dangerous heightening of tension between Israel and the powerful Soviet-backed forces of Syria, which put both countries on full-scale alert, and sparked fears of a full-scale war.

The attack on the Israeli headquarters was carried out by a solitary Shia Muslim who drove a car packed with 1100 lbs of high explosive into the Israeli military compound. Although the Israeli sentries shot the driver dead and stopped the car short of the building, the headquarters was destroyed by the bomb which set off a chain of ammunition explosions which lasted for more than two hours, and which made rescue operations virtually impossible. The death toll was heavy; 28 Israeli soldiers were killed along with 33 Palestinians and Lebanese waiting to be interrogated.

The Israeli reaction was to impose a three-day curfew in the town of Tyre and to attack Syrian, Palestinian and Druse Muslim bases in the Chouf Mountains and the Bekaa Valley. On November 7th 1984 the Syrians called up 100,000 reserves "to face US and Israeli troop concentrations" and the Israeli Defence Forces (IDF) were put on special alert. Syrian anti-aircraft batteries fired on a French aircraft over Beirut and on American aircraft flying reconnaissance flights over the Bekaa Valley. On November 12th 1984 the US Congress voted to stop $125 million worth of aid to Syria because of its "hostile attitude" to the USA.

## ISTANBUL AIRPORT ATTACK, TURKEY. (August 11th 1976). An attack by three Arabs and a Japanese from the POPULAR FRONT FOR THE LIBERATION OF PALESTINE (PFLP) on the passenger terminal at Istanbul International Airport in Turkey in which four people were killed and 20 injured. The gunmen opened fire with automatic weapons and hurled grenades in a transit lounge where passengers were waiting to board an El Al flight to Tel Aviv. Among the dead were two Israelis and Harold W. Rosenthal, aide to a senior US Senator. The Japanese terrorist

was killed in the attack, and one of the Arabs escaped. The two who were captured claimed that the Istanbul raid had been a response to the Israeli hostage-rescue operation following the AIR FRANCE HIJACKING TO MOGADISHU AIRPORT, SOMALIA, earlier in the year. They were tried and sentenced to death, sentences which were later commuted to life imprisonment.

# J

**JACKSON, GEOFFREY**. British Ambassador to Uruguay who was kidnapped in Montevideo in January 1971, held in a "people's prison" for eight months, and then released unharmed. All efforts by the Uruguayan and British governments to trace Jackson failed, and a reward offer of $25,000 put up by the kidnapped diplomat's friends failed to elicit any information. Although suspicion fell on Uruguay's main terrorist group the TUPAMAROS, they denied any responsibility for the kidnapping. As part of the effort to find Jackson the Uruguayan government declared a 90-day "state of emergency". After his release Jackson said that his abductors had "laid on 50 chaps and seven cars" for the kidnapping.

Jackson was snatched on January 8th 1971 only 200 yards from the British Embassy in the centre of Montevideo. The 55-year-old ambassador's car was attacked by armed men who beat his driver and bodyguards unconscious. When efforts by the Uruguayan government failed to recover Jackson the British government sent "security experts" to Uruguay but they were unable to help. Jackson was finally released unharmed on September 10th 1971 having spent eight months in a subterranean "people's prison" somewhere in Montevideo. On his return to the UK he learned that he had been awarded a knighthood.

**JACKSON, GEORGE**. American "black power" propagandist and author who was killed in a gun battle at San Quentin prison in California on August 22nd 1971 while serving a life sentence for the murder of a prison guard. Born in Chicago, Jackson had spent most of his short life in jail and became famous in left-wing and radical circles for his book *Soledad Brother* which was published in 1970 with an introduction by French playwright Jean Genet. Jackson's young brother Jonathan was killed while kidnapping an American judge in an attempt to release his elder brother and two other prisoners. Jackson's funeral on August 29th 1971 was attended by hundreds of young blacks wearing the black beret and leather jacket of the BLACK PANTHER PARTY (BPP). Since his death Jackson's name has been used by various small terrorist groups. One calling itself the "George Jackson Brigade" carried out a series of bank robberies and bombings in the western states of Oregon and Washington in the mid-1970s.

**JAMMU KASHMIR LIBERATION FRONT (JKLF).** One of a number of separatist nationalist movements working for the independence of the State of Kashmir from the Republic of India. The JKLF were responsible for the assassination of Indian diplomat RAVINDRA MHATRE in Birmingham, England, in February 1984.

**JAPANESE AIRLINES HIJACKING TO BENGHAZI, LIBYA. (July 21st 1973).** The hijacking of a JAL jet by Arab gunmen who ordered it to land at Benghazi in Libya. After the passengers were released from the aircraft, it was destroyed on the runway.

**JAPANESE RED ARMY.** See UNITED RED ARMY OF JAPAN.

**JEWISH DEFENCE LEAGUE (JDL).** Right-wing American-Jewish organisation who have taken to violence to defend what they see as Jewish interests world wide. Founded in 1968 by Rabbi Meir Kahane (now an Israeli politician) the JDL have been accused by the FEDERAL BUREAU OF INVESTIGATION (FBI) and the CENTRAL INTELLIGENCE AGENCY (CIA) of being responsible for numerous bombing attacks in the USA.

The JDL are suspected of bombing the Los Angeles office of the American-Arab Anti-Discrimination Committee (ADC) on October 11th 1985, an attack which killed the committee's west-coast director Alex Odeh. The day before he was killed Odeh had appeared on television to discuss the *ACHILLE LAURO* HIJACKING and had said it was time for Americans "to understand the Palestinian side of the story". Rabbi Kahane refused to condemn the assassination of Odeh because he regards the ADC as a front for the the PALESTINE LIBERATION ORGANISATION (PLO).

The JDL are also believed to have been behind the fire-bombing of the ADC's HQ in Washington in December 1985, and the murder in Patterson, New Jersey, of 61-year-old Tscherim Soobzokov a one-time member of the German Waffen SS. The FBI believe there is considerable overlap in membership between the JDL and other Jewish groups such as the Militant Jewish Defence Organisation which offers US Jews free karate and firearms training.

**JONATHAN INSTITUTE, JERUSALEM.** Specialised Israeli "think-tank" set up to study the ramifications of international terrorism. The institute is called after JONATHAN NETANYAHU, the academic-turned-soldier who died leading an Israeli anti-terrorist squad in July 1976 following the LUFTHANSA HIJACKING TO ENTEBBE AIRPORT, UGANDA The Jonathan Institute has published a number of works on terrorism by BENJAMIN NETANYAHU, Jonathan's younger brother and now Israel's ambassador to the United Nations.

**"JONATHAN", OPERATION**. Military codename for the Israeli government's successful operation to rescue the 106 hostages being held at ENTEBBE AIRPORT in Uganda. Operation "Jonathan" was mounted on July 3rd-4th 1976 and was called after its commander Lieutenant Colonel JONATHAN NETANYAHU.

**JUNTA OF REVOLUTIONARY CO-ORDINATION (JRC)**. A Latin-American "terrorist international" established in the early 1970s by the Argentinian EJERCITO REVOLUCIONARIO DEL PUEBLO (EDP), the Uruguayan TUPAMAROS, the Chilean MOVIMIENTO DE LA IZQUIERDA REVOLUCIONARIA (MIR) and the Bolivian Ejercito De Liberacion Nacional (ELN). Most of the estimated $5 million put into the JRC was contributed by the well-organised EDP as a result of which the EDP became the dominant group. The money was used to fund operations throughout Europe, arms procurement, and the production of a revolutionary journal called *Che Guevara*.

# K

**KALASHNIKOV AK-47**. Russian-designed assault rifle much favoured by terrorist and insurgency groups. Robust, simple to use, easy to maintain and cheap to manufacture the AK 47 has been described as the world's most widely used firearm. Just over 34 inches long, weighing 9.45 lb, the AK-47 has a 30-round "banana"-shaped magazine and a rate of fire of up to 600 rounds per minute. The rifle uses 7.62mm rounds. The AK-47 is heavy enough to be accurate and shoots well on automatic without too much vibration. The folding stock version (designed for use by Russian airborne troops) makes the AK-47 easier to conceal and has been much-favoured by terrorists.

Based on the World War II German MP44 "Sturmgewehr" the AK-47 was designed by Michael Kalashnikov and adopted by the Soviet armed forces in 1951. Although now replaced by an improved version (the AK-74) the AK-47 has been manufactured under licence in most Eastern Bloc countries. The Chinese make a version which they call the Type 56 Assault Rifle, and which has a permanently-fixed bayonet under the barrel. The Finnish army's M62 "Valmet" is also based on the AK-47 (although it contains no wooden parts).

**KANAFANI, GHASSAN**. Palestinian poet, novelist and spokesman in Beirut for the POPULAR FRONT FOR THE LIBERATION OF PALESTINE (PFLP) who was believed by Israeli intelligence to have organised the LOD AIRPORT MASSACRE of June 1972. Kanafani was killed by a remote-controlled bomb wired to his car in Beirut on July 8th 1972. His 17-year-old niece died along with him. Kanafani's killing was an Israeli reprisal for the attack on Lod Airport in which 27 people died.

**KANAK SOCIALIST NATIONAL LIBERATION FRONT**. Pro-independence, anti-French movement active in the French Pacific colony of New Caledonia. The Kanak campaign for independence from France has become increasingly violent with a growing number of casualties on both sides. Kanak leaders are known to have been trained in guerrilla and subversion techniques in Libya, while French settlers, suspicious of the intentions of the socialist regime of President Mitterand, have been (illegally) importing large quantities of arms to defend their interests.

In January 1986 the Australian Government warned the Libyan regime of MUAMMUR QADDAFI not to stir up violence in the Pacific. This warning followed an invitation to the Kanak Socialist National Liberation Front to attend a "summit meeting" of liberation movements in Tripoli which Kanak leader Yann Celene Uregei accepted. In December 1985 the French freighter *Ile de Lumiere* was seized in Auckland, New Zealand, after automatic weapons, pistols and more than 8,000 rounds of ammunition was discovered hidden in her hold. The weapons were thought to have been put on board the freighter in Australia, and were bound for French settlers in New Caledonia. It was the third cache of weapons and ammunition discovered on ships heading for the French colony.

**KARAMEH, BATTLE OF. (March 21st 1968).** Set-piece battle at the village of Karameh inside Jordan when 300 or so FATAH guerrillas fought off a column of 15,000 Israeli troops supported by armour and helicopters. Although the Palestinians lost almost half their force, they killed 20-30 Israelis and drove them back. Fatah had been warned in advance of the Israeli raid (probably by the CENTRAL INTELLIGENCE AGENCY (CIA) via the Jordanians) and fought from carefully-prepared defensive positions. Karameh was a watershed in the fortunes of Fatah and the PALESTINE LIBERATION ORGANISATION (PLO). According to the PLO, within 48 hours of the battle at Karameh 5,000 new recruits applied to join Fatah.

**KATKOV, ARKADY.** Cultural attaché at the Soviet Embassy in Beirut who was shot dead by Muslim extremists in October 1985. Katkov was one of four Soviet diplomats who were seized by a little-known organisation called the Islamic Liberation Organisation (ILO), who demanded that Moscow put pressure on Syria to "stop the annihilation of Muslims in Tripoli through Soviet tanks and artillery". Although the Soviets declared their opposition to terrorism they evacuated their Beirut Embassy and conceded to the kidnappers demands by negotiating a ceasefire in Tripoli via the Syrians. Two days after the kidnapping Katkov's body was found on a rubbish dump near the Beirut sports ground. Four weeks later the ILO released Soviet press attaché Oleg Spirin, commercial attaché Valery Mirkov, and Embassy doctor Nikolai Svirsky.

**KENNEDY, JOHN FITZGERALD (1917-1963).** The 35th President of the United States of America, shot dead in Dallas, Texas by, it is alleged, LEE HARVEY OSWALD. The circumstances of John Kennedy's assassination threw up many conspiracy theories, among them one that Kennedy was shot by disgruntled members of the CENTRAL INTELLIGENCE AGENCY (CIA) or by organised crime. Although such theories were dismissed by the US authorities for many years, in 1979 a Congressional committee came to the conclusion that President Kennedy was "probably assassinated as a result of a conspiracy".

Kennedy was shot at 12.30 on November 22nd 1963 as his motorcade was travelling through Dealey Plaza in the centre of Dallas. Although rushed to a local hospital the President was announced dead at 13.00. Within an hour of the shooting a 6.5mm Mannlicher-Carcano rifle was found on the sixth floor of the Texas School Book Depository overlooking Dealey Plaza. One of the book depository's employees, Lee Harvey Oswald, was later arrested by the Dallas police and charged with killing Kennedy, and with the shooting of a Dallas patrolman J. D. Tippit. In the two days he was held by the police Oswald persistently denied shooting either Kennedy or Tippit. On November 24th, while in police custody, Oswald himself was shot dead by JACK RUBY, a Dallas club-owner and petty criminal.

Athough the official US government inquiry into the Kennedy murder (the Warren Commission) concluded that Oswald was the only assassin involved, there were persistent reports from witnesses claiming to have seen and heard shots coming from positions in front of the President's car (and well away from the book depository). And in December 1978 an acoustics expert testified to the House Committee on Assassinations that, based on the evidence of a recently-discovered police radio tape, at least four shots had been fired, and that one of them had come from a position in front of the Kennedy cavalcade.

In the light of the new evidence the committee decided that while there was no evidence that any US government agency (CIA, FBI, or Military Intelligence) had been involved, the killing of John F. Kennedy was almost certainly carried out by more than one gunman. Some committee staff members believed that Kennedy had been killed by organised crime (The Mafia), or anti-Castro

Cubans bitter over the Bay of Pigs débâcle. Others believed that extreme right-wing Texans organised the killing.

**KENNEDY, ROBERT FRANCIS (1926-1968).** US Senator, and younger brother of President John Kennedy, who was shot in a Los Angeles hotel on June 5th 1968 while campaigning for the Democratic Party's presidential nomination. Robert Kennedy's assassin was a young Jordanian called SIRHAN SIRHAN who resented Kennedy's support for Israel. Although Robert Kennedy's murder never generated the number of conspiracy theories which his brother's did, there were suggestions that Sirhan had been hypnotized to carry out the shooting, and that the small-calibre hand-gun he used could not have done the damage it did. None of these suspicions were taken seriously by the authorities. Kennedy was shot in the Ambassador Hotel in Los Angeles late in the evening of June 5th 1968. He was struck by three bullets from a 0.22 Iver Johnson hand-gun, one of which hit him in the back of the head. He died some hours later. His assailant Sirhan Sirhan was captured on the spot.

**KENYATTA, JOMO (1897-1978).** Real name Kamau wa Ngengi. Leading African statesman and politician, and founder of the Kenya African Union (KAU). Kenyatta was accused by the British colonial regime in Kenya of being the driving force behind the MAU MAU terrorist insurgency in the 1950s. A member of the powerful Kikuyu tribe Kenyatta was detained by the British during the emergency. When the British finally pulled out of Kenya in 1963 Kenyatta became Kenya's first President, and rapidly became respected as one of black Africa's most moderate leaders. When cabinet minister TOM M'BOYA, a leader of the Luo tribe was assassinated by a Kikuyu in 1969, only the intervention of Kenyatta saved Kenya from being plunged into inter-tribal warfare.

**KHALAF, SALAH.** One of the four founder-members of FATAH, the militant Palestinian organisation which is now the core of the PALESTINE LIBERATION ORGANISATION (PLO). The son of a Palestinian grocer from Jaffa, Khalaf met YASIR ARAFAT while the latter was studying engineering at the University of Cairo in the 1950s. Khalaf and Arafat remain at the centre of the PLO.

**KHALED, LEILA (born 1948).** Female member of the POPULAR FRONT FOR THE LIBERATION OF PALESTINE (PFLP) who became internationally notorious when one of her hijacks over

Britain was foiled by an Israeli security guard on September 6th 1970 and she was held by the British government. She was freed three weeks later as part of the deal to release the hostages being held in Amman in Jordan after the DAWSON'S FIELD HIJACKINGS. The British government were bitterly criticised by the Israelis for succumbing to the terrorists' demands. At a press conference after her release Khaled described hijacking as "one of the operational aspects of our war against Zionism . . . it was a perfectly normal thing to do, the sort of thing all freedom fighters have to tackle".

A Palestinian who was born in Haifa, Khaled fled with her family to Tyre in Lebanon when she was four years old. She joined the left-wing PFLP following the catastrophic Arab defeat in 1967. On September 6th 1970 Khaled was one of two Arabs who tried to take over an El Al Boeing 707 bound for New York from Amsterdam. At 13.50, when the aircraft was over the south of England, Khaled and her colleague tried to force their way into the cockpit. There was a brief struggle in which an Israeli cabin steward was shot in the stomach (he later recovered) and the male hijacker was shot dead by an Israeli SKYMARSHALL. Khaled was overpowered by an American passenger (although she did throw a grenade which failed to explode). The aircraft made an emergency landing at Heathrow Airport in London where Khaled was handed over to the British police.

But when PFLP gunmen hijacked three jetliners to Dawson's Field in Jordan (and one to Cairo) and held more than 300 passengers and crew hostage, Khaled was one of those who were released in exchange for the safety of the hostages. She was flown out of Britain to Cairo by Royal Air Force Comet on September 30th 1970. In August 1972 Khaled was spotted by Interpol near Schipol Airport in Amsterdam. She is believed to have been involved in the MUNICH OLYMPICS ATTACK in October 1972.

**KHATER, SULEIMAN**. The Egyptian security policeman who went berserk and killed seven Israeli tourists at Ras Burka in Sinai, and then became a national hero to Egypt's Muslim fundamentalists after committing suicide in a Cairo jail. Khater, a 25-year-old conscript in Egypt's Central Security Force, shot and killed four children, two women and an old man at a tourist resort in Ras Burka in the Sinai in September 1985. After being sentenced to life imprisonment for the crimes by an Egyptian court, Khater was found dead in his cell on January 7th 1986. According to Egypt's chief coroner, Khater hanged himself with a

5ft-long strip of bedding. The coroner said there were no drugs in the man's bloodstream and no signs of any resistance which might have suggested that he had been murdered.

But Khater's family and friends (and most of Egypt's political opposition) insist that he was killed in his cell either by Israeli agents, or by the Egyptian government anxious to pre-empt any rescue attempt by terrorists. The Khater affair was a grave embarrassment to the Egyptian government; even before his death the apparently unbalanced young man was made a martyr by Egypt's powerful Muslim fundamentalists, while respectable opposition politicians made pilgrimages to Khater's grave.

**KIDNAPPING**. The taking and holding captive of individuals for political and/or financial reasons. Kidnapping is a terrorist strategy widely and successfully used by Latin American terror groups in the late 1960s and 1970s, and is now regularly deployed by Muslim bands operating in Beirut, Lebanon. Although many kidnap victims have been killed by their captors, (HANNS-MARTIN SCHLYER, ALDO MORO, DAN MITRIONE) most survive, either because their governments (or employers) give in to the kidnappers' demands, or because their kidnapping no longer serves a useful purpose. Occasionally kidnap victims are killed as an act of political revenge. Two Britons, Philip Padfield and Leigh Douglas, who had been kidnapped in Beirut were murdered by their captors because the British government allowed the Americans to use US bases in England for the bombing attacks on Libya in April 1986.

Most national governments take a hard line with terrorist groups who kidnap their citizens, and refuse to make concessions. The US adopts this line, and has been criticised for refusing even to negotiate with kidnappers. The US government argues that if the US gives in to kidnapping then no US citizen, or US institution anywhere in the world would be safe. Much the same argument is advanced by Israel and the United Kingdom. Unlike the kind of hostage-taking situations which develop out of aerial HIJACKING, military solutions are very rarely an option (although the Italian anti-terrorist squad did solve the kidnapping of Major General JAMES DOZIER in 1981).

Kidnapping now appears to be endemic in the political and military chaos of the Lebanon. British, American, French, Soviet, Irish and Iranian citizens have all been kidnapped by various Muslim groups, and some have been killed. The victims include journalists, teachers, diplomats, television crews, university lecturers and UN officials. From 1984 to March 1986 47 foreigners were abducted in the Lebanon, 26 of whom were released and five killed. In March 1986 the ISLAMIC JIHAD killed French TV researcher Michel Seurat who they described as "an espionage specialist". The Lebanese kidnappers appear to hold their Western hostages against some future contingency: very rarely are any specific demands made for their  release. The Britons, Philip Padfield and Leigh Douglas, are reported to have been kidnapped by a "freelance" terrorist group and later sold to the pro-Libyan terrorists who killed them.

In the early 1970s the Argentinian Trotskyist group EJERTICO REVOLUCIONARIO DE PUEBLO (ERP) used kidnapping as a way of raising funds for their terrorist campaign. The ERP strategy was to kidnap industrialists and executives from multinational companies (usually American) and use their safety to extort money from their employers. The ERP received $62,500 from the Swift Meat Packing Company in 1971, and in 1973 extracted $1 million from the Ford Motor Company, $2 million from Acrow Steel, $3 million from Firestone Tyre & Rubber, and $14.2 million from Exxon Oil. The  Argentinian MONTONEROS are reported to have extorted more than $60 million  from multi-national corporations by kidnapping their executives.

Terrorist groups have also used kidnap victims to force national governments to release prisoners. Between 1969 and 1970 terrorists in Brazil forced their government to release 125 terrorist suspects from jail by kidnapping the US, West German and Swiss ambassadors. In 1971 the TUPAMAROS of Uruguay kidnapped the British ambassador GEOFFREY JACKSON who was held for eight months and then released unharmed. In 1970 the FRONT DE LIBERATION DU QUEBEC (FLQ) kidnapped RICHARD CROSS, the British trade commissioner in Montreal and Quebec industry minister PIERRE LAPORT in an attempt to release 25 FLQ men from jail (and $500,000 worth of gold  bullion). The attempt failed, and while Cross was discovered unscathed, Laport was murdered by the FLQ.

## KING DAVID HOTEL BOMBING, JERUSALEM. (July 22nd 1946).

Ninety-one  people were killed and many injured when the Jewish terrorist group IRGUN ZVAI LEUMI (IRGUN) planted a bomb in the south wing of the King David Hotel  in Jerusalem. The hotel was being used by the British authorities as the  centre of the Military Government in the city. Casualties were high because the British ignored a warning from the Irgun that the King David was about to be bombed. At the time of the incident Irgun was led by MENACHEM BEGIN, later to become the Prime Minister of Israel.

**KING, MARTIN LUTHER (1929-1968).** The most important black American civil-rights leader in recent history who was shot dead at a motel in Memphis, Tennessee, on April 4th 1968 by JAMES EARL RAY. King's death sparked off a wave of rioting and bloodshed across the USA. A Baptist minister from Montgomery, Alabama, King's powerful oratory and organising skills made him the most able and influential black leader of his day. In 1964 he was awarded the Nobel Peace Prize. A few weeks after the murder King's assailant was captured at London airport.

King was in Memphis to support a strike by the city's 1,300 (mainly black) garbage collectors when he was shot dead at 18.00 on April 4th 1968 on the balcony of the Lorraine Motel in Memphis. He was rushed to hospital but was found to be dead on arrival, with gunshot wounds to the neck and face. Police discovered that the shots which killed King were fired from a room in a boarding house facing the Lorraine Motel. A high-powered 30.06 calibre rifle with a telescopic sight was discovered in the room covered in Ray's fingerprints.

The assassination of the most powerful figure in the black civil rights movement provoked a wave of racial violence in more than 100 American cities in which almost 40 people died (most of them black), 2,500 were injured, and 14,000 arrested. More than 45,000 National Guardsmen and 21,000 federal agents had to be called out to cope with the violence and destruction. Ironically, King's murder boosted the credibility of the more radical and militant black leaders who used it as proof that the kind of non-violent action which King had advocated was futile.

**KITSON, FRANK.** British soldier and military theorist whose book *Low Intensity Operations – Subversion, Insurgency and Peacekeeping* is regarded as a key piece of anti-terrorist writing. Kitson's book was published when he was serving as commander of the British Army in Belfast, and its advocacy of a specially-trained military force to counter terrorism made Kitson one of the Republican movement's most feared enemies. Such a force was set up a few years later, following the MUNICH OLYMPICS ATTACK in 1972, when the British SPECIAL AIR SERVICE (SAS) was given the funds to establish a permanent Counter Revolutionary Warfare (CRW) unit.

Kitson argued that in the foreseeable future terrorism and insurgency would prove a more common threat to Western democracies than full-scale "conventional" war, and that the West was ill-equipped to deal with it. Kitson pointed out that, typically, the terrorist deploys "a combination of political, economic, psychological and military measures" and that no governmemnt can expect to defeat terrorism unless it does the same. Kitson's conclusion that "the civilian authorities will rightly expect the soldier to know how to use non-military forms of action as part of the operational plan" was regarded by some as an argument in favour of politicising the military.

**KLINGHOFFER, LEON**. Elderly Jewish American who was shot dead during the *ACHILLE LAURO* HIJACKING in October 1985. Klinghoffer's murder outraged the USA, and the American government reacted by intercepting the Egyptian aircraft carrying the hijackers to Tunisia and forcing it back to Italy where the four men were tried by the Italian authorities. Efforts by the American government to have Klinghoffer's murderers extradited from Italy to stand trial in the USA have so far failed. The US government says that because Klinghoffer was an American citizen his murderers can and should be tried in the USA.

Klinghoffer, a 69-year-old retired New York businessman was on holiday with his wife on the *Achille Lauro* when the four hijackers took over the ship. Confined to a wheelchair after suffering two strokes, Klinghoffer was among the American and British passengers singled out by the Arab gunmen. Klinghoffer was then taken away, shot and dumped into the sea along with his wheelchair. A few days later his body was washed up on the coast of Syria where a post-mortem examination revealed that the elderly Jew had been shot in the head and chest. His body was then returned to the USA for burial. Klinghoffer's wife Marilyn died a few months later.

**KOMITET GOSUDARSTVENNOI BEZOPASTNOSTI (KGB).** (Committee for State Security). The Soviet Union's internal-security and intelligence-gathering bureaucracy which operates both within the Soviet Union and throughout the world. Probably the biggest and most formidable secret service on earth, the KGB is thought to consist of almost two million operatives including the élite "border guards" who defend the Soviet Union's huge coastline and land borders. Operated through five "Chief Directorates" the KGB is all-pervasive in Soviet society. Founded by a Polish aristocrat called FELIKS EDMUNDOVICH DZERZHINSKY the KGB (and its predecessors) had its roots in the Tsarist secret police known as the OKHRANA. Since its creation in 1917 the Soviet state security apparatus has been known as the Cheka, the Gpu, the Ogpu, the Nkvd, the Nkgb, the Mvd-Mgb, before becoming the KGB in March 1954. Although the KGB has office buildings throughout Moscow its HQ remains in the converted insurance building at Dzerzhinsky Square. The Chairman of the KGB is normally a full member of the ruling Politbureau and one-time Chairman Yuri Andropov rose to become First Secretary of the USSR. The current Chairman of the KGB is Vitaly Fedorchuk.

The KGB's First Chief Directorate (CD) is responsible for foreign operations, the Second CD is responsible for internal security and surveillance, while the Fifth CD tries to control religious, ethnic and political dissenters. The Chief Border Guards Directorate, a well-trained and well-equipped force more than 350,000 strong, patrol more than 45,000 miles of border. Department V or the Executive Action Department of the First Chief Directorate is believed to be responsible for training the KGB's assassination squads.

The KGB also has at its disposal the large (and usually efficient) intelligence/security services of East Germany, Poland, Czechoslovakia, Bulgaria, Hungary, Rumania, all of whose heads confer with Moscow at least once a year. Western intelligence calculate that the Soviet Union spends more than three billion dollars every year on espionage, propaganda and "disinformation" mainly through the huge network of overt and covert  agencies run by the KGB.

**KU-KLUX KLAN**. American white-supremacist organisation which originated in the southern states after the American Civil War, and which is dedicated to "defending" White America against the advance of blacks and other inferior races. The Klan has a long history of terrorism and violence, mainly against blacks, but also against Jews, Roman Catholics and left-wingers. In recent years the Klan has developed links (and overlapping membership) with other right-wing organisations such as the ARYAN NATIONS, the Posse Comitatus, and THE ORDER. The Klan have been trying to recruit the hard-pressed farmers of the Middle West by blaming the agricultural crisis of the 1980s on "bankers and Zionists operating through the Federal  Reserve System" and warning that "the Jew plan is to steal your land".

The original Ku-Klux Klan was set up in Pulaski, Tennessee, in 1866 with the intention of defending the war-ravaged south against the encroachment of vengeful and ill-educated blacks and self-seeking "carpet-baggers". But when it degenerated into violence and anti-black sadism (more than 1,000 blacks were killed in the 1860s) it was disbanded by its founder Nathan Bedford Forrest, and banned by the US Congress in the early 1870s. The Klan was revived in 1915 in Georgia when it reaffirmed its commitment to "pure Americanism" and its opposition to blacks, Jews, Roman Catholics, birth control, Darwinism, pacifism, and the repeal of prohibition. The organisation reached a peak in the 1920s (when it was reputed to have more than five million members), and in the 1930s it added Communism and Marxism to the alien creeds it was determined to fight.

The Klan had a major resurgence in the late 1950s and early 1960s, mainly in response to the black civil rights movement and the US government's campaign to enfranchise all its citizens and desegregate the schools of the southern states. Probably the most infamous Klan killings of modern times occurred near Philadelphia, Mississippi, in 1964 when three civil rights workers – Michael Schwerner, Andrew Goodman and James Chaney – were shot dead and buried near a dam. They were killed by a Klan lynch mob. Of the 18 whites charged with conspiring to deny the three dead men their civil rights by killing them, seven were found guilty but released on bail, eight were acquitted, and three were released after the jury failed to reach a verdict.

**KURDS.** See PESH MERGA.


**KUWAIT AIRWAYS HIJACKING TO TEHERAN. (December 4th-6th 1984).** The hijacking by four Lebanese Shi'ite Muslims of a Kuwait Airways flight from Dubai to Karachi. The four gunmen forced the aircraft to fly to Teheran in Iran where two American passengers were shot dead, and others brutally treated. Although the hijacking ended when Iranian security forces stormed the aircraft and disarmed the hijackers, the US government insisted that the Iranian regime was involved in plotting the incident. The Iranians denied any complicity in the affair.

The hijacking began in the early hours of December 4th 1984, shortly after the Kuwait Airways Flight 221 left Dubai Airport en route for Karachi. The British captain, John Clark, was ordered to fly to Teheran where the aircraft was allowed to land after the terrorists threatened to kill all 150 passengers and 11 crew. Shortly after landing the Lebanese shot dead Charles Hegna, an American government official, and threatened to kill a passenger every fifteen minutes unless the government of Kuwait released 17 Muslim fundamentalists being held for the KUWAIT BOMBINGS. The Kuwait government refused to negotiate. On December 6th, the third day of the hijacking, the Lebanese shot dead William Stanford, another US AID official, while other American passengers, such as businessman John Costa, were brutally treated. The Lebanese then threatened to kill the rest of the passengers and crew unless the Iranian authorities agreed to broadcast a statement in Iran and Kuwait demanding the release of the 17 "enchained brothers" in Kuwait.

The hijacking ended shortly after midnight on December 9th (the sixth day) when Iranian security men, disguised as a doctor and cleaning staff, overpowered the hijackers after smoke grenades and firearms were used to create a diversion. The US State Department accused the Iranian government of engineering the hijacking. The Iranians responded by saying "If any country other than Iran had handled an instance of air piracy the way Iran did, the world would have praised it."

The Kuwait Airways hijacking caused a considerable amount of diplomatic and political turbulence. During the six days of the hijacking US and British forces in the Mediterranean area were alerted to deal with the crisis if the aircraft was flown to another destination. Because the pilot, John Clark, and his flight engineer, Neil Beeston, were British citizens, the British Army's SPECIAL AIR SERVICE (SAS) were put on alert.

**KUWAIT BOMBINGS. (December 12th 1983).** A series of bomb attacks by Shi'ite Muslims in the Gulf state of Kuwait. In less than two hours bombs were exploded at the AMERICAN EMBASSY, the FRENCH EMBASSY, the Shuaiba Petrochemical Plant, the Kuwait International Airport, the Electricity Control Centre and the living quarters of the Raytheon Corporation. Six people were killed and more than 80 injured, and if the Shuaiba plant had been destroyed it could have crippled the economy of Kuwait. Responsibility for the attacks was claimed by ISLAMIC JIHAD, although most of the 21 men arrested by the Kuwaiti police claimed to be members of the pro-Iranian terror group DAWA. In February 1984, 25 young Shi'ite Muslims were put on trial in Kuwait for attempting to "demolish the values of society through criminal means". Six were sentenced to death (including three tried in absentia), seven to life in prison, and seven to prison terms ranging from five to 15 years.

# L

## "LA BELLE" DISCO BOMBING, WEST BERLIN. (April 5th 1986).

One of the most significant terrorist attacks in post-war history. After a bomb was exploded in a West Berlin nightclub frequented by American servicemen killing one American and injuring 50, the US government claimed that the bombing had been organised by Libyan diplomats, and 10 days later launched bombing raids against the Libyan cities of Tripoli and Benghazi. The raids killed 37 people (including President MUAMMAR QADDAFI's adopted daughter) and were vehemently condemned by the entire Arab world and most of Europe. Britain bore a share of the blame as the F-111 bombers which attacked Libya had flown from bases in England with the approval of the British government. In response, Libyan supporters in Beirut murdered two Britons and one American who were being held hostage.

The Americans were undaunted by the world-wide storm of protest and warned Qaddafi they would strike again if Libya was linked to any further terrorist attacks on US citizens. The American administration also criticised their West European allies (with the exception of Britain) for failing to act against the terrorists, and argued that the military action might not have been necessary if the Europeans had agreed to impose diplomatic and economic sanctions against the Qaddafi regime. There were widespread anti-American protests and demonstrations throughout Europe and the Middle East following the US bombing raids.

The "La Belle" discotheque was devastated by a bomb at 01.50 on April 5th 1986. As the club was a favourite venue with Berlin-based American service personnel it was crowded with about 500 men and women. Sergeant Kenneth Ford, 21, was killed and 50 other Americans were injured, some of them seriously. A young Turkish woman was also killed and 60 German and other civilians were injured. American security officials had received warning of the bomb but it exploded before they could act. Although a German group calling itself the "Holger Meins Commando" tried to claim responsibility for the bombing, the Berlin Police and US intelligence ascribed the act to Arab terrorists. A few days previous a German-Arab club had been bombed and seven Arabs killed.

The Americans claimed that the bombing attack on the "La Belle" disco was the work of terrorists operating under the direction of Libyan diplomats from the "People's Bureau" in East Berlin as a reprisal for US navy operations in the Gulf of Sirte in March 1986 (during which a number of Libyan patrol vessels and radar bases were destroyed). The American (and British) governments also claimed to have intercepted signals between Tripoli and East Berlin "congratulating" the staff of the "People's Bureau" on the success of the "La Belle" night-club bombing. The Americans also claimed that US intelligence had uncovered a plan by Libyan-backed terrorists to attack the line of people applying for US visas at the American Embassy in Paris.

For more than a week after the "La Belle" bombing a high-level US delegation tried to persuade the West Europeans to impose strict diplomatic, economic and financial sanctions against the Qaddafi regime. When that failed President Reagan ordered the US forces to attack "carefully selected targets" in Tripoli and Benghazi, after securing the permission of the British government to use F-111s and jet tankers from US bases in the south of England. At 02.00 on April 15th 1986 American F-111 bombers from Britain attacked Tripoli, while carrier-based aircraft from the US Sixth Fleet attacked Benghazi. Their targets in and around Tripoli were the international airport, the Sidi Bilal Marine training base, a military air base and President Qaddafi's HQ at the Aziziyah Barracks. In Benghazi the American aircraft struck at the Jamahiriya Barracks, Benina military airport, and a variety of radar installations and anti-aircraft bases.

The fierce American action split the European alliance. Only Britain sanctioned the strike against Libya. The Americans were roundly condemned by all the countries surrounding the Mediterranean, and France and Spain refused to allow the British-based F-111s to overfly their territory on their way to Libya. The Libyan government denied any connection with the terrorist bombing in West Berlin and accused President Reagan of waging a campaign of "state terrorism" against Libya. Libya's "revolutionary committees" warned that Libya would "unleash massive retaliation" against the USA and said that "suicide squads" were poised to strike deep inside North America.

**LACOSTE, PIERRE**. French Vice-Admiral and head of the DIRECTION GENERALE DE LA SECURITE EXTERIEURE (DGSE) between 1982 and 1985 who was sacked following the *RAINBOW WARRIOR* ATTACK by DGSE agents in Auckland

Harbour, New Zealand, in July 1985. As head of the French government's foreign intelligence-gathering service Lacoste was held to be responsible for the DGSE operation against the Greenpeace ship which embarrassed the regime of President Francois Mitterrand. Lacoste's resignation was demanded on September 20th 1985, since when he has been acting as military adviser to the Gaullist politician Raymond Barre (a political enemy of President Mitterrand).

**LAGO, VICTOR (1919-1982).** Spanish general and commander of the élite Brunete armoured division who was assassinated on November 4th 1982 by gunmen from the Basque separatist organisation EUSKADI TA ASKATASUNA (ETA). Lago was killed while driving in an army staff car through the western suburbs of Madrid. His car was overtaken by two motorcyclists who opened fire with automatic weapons, killing Lago instantly and badly injuring his driver. A fierce right-wing nationalist, Lago had fought with Franco during the Spanish Civil War and served with Spain's Blue Division on the Russian front during World War II on the side of the German army. He was regarded as one of the mainstays of Spain's right-wing regime, and his death was a personal blow to the ailing Franco.

**LARNACA AIRPORT ATTACK, CYPRUS. (February 19th 1978).** A lethal débâcle at Larnaca Airport between Egyptian commandos and the Cyprus National Guard following the hijacking of a Cyprus Airways jetliner by two Arab gunmen. When Egyptian commandos tried to storm the aircraft at Larnaca Airport they were fired on by the Cyprus National Guard and at least 15 Egyptians were killed. Although the Cypriot authorities arrested, tried and jailed the gunmen, Egypt severed diplomatic relations with Cyprus stating that the Cyprus government had connived at the assassination, hostage-taking and hijacking.

The chain of events which ended in the bloodshed at Larnaca Airport began in the afternoon of February 18th when two gunmen belonging to the ABU NIDAL group shot down Yussuf al-Sibai, secretary-general of the Afro-Asian People's Solidarity Organisation (AAPSO) and a close associate of the Egyptian President ANWAR SADAT. Al-Sibai was killed at the Hilton Hotel in Nicosia from where the two gunmen fled taking with them 30 hostages. The gunmen released 12 of the hostages, and at the Larnaca Airport traded another seven for a Cyprus Airways DC-8 jet airliner to make their escape.

The DC-8 carrying the two gunmen and their 11 hostages took off at 20.30 on February 18th, and wandered the Mediterranean for hours while country after country refused to let it land. Finally the tiny desert state of Dubai allowed the DC-8 to refuel on condition that the aircraft left immediately. At 17.45 on February 19th the DC-8 returned to Larnaca Airport followed closely by an Egyptian C-130 transport aircraft carrying a 75-strong unit of SA'AQA (The Thunderbolt), the Egyptian army's anti-terrorist force. But when the Egyptian unit deplaned and tried to storm the Cyprus Airways jet, they were fired on by the Cyprus National Guard who had surrounded the airport. A 50-minute gun battle ensued in which 15 Egyptians died and their C-130 aircraft was destroyed. A number of Cyprus-based fighters from the PALESTINE LIBERATION ORGANISATION (PLO) were on the scene, and Egypt later claimed that the PLO men had joined the Cyprus National Guard and turned their guns against the Egyptian commandos. Eventually the Egyptians surrendered and were allowed to leave the country.

After the débâcle at Larnaca Airport the Egyptians accused the Cyprus government of conniving in the hostage-taking and the hijacking and on February 22nd severed diplomatic relations with Cyprus. A few days later, on February 27th, the Egyptians revoked all the "special privileges" of the 40,000 or so Palestinians living in Egypt. On April 20th the two gunmen – Samir Mohammed Katar and Zayad Hussein al-Ali – were convicted by a court in Cyprus of the murder of Yussuf al-Sibai and sentenced to death by hanging. Their sentence was later commuted to life imprisonment.

**LARNACA MARINA ATTACK, CYPRUS. (September 25th 1985).** Killing of three Israeli tourists at Larnaca Marina in Cyprus by two Palestinians and a European, claiming to be members of FORCE 17, a unit of FATAH. The three Israelis – Reuben Paltzur, Esther Paltzur and Abraham Avnery – were held hostage for the release of 20 Palestinians jailed in Israel, including Faisal Abu-Shar said to be a senior member of Force 17. When their demands were not met, the three terrorists shot their hostages dead and then surrendered to the police. The men – two Arabs and a European – were named as Elias Yiahia Nassif (24), Mahmoud Khaled Abdullah (24) and IAN DAVISON, a Briton from the north of England.

Despite heavy diplomatic pressure, the Cypriot authorities refused to extradite the three men to Israel, insisting that they must stand trial where the crime had been committed. Both Force 17 and the PALESTINE LIBERATION ORGANISATION (PLO) denied responsibility for the three gunmen, and condemned all attacks on Cyprus soil. One PLO spokesman suggested that the killings were an attempt by anti-PLO groups to discredit the PLO before talks with British Prime Minister Margaret Thatcher. In the event Thatcher refused to meet the PLO delegation.

**LEBANESE ARMED REVOLUTIONARY FACTION (LARF).** Recently-formed group of Arab militants blamed for the attempted assassination of the American Consul General in Strasbourg in March 1986. One of the LARF's leaders is thought to be George Ibrahim Abdalah, currently jailed in Paris and awaiting trial. Some of the recent bombings in Paris have been ascribed to LARF as an attempt to pressure the French authorities into releasing Abdalah.

**LETELIER, ORLANDO.** Chilean exile and one-time member of the left-wing Allende government who was assassinated in Washington DC on September 21st 1976. Letelier (44) was driving to his office with his female assistant when his car was blown up as it was passing the Chilean Embassy on Massachussets Avenue in the centre of the city. Investigations by the US authorities placed the blame on right-wing Cuban exiles acting for the Chilean secret police DINA. The involvement of the Chilean DINA in a killing in the heart of Washington did much to discredit the right-wing regime of General Pinochet, although Pinochet immediately denied that Chile had anything to do with the murder.

Letelier's Chevrolet sedan was blown apart by a bomb at 09.35 on September 21st as he drove down "Embassy Row" in Washington on his way to the Institute for Policy Studies. Letelier and his research assistant, Ronnie Moffit, were killed instantly and Mrs Moffit's husband Michael was injured. Suspicion immediately fell on the Chilean DINA as Letelier had been running a vigorous and outspoken publicity campaign for the suspension of all military and civil aid to the Chilean regime which relied heavily on the USA for financial and political support. Although Chile had just stripped Letelier of his Chilean citizenship (for activities calculated to bring about the "political and cultural isolation of Chile") the regime disclaimed all responsibility for the attack, and condemned all acts of terrorism.

But by the beginning of 1977 it became clear that DINA agents had hired right-wing Cuban exiles to assassinate Letelier. In May 1979 an American-born DINA agent called Michael Townley was jailed for his part in the conspiracy. Townley's testimony convicted two Cubans who were given life sentences (of at least 30 years).

In October 1979 the Chilean government refused to extradite to the United States three DINA agents named by Townley as being part of the plot to kill Letelier.

**LIBERATION THEOLOGY AND TERRORISM.** The United States government has made it plain that it regards the Liberation Theology advocated by many Latin-American Roman Catholics as a neo-Marxist philosophy which not only provokes terrorism but is being manipulated by the Soviet Union and its proxies, Cuba and Nicaragua. The American government takes the view that the Roman Catholic Church should remain aloof from secular politics, particularly those which involve violence and terrorism. This view is rejected by West Europe and Latin-American liberals who point out that the Roman Catholic Church in Latin America has a long tradition of political involvement, although usually in support of the status quo. Pope John Paul II has taken the Liberation Theologians to task for their position which he seems to regard as an unacceptable species of Latin-American Marxism likely to damage the Church.

There is no doubt that Liberation Theology involves a radical departure for the Roman Catholic Church in Latin America. The movement grew from the experience of the Church's "worker priests" many of whom came to the conclusion that Latin American societies were so hopelessly corrupt that the only Christian way forward was to struggle for radical political and social change. This case was argued forcibly by theologians such as Paulo Friere, Camillo Torres and Gustavo Guttierez. Guttierez in particular argued that "Only a radical break from the status quo, that is a profound transformation of the private property system . . . would allow for the change to a new society".

To the alarm of Latin America's more repressive right-wing regimes this thinking was endorsed by the Council of Latin-American Bishops at their conference in Medellin, Colombia, in 1968. More than 900 bishops and priests passed a resolution which stated "We cannot condemn an oppressed people when it finds itself obliged to use force to liberate itself . . . under no circumstances should the unjust violence of the oppressors, who maintain this odious system, be compared with the just violence of the oppressed".

This apparent Roman Catholic blessing for "just violence" was denounced all over Latin America (and in Washington) as naked Marxism. But a similar theology has also been voiced by Latin-American Protestant clergy, particularly by Jose Miquez Bonino who argues that until South America shrugs off its cultural and economic dependence on the United States the "new man" will never emerge. Bonino says that future stress must be on "solidarity and creativity over against the individualistic distorted humanity of the present system".

**LIBERATION TIGERS OF TAMIL EELAM**. (The Tamil Tigers). The largest and most aggressive of the Tamil (Hindu) guerrilla/terrorist groups who are fighting for an independent Tamil state at the northern end of the overwhelmingly Buddhist island of Sri Lanka. The Tamil Tigers have been receiving unofficial but powerful support from their co-religionists in the southern Indian province of Tamil Nadu, a fact which has bedevilled relations between India and Sri Lanka. There is a vociferous lobby within Tamil Nadu which believes that India should invade Sri Lanka on the side of the Tamils. The Tamil Tigers are led by V. Prabhakaran who went underground in south India in October 1985 after the Indian government issued deportation orders against him.

Although the war between the Tamil Tigers and the Sri Lankan security forces has produced some appalling incidents of terror and counter-terror, the conflict spilled onto the world stage in May 1986 with the AIR LANKA BOMBING at Katunayaka Airport near Colombo. The Sri Lankan authorities were quick to blame the Tamil Tigers for the attack, although the separatists denied any responsibility. The Sri Lankan authorities believe that the attack was timed to wreck the prospect of Indian-organised peace talks between the Tamil separatists and the Sri Lankan government.

The long-standing hostility between the Hindu Tamils and Buddhist Sinhalese in Sri Lanka flared into guerrilla warfare and terrorism in 1983 when Tamil activists decided their future lay in an independent Tamil state carved out of Sri Lanka. By the end of 1984 the semi-clandestine warfare was exacting a heavy toll as the Tamil Tigers and other groups mounted a series of raids on police stations, post offices, and military outposts, while the Sinhalese-dominated Sri Lankan army struck back against Tamil villages suspected of harbouring terrorists. In November 1984 more than 140 Sinhalese were killed in the village of Mullaittivu, a massacre that was blamed on the Tamil Tigers.

In April 1984 the Tamil Tigers and three other groups – the Tamil Eelam Liberation Organisation (TELO), the Eelam Peoples Revolutionary Liberation Front (EPRLF) and the Eelam Revolutionary Organisation of Students (EROS) – formed the Eelam National Liberation Front (ENLF) to develop a "joint politico-military strategy" in the battle for a Tamil homeland. Since then there has been constant bickering and occasional bloody clashes between the various Tamil groups, out of which the Tamil Tigers have emerged as the most powerful organisation.

In April 1986 President Junius Jayawardene of Sri Lanka declared that terrorist activity would "never succeed" in setting up a Tamil state, and the best that the Tamil activists could hope for was a pardon from the Sri Lankan government. More moderate Tamils have been pressing the government for a measure of "devolved" power similar to that wielded by the individual states within the Indian Union.

**LIBYAN EMBASSY SIEGE, LONDON. (April 17th-24th 1984).** Police siege of the Libyan Embassy (or People's Bureau) in London after shots were fired from the Embassy killing a young policewoman, WPC YVONNE FLETCHER, and injuring 11 Libyans demonstrating against the regime of MUAMMAR QADDAFI. After the shooting the British government formally severed diplomatic links with Libya and advised the 7,000 or so Britons working in the North African state to return home (advice which was largely ignored). The British press reported that American intelligence had picked up signals from Libya instructing the staff in London to fire on the demonstrators, but that the Metropolitan Police had not been warned in time to prevent the casualties.

The day before the shooting, Libyan diplomats had asked the British authorities to ban the anti-Qaddafi demonstration, warning that it was strongly resented and could generate trouble. Their request was refused. The shooting from the Libyan-owned building in St James's Square in the centre of London happened on the morning of April 17th as a group of 70 demonstrators from the Libyan General Students Organisation (LGSO) were shouting anti-Quaddafi slogans from behind police barricades. The burst of automatic gunfire from the first floor of the People's Bureau mortally wounded WPC Fletcher, and injured 11 of the demonstrating students. British police immediately evacuated and sealed off the square and laid siege to the Embassy. The Libyan press reported – quite falsely – that British police had stormed the building, an act it described as a "barbarous outrage".

The siege ended on April 27th 1984 after ten days of negotiation when the Libyan diplomats and others left the building and were driven to the Sunningdale Civil Service College near London Airport where they were "invited" to help the police with their inquiries. They refused,and were flown home to Libya that same day. A police search of the Embassy revealed six handguns and quantities of ammunition which the Libyans claimed had been "planted" by the British authorities. The British government were criticised at home for not taking "firmer"action against the Libyans, but pointed out that action against a foreign embassy is against all international custom, and that reprisals might be taken against the large British population living and working in Libya.

The shootings and siege at St James's Square had been preceded by a flurry of attacks on anti-Qaddafi Libyans living in Britain, and a series of bombings in London and Manchester. Eleven Libyans were arrested after these incidents, and five were deported. Another 20 people were injured when a bomb was detonated on April 20th at London Airport (Heathrow) an act for which the Libyans were blamed. A spokesman for the anti-Qaddafi Libyan Constitutional Union claimed that the student zealots who had taken over the Libyan Embassy (in February 1984) were under "heavy pressure to do something" about the vociferous anti-regime groups in Britain.

## LILLEHAMMER DEBACLE, NORWAY. (July 21st 1973).

A fatal mistake by an Israeli MOSSAD execution squad in the town of Lillehammer in Norway when they shot dead a harmless Moroccan waiter called Ahmed Bouchiki. The Mossad agents had mistaken him for ALI HASSAN SALAMEH who they regarded as the architect of the MUNICH OLYMPICS ATTACK in October 1972. The bungled operation in Lillehammer was a serious embarrassment to the Israeli government of Golda Meir, particularly as six of the Mossad assassins were quickly picked up by the Norwegian police. The agents were tried in February 1974 and five of them were given jail sentences of up to five years for their part in the second-degree murder of Bouchiki. An internal Mossad inquiry into the Lillehammer débâcle established that in their hunt for Salameh the Mossad team had been misled by an Arab informant who not only "fingered" the wrong man, but also tipped off the Norwegian police.

Ahmed Bouchiki was shot to death in a Lillehammer suburb at 22.40 on July 21st 1973 while walking home with his pregnant Norwegian wife. Two Israeli agents – part of a Mossad killing team which had been shadowing him for days – stepped out of a car and pumped 22 rounds from their Beretta handguns into his body. One of the assassins was a woman. Although the two Mossad killers made good their escape, the Norwegian police arrested six members of the "support team"; Sylvia Rafael, Abraham Gehmer, Dan Aerbel, Marianne Gladnikoff, Zwi Sternberg and Michael Dorf.

After a 26-day trial all the Mossad agents with the exception of the communications man Michael Dorf were jailed for their part in the killing of Ahmed Bouchiki. None of them served their full terms.

The trial of the Mossad "hit team" was, of course, an international sensation, and extracted details of the operation which were a painful embarrassment to the Israeli government. The Arab states made much of the killing and the Moroccan government gave the simple waiter a full-scale military funeral. The Arab press deplored his killing at the hands of "imperial terrorists". The Mossad finally caught up with Ali Hassan Salameh in January 1979 in Beirut where he was killed by a car bomb (which also killed an innocent British secretary).

**LITTLEJOHN, KEITH AND KENNETH.** English-born brothers who, when jailed in Ireland on August 3rd 1973 for a raid on the Allied Irish bank in Dublin in 1972, claimed to have been working for British SECRET INTELLIGENCE SERVICE (SIS). After intense press and parliamentary questioning the British government conceded that the Littlejohn brothers had volunteered their services in the struggle against the PROVISIONAL IRISH REPUBLICAN ARMY (PIRA) and had been "put in touch with the appropriate authorities". The Littlejohns (who had set up a fashion boutique in Dublin) were jailed for 20 and 15 years respectively. They were suspected in the Republic of Ireland of being involved in a series of bomb explosions in Dublin (which led to the tightening of the Republic's anti-terror laws). In 1974 the Littlejohn brothers escaped from jail in the Irish Republic, and Kenneth Littlejohn made his way to England where he was arrested in December 1974. He then moved to the centre of a complex extradition case, in the course of which details of in-camera proceedings of 1973 were revealed to the public and press

The massive publicity in Britain and Ireland generated by the Littlejohn brothers discomfited the SIS who ordered an immediate review of their operations in Northern Ireland and the Republic of Ireland, and of their policy of hiring "sub-agents". The Littlejohn affair advanced the argument of MAURICE OLDFIELD, then Deputy Head of SIS, that intelligence gathering in Ireland (north and south) should be left to the SECURITY SERVICE and military intelligence.

**LOD AIRPORT MASSACRE. (May 30th 1972).** Twenty-seven people were killed and 69 injured when three members of the UNITED RED ARMY OF JAPAN (URAJ) opened fire with automatic weapons in the crowded passenger terminal at Lod Airport near Tel Aviv. Many of the dead were Puerto Ricans on a pilgrimage to the Holy Land. One survivor was heard to ask, "What are Japanese doing killing Puerto Ricans in Israel?" Two of the Japanese were killed in the course of the raid, and the third, 23-year-old KOZO OKOMATO, was captured and jailed (and later released in exchange for Israeli prisoners held in the Lebanon).

The attack was carried out by Kozo Okomato, Yasuda Yasuki and Okudeira Takushi who had flown into Lod Airport on an Air France flight from Rome. At around 22.00 on May 30th the young Japanese removed three Czech-made 7.62 machine-guns from their luggage, and opened fire in the crowded terminal. More than 130 shots were fired in the attack killing 24 people outright, and injuring 72 others (three of whom died). Yasuki and Takushi were killed in the exchange of fire with Israeli security, and Okomato was captured to stand trial a few months later. The Israelis believe that the Japanese had been co-opted by BLACK SEPTEMBER at the Badawi Conference held near Tripoli, Lebanon in May 1972, and that the organiser of the attack was GHASSAN KANAFANI, one-time spokesman for the POPULAR FRONT FOR THE LIBERATION OF PALESTINE (PFLP) in Beirut.

**LONGOWAL, HARCHAND SINGH. (1932-1985).** Indian Sikh holy man and President of the Akali Dal political party assassinated by fellow Sikhs in August 1985 at a Sikh temple in Sherpur in the Punjab. Longowal, one of the most influential and statesman-like of the Sikh leaders, was killed by a 0.455-calibre revolver bullet fired by a young man in the 50,000-strong crowd. Longowal was seen by many Sikhs as a "traitor" who had sold out to the Hindu-dominated government of Rajiv Gandhi. In July 1985, a few weeks before his assassination, Longowal had signed a settlement with Prime Minister Rajiv Gandhi giving the go-ahead to elections in the Punjab in exchange for an investigation into Sikh grievances.

Although a moderate who had rejected the idea of setting up a separate Sikh state to be called Khalistan, Longowal had warned Prime Minister INDIRA GANDHI against any military action against the GOLDEN TEMPLE OF AMRITSAR. Mrs. Gandhi ignored Longowal's advice, went ahead with Operation "BLUE STAR", and was assassinated by Sikh extremists in October 1984. The Longowal/Gandhi agreement was regarded as a sell-out by Sikh militants pressing for a separate Sikh state. Two members of the four-man assassination squad were captured, and the police say that the killing was organised by a Sikh called Jarnail Singh who is still at large.

**LORENZ, PETER**. Prominent West German Christian Democratic politician who was kidnapped in February 1975 by a small left-wing organisation known as the Second of June Movement. Lorenz was held for six days and was released unharmed when the West German government released five members of the left-wing terror group ROTE ARMEE FRAKTION (RAF). The terrorists' demands were met when Lorenz was threatened with the same fate as Chief Justice Gunter Von Drenkmann (who had been murdered by the RAF). The five RAF members were released from a West Berlin jail, transported to Frankfurt where a waiting Boeing 707 flew them to Aden in the South Yemen. Only then was Peter Lorenz released.

**LUFTHANSA HIJACKING TO MOGADISHU AIRPORT, SOMALIA. (October 13th-18th 1977)**. The hijacking of a Lufthansa airliner to Mogadishu Airport in Somalia by Arab terrorists. After five days flying around the Mediterranean (during which the aircraft's captain was shot dead) the hijacking was finally resolved at Mogadishu Airport in Somalia on October 18th 1977 when a team from the West German police anti-terrorist unit GRENZSCHUTZGRUPPE-9 (GSG-9) stormed the aircraft and killed most of the hijackers. The West German unit were assisted by two members from the British Army's SPECIAL AIR SERVICE (SAS).

The hijacking began at 11.30 on Thursday 13th October when a Lufthansa Boeing 737 en route from Majorca to Frankfurt with 86 passengers and five crew aboard was hijacked by four young Palestinian terrorists led by ZOHAIR YOUSIF AKACHE. The others were Wabil Harb, Hind Alameh and Suhaila Sayeh. The terrorists were armed with two 9mm hand-guns, a large quantity of ammunition, six home-made hand-grenades, and about 60lbs of plastic explosive, all of which had been smuggled past the Spanish customs at Palma Airport. The passengers and crew of the jet were held hostage for five days and flown from Majorca to Rome, Cyprus, Bahrain, Dubai, Aden and finally Somalia. In return for the lives of the passengers, and that of kidnapped industrialist HANNS-MARTIN SCHLEYER, the hijackers demanded ransom of $15 million and the release of the 10 ROTE ARMEE FRAKTION (RAF) terrorists held in West German jails, plus two Palestinians known as "Mahdi" and "Hussein" being held in Turkey. At Aden the volatile terrorist leader shot and killed JURGEN SCHUMANN, captain of the *Landshut*.

The incident came to an end at Mogadishu Airport at 02.07 on October 18th when a 26-man police squad from GSG-9, which had been shadowing the captive airliner around the Mediterranean for days, stormed the jet, killed Akache, Harb and Alameh, and released the passengers and crew. The GSG-9 team was commanded by ULRICH WEGENER, and assisted by two members of the SAS (Major ALASTAIR MORRISON and Sergeant Barry Davies). The success of the operation (called "MAGIC FIRE") owed much to the British-designed, magnesium-based "flash/bang" stun-grenades which blinded the terrorists for a crucial six seconds while the Germans stormed the aircraft. The only Palestinian to survive the GSG-9 attack was Suhaila Sayeh.

On hearing of the failure of the hijack ANDREAS BAADER, GUDRUN ENSSLIN, and JAN-CARL RASPE, being held in German federal prison committed suicide. Another RAF terrorist Irmgard Moller was found with stab wounds to the chest, but they were superficial and she recovered.

**LUFTHANSA HIJACKING TO TRIPOLI, LIBYA. (October 29th-30th 1972).** One of the most mysterious hijackings in recent history when a Lufthansa Boeing en route from Beirut to Munich was taken over by a group of Arab gunmen at 06.33 on October 29th 1972 and forced to fly to Zagreb in Yugoslavia. The terrorists demanded the immediate release of the three BLACK SEPTEMBER gunmen who had survived the MUNICH OLYMPICS ATTACK. At 15.30 on the same day the three Arab terrorists were flown to the hijacked Boeing and then to Libya in the early hours of October 30th 1972. After refuelling the Lufthansa jet flew straight back to West Germany. So flawless was the operation that some commentators have argued that the hijacking was pre-arranged by the West Germans and the Palestinians. The Palestinians got their men back, and the West Germans were rid of a potential focus of terrorist trouble.

**LUQA AIRPORT RAID**. See EGYPTAIR HIJACKING TO LUQA AIRPORT, MALTA.

# M

**M-19 (COLOMBIA).** Left-wing Colombian guerrilla/terrorist group led by LUIS OTERO. The M-19 are most notorious for their takeover of the BOGOTA PALACE OF JUSTICE on November 13th-14th 1985 in which more than 100 people were killed. All 24 of the M-19 gunmen, including their leader Luis Otero, died when the Colombian army stormed the building.

**M-62 BOMBING, YORKSHIRE, ENGLAND. (February 14th 1974).** The bombing of a coach filled with off-duty soldiers and their families which killed 12 people, two of them children. A 25-year-old Irishwoman JUDITH WARD was later tried and convicted for the 12 murders. The 50lb bomb planted in the coach's luggage hold blew up shortly after midnight on February 14th as it was travelling on the M-62 motorway between Manchester and Leeds. Twelve of the 56 passengers were killed including four from one family; 23-year-old Corporal Houghton of the Royal Regiment of Fusiliers, his wife Linda, and their children Robert (5) and Lee (2). Two days after the explosion a group calling itself Saor Eire (Free Ireland) claimed responsibility for the attack. On February 19th Judith Ward was charged with the murders at West Riding magistrates court. She was sentenced to life imprisonment on November 4th 1974.

**MA'ALOT MASSACRE, ISRAEL. (May 15th 1974).** A terrorist attack on a school in the northern Israeli town of Ma'alot in which 22 Israeli schoolchildren died. Three Arab gunmen from the DEMOCRATIC FRONT FOR THE LIBERATION OF PALESTINE (DFLP) took over a secondary school filled with 100 children and demanded the release of 26 Arab prisoners. Most of the children who were killed died when troops from the Israeli SAYARET MATKAL tried to rescue them. As the operation was personally supervised by Israel's Defence Minister Moshe Dayan, his handling of the incident was bitterly criticised by the grief-stricken parents of the dead and injured children.

The terrorists took over the school on May 15th (Israel's Independence Day) after killing two Arab women and an Israeli family of three. Four teachers and 100 children were in the school at the time. The terrorists released two of the teachers and some of the children to carry their demands to the Israeli government. The terrorists warned that unless 26 Arab prisoners were released from Israeli jails, the school and its occupants would be blown up. The Israelis tried to negotiate with the DFLP men (with the help of the French and Rumanian ambassadors) but eventually ordered the Sayaret Matkal anti-terrorist squad to storm the building. In the course of the assault all three terrorists were shot dead, but not before 22 of the hostage children were killed and more than 60 injured.

The bitter response of the Israeli public to the Ma'alot killings shook the government of Golda Meir and opened splits between Defence Minister Moshe Dayan and Chief of Staff Mordechai Gur. Dayan had been opposed to any negotiation with the DFLP terrorists and had wanted to mount the rescue operation immediately. The Israeli cabinet had overruled him and tried to negotiate their way out of the crisis with the help of the French and Rumanian ambassadors.

**McALISKEY, BERNADETTE (born 1947).** Also known as Bernadette Devlin. Influential left-wing Irish Republican, and founder-member of the radical IRISH REPUBLICAN SOCIALIST PARTY (IRSP). A leading member of the Northern Ireland Civil Rights Association (NICRA) in the late 1960s, she was the youngest woman ever elected to the British Parliament when she won South Derry in April 1969 at the age of 21. As Bernadette Devlin she took an active part in the "Battle of the Bogside" in Londonderry in August 1969 for which she was jailed in December 1969. She married schoolteacher and fellow Republican Michael McAliskey in April 1973. In 1974 she helped found the IRSP whose military arm, the IRISH NATIONAL LIBERATION ARMY (INLA) became involved in a lethal feud with the OFFICIAL IRA. On 16th February 1981 McAliskey and her husband were shot and seriously wounded by Protestant gunmen at their home in Derrylaughan near Coal Island. Prompt action by a British Army patrol saved their lives. Attempts to resume her political career as an MP in the Dail (the Parliament of the Irish Republic) have, so far, failed.

**McKEAGUE, JOHN. (1930-1982).** Leading Belfast Protestant politician, and one of the founders of the Shankhill Defence Association, shot dead by the IRISII NATIONAL LIBERATION ARMY (INLA) at his shop in Belfast in January 1982. McKeague was widely believed to have been a founder of the illegal RED HAND COMMANDOS although he always denied any connection with that organisation. In 1969 he was cleared of explosives charges, but jailed for unlawful assembly. In the 1970s McKeague grew disillusioned with the United Kingdom and became a powerful advocate of an independent Ulster. In 1977 McKeague was appointed official spokesman of the Ulster Independence Association.

**McKINLEY, WILLIAM. (1843-1901).** Twenty-fourth President of the United States assassinated at the start of his second term in Buffalo, New York on September 14th 1901. A Republican of Scotch-Irish descent, McKinley was on a visit to the Pan-American Exposition in Buffalo when he was shot to death by a Polish-born anarchist called LEON CZOLGOSZ. In the wake of McKinley's assassination the US Congress passed a law in 1903 attempting to ban European anarchists from entering the USA.

**MacSTIOFAIN, SEAN (born 1928).** Chief of Staff of the PROVISIONAL IRISH REPUBLICAN ARMY (PIRA) 1970-1972, and once described as "the only real terrorist" which the post-war Irish conflict produced. Born in London as John Stephenson, MacStiofain served with the Royal Air Force and joined the IRA in the early 1950s. In 1953 MacStiofain and CATHAL GOULDING were jailed for eight years for stealing rifles and machine-guns from an armoury in England. Released in 1959 he moved to Dublin, became fluent in Irish Gaelic, and immersed himself in Republican and IRA affairs. When the IRA split along right-wing/ left-wing lines in 1972 into the PIRA and the OFFICIAL IRISH REPUBLICAN ARMY (OIRA) MacStiofain helped to build PIRA into a formidable organisation. He was arrested in 1972 in the Irish Republic, jailed as a member of the (illegal) IRA, and went on 57-day hunger strike which he ended in January 1973. In 1981 MacStiofain quit PIRA's political affiliate Provisional Sinn Fein when the party's "ard-fheis" (annual conference) abandoned the policy of a four-province Federal Ireland which PIRA had long supported.

**McWHIRTER, ROSS. (1925-1975).** British right-wing author, journalist, and television personality assassinated by the PROVISIONAL IRISH REPUBLICAN ARMY (PIRA) in London on November 27th 1975. McWhirter had antagonised PIRA by setting up an appeal to raise $70,000 to be used as a reward fund for information leading to the conviction of terrorists. McWhirter and his twin brother Norris were founders and co-authors of the famous *Guinness Book of Records*. At the press conference on November 4th 1975 to announce the reward fund, McWhirter agreed that he might be setting himself up as a target for terrorists. Three weeks later he was shot to death by two PIRA gunmen on the doorstep of his home in Enfield, North London. Following the assassination, McWhirter's brother established the Ross McWhirter Freedom Foundation, one of whose sponsors is Margaret Thatcher. British police think that one of McWhirter's assailants was Michael Wilson, captured following the BALCOMBE STREET SIEGE.

**MAFART, ALAIN**. French major and agent of the DIRECTION GENERALE DE LA SECURITE EXTERIEUR (DGSE) involved in the *RAINBOW WARRIOR* ATTACK in Auckland Harbour, New Zealand in July 1985. After the bombing Mafart and his DGSE colleague DOMINIQUE PRIEUR were quickly picked up by the New Zealand police, tried, and convicted for the manslaughter of the ship's photographer FERNANDO PEREIRA. Mafart, 35, was a senior French agent and one-time Deputy Head of the French Navy's underwater combat centre at Aspretto in Corsica who had worked on DGSE clandestine operations in Chad and Lebanon. On November 22nd 1985 Mafart and Prieur were sentenced to 10 years in prison.

**"MAGIC FIRE", OPERATION**. Military code name for the highly successful West German police operation which ended the LUFTHANSA HIJACKING TO MOGADISHU AIRPORT, SOMALIA in October 1977.

**MAGSASAY, RAMON. (1907-1957)**. Philippino politician and statesman who defeated the Communist-led HUKBALAHAP (HUK) insurgency of the early 1950s. The son of a Malay artisan, and a schoolteacher by profession, Magsasay was a wartime guerrilla leader. Appointed Secretary of National Defence in 1950, Magsasay reorganised the unpopular Philippines army, dismissed corrupt and incompetent officers, and set up specially-trained counter-insurgency teams while at the same time improving the conditions of the Philippine peasants. Politically outflanked by Magsasay's reforms the HUK insurgency was virtually over by 1953, and HUK leader LUIS TAROC surrendered in 1954. Magsasay was later elected as President of the Philippines, remained a supporter of US policy in the area, and ensured that the Philippines became a member of the South East Asia Treaty Organisation (SEATO).

**MAHESWARAM, UMA**. Leader of the People's Liberation Organisation of Tamil Eelam (PLOTE), one of the guerrilla/terrorist groups fighting in Sri Lanka to set up a separate Tamil (i.e. Hindu) state at the northern end of the Buddhist-dominated island.

**MAJALLAT AL IKHWAN AL MUSLIMIN**. (The Muslim Brotherhood). Fundamentalist Islamic organisation with a long tradition of political and sectarian violence. Well-organised, well-funded, puritanical, and contemptuous of Western values, the Muslim Brotherhood remains a potent ideological/religious force in the Islamic world. The organisation was founded in Egypt in 1925 by HASAN AL BANNAH, and in 1940 set up a "secret apparatus" or "special order" of armed activists. In 1948, the Muslim Brotherhood was banned in Egypt and responded by killing Prime Minister Nokrashi Pasha. Hassan al Bannah was himself killed by Egyptian police in February 1949. After three years, the Brotherhood were legalised, and then proscribed for a second time. When the Muslim Brotherhood attempted (but failed) to assassinate the Egyptian leader Gamel Abdul Nasser six of their members were hanged and the movement crushed for 20 years. The Muslim Brotherhood was revived in the late 1960s and early 1970s, now has members all over the Islamic world, and is particularly strong in Egypt, Iran, Afghanistan and Lebanon.

**MALAYAN RACES LIBERATION ARMY (MRLA)**. The mainly Chinese guerrilla and terrorist force which fought the British and Malayan authorities during the Malaya Emergency between 1950 and 1960. Led by CHIN PENG, Secretary-General of the Malayan Communist Party, the MRLA numbered no more than 10,000, and often considerably less. Heavily outnumbered by British and Malayan government forces, the MRLA finally conceded defeat in 1960 (although a few hundred ex-MRLA members still inhabit the Malayan forests).

**MALCOLM X. (1925-1965)**. Also known as Al Hajj Malik al-Shabazz. Black American political leader and founder of the ORGANIZATION OF AFRO-AMERICAN UNITY (OAAU) who was assassinated in New York in February 1965. Born Malcolm Little in Omaha, the son of a Baptist preacher, Malcolm X moved to New York as a young man and drifted into a life of petty crime and drug addiction. Sentenced to 10 years in jail in 1946, like many black convicts he was converted to Islam by the NATION OF ISLAM organisation of ELIJAH MUHAMMAD. Malcolm X worked for the Nation of Islam for many years, became a powerful figure in the organisation, and was seen as the heir-apparent to Muhammad. But after growing differences with the Nation of Islam, Malcolm X left in 1963 and founded his own Muslim group, the OAAU. He was shot to death by three (black) gunmen at a public meeting in the Auboadon Ballroom in Harlem on the evening of February 21st 1965. Elijah Muhammad and the Nation of Islam were widely blamed for the death of Malcolm X, although their complicity in his murder was never proved.

**MALIK, MICHAEL ABDUL. (1930-1975).** Also known as Michael X. Self-styled Black Power leader and dubious convert to Islam who was hanged for murder in Trinidad in 1975. Born Michael De Freitas in Port of Spain, Trinidad, he emigrated to England in the late 1950s where he led a life of crime before his "conversion" to Islam and emergence as a British Black Power leader. In 1967 he was jailed under the Race Relations Act for inciting blacks to violence against whites, and after a police investigation into his finances, fled back to Trinidad in 1971. After a series of murders in Trinidad in 1972 (including that of 27-year-old Englishwoman Gale Benson) Malik was arrested in Guyana, extradited to Trinidad, tried, and sentenced to death. Despite repeated appeals to the higher courts (including the Privy Council in London) Malik was hanged at Port of Spain, Trinidad, in May 1975.

**MANDELA, NELSON ROLIHLALA. (Born 1918).** Charismatic black South African politician, and leading member of the AFRICAN NATIONAL CONGRESS (ANC) who has been in prison since 1962. Mandela is now an internationally recognised symbol of black resistance to South Africa's apartheid regime. The South African government have repeatedly offered Mandela his freedom if he will renounce violent revolution, but Mandela has always refused and remains a prisoner in Pollsmoor jail near Cape Town. All efforts to secure his unconditional release have, so far, failed.

The son of the Chief of the Tembu tribe, Mandela became involved in African politics in the 1940s, joined the ANC in 1943, studied law at Witwatersraand University, and set up a legal practice in Johannesburg in 1952 along with OLIVER TAMBO (now Chairman of the ANC). Mandela was unsuccessfully prosecuted for treason in 1956, then arrested when the government banned the ANC following the SHARPEVILLE MASSACRE of 1960. In 1961 Mandela was appointed secretary of the All-African National Action Council (AANAC) and became a founder-member of UMKONTO WE SIZWE (Spear of the Nation), the military arm of the ANC. In 1962 Mandela was arrested and sentenced to five years in jail for travelling abroad without permission, and inciting blacks to strike against the white regime. He was charged again in October 1963 with plotting treason and the overthrow of the South African state.

At his trial Mandela admitted to being both a member of the ANC and a founder of Umkonto We Sizwe. He told the court that "50 years of non-violence had brought the African people nothing but more and more repressive legislation and fewer and fewer rights". Mandela claimed that Umkonto had considered four options – sabotage, guerrilla warfare, terrorism, and open revolution – and had opted for sabotage as the least destructive. The strategy of the ANC he said was to wage economic war against South Africa's industry and scare foreign capital out of the country. The ANC, he claimed " . . . did not want an inter-racial war, and tried to avoid it to the last". Mandela assured the court that the ANC was not a Communist front although there had been "close co-operation" between the ANC and the South African Communist Party. He was sentenced to life imprisonment along with eight other members of the ANC.

In recent years Mandela has received a number of awards for his stance against apartheid; the Jawahardal Nehru Award (1979), the Bruno Kreisky Prize for Human Rights (1981), the Freedom of the City of Glasgow (1981), Honorary Citizenship of Rome (1983), the Simon Bolivar International Prize (1983). He has also been awarded honorary degrees from the National University of Lesotho (1979) and the City College of New York (1983).

**MANO BLANCA (MANO).** (The White Hand). A right-wing terrorist group which operated in Guatamala in the late 1960s and early 1970s. Comprised mainly of renegade policemen and soldiers, MANO specialised in killing left-wingers (real or imaginary) and sending parts of their victims' bodies to relatives.

**MAQUELA MASSACRE, ANGOLA. (February 1976).** Killings at Maquela in Angola of 13 British mercenaries by their own officers and NCOs led by an ex-British Army paratrooper called COSTAS GEORGIOU. All the men were employed by the armed forces of Holden Roberto to fight the Cuban-assisted army of Antonio Agostino Neto. The 13 Britons were "executed" at Maquela for allegedly ambushing their own comrades. The man in charge of the firing party, Sergeant Sammy Copeland, was later killed by another group of British mercenaries led by Peter McAleese. Three months after the killings, Georgiou and other members of the British mercenary force were captured and put on trial in Luanda. Four of the mercenaries – Costas Georgiou, Andrew McKenzie, Derek Barker and Daniel Gearhart (an American) – were sentenced to death and executed by firing squad on July 10th 1976.

**MARCUSE, HERBERT. (1898-1979).** Influential German-born philosopher of the Libertarian Marxist school, much admired and much quoted by the radical and revolutionary students of the USA and Western Europe in the late 1960s. In *One Dimensional Man* Marcuse advanced the theory that the working class of the West were being subtly repressed by affluence while their critical faculties were being suspended, and their revolutionary potential undermined. Marcuse's analysis appealed greatly to the radical students of the time, whose polemic Marcuse grew to dislike, and whose movement he described as "the pubertarian struggle". Born in Berlin of Jewish parents, Marcuse became a Marxist in the 1920s, fled from the Nazis to the USA in the 1930s and published his important study of Hegel, *Reason and Revolution*, in 1941. After some years in the US State Department, Marcuse held professorships at Brandeis University in Massachussets (1953-1965) and the University of California at San Diego (1966-1979).

**MARIGHELLA, CARLOS. (1912-1969).** Brazilian terrorist, revolutionary theorist, and leader of the ACAO LIBERTADORA NACIONAL (ALN), who was killed by the Brazilian police in November 1969. A one-time prominent member of the Brazilian Communist Party, Marighella's hard-line "violence before politics" theories found a wide audience among Latin-American terrorist groups in the late 1960s and early 1970s. Unusually, Marighella's terrorist career began when he was a middle-aged man in his 50s. His terrorist handbook *MINIMANUAL OF THE URBAN GUERRILLA* was translated into a number of languages, and banned in many countries. Marighella's central conviction was that the revolution (and the future) belonged not to tract-writers and politicians, but to people hardened by armed struggle. His most substantial work was *For the Liberation of Brazil*, which was translated into English and published in 1971. Marighella's career as an active terrorist was short; the ALN began their campaign in 1968 and Marighella was killed in a police ambush near São Paulo in November 1969. But his reputation as a theorist of guerrilla warfare and urban terrorism grew strongly after his death.

**MARITA ANNE AFFAIR. (September 29th 1984).** The seizure by the Irish authorities of a consignment of firearms and ammunition from the USA bound for the PROVISIONAL IRISH REPUBLICAN ARMY (PIRA). The consignment consisted of 163 firearms, 71,000 rounds of ammunition, and 11 bulletproof vests, and had been shipped across the Atlantic in a Boston-registered ship *Valhalla* and transferred to the *Marita Anne* off the Irish coast. In April 1986 six members of a Boston criminal gang led by Irish-American Joseph Murray were charged with illegally shipping the firearms (and also importing 31 tonnes of cannabis into the USA). The American authorities claimed that the Murray gang had assembled the arms shipment over six months in 1984, usually buying the weapons and ammunition by post from American gun dealers. American customs officers said that Murray ran his gang like a "paramilitary organisation" of which everyone in the Charlestown area of Boston was afraid. The gang are suspected of being involved in other arms shipments to the PIRA.

**MARKOV, GEORGI. (1930-1978).** Dissident Bulgarian author, playwright and broadcaster assassinated in London by, it is believed, the Bulgarian secret service and/or the Soviet KOMITET GOSUDARSTVENNOI BEZOPASTNOSTI (KGB). Markov's assassin used the point of an umbrella to inject a miniscule pellet of poison into the Bulgarian's thigh. Markov was stabbed in a London street on Thursday September 7th 1978 and died on Monday 11th September after four days of fever and delirium. A post-mortem examination revealed a metal ball lodged in the dead man's thigh, 1.52 millimetres in diameter made from platinum and irridium and containing a lethal poison called ricin. Two tiny holes in the metal were sealed with wax which was melted by Markov's body heat, releasing the ricin into his system. British authorities believe that the the ricin was mixed with a bacteria to create gangrene and increase the poison's potency. Markov's death became famous as the UMBRELLA MURDER. Markov defected from Bulgaria in the early 1970s and worked for the Bulgarian language service of the British Broadcasting Corporation (BBC), and for the Munich-based Radio Free Europe through which he attacked the Bulgarian regime. Markov's last play before he fled Bulgaria was called *The Assassin.*

**"MARTINEZ, CARLOS".** Also "Carlos the Jackal". See SANCHEZ, RAMIREZ ILLICH.

**MARTYR MAHMUD, CAPTAIN.** Nom de guerre of ZOHAIR YOUSIF AKACHE, leader of the Arab terrorists involved in the LUFTHANSA HIJACKING TO MOGADISHU AIRPORT, SOMALIA.

**MARTYR'S MAUSOLEUM BOMBING, RANGOON, BURMA. (October 9th 1983).** A bombing attack by North Korean terrorists on a South Korean delegation to Burma led by President Chun. Chun survived the attack, but five of his cabinet and 15 other people were killed in the blast. A few days later the Burmese tracked down three North Korean suspects, one of whom killed himself. The bombers admitted to being North Korean army officers, a fact which prompted Burma to abandon its neutrality and sever all diplomatic relations with North Korea. In the wake of the Rangoon bombing Japan announced economic and diplomatic sanctions against North Korea.

The bombing happened as the South Korean delegation were paying a visit to the Martyr's Mausoleum on October 9th 1983 to lay a wreathe to Burmese dead. The bomb was exploded before President Chun arrived, but 16 South Koreans were killed and 13 injured. (Burmese casualties were four dead and 32 injured.) The South Koreans who died included Lee Bum Suk, Foreign Minister, Kim Jae Ik, economic adviser to the President, Suh Suk Joon, Deputy Prime Minister, Suh Sung Chul, Minister of Energy and Resources and Kim Dong Whie, Minister of Industry and Commerce. The three terrorists were speedily tracked down by Burmese security, but not before one killed himself with a hand-grenade. The other two were Captain Kang Min Chul and Major Zin Mo of the North Korean Army. At their trial in Rangoon in December 1983 it emerged that the men had entered Burma by ship, stayed in the house of a North Korean diplomat, and planted the bomb at the Martyr's Mausoleum on October 8th. The men were working to Major-General Kang Chang of the North Korean Army. Both were convicted of the murders and sentenced to death.

On November 4th 1983 the Burmese government announced it was breaking off all diplomatic ties with North Korea and gave North Korean diplomats 48 hours to leave Rangoon. The diplomatic move was a departure from Burma's cherished policy of strict neutrality between Communist and Western powers, and was interpreted as a shift to the West. At the same time the isolation of North Korea was intensified.

**MASELHAD, MOHAMMED.** Libyan-born leader of the eight BLACK SEPTEMBER terrorists who mounted the MUNICH OLYMPICS ATTACK in September 1972.

**MASHAD, YAHYA EL.** Egyptian-born nuclear scientist assassinated in Paris on June 14th 1980 possibly by the Israeli MOSSAD or by Syrian agents spying on Iraqi secrets. Mashad was a senior member of the project to build two nuclear reactors at Tammuz near Baghdad, and his death was a blow to the Iraqi nuclear programme as it discouraged other nuclear physicists from working on the project. A year previously, in April 1979, two nuclear reactor-cores bound for Iraq were blown up in a hangar near the French city of Toulon.

A brilliant scientist with degrees from both Russian and American universities, Mashad had been in France to check materials and equipment due to be delivered to Baghdad. After spending a week at various French nuclear-industry centres, Mashad returned to the Hotel Meridien in Paris on June 13th. On the morning of June 14th Mashad was found battered to death in his room. Although the French police were never able to solve the crime they suspect Mashad may have surprised an intruder going through his papers. A young French prostitute, who may have been hired to keep Mashad away from his room for a few hours, was killed shortly afterwards by a hit-and-run driver who was never found. Although it has been suggested that Mashad was killed by Israeli agents to deter other European and Arab scientists from helping Iraq to fulfil its nuclear ambitions, the Israelis have always denied any part in the Egyptian's death. And Egyptian sources have suggested that the killing may have been the work of Soviet-backed Syrians anxious to find out just how far Iraq's nuclear programme had developed. A year after Mashad's death, in June 1981, the TAMMUZ NUCLEAR REACTORS were destroyed by Israeli aircraft.

**MASSU, JACQUES (born 1908).** French general and commander of the élite 10th Parachute Division of the French Army between January 1957 and January 1960 during the Algerian War of Independence. A veteran of World War II, the war in Indo-China and the Suez landings of 1956, Massu was a brilliant, but extremely ruthless counter-terrorist commander. Although General Massu and his subordinates were widely criticised for using torture against Algerian prisoners, they were credited with "winning" the BATTLE OF ALGIERS in early 1957 and reasserting French rule in the city. Massu was recalled to France in disgrace in January 1960 after criticising General de Gaulle's Algerian policy to a West German newspaper. In 1961 Massu was approached by French officers who were planning a putsch against General de Gaulle and invited to lead the movement. Massu refused.

**MAU MAU**. African terrorist organisation which operated in Kenya against the British colonial regime in the struggle for independence between 1953 and 1960. With its roots in the Kikuyu Association (founded in 1921) Mau Mau was drawn from the powerful Kikuyu tribe and was set up in the late 1940s. The organisation acted as a militant/radical wing of the Kikuyu Central Association (KCA) led by JOMO KENYATTA (later President of Kenya) and were strongest in the Aberdare and Mount Kenya areas.

The Mau Mau campaign began in earnest in September 1952, and by 1953 the organisation had killed 18 Europeans, 11 Asians, and 613 Kikuyu but also lost 4,000 dead and captured. Despite their "secret society" nature and their use of witchcraft and terror, Mau Mau proved very susceptible to infiltration by "pseudo" gangs (i.e. terrorists who had been "turned" by the British). The Kenyan police/army strategy was devised by Sir Percy Sillitoe, then head of the British SECURITY SERVICE who was co-opted to help the Kenya Government in November 1952. The seven-year-long Kenya "emergency" was ended on January 12th 1960. In the course of it 78,000 civilians were detained, and 1858 killed (1800 of them Africans). Police and army casualties amounted to 1167 killed and wounded.

**MAZE PRISON HUNGER-STRIKES, NORTHERN IRELAND. (March 1st-August 20th 1981)**. A hunger-strike by convicted terrorists in the Maze Prison near Belfast in which 10 prisoners died. The men who died were from the PROVISIONAL IRISH REPUBLICAN ARMY (PIRA) and the IRISH NATIONAL LIBERATION ARMY (INLA). While the British government refused to concede to the hunger-strikers' demands for political category status, the deaths generated an enormous amount of embarrassing publicity for the British authorities, and fresh support for the Republican cause. The first PIRA man to fast to death was ROBERT ("BOBBY") SANDS who was elected to the British Parliament in the course of his hunger-strike.

The six PIRA men who died were: Robert Sands (27), died May 5th 1981; Frances Hughes (25), died May 12th 1981; Raymond McCreesh (24), died May 21st 1981; Martin Hurson (24), died July 13th 1981; Kieran Doherty (25), died August 2nd 1981; Thomas McElwee (23), died August 8th 1981. The four INLA men who died were: Patrick O'Hara (26), died May 21st 1981; Joseph McDonnell (30), died July 8th 1981; Kevin Lynch (25), died August 1st 1981; Michael Devine (27), died August 20th 1981. Most died around the 60th day of their fast (although Kieran Doherty of the PIRA survived for 73 days).

Despite a sharp increase in violence both north and south of the Irish border the British government refused to back down. The Northern Ireland Minister, Humphrey Atkins, said; "Our position is clear. We do not want any prisoners to die. But if those still on hunger-strike persist, they will not be forcibly fed. If they die, it will be from their own choice." But the British government did try to blunt the pro-Republican publicity by circularising their embassies and consulates abroad with dossiers outlining the hunger-strikers' terrorist activities. The British counter propaganda was largely futile.

**MBOYA, TOM. (1930-1969).** Kenyan politician and cabinet minister assassinated in Nairobi in July 1969. As Mboyo was leader of the Luo tribe and his assailant a Kikuyu, his murder threatened Kenya with inter-tribal war. Only the statesmanlike intervention of Kenya's President JOMO KENYATTA, who had been jailed by the British for leading the MAU MAU terrorists, saved Kenya from disaster. Mboyo's death deprived Kenya of one of her most able politicians. Educated at Roman Catholic mission schools, and at Ruskin College, Oxford, Mboya became a trade union organiser, and was Kenya's first Minister of Labour. Later he became Minister of Justice, and then Minister of Economic Planning.

**MEDIA AND TERRORISM.** One of the most contentious and bitterly argued issues raised by international terrorism is its relationship with the press and broadcast media. Western governments (particularly those of Britain and the USA) have argued that the mass media coverage of protracted terrorist incidents (such as the TRANSWORLD AIRLINES HIJACKING TO BEIRUT in June 1985 or the *ACHILLE LAURO* HIJACKING in November 1985) is playing into the hands of terrorists. Media spokesmen accept the logic of the argument, but insist that terrorism is world news which cannot be downplayed or ignored, and that suppressing freedom of speech would be an even greater danger to the Western democracies than the one posed by terrorism.

In May 1986 the American network NBC irritated the US government by screening an interview with ABU ABBAS who the American authorities believe was behind the *ACHILLE LAURO* hijacking. The network were accused by ROBERT OAKLEY of the US State Department of being an "accomplice" to terrorism by giving air time to Abbas, and he called the arrangement between the Palestinian leader and NBC "reprehensible".

There is no doubt that the international media plays a central role in the thinking and planning of most terrorist groups, and that many terrorist attacks are carried out in order to attract the attention of the world to a particular cause. Some historians of terrorism, notably Walter Laqueur, have argued that terrorism moved out of the countryside and into the cities in the late 1960s and early 1970s in order to be closer to the sources of the press and broadcasting.

The commentator Richard Clutterbuck has argued that television is the most powerful weapon in the terrorist's arsenal. "It magnifies the action of the terrorists," Clutterbuck writes "...brings their violence ... into the home of almost every citizen in the land...we can and do identify with the hostages whose photographs we see in the press and whose tearful families talk to us from the screen in our own homes ... It is all to easy to imagine these families being our own...". Clutterbuck contends that the relentless outpouring of such images often leads democratic governments "...to give way to terrorists, multilaterally or unilaterally...".

The *Columbia Journalism Review* has succinctly described the dilemma of the democracies: "Of all the foundations of a free democratic society, that most basic – the freedom to know, to be informed – has guaranteed that such knowledge and such information can be fashioned by the fanatic through the conduit of the media eye. To close that eye would erode a fundamental right, would close an open society. Yet not to do so assures future massacres, further terrorist-events with little hope of audience saturation."

But as well as providing a platform for the terrorists, the media can become so enmeshed in the confrontation between terrorists and the authorities that they are a positive obstruction and danger. During the LUFTHANSA HIJACKING TO MOGADISHU

AIRPORT, SOMALIA, for example, radio broadcasts revealing that the captain of the hijacked aircraft had managed to pass on information to the authorities led to the captain being killed. The media trying to make direct contact with hostage-takers (usually by telephone) can tie up lines of communication that are badly needed by hostage negotiators. The kind of powerful floodlights used by television crews can endanger police marksmen trying to conceal themselves.

On the other hand, it was radio reports that the London police had brought in the SPECIAL AIR SERVICE (SAS) which brought an end to the BALCOMBE STREET SIEGE in December 1975. The world-wide coverage of the SAS rescue operation at the IRANIAN EMBASSY SIEGE in 1980 boosted the regiment's reputation and did the government of Margaret Thatcher no harm. President Reagan's massively-publicised counter-terrorist raids against Libya in April 1986 generated enormous political support in the USA, and have been described as America's favourite television; a small war far away which cannot be lost.

What has been described as the "symbiotic relationship" between terrorism and the world's media has been growing increasingly powerful since the late 19th century when the anarchists of France, Italy and the USA formulated the idea of "propaganda of the deed". Their theory (and practice) was based on the knowledge that acts of violent terrorism must attract the attention of the world's rapidly-growing press, thus airing the grievances of the terrorists. Interestingly, the notion of exploiting the mass media for political purposes coincided with the advent of the linotype printing machine which proliferated newspapers and magazines throughout the world. Similarly, the upsurge of modern terrorism has coincided with the advent of satellite television coverage, the hand-held "minicam" (portable TV camera), and a world-wide network of telephone, telex, and now facsimile transmission machines.

**MEIBION GLYNDWR.** (The Sons of Glendower). Welsh nationalist extremists who have specialised in arson attacks on English-owned holiday cottages in rural Wales. Owen Glendower was a 15th-century Welsh leader who led the resistance to English rule of Wales. Since the arson attacks began in 1979 more than 100 cottages and houses have been burned and 19 people have been convicted for 14 of the attacks. In recent years the attacks have been more sophisticated. Welsh police believe that the attacks are not the result of a co-ordinated campaign but the work of individuals who have little or nothing to do with one another. Responsibilty for some of the arson attacks has been claimed by a group calling itself Cadwyr Cymru (The Defenders of Wales).

**MEINHOF, ULRIKE (1934-1976).** West German terrorist leader and one of the eponymous members of the BAADER-MEINHOF GANG, also known as the ROTE ARMEE FRAKTION (RAF). After a brief but well-publicised career as a terrorist leader, Meinhof hanged herself in her cell at the top-security Stammheim Prison on 9th May 1976.

Born in Lower Saxony but orphaned at an early age, Meinhof was brought up by the Marxist historian Professor Renate Reimeck. A journalist by profession, Meinhof edited the left-wing magazine *Konkret* from 1960 to 1964. She was converted to the use of violence after an attempt on the life of German student leader Rudi Dutschke in April 1968. Reputedly trained by Palestinian guerrillas, Meinhof organised a number of bomb attacks on the US Army in West Germany, and at one stage plotted the kidnap of Chancellor Willy Brandt. Her most spectacular armed raid was the one on the West Berlin prison library on May 14th 1970 which freed fellow terrorist ANDREAS BAADER. Thereafter the West German press dubbed the group the Baader-Meinhof Gang, although they called themselves the Rote Armee Fraktion (RAF). After one of the longest and most intensive police hunts in West German history, Meinhof was captured in Hanover on June 16th 1972.

In September 1974 Meinhof was sentenced by a West Berlin court to eight years in prison for the raid which freed Baader. She was brought to trial again in May 1975 along with Baader, GUDRUN ENSSLIN, and JAN-CARLE RASPE. The group were convicted of five murders, 54 attempted murders, and membership of a criminal organisation. On May 9th 1976, almost a year into the trial, Meinhof killed herself in her cell at Stammheim Prison. She was 41 when she died.

**MHATRE, RAVINDRA. (1936-1984).** Assistant Commissioner at the Indian High Commission in Birmingham, England, assassinated in February 1984 by members of the JAMMU KASHMIR LIBERATION FRONT (JKLF). Ravindra was abducted in a Birmingham street, and his body was found a few days later in the nearby countryside. Two members of the JKLF were later tried and convicted of his murder. On September 6th 1985 six members of the JKLF were arrested by British police under the Prevention of

Terrorism Act. They included Amanullah Khan, head of the JKFL in Britain who was arrested at the organisation's headquarters in Luton, Bedfordshire.

**MI5.** See SECURITY SERVICE, BRITISH.

**MI6.** See SECRET INTELLIGENCE SERVICE, BRITISH.

*MINIMANUAL OF THE URBAN GUERRILLA.* A notorious guerrilla/terrorist handbook written in the late 1960s by the Brazilian revolutionary CARLOS MARIGHELLA and translated into at least 15 languages. Widely banned throughout the world, Marighella's *Minimanual* was an influential document among Latin-American and West European terrorist groups in the early 1970s. The *Minimanual* analyses the complexity of modern urban societies and describes how they can best be disrupted and terrorised. Marighella also describes the tactics of political kidnapping, selective assassination, bombings, bank robberies and hijacking. Marighella said that the purpose of the document was to bring down the "great industrial financial economic political cultural military police complex" which sustains "fascism and colonialism". The duty of the urban guerrilla, he writes, is to "attack and survive".

But for all its world-wide notoriety, the *Minimanual* is an unremarkable document which rehashes a variety of well-known theories of guerrilla warfare. Marighella incites the urban guerrilla to be politically aware, morally superior, fit, brave, well-trained, resourceful and canny. He should also be mechanically adept, skilled at electronics, a good driver, pilot, gunsmith and saboteur. According to Marighella the urban guerrilla's best weapon is the modern light machine-gun (LMG), followed by the 0.38 revolver. He recommended that urban guerrillas should operate in five-man "firing groups" at least one member of which should be adept with an LMG. While stressing the "moral superiority" of the urban guerrilla over the forces of repression he advocates terrorism. "It is an action the urban guerrilla must execute with the greatest coldbloodedness, calmness and decision," Marighella wrote. "Terrorism is an arm the revolutionary can never relinquish."

**MISHIMA, YUKIO. (1930-1970).** Right-wing Japanese poet, novelist and essayist and founder of the SHIELD SOCIETY who publicly committed "seppuku" (suicide) at Japanese Army HQ in Tokyo on 25th November 1970 after failing to incite Japanese troops to rebel against Japan's post-war "Peace Constitution".

Mishima was founder member of a small quasi-fascist group called the Shield Society dedicated to the cult of the Emperor, the Samurai way of life, and the overthrow of the post-war constitution forced on the Japanese by the USA. When Mishima's impassioned speech met no response from the soldiers, he disembowelled himself with his Samurai sword, and was then decapitated by his follower Kazumasa Morita. Police investigations showed that Mishima had hoped to incite the 32nd Infantry Regiment to stage a coup d'etat against the Japanese government. Mishima was one of Japan's most famous novelists, and had been nominated for the Nobel Prize for Literature. His work, particularly *After The Banquet* (1960) and *The Voices Of The Heroic Dead* (1966) were explorations of nationalism, obsession, loyalty and political violence. Mishima's strange and dramatic story was made into a feature film in 1984 by the American film-maker Paul Schrader.

**MISURA**. The largest and most militant of the anti-government organisations set up by the Miskito indians of north-east NICARAGUA. Misura, like the other Miskito organisations, claim they are being harassed and persecuted by Nicaragua's left-wing SANDINISTA government, and that an estimated 50,000 Miskito people have been forced to flee for their lives to other parts of Nicaragua and into neighbouring Honduras. Despite the existence of a "peace" faction inside Misura, in September 1985 Misura voted to abandon negotiations with the Sandinistas, and throw in their lot with the Nicaraguan Opposition Union, an alliance of right-wing CONTRA guerrilla groups. As members of the "Union" the Misura will qualify for a share of the $27 million "humanitarian aid" granted to the Contras by the US Congress.

**MITRIONE, DAN**. A 49-year-old American police official and adviser to the Uruguayan government who was kidnapped and killed by the left-wing TUPAMAROS. Mitrione was snatched in the street on July 31st 1970 as he was driving to work. His kidnappers demanded the release of all the "political prisoners" being held in Uruguay, and an aircraft to fly them to Mexico, Peru and Algeria. The Tupamaros set a deadline of noon on August 9th for their demands to be met. The Uruguayan authorities refused, and despite a last-minute appeal by the American ambassador for Mitrione's life, the American official was duly shot. His body was found in the boot of a car in a Montevideo street a few hours after he had been killed (by two bullets in the head). A massive police hunt (involving an estimated 10,000 police) failed to track down Mitrione's killers.

But in March 1973 a Spanish-born member of the Tupamaros called Antonio Mas Mas was charged with Mitrione's death. In 1977 Mas Mas was sentenced to 30 years in jail for the murder.

**MOGADISHU RESCUE**. See LUFTHANSA HIJACKING TO MOGADISHU AIRPORT, SOMALIA.

**MOHAMED, ABBAS**. One of the four fundamentalist gunmen who shot and killed ANWAR SADAT, President of Egypt, on 6th October 1981. Mohamed was an expert army-trained marksman, and it is likely that his bullet was the one which killed Sadat.

**MOLKY, MAJED YOUSEF AL**. One of the four young Arabs who hijacked the Italian cruise liner *Achille Lauro* in October 1985.

**MONTONEROS**. Left-wing Argentine terrorist group active between 1970 and 1976, and drawn mainly from the left wing of the Peronist movement. The Montoneros made a much-publicised debut when they kidnapped and then killed ex-president PEDRO ARAMBURU in May 1970. Led by MARIO FIRMENICH at their height the Montoneros claimed a membership of 25,000. Like most Latin American terrorist groups the Montoneros received little or no outside support and financed their activities by bank robberies, extortion and kidnapping. They campaigned for the return from his exile in Spain of Juan Peron, but during the preparations for Peron's homecoming they were involved in a gun battle at Ezeiza Airport on 20th June 1973 which left 13 people dead and 100 wounded. They were later denounced by Peron as terrorists and saboteurs. The Montoneros' campaign of bombing, killing and extortion in Argentina reached a peak in 1975/76, and did much to provoke the military coup of 1976 and the notorious "dirty war" that followed.

**MOORE, SARAH JANE**. The 45-year-old woman who tried to assassinate President Gerald Ford of the USA in San Francisco on September 21st 1975. Moore shot at President Ford as he was leaving a San Francisco hotel, but her firearm was deflected by a bystander. At her trial in January 1976 it emerged that Moore had been a member of various radical organisations in California and was a paid informer of the FEDERAL BUREAU OF INVESTIGATION (FBI). The day before the assassination attempt Moore had asked the San Francisco police to lock her up before she decided to "test the system". The defence tried to argue that Moore was unfit to plead but she was judged fit, found guilty and jailed for life. A few months earlier another woman, LYNETTE FROMME, had also tried to shoot President Ford.

**MORO, ALDO (1916-1978).** Italian politician, President of the Christian Democratic Party and six times Prime Minister of Italy who was kidnapped and then killed by members of the BRIGATE ROSSE in 1978. Moro's kidnapping and subsequent death provoked a political crisis in Italy in the course of which the Interior Minister resigned.

Moro was seized in Rome on Sunday 16th March 1978 on his way home from church. During the attack four of his bodyguard were killed and another mortally wounded. The veteran politician was held by his captors for almost two months, while the Brigate Rosse tried to secure the release of colleagues being tried by Italian courts. The Italian government, however, refused to concede anything, and on April 15th he was declared "guilty" by a Brigate Rosse "people's court" and sentenced to death. On May 9th Moro's body was found in a car in the centre of Rome near the headquarters of the Christian Democratic Party. He had been shot 11 times. On June 5th and 6th eight members of the Brigate Rosse were charged with the kidnap and murder of Moro. The police investigation was assisted by two members of the British Army's SPECIAL AIR SERVICE (SAS). Later in the year police raids in Milan uncovered documentary evidence of Moro's captivity and "trial", including papers in which Moro is alleged to describe corruption inside the Italian government. As these were plainly written under duress, their publication had little political effect.

**MORRISON, ALASTAIR.** British Army major from the SPECIAL AIR SERVICE (SAS) who advised the West German GRENZSCHUTZGRUPPE-9 (GSG-9) anti-terrorist unit during "MAGIC FIRE", the operation to free the hostages following the LUFTHANSA HIJACKING TO MOGADISHU AIRPORT, SOMALIA in 1977.

**MOSSAD LE ALIYAH BETH.** (The Mossad). Institution for Intelligence and Special Services. The largest and most aggressive of Israel's intelligence-gathering and special-operations services. The Mossad is Israel's main external espionage organisation, with agents in most parts of the world. Mossad officers have been responsible for carrying out some of Israel's most successful sub rosa operations such as the kidnapping of Adolf Eichmann, the attacks on German rocket scientists working for Egypt and the hijacking of

Israeli-ordered gunboats from French shipyards. Although officially constituted in 1952 under the leadership of ISSER HAREL, the post-war Mossad was built on the intelligence arm of the pre-war HAGANAH. The other two main arms of Israeli secret service are the SHIN BET and the Aman.

**"MOTORMAN", OPERATION. (July 31st 1972).** The code name of the British operation to clear the barricades and reassert law and order in the Catholic/Republican "no go" areas in Londonderry, Northern Ireland. Around 21,000 British Army regulars, plus 9,000 men from the ULSTER DEFENCE REGIMENT (UDR) and 6,000 policemen from the ROYAL ULSTER CONSTABULARY (RUC) were involved in Operation "Motorman". Apart from small-scale sniping there was little resistance, but two civilians were killed. The British government said the purpose of "Motorman" was to "remove the capacity of the IRA to create violence and terror".

**MOUNTBATTEN, LORD LOUIS (1900-1979).** Senior member of the British Royal Family, war-time leader, and the last Viceroy of India, who was assassinated by the PROVISIONAL IRISH REPUBLICAN ARMY (PIRA) on 27th August 1979. His boat *Shadow V* was blown up with a bomb a few hundred yards from the coast of County Sligo in the Republic of Ireland. Mountbatten, his grandson Nicholas (14) and boatman Paul Maxwell (17) were killed, and other members of Mountbatten's family were seriously injured. PIRA said that the Mountbatten's 30ft boat had been destroyed by 50lbs of explosive detonated by remote control from the shore. The bomb was hidden in a lobster pot which Mountbatten had gone to collect for a fishing trip. The same day that Mountbatten was murdered, 18 British soldiers were killed in the WARREN POINT BOMBINGS in Northern Ireland.

**MOUSSA, ABU.** One of the commanders of the Palestinian group FATAH who led a mutiny against the leadership of YASIR ARAFAT and, with Syrian assistance, drove the mainline Fatah forces out of Tripoli in Lebanon in 1983.

**MOUVEMENT DEMOCRATIQUE DE RENOVATION MALGACHE (MDRM).** (Democratic Movement for the Renewal of Malagasy). Insurrectionary nationalist movement which emerged in the French colony of Madagascar in 1947. The MDRM insurrection was launched on 29th March 1947 with concerted attacks on military depots, railway stations and telegraph communications mainly in the east of the island. The MDRM were banned by the French Cabinet on May 10th 1947, although two of their members had been elected to the French Chamber of Deputies. An estimated 11,000 people were killed during the emergency. In September 1958 the people of Madagascar voted to set up an independent Malagasay Republic ending 62 years of French colonial rule.

**MOUVEMENT POPULAIRE FRANCAISE (MPF).** (Movement of the French People). Small French Nazi group which began as the Mouvement National Citadelle, was renamed the Parti Socialiste Française, later the Phalange Française, and became the MPF in 1958.

**MOVIMIENTO DE ACCION REVOLUCIONARA (MAR).** (Revolutionary Action Movement). Small group of Communist-trained urban guerrillas which operated in and around Mexico City in the early 1970s. The MAR consisted of around 40 Mexican leftists who had been trained in the Soviet Union and in North Korea in the late 1960s. The organisation's campaign of bank raids and sabotage was swiftly put down by the Mexico City police. But suspicion that the MAR were being "run" from the Soviet Embassy led to the expulsion of five Soviet diplomats from Mexico in March 1971.

**MOVIMIENTO DE LA IZQUIERDA REVOLUCIONARIA (MIR-CHILE).** (Movement of the Revolutionary Left). Left-wing, largely middle-class guerrilla terrorist group founded in Chile in 1965. When the Pinochet junta came to power in 1973 the MIR were too weak to put up much resistance. When MIR leader Miguel Enriquez was killed in October 1974, his place was taken by Andreas Allende, nephew of the president who had been toppled in the military coup. The "Miristas", as they were known, survived into the 1980s but made little impact on the Pinochet regime.

**MOVIMIENTO DE LA IZQUIERDA REVOLUCIONARIA (MIR-VENEZUELA).** (Movement of the Revolutionary Left). Venezuelan terrorist organisation active in the early 1960s. MIR's vaguely left-wing aims were poorly defined, and came to nothing when resisted by the elected government of the Accion Democratica Party. After alienating Venezuela's urban population by a series of bank robberies, hijackings and kidnappings (including popular football players) the MIR abandoned their urban struggle and took to the countryside to follow Fidel Castro's maxim, "All guns, all bullets, all reserves to the Sierra".

**MOVIMIENTO DE LIBERACION NACIONAL (MLN).** (National Liberation Movement). Better known as the TUPAMAROS (after the Inca "Robin Hood", Tupac Amaru). Left-wing revolutionary terror group founded in 1965 in Uruguay, and suppressed by the Uruguay security forces in the early 1970s. It has been argued that the terrorist activities of the Tupamaros transformed Uruguay from a liberal democracy to a right-wing police state, and that their left-wing rhetoric and violence worked the opposite of what they sought to achieve.

Mainly middle-class and academic in membership, the Tupamaros were one of the most politically sophisticated, influential and least violent of the Latin-American groups. In the late 1960s they concentrated on raiding banks, businesses, arsenals, and at one stage published a series of documents proving corruption at high levels in the Uruguay government. Tupamaros guerrillas once robbed a casino of $250,000 and distributed the money among the staff. But they grew more violent as their campaign progressed, and in the early 1970s began killing policemen and soldiers. One of their victims was the American DAN MITRIONE. Although they operated under the slogan, "The Tupamaros are the people and the people are the Tupamaros", they had no real political programme, and made little political impact. The party they supported in the 1971 general election – the Fronte Amplio – won only 20% of the popular vote. A new group named after Tupac Amaru has recently emerged in Peru.

**MUHAMMAD, ELIJAH. (1897-1975).** American Muslim and most important leader of the once-influential NATION OF ISLAM. Denounced in the USA as a racist and anti-white fanatic, Muhammad's puritanical religious sect reached a peak in the 1960s then steadily decreased in power and influence, particularly after Muhammad's death in 1975.

Born Elijah Poole, the son of poor Georgia farmers, he moved in 1923 to Detroit where he came under the influence of the Black Muslim leader W. D. Fard (also known as Noble Drew Ali). Poole changed his name to Muhammad and after the mysterious disappearance of Fard, became a leading light in the Nation of Islam, and moved in 1934 to Chicago where he took the title of "Prophet" and founded a new Black Muslim temple. Muhammad's brand of Islam forbade tobacco, drink, drugs, gambling, extramarital sex, and traditional "Negro" food such as pork and greens. After a spell in prison during the war (for advocating resistance to the draft) Muhammad steadily increased his influence, particularly among the disaffected blacks of the northern states. His doctrine of self-discipline, and self-respect, found response in many young blacks. Although Muhammad built up a powerful religious/political movement, the emergence of the charismatic MALCOLM X created tensions and eventually a split. Elijah Muhammad and his followers were blamed (but never convicted) for the assassination of Malcolm X in New York in 1965.

**MUJAHADEEN**. (The Soldiers of God). The fiercely orthodox Islamic guerrillas of Afghanistan who have been fighting the Communist government of Afghanistan and its Soviet allies since the Soviet invasion of Afghanistan at the end of December 1979. Despite a large Soviet force estimated at 100,000 to 150,000 strong equipped with helicopters and armoured vehicles, the Mujahadeen continue to control many parts of the mountainous countryside, and retain the ability to strike at the cities. Armed with a wide variety of weapons (many of them captured from Soviet forces and the Afghan army) the Mujahadeen specialise in mining roads used by the Soviet columns, ambushing Soviet patrols, attacking isolated garrisons, and assassinating Soviet and pro-Soviet officials. The greatest threat to the Mujahadeen proved to be the Soviet SPETSNAZ units, the élite special forces trained in counter-insurgency operations and skilled at exploiting the tribal vendettas which plague the Mujahadeen resistance groups.

**MUJIBAS**. Young Africans used as scouts, political organisers, intelligence-collectors, fund-raisers, and occasionally guerrilla soldiers by the ZIMBABWE AFRICAN NATIONAL LIBERATION ARMY (ZANLA) during the Rhodesia insurgency of 1972-1978. Mujibas were described by one left-wing writer as ZANLA's "unique contribution to the practice of people's war".

**MUNICH "OKTOBERFEST" BOMBING. (September 26th 1980)**. A bombing incident which killed 13 people and injured 72 at Munich's famous beer festival. The bomb was planted by Gundolf Kohler, a Bavarian Neo-Nazi who belonged to no organisation, and who died in the blast.

**MUNICH OLYMPICS ATTACK. (September 5th-6th 1972)**. An attack by Arab BLACK SEPTEMBER terrorists on the Israeli Olympic team during the 1972 Munich Olympic Games which killed

11 Israeli athletes and team coaches. Two of the Israelis were killed when the Arabs broke into the Olympic Village in Munich, and nine were killed at Munich airport when the Bavarian police operation went disastrously wrong. The débâcle at Munich led to a complete reorganisation of the anti-terrorist forces of Western Europe (and the setting up of MOSSAD "hit teams" to take vengeance on Black September). The Israelis believe that the Munich massacre was conceived and ordered by ALI HASSAN SALAMEH, head of security to FATAH.

The Munich tragedy began around 04.00 on 5th September 1972 when the Arab terrorists, dressed in track suits and armed with KALASHNIKOV AK-47 assault rifles, climbed the six-foot-high wire fence surrounding the Olympic village, and broke into the block housing the Israeli Olympic team. The Arab group were led by a Libyan named MOHAMMED MASALHAD. Wrestling coach Moshe Weinberger and weightlifter Yossef Romano were shot dead in the Olympic village when they tried to resist. Nine athletes and coaches were captured. In return for the safety of the Israelis the terrorists demanded the release of 234 prisoners held in Israel, plus the leading members of the ROTE ARMEE FRAKTION (RAF) imprisoned in Germany. Their list included KOZO OKOMATO, the surviving gunman from the LOD AIRPORT MASSACRE of May 1972. After 17 hours of negotiations (during which the Israeli government refused to make any concessions although the West Germans wanted a deal) the terrorists and their nine hostages were helicoptered to Furstenfeldbruk Airport 15 miles from Munich where a Boeing 727 was, ostensibly, being prepared to take them to Cairo. When four of the Arabs climbed out of the helicopters, they were shot at by German police marksmen, from a great distance and in extremely poor light. In the exchange of fire, two of terrorists were killed, others injured, and the two German helicopter pilots wounded. Shortly after midnight on September 6th the German police launched an attack (with six armoured cars) to which the terrorists responded by destroying the helicopter holding five of the bound and gagged Israelis. However post-mortem examination proved that the Israelis had been shot to death before the helicopter burst into flames. The four Israelis in the second helicopter were also killed. The Israelis who died were Moshe Weinberg, Yosser Romano, David Berger, Mark Slavin, Eliezer Halfin, Zeev Friedman, Amitzur Shapira, Andrei Spitzer, Kehat Shorr, Yacov Springer, Yossef Gutfreund.

The Munich tragedy was one of the most significant terrorist attacks in post-war years. The global publicity involved, and the ineptitude of the Bavarian police operation rocked the West German government and disgusted the Israelis who felt they were winning the anti-terrorist war within their own borders only to lose it in Western Europe. The Munich massacre led to the setting up of the specialised anti-terrorist force GRENZSCHUTZGRUPPE-9 (GSG-9) in Germany, the GROUPE D'INTERVENTION DE LA GENDARMERIE NATIONALE (GIGN) in France , while in Britain the SPECIAL AIR SERVICE (SAS) were given the resources to form a permanent Counter Revolutionary Warfare (CRW) unit.

**MUSLIM BROTHERHOOD**. See MAJALLAT AL IKHWAN AL MUSLIMIN.

**MUSSOLINI ACTION SQUADS**. See SQUADRE D'AZIONE MUSSOLINI.

**MUSTAPHA, SALAH**. Egyptian military attaché in Jordan killed by a parcel bomb on 14th July 1956. Mustapha was a colonel in Egyptian Army Intelligence, and was believed by MOSSAD to be second-in-command of the Egyptian organisation training Palestinian and Jordanian terrorists against Israel. Mustapha's superior MUSTAPHA HAFEZ was killed in similar circumstances three days previously. Both men were early victims of letter and parcel bombs, but the Mossad used similar devices to devastating effect in the 1960s against German rocket scientists working in Egypt.

# N

**NARCO-TERRORISM**. The phrase coined to describe the apparently growing tendency of some terrorist organisations to finance their activities by buying and selling drugs like cocaine and heroin. Some American researchers claim that the left-wing terrorist/guerrilla groups of Colombia, Peru, Thailand and Burma are pumping drugs into the USA and Western Europe. They contend that the governments of Nicaragua and Cuba are actively abetting the drug traffickers, and quote the evidence of Antonio Farach, a one-time member of the Nicaraguan government, to a US Senate Drug Enforcement Caucus in 1983. "The drugs were destined for the United States," Farach told the Senators. "Our youth would not be harmed, but rather the youth of the United States, the youth of our enemies."

Professor Michael Ledeen told a Presidential committee that drug-running is "ideologically attractive" to terrorist groups. "Drugs go to the bourgeois countries, where they corrupt and they kill, while the arms go to the pro-Communist terrorist groups in the Third World." Rachel Ehrenfeld of Columbia University and Michael Kahan of the City University New York claim they can produce 100 references in the last 12 years linking the PALESTINE LIBERATION ORGANISATION (PLO) to narcotics operations. Other researchers regard fears about narco-terrorism as inflated, and argue that terrorist organisations (particularly the nationalist/separatist variety) tend to be puritanical and implacably opposed to drug-taking and drug-dealing.

**NARODNAYA VOLYA**. (The People's Will). Short-lived but influential Russian revolutionary terrorist movement active between 1878 and 1881 whose members were responsible for the death of Tsar ALEXANDER II in March 1881. At the height of its activities the Narodnaya Volya had around 500 members (although only about 50 real activists) drawn mainly from Russia's upper classes. As well as the Tsar, Narodnaya Volya members succeeded in assassinating the governor-general of Saint Petersburg and General Mezentsev, head of the hated "third section" of the Tsarist OKHRANA. Although the movement was rooted out by the Tsarist authorities in the 1880s, the theories of the Narodnaya Volya continued to influence terrorist groups throughout Europe, and later generations of Russian revolutionaries.

Narodnaya Volya grew out of an earlier clandestine organisation known as "Land and Liberty" whose "Disorganising Section" carried out a number of sporadic assassinations of minor Tsarist functionaries in the 1870s. When "Land and Liberty" split in 1878 the hard-line revolutionaries among them went on to form Narodnaya Volya which was dedicated to violent change, and one of whose first acts was to condemn the Tsar to death. One of the Narodnaya Volya's most spectacular attempts on the Tsar's life was in February 1880 when one of their explosives experts succeeded in penetrating the security at the Winter Palace in St Petersburg and dynamiting the Tsar's dining room. The Royal family survived, but 10 members of the Palace Guard were killed and 55 people were injured. But the campaign to "execute" the Tsar was pursued with determination, particularly by 27-year-old SOPHIA PETROVSKAYA, one of the organisation's most fanatical leaders. Ultimately Petrovskaya and her colleagues were successful, and Tsar Alexander II was assassinated by a terrorist bomb in March 1881.

What marked Narodnaya Volya out from previous (and subsequent) terrorist groups was their concern for the ethics of what they were doing. Most of them seemed to regard terrorism as a last resort against an overwhelmingly brutal tyranny. When, for example, President JAMES GARFIELD of the USA was assassinated in 1881, the Narodnaya Volya published a pamphlet deploring the act on the grounds that in a democratic society such as the USA assassination could never be justified. One of the group's most influential theorists was Nikolai Morozov who argued that however repressive and systematic a regime might be, it would always be vulnerable to inventive methods of terrorism. Morozov and his colleagues saw themselves as tyrannicides rather than regicides. And Narodnaya Volya member Gerasim Romanenko argued that brutal as it was, political terrorism was infinitely more humane than mass revolution in terms of lives lost and damage done.

**NATION OF ISLAM**. See BLACK MUSLIMS.

**NAXALITES**. Collective title of an assortment of left-wing, mainly Maoist, groups which emerged in Bengal in northern India in the late 1960s, and which tried to provoke a rural insurgency against the Indian authorities. In 1969 the Naxalites adopted the so-called "annihilation tactic" and in the late 1960s and early 1970s killed many rural landlords and moneylenders, a class the Naxalites regarded as being directly responsible for the misery of the Bengal peasantry. Like left-wing West European terrorist groups such as the ROTE ARMEE FRAKTION (RAF) or ACTION DIRECTE (AD) the Naxalites are mainly well-educated, middle-class young men and women who have despaired of the political process. Although greatly reduced in numbers the Naxalites survive in parts of Bengal.

Called after the West Bengal village of Naxalbara (where the Maoists organised a short-lived peasants revolt in 1967) the Naxalites were at their most dangerous in and around Calcutta in the early 1970s. But the Naxalite "Red Terror" campaign of killing policemen, soldiers and "bourgeois capitalists" was more than matched by a wave of police repression from which the Naxalite movement never really recovered. Thousands of Naxalites (and alleged Naxalites) were interned during the 1975-1977 state of emergency although most were released in 1977 after promising to renounce political violence. But in 1978 Naxalite violence flared again with a series of attacks on police stations, and a bombing raid on the Soviet Trade Mission in Calcutta since when it has diminished. By the mid-1980s the various Naxalite organisations were capable of mounting only occasional small-scale terrorist incidents.

**NEAVE, AIREY (1916-1979).** British Member of Parliament and the Conservative Party's spokesman on Northern Ireland who was killed on March 30th 1979 by a bomb planted in his car by the IRISH NATIONAL LIBERATION ARMY (INLA). A World War II hero and a close friend and political associate of Margaret Thatcher, Neave's death was a bitter blow to the Conservatives. He was killed by a sophisticated explosive device planted in his car while he was driving out of the House of Commons car park. The killing shocked Westminister into tightening the security surrounding the House of Commons and the House of Lords. In his four years as Conservative spokesman on Northern Ireland Neave had been a sharp critic of the Labour government's policy in the province, and consistently pressed for an increased use of covert operations (by both police and army) in Northern Ireland against the terrorist groups.

**"NECKLACING".** Particularly unpleasant terror tactic widely used in the African townships of South Africa to punish alleged police informers and supporters of the apartheid regime. A rubber tyre is filled with petrol, draped round the victim's neck, and set alight. Dozens of blacks have been burned to death in this manner. According to Sikh newspapers the same device was used against Sikhs in the wave of inter-communal violence which swept India following the assassination of INDIRA GANDHI in 1984.

**NEGRI, TONI**. Italian left-wing theorist, and professor at the University of Padua whose writings were influential among terrorist groups such as the BRIGATE ROSSE and the PRIMA LINEA. Some of Negri's works were published in Milan by the publishing house once owned by GIANGIACOMO FELTRINELLI. Negri argued that most forms of politicised violence – sabotage, violent strikes, shootings, etc. – were justified against a repressive capitalist society. Negri later apologised (at his trial in 1983) for the more extreme of his 1970s writings, and for the encouragement they gave to political terrorism. Unlike other West European (and North American) radical theorists, Negri had some influence among the country's industrial workers and trade union membership.

**NEJAD, FOWZI**. The young Iranian Arab who was the only surviving terrorist from the IRANIAN EMBASSY SIEGE, LONDON, in April-May 1980. During the siege Nejad called himself "Ali". The youngest member of the terrorist team, Nejad's life was saved during the British Army rescue assault by the hostages who pleaded with the soldiers not to harm him. Nejad was later tried in London, and jailed for life for his part in the Iranian Embassy siege and the killings that it involved.

**NETANYAHU, BENJAMIN**. Israel's Ambassador to the United Nations and younger brother of Lieutenant Colonel JONATHAN NETANYAHU who was killed leading an anti-terrorist operation in 1976. As a tribute to his brother, Benjamin Netanyahu set up the JONATHAN INSTITUTE in Jerusalem to study terrorism. In 1986 Netanyahu published a study entitled *Terrorism: How the West Can Win* in which he characterised international terrorism as "overwhelmingly an extension of warfare sustained and supported by the states built on the foundations of Marxism and radical Islam". But Netanyahu went on to argue that it was well within the capacity of the West to defeat terrorism so long as Western governments abandon "rules of engagement" which have become "so rigid that governments often straitjacket themselves in the face of unambiguous aggression". In Netanyahu's view (which is also the view of the Jonathan Institute) a sustained campaign of political and economic pressure, combined with military action where and when necessary would undermine international terrorism.

**NETANYAHU, JONATHAN**. Israeli army officer and leader of the SAYARET MATKAL force which rescued more than 100 Israeli hostages being held after the AIR FRANCE HIJACKING TO ENTEBBE AIRPORT, UGANDA. The military code name for the Entebbe rescue was Operation "JONATHAN" after its commander who was killed during the assault. A hero of the Golan Heights campaign in the "Yom Kippur" War of 1973, Netanyahu was born in the USA, the eldest son of a distinguished Jewish scholar. In fact Netanyahu abandoned a promising academic career at Harvard University to join the Israeli Defence Forces (IDF). Most of Netanyahu's military career was spent with the Sayaret Matkal, the Israeli special forces unit which is answerable directly to the head of military intelligence. He was killed at Entebbe Airport on July 4th 1976, the only Israeli military casualty.

**NEWTON, HUEY (born 1942)**. American radical and one of the founder-members of the militant all-black BLACK PANTHER PARTY (BPP). A native of the south, Newton moved to California as a young man and became involved in the riots in the Los Angeles suburb of Watts in 1965. An avid reader of Marxist and other socialist tracts, Newton is said to have introduced fellow radical ROBERT ("BOBBY") SEALE to Marxism-Leninism, and together they founded the Afro-American Party out of which grew the BPP. In the late 1960s Newton was convicted of manslaughter, but the conviction was quashed on appeal in 1970. He was later jailed for contempt of court.

**NEW PEOPLE'S ARMY (NPA)**. Maoist guerrilla army operating inside the Philippines mainly from jungle sanctuaries on Luzon, Mindano, Samar and Negros which posed a serious threat to the corrupt and ailing regime of President Ferdinand Marcos. The new government of President Cory Aquino are now trying to defuse the NPA's political threat by reforming Philippines society and releasing hundreds of political prisoners from jails. The Aquino government has warned the NPA that further armed insurrection will be met by overwhelming force, but the NPA have continued their guerrilla/terrorist campaign.

Estimated at around 20,000 strong, the NPA have been increasingly effective over recent years, and were reputedly inflicting serious casualties on the 200,000-man Armed Forces of the Philippines (AFP). The NPA is part of the New Democratic Front, a banned left-wing coalition (which includes the Communist Party of the Philippines). The guerrillas of the NPA are now operating in over more than half of the 73 provinces in the Philippines, (including the capital Manila) and in 1985 were reported to be killing AFP soldiers at the rate of more than 100 per month. In 1985 the United States despatched two special-forces counter-insurgency teams to the Philippines to help the Marcos regime stiffen the AFP, (and help protect the Clark airforce base and Subic Bay naval base, the leases for which run out in 1991).

**NEW WORLD LIBERATION FRONT (NWLF)**. A two-man radical group based in and around San Francisco, active in the mid-1970s. According to the FEDERAL BUREAU OF INVESTIGATION (FBI) between 1974 and 1978 the NWLF were responsible for almost 100 bombings in the San Francisco Bay area. Their targets were mainly banks, business premises, police stations etc. The activities of the NWLF ended abruptly in September 1979 when the NWLF leader was arrested for the axe murder of his revolutionary colleague (and lover). The title of the NWLF was also used by members of the SYMBIONESE LIBERATION ARMY (SLA) who kidnapped and "turned" heiress PATRICIA HEARST.

**NEWRY POLICE STATION ATTACK, NORTHERN IRELAND**. (February 21st 1985). One of the worst terrorist attacks against the ROYAL ULSTER CONSTABULARY (RUC) when the PROVISIONAL IRISH REPUBLICAN ARMY (PIRA) launched a mortar attack on the heavily defended RUC station at Newry. Nine RUC officers were killed when the mortar bomb struck the station canteen in which they were having a meal. The victims were WPC Rosemary McGookin, Sgt Thomas Dowd, WPC Ivy Kelly, PC Sean McHenry, PC Paul McFerran, PC Denis Price, PC David Topping, Chief Inspector Alexander Donaldson, and Reserve Constable Geoffrey Campbell. The mortars were launched from home-made launching tubes fixed onto the back of an ordinary truck.

**NIDAL, ABU (born 1935)**. Real name Sabry Khalil Bana. Palestinian terrorist organiser (his nom de guerre means "Father of the Struggle") who is thought to be behind many important terrorist incidents including the EGYPTAIR HIJACKING TO LUQUA AIRPORT, MALTA in November 1985 and the attacks at ROME AIRPORT and VIENNA AIRPORT in December 1985. A hard-line believer in armed force, Nidal has been outside the mainstream of the PALESTINE LIBERATION ORGANISATION (PLO) since the early 1970s. A dedicated enemy of PLO chairman YASIR ARAFAT (whom he has tried to kill a number of times) Nidal is reputedly supported by Syria and Libya.

Born into a prosperous middle-class family in Jaffa (then part of Palestine) Nidal's family fled in 1948 to Beirut where it is believed Nidal was educated at the American University. After the 1967 "Six-Day War" Nidal joined FATAH and quickly rose through the hierarchy. In 1970 he opened a PLO office in Khartoum where he alienated the Sudanese government by recruiting exiled Palestinian students. Ousted from the Sudan, Nidal then became the PLO's chief representative in Iraq with whose government he became very close. By the early 1970s Nidal had come to believe that the policies of PLO chairman Yasir Arafat were futile and harmful to the Palestinian people. In 1973 Nidal set up his own military organisation, the FATAH REVOLUTIONARY COUNCIL (FRC) which tried to assassinate Arafat in 1974. The PLO's response was to condemn Nidal to death, since when the two organisations have been locked in bitter struggle. Operating out of Baghdad and then Syria, Nidal's men have assassinated PLO representatives in London, Kuwait, Paris and Portugal, and launched attacks on Egyptians, Jordanians and European Jews in Vienna, Rome and Paris.

Western authorities claim that Nidal's main support comes from the Libyan regime of MUAMMAR QADDAFI although the FRC has offices in Syria and a training camp in the Lebanon. While the FRC is Nidal's "core" organisation, his men have operated under various names including BLACK JUNE, the Arab Revolutionary Brigades, and the REVOLUTIONARY ORGANISATION OF SOCIALIST MUSLIMS (ROSM). Nidal's strategy seems to be to use seasoned fighters to plan and equip attacks, and use young, usually inexperienced men as front-line terrorists. The casualty rate among the latter has been high. Nidal's Arab Revolutionary Brigades have specialised in attacking Israeli settlements on the West Bank of the Jordan.

And Nidal's organisation is thought to have been behind the attempt to kill SHLOMO ARGOV, the Israeli ambassador in Britain in June 1982. The attempt on Argov's life precipitated the Israeli invasion of Lebanon later that month. Nidal is believed to control more than 500 agents and told a Kuwaiti newspaper, "Give me $400 million and in five years I'll change the face of the Middle East."

# O

**OAKLEY, ROBERT (born 1931).** Head of the US State Department's OFFICE FOR COMBATTING TERRORISM (OCT). Before joining the OCT Oakley served as the US Ambassador in Zaire (1979-1982) and Somalia (1983-1984). Earlier in his diplomatic career he was a foreign service officer in Khartoum, Sudan (1958-60), Ivory Coast (1963-1965), Saigon (1965-1967), Paris (1967-1969), the United Nations (1969-1971). He also served as political counsellor to the US Embassy in Beirut (1971-1974) and served on the staff of the National Security Council (1974-1977).

**O'CONAIL, DAITHI (born 1937).** One-time strategist and Chief of Staff of the PROVISIONAL IRISH REPUBLICAN ARMY (PIRA) who later became heavily involved with Provisional Sinn Feinn, widely recognised as the political arm of the PIRA. O'Conail was one of the PIRA leaders involved in the "peace talks" with various Church leaders in 1974. An advocate of the "Eire Nua" policy of a united Ireland based upon the ancient provinces of Ulster, Munster, Leinster and Connaught, O'Conail's weight within the Republican movement dwindled after that policy was rejected by the Republican movement in 1981.

Born in Cork, O'Conail joined the IRA at an early age, was wounded in the campaign of the 1950s and received his first jail sentence (eight years) in 1960 for carrying weapons "with intent to endanger life". After organising a large consignment of Czech arms in 1971 he narrowly escaped arrest in Holland when the guns were discovered. He was jailed in Dublin in 1975, and again in 1976. After his release in 1977 he concentrated on his political work which was virtually destroyed when the Provisional Sinn Feinn's "Ard Fheis" (annual conference) of 1981 rejected the Eire Nua policy so fiercely held by O'Conail.

**OFFICE FOR COMBATTING TERRORISM (OCT).** Special unit of the American State Department, set up in 1972 after the MUNICH OLYMPICS ATTACK, and now headed by Ambassador ROBERT OAKLEY. Made up of senior officials from a number of US government agencies (including State, Defence, Justice, Treasury and the CENTRAL INTELLIGENCE AGENCY) the OCT has the job of coordinating the American government's campaign against internal and external terrorism. The OCT's first director Ambassador Anthony C. E. Quainton declared that the policy of the US government would be to refuse to concede to any "terrorist blackmail" on the grounds that to do so would only encourage future blackmail. The OCT works from an Operations Centre in Washington DC and is responsible to the National Security Council (NSC).

**OFFICIAL IRISH REPUBLICAN ARMY (OIRA).** See IRISH REPUBLICAN ARMY (OFFICIAL).

**OKHRANA.** The internal security/secret-police force of Tsarist Russia. The Okhrana burgeoned in late-19th, early-20th century Russia in response to the activities of terrorists from such groups as the NARODNAYA VOLYA, and the Social Revolutionary Fighting Organisation. By 1912 the Okhrana were employing a huge apparatus of 50,000 or so full-time staff, and a network of 26,000 part-time agents and informers. The brutally efficient espionage/security apparatus set up by the Soviets was based on techniques and methods inherited from Okhrana.

In the 1880s and 1890s the Okhrana were subsidising many of Russia's most radical journals in an effort to discredit the radicals by gross exaggeration. One of the Okhrana's most effective ploys (dreamed up in the early 1900s by Colonel S. V. Subatov, head of the Moscow Okhrana) was to set up state-organised trades unions at a time when trade unionism was banned. This had the short-term effect of defusing the pressure building up from the Russian working class, and allowing the Okhrana to supervise the organisations. These unions were dominated by Okhrana agents briefed to agitate for better pay and conditions, and divert the minds of the workers from deeper social/political problems.

The Okhrana were successful in penetrating most of Russia's radical groups with double agents and agents provocateur, the most extraordinary of whom was a Jewish engineer called Yevno Azev. Azev was so effective that he rose to become the leader of the Social Revolutionary Fighting Organisation, one of the most active of the radical/terror groups. While Azev betrayed many of his comrades by setting up assassinations and terrorist attacks and then informing the Okhrana, he also organised many terrorist operations without informing his superiors. In fact Azev was behind the assassinations in 1904 and 1905 of V. K. Plevhe (the Minister of the Interior) and the Tsar's brother, Grand Duke Serge Alexeivich. Azev's career as a terrorist-cum-double-agent came to a grimly-suitable end in 1908 when the Okhrana betrayed him to the Social Revolutionary Fighting Organisation.

**OKOMATO, KOZO.** One of the three members of the left-wing UNITED RED ARMY OF JAPAN (URAJ) who carried out the LOD AIRPORT MASSACRE in June 1972 in which 27 people were killed and dozens were injured. Okomato was the only member of the three-man assassination squad to survive, and was later tried and jailed in Israel. The decision by the Israeli government to include Okomato among the 1150 prisoners released in May 1985 in exchange for three Israelis caused a political furore inside Israel. In his confession to the Israeli security forces in 1972 Okomato wrote, "We three soldiers, after we die, want to become three stars of Orion."

After joining the URAJ in September 1970, Okomato was trained in the Lebanon in 1971, and in February 1972 flew back to Beirut (via Vancouver, New York, Paris and Rome) for three weeks intensive training in the terrorist camps in the Bekaa Valley. In June 1972 the Japanese group flew from Beirut to Frankfurt and Rome, from where they flew into Lod Airport to carry out the massacre. Okomato's two companions were killed in the shooting that followed, while Okomato was captured on the airport runway.

Okomato only confessed to the Israelis after being duped by the military interrogator; he was promised a revolver and ammunition to kill himself if he wrote a full confession. In July 1972 he was tried by a military court under the Defence (Emergency) Regulations of 1945, found guilty, and sentenced to life imprisonment. He served less than 13 years of his sentence, and was released on May 20th 1985 in an exchange of prisoners.

**OLDFIELD, MAURICE (1915-1981).** One of Britain's most effective and subtle intelligence officers who was head of the SECRET INTELLIGENCE SERVICE (SIS) between 1973 and 1978. Oldfield was taken out of retirement in 1979 to act as "security co-ordinator" in Northern Ireland, and is reputed to have done much to reform and improve the British security forces in the province. Oldfield is rumoured to be the model for John Le Carré's famous fictional spymaster George Smiley.

Oldfield joined the SIS in 1947 after a brilliant academic career in England, France and Germany, having spent World War II with

British military intelligence in the Middle East. In the course of his career with the SIS Oldfield operated in Singapore, Hong Kong, Bangkok and Washington (where he was SIS liaison with the CENTRAL INTELLIGENCE AGENCY). Oldfield rose steadily up through the SIS bureaucracy to inherit the near-legendary position of "C" (head of the SIS) in February 1973. In his five years in the job Oldfield is credited with defining the organisation's role more clearly, and making it more effective. Oldfield proved particularly adept at forging and improving links with friendly intelligence services which provided him with a worldwide network of information on, for example, the shipment of arms by the PALESTINE LIBERATION ORGANISATION (PLO) to the PROVISIONAL IRISH REPUBLICAN ARMY (PIRA) and other Republican groups in Northern Ireland.

After the assassination of AIREY NEAVE in the summer of 1979 Oldfield was asked by the British government to come out of retirement and take the job as "security co-ordinator" in Northern Ireland where relations between the British Army, the ROYAL ULSTER CONSTABULARY (RUC), the SECURITY SERVICE (MI6) and the Irish Republic's police were at an all-time low. The British government were also concerned about the flourishing contacts between PIRA and the various Arab terrorist groups, and felt Oldfield's SIS experience would prove useful. According to most accounts, Oldfield used all his legendary tact and patience to smooth relations between the British Army and the police. Dubbed "Maurice the Mole" by the PIRA, Oldfield never granted interviews to the media, never met politicians (other than government ministers), and kept as deeply in the background as he was able. Ill health forced Oldfield's resignation in the summer of 1980, and he died of cancer in March 1981. In the months before his death he was subjected to a "smear" campaign which hinted at scandals, and suggested that he had left Northern Ireland because he had failed to pass the government's "positive vetting" procedures.

**OMEGA-7**. Right-wing group of anti-Castro Cuban exiles based in the USA which has been responsible for a number of attacks on Cuban institutions and individuals in the USA. Omega-7 are regarded by the FEDERAL BUREAU OF INVESTIGATION (FBI) as one of the most dangerous terrorist groups in the USA. The group have staged firebomb attacks on radio stations, publishing houses and newspaper offices which they have considered sympathetic to the Castro regime. In 1980 Omega-7 placed a bomb under the car of the Cuban ambassador to the United Nations which failed to explode. An Omega-7 bomb exploded in Kennedy International Airport in New York shortly before the luggage in which it was hidden was put onto an aircraft bound for Los Angeles. The group were thought to have been connected with the assassination of the Chilean exile ORLANDO LETELIER in Washington in September 1976, but this was never proved.

**OPEC ATTACK, VIENNA. (December 21st-23rd 1975).** An attack on the Organisation of Oil Exporting Countries (OPEC) headquarters in Vienna by a group calling themselves the "Arab Revolution", a cover-name for the POPULAR FRONT FOR THE LIBERATION OF PALESTINE (PFLP). Led by ILLICH RAMIREZ SANCHEZ ("Carlos the Jackal") the terrorists seized 70 hostages (including 11 oil ministers) and barricaded themselves in the OPEC offices. Three people were killed in the attack. After 36 hours of negotiations the Austrian government allowed the terrorists and 42 of their hostages into an aircraft which flew them to Algeria, Libya, and then back to Algeria. The Saudi Arabian and Iranian governments paid large sums of money (possibly as much as $50 million) for the return of their nationals. Extortion rather than politics is thought to have been the real purpose of the OPEC raid.

The OPEC attack attracted world-wide publicity (one of the hostages was the famous Saudi Arabian oil minister Sheikh Yamani) and the Austrian government of Chancellor Bruno Kreisky was heavily criticised for giving in to the demands of the terrorists. Although the attack on OPEC raised large sums of cash for the attackers, politically it was obscure to the point of futility; the only political demand the kidnappers made was to insist that the Austrian authorities broadcast a political statement couched in terms incomprehensible to the average Austrian.

Sanchez and his five-strong group (which included the West German terrorist GABRIELE TIEDEMANN) invaded the OPEC oil ministers meeting at 11.40 on December 21st 1975, killing an Austrian guard, a Libyan economist, and an Iraqi security man. When the police surrounded the building a gun battle ensued in which one of the German terrorists, Hans-Joachim Klein, was badly injured. After a seige lasting more than 36 hours, the Austrian government eventually agreed to the Sanchez group's demands; the broadcasts of the political statement, a bus to the airport, and an aircraft to take the terrorists and some of their hostages out of the country. In the afternoon of December 22nd the terrorists and 42 of their hostages (including all 11 oil ministers) were driven to

Vienna International Airport where they boarded a DC9 jet. After first flying to Algiers (where the wounded terrorist Klein was taken to hospital) the jet was directed to Tripoli in Libya, and then back to Algiers. The terrorists finally surrendered on December 23rd 1975 (after huge sums of money had been transferred to a bank in Aden).

**ORDER, THE**. American neo-Nazi, white-supremacist organisation founded in 1983 by 31-year-old Robert Matthews who was killed in a shoot-out with the police in December 1984 at Whidbey Island, Puget Sound, Washington State. The Order have evolved into a paramilitary group with a sophisticated armoury (including Ingram MAC-11 submachine-guns), and have staged a number of armed robberies, including the ambush of a Brinks security van near Ukiah, California, in June 1983 which netted the group $3.6 million. A few months later, in Seattle, The Order robbed another security van of $500,000. In June 1984 members of The Order murdered the Jewish radio commentator Alan Berg with a fully-silenced MAC-11 submachine-gun and they are known to have drawn up a hit-list of prominent Americans many of whom are Jewish.

The Order take their philosophy from an apocalyptic novel by the American writer William Pierce called *The Turner Diaries* in which a right-wing terrorist group (also called The Order) stage a coup d'état in the USA, take over the nuclear arsenal and bomb Israel out of existence. In the group's literature (most of which was written by Matthews) The Order declare their intention to make the USA a "white, Christian society" and regard the Jews as an evil influence which must be rooted out. All non-whites are seen as "mud people" and members are encouraged to become "Aryan Warriors" by killing Jews, liberals, blacks, Federal Judges and government agents.

When Robert Matthews was killed in December 1984 his house was found to contain a huge quantity of arms and ammunition (including automatic weapons), forged identity papers, $64,000 in cash, and a "Declaration of War" against the USA signed by members calling themselves the "Aryan Resistance Movement". In 1985 12 members of The Order were arrested in 12 different states. But The Order is thought to maintain a network of "safe houses" and support organisations throughout the southern United States.

**ORGANISATION ARMEE SECRETE (OAS)**. (Secret Army Organisation). The terror group set up by disaffected French "colons" in the latter stages of the Algerian war of 1954-1962. Incensed by the idea that France was about to sell out to the Algerian nationalists, the OAS waged a lethal terrorist campaign in Algeria (and in France) between 1961 and 1962 in which hundreds of Algerian Arabs (and many Europeans) were killed and maimed. The OAS were also heavily involved in the French Army's attempted putsch in 1961, and twice tried to assassinate French President Charles de Gaulle. Eventually, in June 1962, the OAS made a truce with the leadership of the Arab movement, FRONT DE LIBERATION NATIONALE (FLN), after which most of the "colons" in Algeria fled back to metropolitan France.

The OAS emerged in Algiers in January 1961 when two ex-soldiers murdered a lawyer sympathetic to the Arab cause. Led by a fanatical young right-winger called Jean-Jacques Susini the OAS quickly grew into a well-organised clandestine terrorist organisation against which the French authorities in Algeria seemed powerless to act. The organisation's most formidable operator was an embittered ex-foreign legionnaire called ROGER DEGUELDRE who was obsessed by the idea that Algeria must remain French. The OAS were described by de Gaulle as "thugs consumed by totalitarian passion ... deserters and fanatics who were the scum of the army, particularly of the Foreign Legion units ... ".

The cutting edge of the OAS were Degueldre's "Deltas" which the authorities tried to attack by setting up a special undercover anti-terror unit which was promptly dubbed "Les Barbouzes" (false beards – French argot for secret agents). But the small group of Barbouzes proved no match for Degueldre's wily and ruthless ex-paras and legionnaires who hunted them down, and finally destroyed their clandestine headquarters, killing their leader Jim Alcheik and 18 of his team. It is possible, however, that the Barbouzes were set up as an easy target to divert the OAS from their real enemy, the police intelligence unit which eventually traced, arrested and convicted many of the OAS killers.

At the beginning of 1962 the OAS campaign reached its climax, with as many as 30-40 killings every day in Algiers alone. In February 1982 the death toll rose to 553 men, women and children in one month; harmless Muslims, liberal Frenchmen, minor officials, French gendarmes, FLN terrorists and OAS waverers. And in an attempt to bring Algeria grinding to a halt the OAS Delta squads killed postmen, tram drivers, power-station workers, railwaymen, doctors, pharmacists, even the harmless street-corner flower sellers.

In March 1962, following the Evian Agreements between the French government and the Algerian nationalists, the OAS stepped up their campaign of terror, and concentrated their fire against the French army and the French police, and in one incident massacred a party of young French conscripts. But the OAS campaign against the French forces undermined their support in Algeria. In April the OAS "commander-in-chief" Raoul Salan was captured, and in June 1962 the OAS signed a truce with the FLN. Most of them fled back to France where their embittered presence plagued French politics for many years.

**OSWALD, LEE HARVEY (1939-1963).** The 24-year-old ex-Marine who was accused of the assassination in Dallas, Texas, of President JOHN FITZGERALD KENNEDY on November 22nd 1963, and who was shot to death by JACK RUBY on November 24th while in police custody. While Oswald has never been "cleared" of Kennedy's assassination, in 1979 a Congressional Committee investigating the assassinations concluded that it was "probable" that Kennedy had been killed by more than one gunman. Some assassination experts have tried to link Oswald with the KGB, others claim that he was acting for renegade elements of the CENTRAL INTELLIGENCE AGENCY (CIA), while others have suggested that he was manipulated by organised crime.

A solitary, troubled young man from New Orleans, Oswald developed an early taste for left-wing propaganda and polemic. After three years service in the US Marine Corps (where he was a "sharpshooter") Oswald defected to the Soviet Union, returning in June 1962 with his baby daughter and his Russian wife, Marina. In 1963 Oswald became involved in the left-inclined "Fair Play for Cuba" campaign, and, it is believed, made an attempt on the life of General Edwin Walker. In September 1963 Oswald travelled to Mexico City in an attempt to get a visa to visit Cuba. In October 1963 Oswald got a job in the Texas School Book Depository in Dealey Plaza, Dallas.

On November 22nd 1963 Oswald was arrested and charged with the murder of John F. Kennedy after a rifle and cartridge cases were found on the sixth floor of the book depository. He was also charged with the shooting of Dallas policeman J. D. Tippit. Although the rifle had been mail-ordered by Oswald (under the name of "A. J. Hidell") he consistently denied both murder charges under police interrogation. On the morning of November 24th 1963, while he was being moved from the Dallas police headquarters to the county jail, Oswald was shot dead by JACK RUBY, a Dallas night-club owner who had links with organised crime. Oswald was buried at Rose Hill Cemetery, Fort Worth, Texas.

**OTERO, LUIS**. Leader of the left-wing Colombian guerrilla/terrorist group known as M-19 which was involved in the BOGOTA PALACE OF JUSTICE SIEGE in November 1985. Otero died along with all his colleagues when the Colombian army stormed the building.

# P

**PAGLIAI, PIERLUIGI.** Italian neo-fascist and close associate of terrorist organiser STEFANO DELLE CHIAIE who fled to Latin America after a series of terrorist incidents in Italy. Pagliai and Delle Chiaie helped various right-wing regimes (in Argentina, Chile, Nicaragua and El Salvador) set up anti-left terror networks, and planned what has been called a "Fourth Reich" throughout Latin America. A handsome, sadistic man in his late 20s, Pagliai was wanted by the Italian police for his part in right-wing terrorist bombings in Italy, and in September 1982 was finally tracked down to the town of La Paz in Bolivia with the help of the American CENTRAL INTELLIGENCE AGENCY (CIA). On October 10th 1982 Pagliai was shot and wounded in a La Paz street while being arrested by the Bolivian police. Badly injured, he was immediately extradited to Italy where he died of his wounds a few weeks later without having talked to the police.

**PALESTINE LIBERATION FRONT (PLF).** The title of three separate Palestinian military groups which splintered from the POPULAR FRONT FOR THE LIBERATION OF PALESTINE – GENERAL COMMAND (PFLP-GC). The most important of the three factions is the pro-YASIR ARAFAT organisation led by ABU ABBAS, which became notorious in October 1985 during the *ACHILLE LAURO* HIJACKING. The PLF broke off from the PFLP-GC in the mid-1970s and for the first few years was led by Talaat Yaqub. Following the expulsion of the PLO from Lebanon in 1982, the PLF split into three parts; one led by Abdel Fatah Ghanem sided with the Syrians, another led by Talaat Yaqub maintained a nominal independence and a third led by Abu Abbas aligned itself with Yasir Arafat and the PLO mainstream. The Abbas group is by far the most influential of the PLF organisations, although the *Achille Lauro* hijacking and the high-level diplomatic furore it generated appears to have dented the credibility of Abu Abbas.

**PALESTINE LIBERATION ORGANISATION (PLO).** The main political and diplomatic vehicle of the Palestinian cause, and effectively the "government in exile" of the Palestinian people. Although regarded by Israel as a "terrorist organisation" dedicated to the destruction of the Jewish state, since 1974 the PLO has been recognised by the Arab nations as "the sole legitimate representative of the Palestinian people". The PLO is made up of a number of components the largest and most powerful of which is the military wing FATAH whose leader YASIR ARAFAT is also the PLO's chairman. The PLO is currently based in Baghdad, Iraq, having been expelled from Tunisia in 1985 after an Israeli bombing raid on their headquarters. Three years previously, in the autumn of 1982, the PLO were driven out of Lebanon by the Israeli invasion in June 1982 and their fighters scattered around the Arab world. Recently, however, the PLO are known to have been filtering back into Lebanon to continue their long war against Israel.

Although the PLO is widely recognised as a legitimate diplomatic vehicle for the Palestinians, the fact that it incorporates terrorist groups such as the POPULAR FRONT FOR THE LIBERATION OF PALESTINE (PFLP), SA'AQA, and the DEMOCRATIC FRONT FOR THE LIBERATION OF PALESTINE (DFLP) has made many Western nations uneasy about establishing close contacts. While the PLO receives large sums of money from oil-rich Arab states such as Saudi Arabia and Kuwait, and from collections in the large Palestinian diaspora, most of its annual income of $900 million or so, is believed to come from the organisation's sophisticated programme of investments in the Western economies. Most of these investments are handled through the Palestinian National Fund (PNF) and the Arab Bank.

Founded in 1964 and originally led by Ahmed Al-Shukeiry, the PLO was overtaken in militancy by Arafat's Fatah group of guerrillas, and following the humiliation of the Arab nations in the "Six-Day War" of 1967, the PLO succumbed to Fatah control in 1969. But in 1970 the PLO suffered its first major reverse when it was hounded out of its bases in Jordan and into exile in Syria and Lebanon following the DAWSON'S FIELD HIJACKINGS. King Hussein of Jordan saw the hijackings as a direct challenge by the PLO to his authority (although they were the work of the militant PFLP).

The PLO's most important policy statement is the "Palestinian National Charter" issued in Cairo in 1968. This document describes the state of Israel as "illegal" and declares Palestine as the "homeland of the Arab Palestinian people". It also declares that "Armed struggle is the only way to liberate Palestine" and that "Commando action constitutes the nucleus of the Palestinian popular liberation war". In November 1974 the PLO won a major break-through when Arafat addressed the United Nations (UN) General Assembly in New York, which was reinforced a year later when the UN accepted a resolution denouncing Zionism as "racism", and accorded the PLO "observer status" on a number of UN committees.

But Arafat's strategy to "legitimise" the PLO on the world stage, to bring diplomatic, political and economic pressure to bear on Israel was not accepted by all the Palestinian groups. Some of them – notably the PFLP and its offshoot the POPULAR FRONT FOR THE LIBERATION OF PALESTINE – GENERAL COMMAND (PFLP-GC) – formed a "Rejection Front" to continue the military (i.e. guerrilla/terrorist) battle against Israel. And between 1976 and 1982 the PLO was drawn inexorably into the civil war in Lebanon, and at one stage suffered grievously at the hands of the Syrians who were determined not to allow the PLO enough power to challenge Syria's influence in Lebanon (which many Syrians see as part of greater Syria).

After the Israeli invasion of Lebanon in the summer of 1982 (the purpose of which was to destroy the PLO) the PLO suffered a major split, with a Syrian-backed faction of Fatah led by ABU MOUSSA waging war on Arafat loyalists around Tripoli. Eventually Yasir Arafat and his men were driven out of Lebanon and into exile around the Arab world. The PLO set up its new headquarters near Tunis, while their fighters were installed in bases in Algeria, Iraq, Sudan and the Yemen. But following the destruction of the PLO HQ in Tunisia by the Israeli air force, the various PLO groups scattered around the Arab world were exiled once more. Only Iraq was prepared to play host to the PLO and their 5,000 or so full-time fighters, but under strict Iraqi control.

**PALME, OLOF. (1927-1986).** Socialist Prime Minister of Sweden and world statesman who was shot dead in a Stockholm street on March 2nd 1986. Palme's assassin escaped into the centre of Stockholm and was never traced. Although a telephone call said to be from the West German ROTE ARMEE FRAKTION (RAF) claimed the killing, Swedish police think the assassin may have been an individual with a grudge against the Prime Minister. Palme had held office for 10 of the 16 years before his death. In 1982 the Swedish secret police had begged Palme to tighten up on his personal security, but all Palme would accept was a small bodyguard with whose services he frequently dispensed. There was immediate speculation that Palme's assassin may have come from one of the many refugee groups (Palestinian, Croatian, Chilean, Kurdish, Syrian or Iranian) which have found shelter in Palme's liberal Sweden.

Palme was shot while walking in the centre of Stockholm with his wife, Lisbet, late on March 2nd 1986. He was shot twice in the back with copper-cased lead-tipped bullets which the police think were fired from a large 0.357 Smith & Wesson "Magnum" handgun. His assassin, described as tall, dark and wearing a three-quarter length coat, fled across the street and up a staircase. An attempt by a passing nurse to resuscitate the Prime Minister failed, and Palme died shortly after the attack. His wife was slightly hurt. Although born into a wealthy Swedish family, Olof Palme was a passionate democratic socialist and champion of Third World causes. An admirer of the United States of America, he was nevertheless a fierce opponent of that country's war in Vietnam, and of the Soviet Union's invasion of Czechoslovakia in 1968. Palme first became Prime Minister in 1969, then when his party (the Social Democrats) was defeated in 1976 became a member of the Brandt Commission which studied the problems of the Third World. In 1982 Palme became Prime Minister again when the Social Democrats were re-elected.

**PEREIRA, FERNANDO.** **(1950-1985).** Portuguese-born photographer who was killed in the *RAINBOW WARRIOR* ATTACK in Auckland Harbour, New Zealand, in July 1985. The bombing was carried out by agents of the French secret service two of whom, DOMINIQUE PRIEUR and ALAIN MAFART, were later jailed for Pereira's manslaughter. Pereira had fled Portugal at the age of 20 to avoid serving in the dictator Salazar's armed forces, and ended up in Amsterdam where he married a Dutch woman, and became a photographer working mainly for left-wing newspapers and radical organisations. When French combat swimmers attached bombs to the *Rainbow Warrior* in Auckland Harbour to prevent Greenpeace embarrassing the French nuclear test programme, the first bomb-blast left Pereira unharmed. But when he returned to the ship for his cameras he was stunned by the second blast, and drowned by the inrush of water. His body was later found with one of his cameras slung round his neck. Pereira's remains were flown back to Amsterdam for burial, and the French government agreed to compensate his estranged wife and two children.

**PEROVSKAYA, SOPHIA.** Leader of the NARODNAYA VOLYA group of terrorists which emerged in Tsarist Russia in the late

1870s and which assassinated Tsar ALEXANDER II in 1881. Fanatical and single-minded, the 27-year-old Perovskaya was the daughter of a Russian general who had been Governor-General of Saint Petersburg but was sacked after an attempt on the Tsar's life. Described as small, fair-haired, blue-eyed, and "doll-like", Perovskaya was the most dedicated and implacable of the Narodnaya Volya terrorists, and the driving force behind the conspiracy to assassinate the Tsar. She was in charge of the five-man team of terrorists which killed the Tsar with a bomb in St Petersburg in March 1881. Perovskaya and her colleagues were quickly arrested by the Tsarist police, tried, and publicly hanged for their crime.

**PESH MERGA**. (Those Who Precede Death). The armed forces of the Kurdish nationalist movement which is fighting for an independent Kurdistan in territory which is currently part of the USSR, Iraq, Iran, Turkey and Syria. Most of the Pesh Merga's attacks have been directed against Iraq, and the organisation has taken advantage of the Iraq-Iran war to mount raids against the armies of both countries. Iraqi reprisals have been formidable, however, and in December 1985 it was reported that the Iraqi army had pushed into the Kurdish region of the country and killed more than 300 Kurdish fighters. Reports of mass extra-judicial executions of Iraqi Kurds were referred by Amnesty International to President Saddam Hussein for investigation. There have also been large-scale Iranian attacks on the Pesh Merga guerrillas operating on the Iranian side of the border. The Kurdish population of the Middle East now numbers more than 10 million and Kurdish nationalists have been agitating for an independent homeland since the late 19th century.

*PHOENIX* **PROGRAMME**. Counter-terrorist programme devised by the American CENTRAL INTELLIGENCE AGENCY (CIA) in South Vietnam between 1968 and 1971 in which at least 20,000 people were killed. Although the *Phoenix* Programme became notorious throughout the world, it was described by CIA director William Colby as "an attempt to bring some order and propriety and effectiveness to the government side of the struggle against the secret apparatus of the Communists in Vietnam". According to Colby the CIA compiled dossiers on three categories of Vietnamese; a) the leaders, b) the cadre, and c) the "ordinary, casual supporters". The CIA concentrated their counter-insurgency efforts on the first two categories. The CIA claim that more than 17,000 Vietnamese accepted the official amnesty by 1971, another 28,000 were captured, and around 20,000 were killed. The CIA's critics claim that the number killed was much higher, and that many of them were innocent men, women and children.

**POPULAR FRONT FOR THE LIBERATION OF PALESTINE (PFLP)**. One of the most militant and ingenious of the Palestinian groups associated with the PALESTINE LIBERATION ORGANISATION (PLO) which has been led since its inception by GEORGE HABASH. Formed in 1967 out of an assortment of groups including the National Front for the Liberation of Palestine, the Arab Nationalist's Movement, and The Heroes of the Return, the left-inclined PFLP has proved to be one of Israeli's most determined and dangerous enemies. They have also mounted two serious challenges to the FATAH leadership of the PLO which they regard as "surrenderist" and ineffective.

The PFLP were the first of the Arab groups to use aerial hijacking as a military tactic. Beginning in July 1968 the PFLP's "external operations" branch led by Wadi Haddad organised some of the most spectacular terrorist operations in post-war history including the ZURICH AIRPORT ATTACK in 1969, the DAWSON'S FIELD HIJACKINGS in September 1970 (which brought down the wrath of the Jordanian army on the Palestinians) and the LUFTHANSA HIJACKING TO MOGADISHU AIRPORT, SOMALIA, in 1977. The PFLP are also thought to have engineered the OPEC ATTACK, VIENNA in December 1975 which was mounted by the notorious ILLICH RAMIREZ SANCHEZ ("Carlos the Jackal").

In September 1974 the PFLP broke with the PLO over the latter's "moderation", and led the Iraqi-sponsored "Rejection Front", which also included the POPULAR FRONT FOR THE LIBERATION OF PALESTINE – GENERAL COMMAND (PFLP-GC). The PFLP-led Rejection Front lasted from 1974-1978 in the course of which the PFLP tried to challenge Fatah's leadership of the PLO, but were never militarily or politically strong enough to topple YASIR ARAFAT. In recent years the PFLP and Fatah appear to have sunk their differences and Habash has made a number of appearances in public at Arafat's side. To some extent the long struggle between the PFLP and Fatah for the control of the PLO has been philosophical; the left-wing PFLP are passionate believers in Pan-Arabism, and are convinced that until the "Arab masses" combine, the fight against Israel will never be won. Fatah, on the other hand, have long adopted a pragmatic "Palestine-first" ideology.

**POPULAR FRONT FOR THE LIBERATION OF PALESTINE – GENERAL COMMAND (PFLP-GC).** An offshoot of the PFLP which emerged in October 1968, shortly after the PFLP had been formed. Led by an ex-Syrian army officer called Ahmed Jibril the PFLP-GC joined the Iraqi-backed "Rejection Front" which opposed (sometimes violently) the policies of the mainstream PALESTINE LIBERATION ORGANISATION (PLO). In 1977 the PFLP-GC split when Jibril's second-in-command ABU ABBAS formed the breakaway PALESTINE LIBERATION FRONT (PLF). The PFLP-GC were blamed for a massive explosion in Beirut in August 1978 which destroyed the headquarters of the Abu Abbas organisation, killing more than 200 people in the process. Jibril's PFLP-GC are now a hard-line "physical force" group based in Damascus.

**PRICE, DOLOURS AND MARIAN.** Two young Irish sisters from Belfast who were jailed for life in November 1973 for their role in a series of bombing attacks in London earlier in 1973. The Price sisters (both student teachers at St Mary's College, Belfast) were convicted of planting bombs in an army recruiting office near Trafalgar Square and at the Central Criminal Courts. They are also believed to have been involved in the bombing outrage in Belfast known as "BLOODY FRIDAY". It was claimed that Dolours Price (the elder of the two) was the leader of the bombing gang, while her sister Marian was an expert shot and had been dubbed "The Armalite Widow" by British soldiers in Northern Ireland. In 1975 the Price sisters staged a hunger-strike as part of their campaign to be allowed to serve out their sentences in Ireland. They were transferred to the Armagh woman's prison in March that year. In 1982 Marian Price was released from jail for medical reasons, and was said to be suffering from severe mental illness.

**PRIEUR, DOMINIQUE.** One of the two French agents of the DIRECTION GENERALE DE LA SECURITE EXTERIEURE (DGSE) jailed for the *RAINBOW WARRIOR* ATTACK in Auckland Harbour, New Zealand, on July 10th 1985. The 36-year-old Prieure (a DGSE captain) and her colleague ALAIN MAFART were sentenced to 10 years in jail by a New Zealand court in November 1985. Attempts by the French government to have them extradited to France have so far failed, and the New Zealand authorities are insisting that Prieur and Mafart must serve their sentence in a New Zealand prison. The wife of a senior Paris fire-brigade officer, Prieur has been described as one of the "new generation" of intellectually-inclined DGSE officers. She studied sociology and politics at Nanterre University where she wrote a dissertation on the politics of Libya and the influence of the *Green Book* of MUAMMAR QADDAFI. As a DGSE officer she rose quickly through the ranks by specialising in gathering intelligence on West European peace groups and environmental movements.

**PRIMA LINEA**. (The Front Line). A left-wing Italian terrorist group similar to the larger BRIGATE ROSSE with which it had a number of contacts. The organisation's most notorious act was the killing in January 1979 of Emilio Allesandrini, the magistrate who had been assigned to investigate the murky financial affairs of the Banco Ambrosiano. Allesandrini had also specialised in investigating both the left and right-wing terrorist groups which plagued Italy during the late 1960s and 1970s.

**PRINCIP, GAVRILO (1894-1918)**. The young Serbian student who assassinated Archduke FRANZ FERDINAND, heir to the throne of Austria-Hungary and his wife in Sarajevo, on June 28th 1914. Princip was a member of the illegal nationalist organisation Young Bosnia, which wanted to separate Bosnia-Herzegovina from the Austro-Hungarian Empire. The wider conspiracy involved officers within Serbian military intelligence, and The Black Hand terrorist organisation. After the killings there was widespread rioting in Bosnia, and the trial and execution of many Serbians. Ironically perhaps, Princip himself was too young to be executed for murder, but he died in hospital of tuberculosis in 1918.

**PRIVATE SECURITY AND TERRORISM**. Since the growth of national and international terrorism there has been a corresponding growth of private-enterprise security companies set up to protect their clients against the activities of the terrorists. Most of these are straightforward, overt operations which provide uniformed security guards, night watchmen, dog handlers etc., and generally fulfil many of the low-level functions of hard-pressed police forces. Others specialise in selling (often sophisticated) surveillance equipment, baggage x-ray machines, battery-powered metal detectors, explosives-sensing devices etc.

But many security organisations are more than that. A recent American study revealed at least 40 companies who provided specially-trained (and armed) bodyguards, anti-terrorist driving skills for chauffeurs, and even high-grade intelligence on terrorist groups and individual terrorist leaders. Others specialise in acting as "hostage negotiators" in the event of company executives being kidnapped by terrorists. A few private security firms offer "paramilitary" units ready to stage hostage-rescue operations or "pre-emptive strikes" against terrorist groups. In May 1986 there were reports that one London-based private security firm (staffed mainly by ex-members of the British Army's SPECIAL AIR SERVICE (SAS)) were assisting the government of Sri Lanka in their campaign against the Tamil separatists.

In 1978 one such company mounted a successful "private enterprise" commando raid on a prison in Iran to release two employees of Texas industrialist H. Ross Perot. Perot explained that he had paid the private firm to release his employees because the US government were refusing to help his employees. "Private companies, private individuals shouldn't be involved in this sort of thing," Perot told the press, adding that if the government was not prepared to help "you have an obligation to get them out of there." In Northern Ireland private security firms are notorious for being cash-gathering "front" operations for both the PROVISIONAL IRISH REPUBLICAN ARMY (PIRA) and/or the ULSTER DEFENCE ASSOCIATION (UDA) or ULSTER VOLUNTEER FORCE (UVF). There are now more than 60 private security firms in the Belfast telephone directory compared to less than a dozen 15 years ago.

**PROVISIONAL IRISH REPUBLICAN ARMY (PIRA)**. See IRISH REPUBLICAN ARMY.

**PSYCHOLOGY OF TERRORISM**. A subject which has been the source of much study and speculation by psychologists and psychiatrists since the late 1960s. Most anti-terrorist agencies in Western Europe and the USA have a psychiatrist or psychologist on whom they can call to try to understand terrorist groups, individuals, and/or their hostages. In an attempt to define the psychiatrist's role in coping with terrorism, a few years ago the American Psychiatric Association (APA) set up a special "Task Force" on the "Psychiatric Aspects of Terrorism".

Work by the FEDERAL BUREAU OF INVESTIGATION (FBI) Special Operations and Research Unit suggests that the individuals who make up many terrorist groups can be divided into three main psychological types.

1; The Leader, very often a woman such as Nancy Ling Perry of the SYMBIONESE LIBERATION ARMY (SLA) or ULRIKE MEINHOF of the West German ROTE ARMEE FRAKTION (RAF). The Leader is normally dedicated and inflexible to the point of fanaticism, a perfectionist who specialises in manipulating the opinions and attitudes of her subordinates.

2; The Opportunist, usually male, very often with a criminal background (such as Donald De Freeze of the SLA), and familiar with violence and weaponry which gives him a lurid glamour in the eyes of the group. Both ANDREAS BAADER and Hans Joachim Klein of the RAF fit into this category. The Opportunist is often recruited from the prison population, and occasionally challenges the authority of The Leader.

3; The Idealist, who normally plays the part of the faithful follower, easily biddable by The Leader, and easily deceived by The Opportunist. Usually The Idealist comes from a "good", although often disturbed, social background.

A West German study of members of the RAF revealed that 25% of the terrorists had lost one or both of their parents by age 14, that 33% of them had been in trouble with the juvenile courts, and that many of them were school or college drop-outs and/or individuals who had trouble holding down a job. Some psychologists claim there are marked differences between the psychological make-up of left-wing revolutionaries (such as the members of the RAF or the Italian BRIGATE ROSSE) and that of "nationalist separatist" activists. The revolutionaries tend to reject both their own families and their societies, while the separatists retain powerful links with their family backgrounds, and indeed often see themselves as carrying on a family tradition (which in many cases they are).

There is a general agreement among psychologists that the terrorist groups provide a kind of mutually-supporting "family" environment in which attitudes and behaviour are powerfully reinforced, often by the threat of extreme violence, but usually by subtler pressures. Typically, the standards of the group become the norm while the standards of the world become alien and evil. The function of the group is to commit acts of terrorism, and if this is not done the group loses its reason to exist, hence the resort to terrorism almost for its own sake. Terrorist groups appear to be characterised by excessive optimism, excessive risk-taking, feelings of moral superiority, a perception of the "status quo" as evil, and with little tolerance for internal dissent (which when it does happen, often leads to extremely violent splits).

One analysis suggests a distinction between terrorists operating on their own patch, and terrorists operating "trans-nationally". The "domestic" terrorist is susceptible to the opinions of the public he hopes to influence and is therefore more selective in his targeting. The terrorist operating abroad, however, regards the shock and outrage of the foreign public as a "bonus", evidence that he has harmed the enemy, and is inclined to be the more ruthless. And more than one writer on the subject has pointed to the "ecstasy factor" in terrorism, where gunmen and bombers are reckless to the point of self-destruction, and go into a "killing frenzy". The LOD AIRPORT MASSACRE of 1972 is often cited as a case of "ecstatic" terrorism. And the Arab gunmen who carried out the ROME AIRPORT ATTACK in December 1985 were found to have quantities of drugs in their bloodstreams, which may have induced ecstasy by chemical means.

# Q

**QADDAFADEM, SAYED**. One-time head of Libya's state security apparatus, head of Libya's arms purchasing agencies, and cousin to MUAMMAR QADDAFI, President of Libya. A close confidant of the President, and a Qaddafi loyalist, Qaddafadem played a major role in building up Libya's military forces in the 1970s. After a short period in charge of Libya's internal security apparatus Qaddafadem was given command of a military unit which is particularly faithful to President Qaddafi. Described as a sophisticated and cosmopolitan man with little taste for the anti-Western rhetoric of the Muslim zealots, in the mid-1970s Qaddafadem was charged with acquiring the weaponry the Libyan regime needed to support itself and suppress its opponents. Based in London with an almost unlimited budget, Qaddafadem became the centre of an arms-purchasing operation that attracted some shady people including the renegade CENTRAL INTELLIGENCE AGENCY (CIA) man EDMUND WILSON. In 1976 Qaddafadem was suspected by the British authorities of plotting the assassination of Libyan emigrés in London, and was forced to leave Britain in some haste.

**QADDAFI, MUAMMAR (born 1941)**. President of Libya since 1969, and widely regarded in the West (and particularly in the United States) as one of the main instigators and supporters of international terrorism. This charge Qaddafi has consistently denied, although he claims the right to export "the revolution" throughout the world. He was once described by President Ronald Reagan of the United States as "the most dangerous man in the world". US reaction to Qaddafi's activities flared into open warfare in March and April 1986 when the US Sixth Fleet destroyed Libyan gunboats in the Gulf of Sirte, and then US aircraft attacked what the Americans described as "terrorist bases" in the cities of Tripoli and Benghazi. Qaddafi's response was to denounce the US action as "state terrorism", call for the support of the entire Arab world, and proclaim that the American attacks would not divert Libya from its revolutionary path.

Qaddafi has long been believed by the United States to be one of the "godfathers" of international terrorism, and responsible for the funding and training of many Arab and non-Arab terrorist groups. Following terrorist attacks at ROME AIRPORT and VIENNA AIRPORT in December 1985 (in which 19 people died) the US government denounced Qaddafi as masterminding the operation, and imposed economic sanctions on Libya, and ordered all US citizens out of the country. The American government then launched a campaign to persuade its European allies to join the USA in isolating Qaddafi and his regime. But the Europeans refused to go along with the American strategy, partly out of self interest, and partly because the evidence of the Rome and Vienna attacks suggested that the terrorists had been trained in Syria. In fact, ROBERT OAKLEY, head of the US State Department's anti-terrorist unit, admitted in January 1986 that there was little or no evidence to link Qaddafi with the attacks at Rome and Vienna. But he insisted that Qaddafi has a "master plan" to step up the level of terrorism in the West and the Middle East. For his part Qaddafi tried to blunt the US accusations by urging Palestine "freedom fighters" to confine their campaign to "military Israeli targets" although he pledged Libya's continued support for the Palestinian cause.

In May 1986 a new twist to Qaddafi's alleged support for terrorism emerged when a right-wing Spanish army officer called Colonel Meer de Ribera admitted that he had been negotiating with Qaddafi for funds and arms for a campaign of anti-American attacks throughout Europe. The Spanish extreme right shares Qaddafi's distaste for the USA, and for the Western democracies. Qaddafi's anti-Zionism is echoed in the anti-Semitism of the high Roman Catholicism of the Spanish extremists. Although the Libyan government denied any contacts with the Spanish right-wing groups, the Spanish government registered a formal protest claiming that Libyan diplomats have been dabbling in Spanish politics.

Coping with Qaddafi has put a variety of strains on the Western Alliance. In the course of their diplomatic offensive against the Libyan leader in early 1986 the US government accused a number of European countries (particularly France and Italy) of doing secret deals with Qaddafi in the 1970s to spare their cities from terrorist attacks. The French refused to confirm or deny the assertion while the Italian government admitted that their intelligence services had been in contact with Libya and said, "Qaddafi was giving us information on terrorism and other issues."

Unpredictable but extremely shrewd, Qaddafi was trained at the Military Academy in Benghazi and at the British Army's signal school in England. A devout Muslim and a Bedouin by background, Qaddafi developed a "military cabal" inside the Libyan army, and came to power when he staged a (relatively) bloodless coup against the corrupt monarchy of King Idris in September 1969. In 1972 Libya ended the Anglo-Libyan treaty of friendship, and nationalised British oil interests. Initial Western hopes that Qaddafi's Muslim zeal would make him hostile to the Soviet Union were dashed when the Libyan began building up his armed forces with Soviet arms and equipment such as MiG aircraft and T-72 tanks. Since 1969 Qaddafi has survived a number of attempts on his life including one in March 1985 after which 15 army officers were hanged.

Qaddafi did much to distribute Libya's oil wealth among the three million population (with whom he remains very popular) and launched a huge programme of building schools, hospitals, houses, roads, universities etc, all of which Libya badly needed. But he also built up a large military/security apparatus which his opponents claim has converted Libya into a police state from which around 30,000 of its best-educated people have fled. In recent years the collapse of the oil price has slashed Libya's oil income from around $20 billion a year to around $6 billion, and stressed the Libyan economy.

In 1981 the Qaddafi regime was denounced by Amnesty International for its "systematic" use of torture, and its practice of highly-public (often televised) executions. A fanatical believer in Arab unity, Qaddafi has supported the Palestinian cause enthusiastically, but is viewed with considerable suspicion by his Arab neighbours in whose affairs he has meddled. There have been a number of border clashes between Qaddafi's army and Egypt, and only fear of internal Muslim fundamentalism has stopped Egypt invading Libya in an attempt to topple Qaddafi.

Although Qaddafi denies funding and supporting terrorism, he insists on his right to "export" the revolution, and one way or another he has been connected with a number of serious terrorist incidents over the past 15 years. Among them are the SAUDI ARABIAN EMBASSY ATTACK, KHARTOUM in 1973, the ATHENS AIRPORT ATTACK in 1973, the ROME AIRPORT ATTACK, 1973, the "VORI" HIJACKING in Pakistan in 1974, the OPEC ATTACK in Vienna in 1975, the ISTANBUL AIRPORT ATTACK, 1976. Qaddafi's hand is also thought to have been behind many other terrorist incidents including the EGYPTAIR HIJACKING TO LUQUA AIRPORT, MALTA, in December 1985. In January 1980 Qaddafi broke off relations with YASIR ARAFAT of the PALESTINE LIBERATION ORGANISATION (PLO) and is known to have supported the anti-Arafat organisation of ABU NIDAL. In January 1986 Abu Nidal praised Qaddafi as having been "of great help to us . . . an honest man with whom we have strong ties".

Qaddafi's agents have carried out numerous assassinations of Libyan "stray dogs" (political opponents) throughout the world. In 1980 at least 10 Libyan exiles in Rome, London, Athens, Milan, Bonn and Manchester were assassinated. In April 1984 after the LIBYAN EMBASSY SIEGE, LONDON, the British government severed all diplomatic relations with the Qaddafi regime. In January 1986, following the killings at Rome and Vienna, President Reagan denounced Qaddafi as "flaky" (crazed) and accused him of "armed aggression against the United States". Qaddafi reciprocated by describing Reagan as "mad" and professed his amazement that the American people would want to support such a man. He also threatened to respond to American attacks on Libya by taking the war into the streets of American cities.

**QUTB, SAYYID (1906-1966).** Radical Muslim philosopher and theologian, and important member of the MAJALLAT AL IKHWAN AL MUSLIMIN (MUSLIM BROTHERHOOD), whose interpretation of the Islamic texts is regarded as an important source of the current wave of Muslim fundamentalism. Qutb was executed for his religious views in Egypt in 1966. A passionate believer that Islam had been brought into the world to unify mankind, Qutb argued that those who rejected Islam (such as the Western countries) had to be fought against in a "jihad", or holy war, until they saw the error of their ways. "Those who believe fight for the sake of God," he wrote in one of his books. "And those who disbelieve fight for the sake of idols. Fight, then, the followers of Satan . . . " In one of his texts Qutb frankly advocated a return to Islamic conquest. Born in Egypt, Qutb spent a few years (1949-1951) in the USA where he learned to detest Western civilisation and its apparently implacable support for the newly-fledged state of Israel. On his return to Cairo in 1951 Qutb joined the Muslim Brotherhood which was then regarded as a subversive organisation by the Egyptian government. In 1954 he was sentenced to 15 years in jail, released in the early 1960s, jailed again in 1965 and executed in 1966.

# R

*RAINBOW WARRIOR* **ATTACK**. (July 10th 1985). Bombing attack by French secret service agents on the Greenpeace ship *Rainbow Warrior* in Auckland Harbour, New Zealand. The ship was sunk by two bomb blasts one of which killed the ship's photographer FERNANDO PEREIRA. The revelation that the bombing had been carried out by French agents eventually led to the resignation of the French Defence Minister Charles Hernu, and the sacking of Admiral PIERRE LACOSTE, head of the DIRECTION GENERALE DE LA SECURITE EXTERIEURE (DGSE) in September 1985. The bombing and the subsequent cover-up has been described as the French "Watergate". Two French DGSE agents, DOMINIQUE PRIEUR and ALAIN MAFART were convicted in New Zealand for their part in the bombing, and sentenced to 10 years in jail.

The refusal of the New Zealand government to hand over Prieur and Mafart to the French government is being viewed by the regime of Jacques Chirac as a near-hostile act. Chirac has said that if New Zealand does not grant amnesty to the two French agents it would have "placed itself in the camp of the adversaries, even the enemies of France, and it must then suffer the necessary consequences". Prime Minister David Lange of New Zealand, however, has reiterated that the French agents must serve out their sentences under New Zealand law.

The converted trawler *Rainbow Warrior* was due to lead a "peace flotilla" of small ships to the French nuclear test site at Mururoa Atoll in the Pacific when it was attacked by the DGSE agents. Although initially the French denied that the bombs were planted by the DGSE, the New Zealand government insisted France was responsible, and demanded an unqualified official apology. They also demanded compensation, and the prosecution of the DGSE agents responsible for the attack. On the 13th July 1985 the New Zealand police arrested Captain Dominique Prieur and Commander Alain Mafart, two DGSE agents travelling on forged Swiss passports under the name of "Turenge". Both were subsequently charged with murder. Three other Frenchmen – Raymond Velche, Eric Augrenc, and Jean-Michel Berthelo – were questioned by New Zealand police on Norfolk Island but released.

Although the "immediate and rigorous" inquiry ordered by President Mitterrand at first absolved the DGSE from blame, leaks to the French press made it clear that the DGSE had been responsible, and led to the downfall of Hernu and Lacoste. The French press claimed that three DGSE teams had been involved, including a group of underwater swimmers who had never been traced. In September three DGSE officers were arrested for leaking "sensitive" information to the press, creating speculation that the press leaks were an effort by right-wingers in the DGSE to discredit the socialist government of François Mitterrand. On 25th September 1985 French Prime Minister Laurent Fabius announced that compensation would be immediately paid to the family of the Portuguese-born photographer killed in the blast, but he failed to make any official apology to New Zealand.

In October 1985 Dominique Prieur and Alain Mafart were both sentenced to 10 years in prison for their part in the sinking of the "Rainbow Warrior" and the death of Fernando Pereira. The French public, however, have taken the view that the two agents were simply doing their job, and their jailing has created an upsurge of anti-New Zealand feeling. In April 1986 the owner of one of the biggest supermarket chains in France announced that he would not stock New Zealand produce so long as Prieur and Mafart were in New Zealand jails. In July 1986 it was agreed that Mafart and Prieur should serve their sentences in a French Pacific jail.

**RASHTRIYA SWAYAMSEVAK SANGH (RSS).** Right-wing fundamentalist Hindu organisation one of whose members NATHURAM VINAYAK GODSE assassinated MAHATMA GANDHI in January 1948. Described by Gandhi as a "body with a totalitarian outlook" the RSS were founded in 1925 by a Hindu doctor called Keshav Hedgewar. The RSS quickly evolved into a paramilitary organisation with a vision of an all-Hindu India stretching from Afghanistan to the tip of the subcontinent. Drawn mainly from lower-middle-class merchants and white-collar workers, RSS activists have been among the most virulent and dangerous anti-Muslims in India. Hedgewar himself regarded all Muslims as "snakes" and was bitterly opposed to Gandhi's attempts to create an India which would embrace all religions and creeds. After Gandhi was killed in January 1948 the RSS was proscribed by the new Indian government but was legalised again in 1949 after swearing to give up politics and "abjure violence and secrecy". The RSS were banned again in the state of emergency between 1975 and 1977. In recent years the RSS have acted as a kind of "protection agency" for Hindu businessmen in some parts of India against the Muslim-dominated underworld.

**RASPE, JAN-CARLE**. Leading member of the West German terrorist group ROTE ARMEE FRAKTION (RAF) who killed himself in Stammheim jail near Stuttgart on October 18th 1977 after the successful West German police rescue operation following the LUFTHANSA HIJACKING TO MOGADISHU AIRPORT, SOMALIA. Raspe was found dead in his cell at 07.41 on October 18th 1977 with a gunshot wound in the head from a weapon which had been smuggled into the prison. Although still alive, Raspe died in a Stuttgart hospital two hours later. Raspe's suicide coincided with that of ANDREAS BAADER and GUDRUN ENSSLIN. Like most members of the RAF Raspe was an intellectually-inclined product of the German middle class who had become convinced that Western society was terminally "sick" and deserved to be overthrown.

**RAY, JAMES EARL (born 1928)**. Also known as Eric Stavro Galt. Right-wing American racist who assassinated American civil rights leader MARTIN LUTHER KING in Memphis, Tennessee, on April 4th 1968. Ray fled from the scene of the crime leaving a high-powered rifle with telescopic sight on which his fingerprints were visible. After the FEDERAL BUREAU OF INVESTIGATION (FBI) issued a warrant for his arrest Ray was eventually picked up at Heathrow Airport, London, on June 8th 1968 while travelling on a false Canadian passport. A revolver and ammunition were found in his luggage. Ray had, in fact, escaped on April 23rd 1967 from Missouri State Penitentiary where he had been serving 20 years for armed robbery. After pleading guilty to the murder of Martin Luther King, Ray was sentenced to 99 years in prison. Ray later applied for a retrial but was refused.

**RED ARMY FACTION (RAF)**. See ROTE ARMEE FRAKTION.

**RED BRIGADES**. See BRIGATE ROSSE.

**RED HAND COMMANDOS (RHC)**. Small but violent Ulster "loyalist" group which emerged in Northern Ireland in 1972 and is believed to have been responsible for a number of sectarian murders of Roman Catholics. The British government declared the RHC illegal in 1973 at the same time as they proscribed the ULSTER FREEDOM FIGHTERS (UFF). In 1974 the RHC issued a statement to local newspapers declaring that for every Protestant killed in the border areas of Fermanagh and South Tyrone four Roman Catholics would be shot. The RHC were closely associated with the larger ULSTER VOLUNTEER FORCE (UVF) and at a meeting with the British government in 1974 the UVF delegate said he was also speaking on behalf of the Red Hand Commandos.

**REGENT'S PARK BOMBING, LONDON. (July 20th 1982).** One of two bomb attacks in London on the same day. Six soldiers of the Royal Green Jackets military band were killed, and 28 injured when a bomb placed under the bandstand on which they were giving a concert in Regent's Park exploded at 12.55. Four civilians were also injured and a seventh bandsman died a few days later. The bombing occurred two hours after the HYDE PARK BOMBING which caused carnage among the men and horses of the Household Cavalry.

**REVOLUTIONARY ORGANISATION OF SOCIALIST MUSLIMS (ROSM).** One of the names used by the ABU NIDAL organisation. The ROSM have claimed responsibility for a series of attacks on British individuals and institutions in Greece, Lebanon, India and Italy. The ROSM were first heard of in March 1984 when they admitted killing Kenneth Whitty, a British official based in Athens. In November of the same year the ROSM assassinated Percy Norris, Britain's deputy high commissioner in Bombay. In August 1985 the group attacked The London Hotel in Athens injuring 13 people, six of them British. On September 3rd 1985 they launched a grenade attack on the Glyfad Hotel in a holiday resort near Athens, injuring 19 British tourists. The organisation also claim to be holding Alex Collett, a British journalist kidnapped in Lebanon in March 1984.

On September 16th 1985 the ROSM bombed the Café De Paris in Rome injuring 39 people, and 10 days later injured 14 people in an attack on the British Airways office in Rome. In messages to news agencies in Beirut, Paris and London the ROSM have warned the British to "stop their aggressive attacks" and to "release all Muslim freedom fighters from British imperialist jails". The latter demand is thought to refer to two Palestinians jailed in Britain for the attempted murder of the Israeli ambassador SHLOMO ARGOV in London in June 1982.

**REVOLUTIONARER ZELLEN (RZ).** (Revolutionary Cells). Left-wing West German terror group which was formed in the 1970s, and which specialised in attacking American multinational companies (which RZ activists believe are dominating the governments of the world). Less intellectually élitist than the ROTE ARMEE FRAKTION (RAF), the RZ are regarded by West German authorities as the most active and dangerous of the left-wing groups. Their numbers appear to have dwindled from 200 activists to around 80. In December 1980 the RZ shot and killed Hans-Herbert Karry, the State of Hessen's finance minister. The group later claimed that they only intended to wound Karry. The RZ are organised in "cells" of five or six people which operate independently of one another. In recent years RZ bombers have attacked a chemical plant in Cologne, the Deutsche Bank in Dusseldorf and a NATO pipeline near Frankfurt. In 1984 they bombed West German companies who had "fought against the striking miners" of Britain.

**REZAQ, OMAR MOHAMMED ALI**. A 22-year-old Palestinian, and the only survivor of the four-man terrorist group involved in the EGYPTAIR HIJACKING TO LUQA AIRPORT, MALTA, in November 1985. Rezaq is now being held in a Malta jail waiting trial, and efforts by the Egyptian government to have him extradited to stand trial in Egypt have failed.

**RHODESIAN SPECIAL AIR SERVICE (RSAS)**. The Rhodesian version of the British Army's SPECIAL AIR SERVICE (SAS) which formed one of the illegal white regime's main anti-terrorist units in the war against the ZIMBABWE NATIONAL LIBERATION ARMY (ZANLA) and the ZIMBABWE PEOPLE'S LIBERATION ARMY (ZIPRA) between 1966 and 1980. The RSAS were used as a counter-terror force inside Rhodesia and for "search and destroy" missions into Angola and Zambia. The all-white unit was disbanded in 1980, and many of its members joined the South African Defence Force (SADF).

**"RICE BOWL", OPERATION**. Military code name for the preparatory and planning stage of the abortive operation by US special forces to resolve the AMERICAN HOSTAGE CRISIS, TEHERAN. The military operation itself was dubbed "EAGLE CLAW".

**RODE HULP (RH)**. (Red Help). Dutch left-wing "support" group set up in 1973 to agitate for the release of Dutch radicals jailed in Holland. The RH had some contact with the Palestinian movement, and in July 1976 10 RH members spent three weeks in South Yemen being trained by the POPULAR FRONT FOR THE LIBERATION OF PALESTINE (PFLP). In return the RH agreed to attack Tel Aviv airport but their plan was thwarted by Israeli intelligence, and RH members Ludwina Janssen and Marius Nieuwburg were arrested in Israel.

**RODE JEUGD (RJ).** (Red Youth). A Maoist splinter group of the Communist Party of the Netherlands which advocated the writings of the Brazilian urban guerrilla theorist CARLOS MARIGHELLA and which tried to "radicalise" street demonstrations into battles with the Dutch police. In 1972 RJ activitists attacked the Holiday Inn hotel in Utrecht, and the Phillips Corporation buildings in Rotterdam and Eindhoven. Later that year the RJ dissolved itself and set up RODE HULP.

**RODE VERZETSFRONT (RVF).** (Red Resistance Front). One of a number of small left-wing Dutch groups which emerged in the 1970s. Although the RVF confined themselves mainly to graffiti-painting, leafleting, and occupying offices etc, in 1979 they did make an armed assault on a government building at Groningen in an attempt to steal blank passports. Two RVF members – Johannes Bolt and Ferdinand Western – were later jailed.

**ROME AIRPORT ATTACK. (December 17th 1973).** An attack on an American airliner at Rome Airport by two Arab terrorists which killed 33 people and injured more than 40. The gunmen then took six hostages, commandeered another aircraft and flew to Athens, Damascus, and then to Kuwait where they surrendered. Efforts by the Italian government to extradite the terrorists to stand trial failed as the Kuwaiti authorities argued that the men were "political" activists and not criminals. But in March 1974 the men were flown to Cairo where they were tried in secret by a Palestinian court.

The attack began when the two Arabs drew automatic weapons and grenades from their hand luggage, sprayed the airport terminal with automatic fire, and then lobbed phosphorus grenades into the open doorways of a Pan-American Airways airliner. Most of the 90 passengers on board were strapped into their seats, and the attack killed 32 of them and injured another 40. An airport worker was also shot to death. The Arab gunmen then took six hostages (five Italian policemen and an Ethiopian airport worker), seized a Lufthansa Boeing 737 and a crew of six and forced it to take off for the Middle East.

After being refused permission to land at Beirut Airport the gunmen ordered the Lufthansa jet to Athens airport where they landed, shot one of their Italian hostages, and warned the Greeks that the others would be killed unless two Arabs being held in Greece were released. The two jailed Arabs refused to join the hijackers because they belonged to a different terrorist group. The 737 then left for Baghdad (where it was refused permission to land), refuelled at Damascus, and finally landed in Kuwait where the gunmen surrendered to the Kuwaiti authorities who refused to extradite them to Italy. The Kuwaitis said the attack on Rome Airport had been "political" and therefore the men could not be handed over to Italian justice. But the outrage put heavy pressure on YASIR ARAFAT and the PALESTINE LIBERATION ORGANISATION (PLO) and on March 3rd 1974 the gunmen were flown to Cairo where they were tried in secret by a PLO court.

**ROME AIRPORT ATTACK. (December 27th 1985).** Fifteen people died and more than 70 were injured when four Arab gunmen opened fire and threw grenades into a crowded passenger terminal at Leonardo Da Vinci Airport in Rome. Three of the gunmen were killed by Israeli and Italian security men and one was captured. At the same time another group attacked the passenger terminal of VIENNA AIRPORT. Although both attacks were immediately blamed on the Palestinian group controlled by ABU NIDAL, the American and Israeli governments accused Libya and Syria with aiding and abetting the terrorists. Fearing US and/or Israeli reprisals the Libyans denounced the attacks at Rome and Vienna, but warned that Libyan "suicide squads" were ready to take the war "into the streets of American cities".

The four Arabs responsible for the Rome outrage launched their attack at 08.15 on December 27th 1985 by throwing hand grenades into the queues standing at the El Al and TWA ticket desks. They then opened fire with KALASHNIKOV AK-47 assault rifles. Most of the people who died were Israelis and Americans, but Greeks, Mexicans, and two Arab passengers were among the dead. After a brief gun battle with Israeli security men and Italian police, three of the terrorists were killed and one wounded and captured. He was MOHAMMED SHARAM (19). A note found on one of the Arabs warned all "Zionists" that "The tears we have shed will be exchanged for blood. The war started from this moment." The note was signed "The Martyrs of Palestine".

The PALESTINE LIBERATION ORGANISATION (PLO) were quick to condemn the Rome and Vienna attacks and to disclaim the attackers. Some observers believe that both attacks were calculated to discredit the PLO and were part of Abu Nidal's long-running campaign against Yasir Arafat. Both Italy and Austria are among the European countries well disposed to the Palestinian cause. Israel and the USA blamed the Libyan and Syrian governments for financing and supporting the Abu Nidal terrorists. A few days after the shootings in Rome and Vienna, the Americans moved a task force from the US 6th Fleet towards the coast of Libya, which prompted the Libyan government to put its forces on alert. The Americans also put pressure on their West European allies to impose economic and political sanctions against Libya and Syria.

**ROME AIRPORT, ATTEMPTED MISSILE ATTACK. (September 5th 1973).** A plan by Arab terrorists to shoot down an Israeli aircraft at Fiumicino Airport, Rome, using a Soviet-made SA-7 surface-to-air missile. The attack was foiled when Italian police raided a flat at Ostia near the airport in the early hours of September 5th 1973, and arrested five Arabs (a Libyan, an Iraqi, a Lebanese, a Jordanian and an Algerian). Two SA-7 rocket launching systems were found in the apartment. Italian police claimed that the Arabs were arrested only hours before they planned to use the heat-seeking anti-aircraft missiles to down an El Al civilian airliner. The police pointed out that the SA-7 is a "man-portable" system with a range of 9-10 kilometres which had been sold to a number of Third World countries including Egypt, Syria, South Yemen, Morocco and Cuba.

Alarmed at the prospect of such weapons being used against their civilian aircraft, the Israeli government fiercely denounced the Arab states which had supplied the terrorists "with this means of slaughter". On September 10th 1973 Israel complained to the International Civil Aviation Organisation (ICAO) meeting in Rome that the SA-7 missiles had been supplied to the terrorists by either Egypt, Syria or Iraq, and described their complicity as "an unspeakable act". The three accused governments rejected the Israeli charge, and counter-charged Israel of seeking to justify "future illegal actions".

**ROMERO, OSCAR (1917-1980).** The Archbishop of San Salvador, El Salvador, who was shot to death on March 24th 1980 while holding Mass at a hospital chapel in San Salvador. An outspoken critic of El Salvador's repressive right-wing regime, Romero had received many threats on his life. On the day before his murder the 63-year-old Romero was denounced by the regime for calling on Salvadoran soldiers not to carry out military orders which were "contrary to God's law". At Romero's funeral on March 30th 1980 an estimated 39 people were killed and 50 injured when firing broke out. The El Salvador government tried to accuse leftists in the crowd for starting the shootings in an attempt to steal Romero's body. But the 26 foreign prelates and other churchmen in the procession insisted that the firing was instigated by government troops. Shortly before his death Romero was nominated for the Nobel Peace Prize by a group of British Parliamentarians.

**ROTE ARMEE FRAKTION (RAF)**. (Red Army Faction). Left-wing German terrorist organisation also known as the Baader-Meinhof Gang. Founded in 1967 by ANDREAS BAADER, ULRIKE MEINHOF and GUDRUN ENSSLIN, the RAF was responsible for a large number of attacks throughout Western Europe, often in co-operation with other left-wing and Palestinian groups. The RAF are usually regarded as the most violent and effective of the West German terror groups, and have been responsible for dozens of bombings and assassinations throughout West Germany. RAF members were also involved in the OPEC ATTACK in December 1975, the AIR FRANCE HIJACKING TO ENTEBBE AIRPORT in June 1976 and the LUFTHANSA HIJACKING TO MOGADISHU AIRPORT in October 1977. Although the RAF's founders and ringleaders were jailed in 1972, and all committed suicide in 1976 and 1977 the RAF continues to operate in West Germany. In January 1985 the RAF announced the formation of a "Political Military Front" with the French left-wing group ACTION DIRECTE (AD) to attack NATO bases and those companies working for NATO.

In July 1985 the RAF mounted the AMERICAN AIR FORCE BASE ATTACK, RHEIN-MAIN, killing one US serviceman and the wife of another. The same week the RAF/AD planted incendiary bombs (which failed to ignite) on a US troop train, and attacked a US depot at Monchen-Gladbach. The RAF are believed to have carried out 40 bombing and arson attacks in 1985, and operate through a network of 20 activists and around 100 supporters.

Like other West European terrorist groups the RAF grew out of the political turbulence of the late 1960s and the apparent failure of the New Left to effect radical change in Western society. Formed in 1967, the RAF launched their campaign against Western capitalism in 1968 by planting incendiary bombs in a Frankfurt department store. After a period of study and training in Palestinian camps in the Middle East, the nucleus of the RAF returned to Europe and began bombing US military bases, police stations, and the offices of the right-wing Springer press. The West German government response was to step up police efficiency, and in 1972 Baader, Meinhof and Ensslin and 18 RAF members were arrested and jailed at Stammheim high security prison.

Successive attempts by the terrorists to force the West German government to release the RAF leaders failed, although the government did release five minor RAF members in exchange for PETER LORENZ, a West Berlin Christian Democrat who had been kidnapped by one of the RAF's allied groups in February 1975. In April 1975 the RAF took over the West German Embassy, Stockholm, and held the ambassador and some of his staff hostage demanding the release of Baader, Meinhof and Ensslin. The government refused, although the refusal cost two lives.

In the 1970s the RAF were an active part of the international network, and established close contacts with a number of Palestinian groups. The notorious ILLICH RAMIREZ SANCHEZ recruited RAF members for a rocket attempt against an Israeli aircraft at Orly airport, Paris, for the raid on the OPEC headquarters in Vienna, and for the Air France hijacking to Entebbe Airport, Uganda. The RAF terrorists involved in the hijacking were Brigitte Kuhlmann and Wilfried Bose. The RAF suffered its worst blow in October 1977 when the attempt to force the release of Baader and Ensslin by the hijacking to Mogadishu came to nothing when the German police GRENZSCHUTZGRUPPE-9 (GSG-9) squad stormed the aircraft. After the failure of the Mogadishu operation RAF leaders Baader, Ensslin and JAN-CARLE RASPE committed suicide in Stammheim Prison.

Although deprived of it founder-members, the RAF probably reached a peak in 1977 when the organisation killed Attorney General Siegfrid Buback (and his guards), Hanns-Martin Schleyer (and his guards) and mounted a rocket attack on the Federal justice department offices. In June 1979 the RAF made a serious attempt on the life of Alexander Haig, then head of NATO forces in Europe. In February 1985 the RAF killed West German arms manufacturer Ernst Zimmerman at his home near Munich.

**ROYAL ULSTER CONSTABULARY (RUC).** The largely Protestant, civilian police force of the British province of Northern Ireland. Formed out of the old Royal Irish Constabulary following the partition of Ireland in 1921, the RUC was officially instigated in June 1922, and has borne the brunt of the various terrorist onslaughts ever since. Until 1970 the RUC was supported by the

Ulster Special Constabulary (USC), a force which was bitterly resented by most Northern Ireland Catholics as sectarian and anti-Catholic. Despite strenuous efforts in recent years to recruit more men and women from the Catholic community, the RUC remains a mainly Protestant force and is unwelcome in many hard-line Republican areas of Northern Ireland. Since being set up in June 1922 the RUC has lost 242 officers to terrorist attacks, 214 of them since the modern troubles began in 1969. The most serious single incident was the NEWRY POLICE STATION ATTACK in February 1985 which killed nine RUC officers.

Following the bitter riots of August 1969 a British government commission decided that the RUC had been "seriously at fault" in at least six incidents, and that there was a "fateful split between the Catholic community and the police" which had to be healed (if possible). In 1970 the RUC was reorganised along British mainland police force lines, the USC were stood down, and the RUC establishment was increased from 3,500 to over 4,000 and has grown steadily ever since to around 8,000 regular police officers and 5,000 reservists. Despite the hazards of the job, in 1985 the RUC received applications from 4,000 men and women for 390 places.

Since 1979 the RUC has been co-operating closely with the Garda Siochana (the police of the Irish Republic) which has produced some successful arms seizures on both sides of the border. In the last 16 years the RUC has confiscated 9,281 firearms, 82 tons of explosives, more than a million bullets, and charged almost 8,000 people with terrorist offences. In recent years the RUC has been heavily criticised (both inside and outside Northern Ireland) for their extensive use of "supergrass" informers, usually terrorists who have been "turned" in exchange for immunity from prosecution.

And after a series of shooting incidents in Armagh in 1982 (in which six people were killed) the RUC was accused of operating a "shoot to kill" policy against suspected Republicans. The charges were made by Roman Catholic leaders against undercover policemen from the RUC's Divisional Mobile Support Unit, and led to an investigation into the activities of the RUC in Armagh by a senior English policeman, John Stalker. Stalker's report was submitted to the Director of Public Prosecutions in February 1986.

Although the RUC has always been regarded by Northern Ireland's Roman Catholics as a Protestant (and therefore "Loyalist") force, following the British-Irish agreement giving Dublin a say in the running of the province, the RUC came under bitter attack from the Protestant side. In an attempt to weaken the British government's authority and make Ulster ungovernable hundreds of attacks were made upon the homes of RUC men. Many officers and their familiies were driven out by bricks, firebombs and even bullets and were forced to seek "secure" quarters elsewhere. Dozens of officers have applied for transfers to police forces on the British mainland.

**RUBY, JACK. (1911-1967).** Real name Jacob Rubenstein. The Polish-born American night-club owner and petty criminal who shot dead LEE HARVEY OSWALD on November 24th 1963 in the basement of the Dallas police headquarters. Ruby committed the crime in full view of the television cameras. Oswald had been charged with the murder of President JOHN F. KENNEDY at Dealey Plaza, on November 22nd 1963. How Ruby contrived to infiltrate the Dallas police headquarters and shoot Oswald in the stomach has never been satisfactorily explained. Before he died of cancer in 1967 Ruby said that he had been "framed" into shooting Oswald and that "the world will never know the true facts of what occurred". What is known is that Ruby had long-standing contacts with organised crime, and with the anti-Castro Cubans of the American south-west.

**RUE COPERNIC SYNAGOGUE BOMBING, PARIS. (October 3rd 1980).** Four people were killed and 15 were injured when terrorists attacked the Jewish synagogue in the Rue Copernic in Paris. One of the dead was an Israeli woman. The bombing of the synagogue was one of a series of attacks on Jewish (as distinct from Israeli) targets in France in the early 1980s. A demonstration in Nice protesting at the Rue Copernic bombing was itself attacked by a hand grenade (although there were no casualties).

# S

**SA'AQA**. (The Thunderbolt). Egypt's élite anti-terrorist group which has been used a number of times to resolve hijackings, including the EGYPTAIR HIJACKING TO LUQA AIRPORT, MALTA in December 1985. Western governments believe that Sa'aqa contains 500-700 men some of whom have been trained by US and West German special forces. Although Sa'aqa has had its successes (in 1975 they were responsible for releasing all the passengers from a Boeing 737 hijacked at Luxor in Upper Egypt) the unit were involved in the LARNACA AIRPORT ATTACK in 1985 when a Sa'aqa team tried to storm a hijacked Cyprus Airways jet without informing the Cyprus authorities. The Sa'aqa unit were heavily criticised for the way they handled the rescue attempt at Luqa Airport. Some critics say the Egyptians moved for political reasons before the the operation could be taken over by US anti-terrorist forces. British SPECIAL AIR SERVICE (SAS) claimed that the Sa'aqa teams failed to gather enough information about the hijackers and their captives, failed to divert the hijackers' attention, mistimed their attack, took too long to carry out the operation, and failed to use the kind of "flash-bang" stun grenades which had proved so successful in the rescue operation after the LUFTHANSA HIJACKING TO MOGADISHU AIPORT, SOMALIA in 1977.

**SA'AQA**. (The Thunderbolt). The military arm of the Pro-Syrian Palestinian organisation known as The Vanguards Of The Popular War Of Liberation (The Vanguards). Close allies of the mainstream guerrilla organisation FATAH, Sa'aqa have one seat on the influential Executive Committee of the PALESTINE LIBERATION ORGANISATION (PLO). Sa'aqa's close connections with the ruling Ba'ath party in Syria have made the organisation vulnerable to Syrian internal disputes. From time to time the Syrian military have purged Sa'aqa of its leadership and replaced it with Syrian appointees. In 1970 the Syrians installed a veteran Ba'athist called Zuhair Muhsin to lead Sa'aqa but he was driven out of Beirut in 1976 by Fatah guerrillas and eventually assassinated in Cannes in July 1979 (on his way back to his apartment from a Cannes casino).

Sa'aqa units based in Lebanon have played an active part in that country's civil wars, but the credibility of the Sa'aqa fighters was badly damaged when the Syrian army withdrew from key points during the Israeli invasion of June 1982.

**SABENA HIJACKING TO LOD AIRPORT, ISRAEL. (May 9th 1972).** The hijacking of a Belgian-owned airliner to Lod Airport in Israel by four BLACK SEPTEMBER terrorists who threatened to blow up the jet and its 90 passengers unless the Israelis released 371 Arab prisoners. The aircraft was stormed by men of the Israeli anti-terrorist squad SAYARET MATKAL who killed two of the four hijackers. One passenger was also killed in the exchange of fire. The incident at Lod Airport was the first time that a captured airliner was successfully stormed by security forces.

Flight 517, a Sabena Boeing 707 with 100 passengers and crew aboard was en route from Brussels to Tel Aviv on May 9th 1972 when it was taken over by four armed terrorists (two men and two women). The terrorists ordered the pilot to fly direct to Lod Airport in Israel where the aircraft landed. The Israeli government were warned that unless they released 371 Arabs being held prisoner in Israel the aircraft and its 100 passengers and crew would be blown up. Playing for time, the Israelis pretended to negotiate through the good offices of the International Red Cross (IRC). While the negotiations were going on, the Sayaret Matkal team were practising their assault techniques on another Boeing 707 in a nearby hangar. Then disguised as mechanics the Israelis approached the aircraft and burst through the doors killing the two male hijackers and wounding one of the women. One female passenger was also killed in the assault. Later the International Red Cross complained that they had been "used" in bad faith by the Israeli authorities.

**SABRA AND SHATILA MASSACRES, BEIRUT. (September 16th-18th 1982).** Massacre of Palestinian and other Arab men, women and children in two refugee camps in Beirut by Lebanese Christian militiamen taking revenge for the assassination of President-elect BASHIR GEMAYEL. It is estimated that anything from 800 to 2,000 people died in the killings. The slaughter shocked the world, particularly as the Israeli Defence Forces (IDF) had allowed the Christians to enter the camps and held the perimeter while the massacres went on. The Israeli government set up the Kahan Commission to investigate the Sabra and Shatila incident. When the commission decided that Israel's minister of defence, Ariel

Sharon bore "personal responsibility" for the massacres Sharon resigned.

The killings began at dusk on September 16th 1982 when 200 or so Christian militiamen crossed Israeli lines and moved into the Sabra and Shatila refugee camps in the southern surburbs of Beirut. The camps were heavily populated by Palestinian women and children, but most of the Palestinian fighters had been driven northwards by the Israeli invasion. Many of the dead – perhaps as many as half – were Lebanese Shia Muslims. Egyptians, Syrians, Jordanians and Kuwaitis also died in the attack.

For almost 38 hours the Christian militiamen butchered their way through Sabra and Shatila, killing, raping, mutilating and torturing, even booby-trapping bodies and burying many of their victims in the rubble of bull-dozed houses. The true death toll will never be known but at least 800 people died in the camps, and many Lebanese and Palestinians believe the figure is nearer 3,000. The killings came to an end when press reports began to leak out to the severe embarrassment of the Lebanese Christian authorities and the Israeli Defence Forces (IDF). In the face of world outrage the Israeli government asked the Kahan Commission to investigate the atrocities. Kahan and his colleagues reported on February 7th 1983 and came to the conclusion that the IDF commanders should have known that turning the Christians loose on Sabra and Shatila could have disastrous consequences.

Kahan and his colleagues concluded that Defence Minister Ariel Sharon bore "personal responsibility" for the atrocity and that if he did not resign he should be sacked. They also arrived at "grave conclusions" concerning the Chief of Staff, Rafael Eitan. The Kahan Commission accepted the difficulties of waging war in an urban maelstrom like Beirut where alliances shifted daily, and agreed that the IDF had to pursue their objectives with single-minded toughness. But they warned that "the end never justifies the means, and basic ethical and human values must be maintained in the use of arms".

**SADAT, ANWAR. (1918-1981).** President of Egypt who was assassinated by fundamentalist Muslims on Tuesday 6th October 1981 while taking the salute at a military parade in Cairo. The attack was led by KHALED EL-SAMBOULI, an Egyptian army lieutenant who contrived to replace members of his military unit with three Muslim extremists, Abdul Salam, Abbas Mohammed and Ataya Reheil. Sadat died in a hail of gunfire from the four assassins, one of whom, Abbas Mohammed, had been one of the

Egyptian army's best marksmen. Seven other people – including a Coptic bishop – died along with Sadat, and 28 were injured. The assassins believed that Sadat's death would spark off an uprising by Egypt's Muslim fundamentalists which would topple the pro-Western regime. In April 1982 El Sambouli, Salam, Mohammed and Reheil were executed along with fellow conspirator Abdel Salem Farag.

Sadat's assasination was plotted by an 'anqud (or cell) of Muslim fundamentalists led by Farag, a 28-year-old electrical engineer and author of a religious work called *The Absent Prayer*. This privately printed book influenced the already pious Khaled El Sambouli, already hostile to Sadat's policies. His brother Mohammed had been arrested in September 1981 for anti-Sadat activities, and was in Mecca in December 1979 when Moslem fundamentalists attacked the GREAT MOSQUE OF MECCA.

El Sambouli and his accomplices were armed with four submachine-guns and a few hand grenades which were used as a diversion. Three of the assassins were wounded in the counter-fire. When Sadat was rushed to the Maadi Hospital in Cairo he was found to be suffering from bullet wounds to his neck, chest, legs, arms and face. At 14.40 Sadat was declared dead. Ironically, Sadat had refused to wear his bullet-proof undervest that day because he felt it spoiled the line of his new, London-tailored uniform.

Although Colonel ABBOUD ZUMR, the military leader of the 'anqud, was against the murder of Sadat, he was overruled. Farag, El Sambouli and the others firmly believed that the death of Sadat would spark off an uprising by Egypt's fundamentalists which would rid the country of the Westernised Egyptians who had struck an accommodation with Israel. Sadat's murder led to a purge of radical Muslims from the Egyptian army. The police investigation into the killing of Sadat and the others uncovered a wide conspiracy. Twenty-four people were tried for the shootings in Cairo between November 1981 and March 1982. Twenty-two were found guilty, 17 were jailed for life, and five sentenced to death. On April 15th 1982 El Sambouli and Mohammed were shot, while Reheil, Salam and Farag were hanged.

**SADR, MUSA AL**. Iranian-born Muslim "Imam" (holy man) and head of the Shia Muslims of Lebanon who disappeared in September 1978 during a trip to Libya. Although the regime of MUAMMAR QADDAFI have always denied any knowledge of Imam Sadr's disappearance, most Lebanese Shias believe that the Libyan leader was responsible. Sadr and two of his Lebanese colleagues disappeared after a session of talks with Qaddafi and his aides in which Sadr was pleading for assistance and support for the oppressed Shias of southern Lebanon against the Israeli and Palestinian occupiers. The missing Lebanese were due to catch a flight from Tripoli to Rome; their luggage arrived but the Imam and his associates did not. As the spiritual leader of Lebanon's one million Shi'ites, Musa Al Sadr's unexplained disappearance became a Shi'ite cause, and a number of hijackings, attacks and kidnappings have been perpetrated by Shi'ites in the name of their missing Imam.

**SALAMEH, ALI HASSAN**. Also known as Abu Hassan and "The Red Prince". Senior security aide to YASIR ARAFAT, head of the Palestinian FATAH, and the man believed by the Israelis to have been responsible for the planning and organisation of the MUNICH OLYMPICS ATTACK in 1972. Salameh was at the head of the Israeli MOSSAD's hit list for most of the 1970s until he was finally killed by a car bomb in Beirut in January 1979. Salameh's death was widely regarded as a severe blow to Yasir Arafat and the Fatah command.

Following the BLACK SEPTEMBER attack on the Munich Olympic Games (in which 11 Israeli athletes died) Salameh was blamed by the Israelis for setting up the entire operation. The Mossad "WRATH OF GOD" assassination squads which were set up by Golda Meir after the Munich débâcle spent seven years trying to kill Salameh. One of the Israeli teams caused a major diplomatic incident in July 1973 in the LILLEHAMMER DEBACLE, when they mistakenly killed a harmless Moroccan waiter they thought was Salameh.

The son of a Palestinian Arab who had waged bitter war against the Jews and was killed by a HAGANAH bomb, Ali Hassan Salameh grew up as a refugee in the West Bank town of Nablus. Like many bright young Palestinians he studied at the American University in Beirut where he attracted the attention of Yasir Arafat who recruited him into the PALESTINE LIBERATION ORGANISATION (PLO) and sent him to Egypt to study intelligence work. Salameh became one of the group of Palestinian radicals who formed the Black September arm of Fatah following the PLO's expulsion from Jordan by King Hussein's army in September 1970. Salameh was finally assassinated in Beirut (almost certainly by Mossad agents) on January 23rd 1979 when a remote-controlled bomb in a parked car exploded as he drove past. The blast killed Salameh, four of his bodyguards, and a number of passers-by, including 34-year-old Susan Wareham, a British secretary working in Beirut.

**SALEH, MAHMOUD.** One-time representative of the PALESTINE LIBERATION ORGANISATION (PLO) in Paris who was shot dead outside his bookshop on January 3rd 1977. Indirectly, Saleh's death caused a major diplomatic incident when the one of the PLO delegation to his funeral was arrested and then released by the French authorities. Although the PLO man was travelling on an Iraqi passport under an assumed name he was, in fact, ABU DAOUD believed by the Israeli and West German governments to have been one of the organisers of the MUNICH OLYMPICS ATTACK in October 1972. The PLO blamed the Israeli MOSSAD for Mahmoud Saleh's death.

**SAMBOULI, KHALED EL.** The Muslim fundamentalist Egyptian army lieutenant who led the group which assassinated Egyptian President ANWAR SADAT on October 6th 1981. A devout young Muslim whose brother had been arrested for anti-Sadat activities, El-Sambouli reorganised his army unit to include the four-man assassination team of Muslim extremists. After a lengthy trial he was executed on April 15th 1982 along with the other assassins.

**SANCHEZ, ILLICH RAMIREZ (born 1950).** Also known as "Carlos the Jackal". Venezuelan-born terrorist organiser responsible for the killing of the Palestinian Michael Moukharbel and two French secret service agents in Paris in 1975, and for the OPEC ATTACK, VIENNA, in December 1975. Believed to have contacts with many of the Arab and European terrorist groups, Sanchez is also suspected of being involved with the AIR FRANCE HIJACKING TO ENTEBBE AIRPORT, UGANDA, in June 1976. Sanchez is now thought to be based in Iraq. Some commentators believe that far from being a "freelance" terrorist Sanchez is, in fact, an officer of the Soviet KOMITET GOSUDARSTVENNOI BEZOPASTNOSTI (KGB).

Born into a middle-class Communist family in Venezuela (his father was a lawyer and Sanchez's first name is a tribute to Vladimir Illich Lenin) Sanchez spent some time in a Cuban training camp, then a period in London and Paris, and was finally sent to the Patrice Lumumba University in Moscow where he learned French, Arabic and German, but was expelled in 1971. Some writers claim that his expulsion was a cover story to "distance" him from the Soviet authorities. After a short spell teaching in London,

Sanchez went back to Paris to take over the terrorist organisation of the slain Algerian Mohammed Boudia (which Sanchez renamed the "Boudia Commando").

Sanchez is believed to have been responsible for the attempt on the life of Lord Sieff on December 30th 1974, a series of bombings of pro-Israeli newspapers and institutions in France, and a rocket attack on an Israeli airliner at Orly Airport in Paris. In June 1975 Sanchez was almost trapped in a Paris apartment by the French secret service, but shot his way out of trouble, killing two French agents and an Arab informer in the process. A few months later he organised the attack on OPEC, the political purpose of which is obscure, and which may have been a terrorist fund-raising operation. Sanchez is still being sought by the police and intelligence agencies of almost every Western country.

**"SANDINISTAS".** See FRENTE SANDINISTA DE LIBERACION NACIONAL (FSLN).

**SANDINO, AUGUSTE CESAR.** Nicaraguan political and guerrilla leader who waged a bitter resistance campaign against the US military domination of Nicaragua, and after whom the FRENTE SANDINISTA DE LIBERACION NACIONAL ("Sandinistas") take their name. Sandino was eventually assassinated on February 11th 1934 by the US-trained National Guardsmen of ANASTASIO SOMOZA whose family went on to run Nicaragua as dictators for more than 40 years until being overthrown by the left-wing Sandinistas in 1979.

**SANDS, ROBERT ("BOBBY") (1954-1981).** Irish Republican and elected member of the British Parliament who starved himself to death in May 1981 during the MAZE PRISON HUNGER-STRIKES. While on hunger-strike Sands was elected MP for the constituency of Fermanagh and South Tyrone. His death prompted a wave of support for the Republicans in Northern Ireland and elsewhere, and he became one of the martyrs of the Republican cause.

Born into a Republican family in Belfast, Sands had been involved with the PROVISIONAL IRISH REPUBLICAN ARMY (PIRA) since he was a teenager and when he was 19 he was sentenced to five years in prison on arms charges. In 1977 he was jailed for 14 years after being found in a car packed with weapons, and in 1980 he became leader of the PIRA prisoners in the Maze Prison's notorious H-Blocks. Sands began his "fast unto death" on March

1st 1981, and he died on May 5th on the 65th day of his hunger-strike. Despite pleas from Irish MPs, family, and a special Papal emissary (who gave him a crucifix sent by the Pope) Sands refused to abandon his fast.

***SANTA MARIA* HIJACKING. (January 23rd-February 2nd 1961).** The hijacking of a Portuguese-owned cruise-liner by a group of Portugese exiles opposed to the right-wing dictatorship of Antonio Salazar. The 24-strong group were led by a disaffected ex-army officer, Captain Henrique Galvao. Although one of the ship's officers was killed when the *Santa Maria* was taken over, the hijacking ended peacefully when the liner sailed into Recife in Brazil escorted by American warships. The hijackers surrendered and were given political asylum by the Brazilian government. The *Santa Maria* incident was one of the relatively few examples of marine hijacking in the annals of post-war political terrorism.

The 22,000-ton liner, with 550 American, Venezuelan, Dutch and Spanish passengers aboard was taken over in the Caribbean en route from Curaçao and Florida. The heavily-armed Portuguese killed the officer of the watch and turned the ship round to head for the coast of West Africa pursued by naval ships from America, Portugal, Britain and Holland. On January 24th 1961 the hijackers radioed that the ship had been taken over by the Independent Junta of Liberation led by the exiled General Humberto Delgado (one of Salazar's most dedicated political opponents). On January 25th 1961 the *Santa Maria* was spotted by an American aircraft, waylaid by a flotilla of American warships on January 27th 1961, and escorted into Recife harbour on February 2nd 1961. The passengers were released unharmed, and on February 3rd 1961 Galvao formally surrendered the ship to the Brazilian navy. Galvao and his 23 men were given political asylum by the Brazilian government. It was later revealed that Galvao's plan was to sail the cruise-liner to the Spanish island of Fernando Po from which he hoped to launch revolutions against the right-wing regimes in Portugal and Spain.

**SANTUCHO, MARIO.** Left-wing Argentine urban guerrilla leader and founder of the EJERCITO REVOLUCIONARIO DEL PUEBLO (ERP), one of the best organised and most troublesome of the Latin-American terrorist groups. Captured three times by the Argentinian security forces only to escape each time, Santucho became something of a legend to Argentina's working class. Santucho's career as an insurgent began in 1969 when he founded the ERP, and ended when he was killed by Argentine police in a suburb of Buenos Aires on July 19th 1976. The activities of Santucho's ERP (and the MONTONEROS) brought Argentine near to chaos which ended when the Argentine military took over the country in March 1976. One of the military's first tasks was to set up a small special unit led by an army captain to track down Mario Santucho. On July 19th 1976 the Trotskyist leader was cornered with three of his lieutenants in a second-floor apartment in a Buenos Aires suburb. All four ERP men were killed. An air ticket to Havana was discovered on Santucho's body.

**SARTAWI, ISSAL.** Moderate member of the PALESTINE LIBERATION ORGANISATION (PLO) who was shot dead in a Portuguese hotel on April 10th 1983 while attending a conference of the Socialist International. Although the killer was never captured, Sartawi's known hostility to the activities of ABU NIDAL and his organisation made Nidal a prime suspect. Sartawi's death was regarded by many Arabs and Israelis as a serious blow to the peace process; for some time he had believed that the Arabs had to recognise Israel's right to exist, and had been the PLO's link with left-wing Israeli politicians. Sartawi was shot in the lobby of the Montochero Hotel in Albufeiro, Portugal. The gunman was pursued by the police but escaped.

**SAS.** See SPECIAL AIR SERVICE REGIMENT.

**SAUDI ARABIAN EMBASSY ATTACK, KHARTOUM, SUDAN.** (March 1st 1973). A raid by seven BLACK SEPTEMBER gunmen on the Saudia Arabian Embassy in Khartoum during a reception for American diplomat George Moore. All the hostages were released except Moore, his colleague Cleo Noel, the Saudi ambassador, the Jordanian chargé d'affaires, and Belgian chargé d'affaires Guy Eid. The terrorists demanded the release of ABU DAOUD and 16 other Black September activists jailed in Jordan, and two female Black September members who had been captured at Lod airport. They also demanded that the USA should release SIRHAN SIRHAN, the assassin of ROBERT KENNEDY, and that the West Germans should free the imprisoned members of the ROTE ARMEE FRAKTION (RAF). When none of the governments involved would concede to their demands, on March 2nd 1973 the Arab gunmen shot and killed the two Americans, George Moore and Cleo Noel, and the Belgian, Guy Eid. They then surrendered to the Sudanese police who discovered that the group had been led by

Rizig Abu Gassan, Deputy Head of the PALESTINE LIBERATION ORGANISATION (PLO) in Sudan.

**SAYARET MATKAL.** (General Staff Reconnaissance Unit). The Israeli government's élite anti-terrorist force who have been responsible for many of Israel's counter-terrorist operations such as the raid to release the hostages taken during the AIR FRANCE HIJACKING TO ENTEBBE AIRPORT, UGANDA, in June/July 1976. One of the unit's most famous officers was Lieutenant Colonel JONATHAN NETANYAHU who was killed leading the raid on Entebbe. The Sayaret Matkal are answerable directly to the Chief of Military Intelligence, and are never mentioned by name in Israeli military communiqués. The unit is known colloquially as "Ha Yehida" (The Unit) and its members as "Ha Hevreh" (The Guys). Sayaret Matkal personnel were involved in the BEIRUT AIRPORT ATTACK in 1968, the SABENA HIJACKING TO LOD AIRPORT, ISRAEL, in 1972, the BEIRUT RAID of 1973, plus Israel's major wars with her Arab neighbours. They also operate undercover in the streets of Beirut and in rural Lebanon.

According to authors Christopher Dobson and Ronald Payne the training of the Sayaret Matkal is similar to that of the British Army's SPECIAL AIR SERVICE (SAS); fitness and endurance training plays a large part, along with navigation, desert survival, marksmanship (particularly with the UZI submachine-gun and the KALASHNIKOV AK-47 assault rifle), explosives and close quarters battle (CQB). The unit's emphasis is on speed, decisiveness and the art of the pre-emptive strike.

**SAZMAN-E ETTEL'AT VA AMNIYAT-E KESHVAR (SAVAK).** (National Information & Security Organisation). Much-hated internal security/secret police organisation of the Shah of Iran. SAVAK's brutal activities were feared by Iranian dissidents both inside and outside Iran, and the organisation's methods almost certainly contributed to the downfall of the Shah's regime in 1979. SAVAK was set up in 1957 with the assistance of the American CENTRAL INTELLIGENCE AGENCY (CIA), "For the purpose of the security of the country and prevention of any kind of conspiracy detrimental to the public interest . . . " according to its articles of incorporation. Although the Shah claimed (in the mid-1970s) that SAVAK numbered no more than 4,000 full-time agents, Western sources estimated the real number to be around 30,000 full-time staff, plus a much larger number of part-time spies, informers, messengers etc. SAVAK's formidable bureaucracy was headed by a Special Assistant to the Prime Minister, who answered directly to the Shah himself.

**SCHLYER, HANNS-MARTIN. (1915-1977).** Influential West German industrialist kidnapped in September 1977 and later killed by the left-wing ROTE ARMEE FRAKTION (RAF). A leading member of the Confederation of German Industry and the Federation of German Employers, Schlyer was snatched from his car at 17.30 on September 5th 1977 in a Cologne suburb. Four of Schlyer's police bodyguards were killed in the attack. On September 6th 1977 the authorities received a note demanding the release of 10 RAF prisoners (including ANDREAS BAADER) being held in German prisons. The same demand was made by the four Palestinians who mounted the LUFTHANSA HIJACKING TO MOGADISHU AIRPORT, SOMALIA. The hijacked Lufthansa jet was successfully stormed on the ground at Mogadishu by a West German police anti-terrorist squad, and the passengers released.

Although Schlyer's family and colleagues were willing to negotiate with the kidnappers and were prepared to offer large sums of money, the West German government refused to concede to the terrorists' demands. On October 19th 1977 (three days after the deadline issued by the RAF) Schlyer's body was found in the boot of an Audi car in the Rue Charles Peguy in Paris after a "communiqué" to the newspaper *Liberation*. In their note the RAF said they had ended "Hanns Martin Schlyer's lamentable and corrupt existence". He had been shot three times in the head some time the previous day. Schlyer was buried in Stuttgart on October 25th 1977.

**SCHUMANN, JURGEN.** Lufthansa captain who was shot dead by Arab gunmen during the LUFTHANSA HIJACKING TO MOGADISHU AIRPORT, SOMALIA, in October 1977. Schumann's *Landshut* airliner was hijacked while en route from Majorca to Hamburg, and flown to Mogadishu via Aden. An ex-Starfighter pilot, Schumann intervened constantly to save the lives of his passengers and crew, until he was eventually shot dead at Aden Airport in the South Yemen. He was killed by the leader of the terrorist group ZOHAIR YOUSIF AKACHE. .

**"SCORPION" MACHINE PISTOL.** Light and easily concealed Czech-built machine pistol often used by Palestinian and other terrorists. Manufactured by Czech State Arsenals, the Scorpion uses

7.65mm ammunition in magazines of 10 or 20, has a barrel length of 4.4 inches, weighs only 3.5 lbs, but can fire 840 rounds per minute (14 rounds per second). It can be used as a handgun, or the wire shoulder stock can be folded down for use as a shoulder weapon. It can also be fitted with a silencer. The weapon can be dangerous to fire from the hip, as the shell cases are ejected vertically and can hit the user on the face. The original Scorpion (the CZ61) was a 0.32 calibre weapon designed to be used for self-defence by Czech tank crews. A version of the Scorpion is manufactured in Yugoslavia, and is distinguishable from the Czech original by its plastic (rather than wooden) pistol grip. The Scorpion has been exported from both countries to a number of African states from where they find their way into the hands of terrorist groups.

**SCOTTISH NATIONAL LIBERATION ARMY (SNLA).** Small group of Scottish extremists who have specialised in sending letter and parcel bombs through the post to British government ministers (normally the Prime Minister and the Secretary of State for Scotland). Like the other Scottish groups which have emerged over the past 15 years (such as the ARMY OF THE PROVISIONAL GOVERNMENT or the Tartan Army) the SNLA want to see the Treaty of Union of 1707 between Scotland and England revoked, and an independent Scotland re-established.

**SEALE, ROBERT ("BOBBY") (born 1937).** Black American radical and one of the founder-members of the BLACK PANTHER PARTY (BPP) which was set up in Oakland, California, in 1967. Seale was introduced to Marxism-Leninism by HUEY NEWTON with whom he founded the BPP. An ex-serviceman, Seale was charged with killing a policeman in Chicago, but escaped from jail. After being rearrested his conviction was quashed on appeal.

**SECRET INTELLIGENCE SERVICE (SIS), BRITISH.** Also known as MI6. The British government's main intelligence-gathering bureacracy which over the years has been racked by scandals caused by the activities of Soviet "moles" such as Guy Burgess, Donald Maclean, Kim Philby and Anthony Blunt. The SIS are responsible to the British Foreign Secretary, and their last published accounts (1982) revealed a (relatively modest) budget of around $100 million. The most famous recent head of the SIS was the late MAURICE OLDFIELD who was brought out of retirement by the British government to act as "security co-ordinator" in Northern Ireland. The overlapping security operations in Northern

Ireland led to some awkward bureaucratic clashes between SIS and the British SECURITY SERVICE (MI5).

**SECURITY SERVICE, BRITISH**. Also known as MI5. The British government's main security organisation responsible for a wide range of activities from spy catching to counter-subversion work. The Security Service are also responsible for most of the "positive vetting" (i.e. security screening) of people for sensitive posts in government and industry. Since the latest round of Irish troubles began in 1969 Security Service agents have been heavily involved in anti-terrorist work both in mainland Britain and in Northern Ireland. Unlike the American FEDERAL BUREAU OF INVESTIGATION (FBI) the British Security Service gives their agents no powers of arrest, for which they rely on the "special branches" of Britain's police forces.

**SELOUS SCOUTS**. One of the anti-terrorist forces of the illegal white regime in Rhodesia (now Zimbabwe). Named after the legendary white hunter Frederick Selous, the unit was around 1,000 strong, and unlike the all-white RHODESIAN SPECIAL AIR SERVICE (RSAS) or the Rhodesian Light Infantry (RLI) the Selous Scouts enlisted black troops (some of them "turned" terrorists). The unit was commanded by Ron Reid-Daley, one-time member of the British Army's SPECIAL AIR SERVICE (SAS). The Selous Scouts specialised in tracking and "hot pursuit" anti-terrorist operations, often across the borders of Zambia and Angola. They were among the Rhodesian units most feared by the insurgents of the ZIMBABWE AFRICAN NATIONAL LIBERATION ARMY (ZANLA) and the ZIMBABWE PEOPLE'S LIBERATION ARMY (ZIPRA).

**SENDERO LUMINOSO**. (The Shining Path). The Maoist guerrillas of Peru who have been waging war against the repressive and often corrupt governments of Peru since 1980. The Sendero Luminoso guerrilla campaign and the Peruvian counter-action cost more than 6,000 lives between 1980 and 1985. The Sendero Luminoso terrorists operate mainly from bases in the remote mountainous regions of the country, and try to cultivate the grievances of the Peruvian peasants. In an attempt to undermine the political raison d'être of the Maoist guerrillas, the government of Alan Garcia Perez tried to purge the Peruvian army and police of corruption and brutality, and instigate the kind of social and land reforms which have helped defeat left-wing insurgencies elsewhere.

**SHARAM, MOHAMMED**. The only survivor of a group of four Arab terrorists involved in the ROME AIRPORT ATTACK in December 1985. Wounded in the arm and shoulder in the exchange of fire with the Italian police and Israeli security men, Sharam (19) tried to escape but was felled by a blow from an Italian policeman. He later told the Italian authorities that he was a "Palestinian fighter" who had been born in the Shatila refugee camp in Beirut. Medical examination revealed that Sharam had considerable quantities of amphetamines in his blood. Sharam told the Italian investigators that the mission had been instigated in November 1985 when a terrorist organiser from the ABU NIDAL organisation toured the Sabra and Shatila refugee camps in Beirut looking for volunteers for a suicide mission. According to Sharam eight men were selected, dubbed the "Martyrs of Palestine", and were despatched to Rome and Vienna to attack the airport terminals.

**SHARPEVILLE MASSACRE, SOUTH AFRICA. (March 21st 1960)**. The killing of 67 Africans and the wounding of more than 200 by South African police armed with automatic weapons in the African township of Sharpeville near Johannesburg. The killings brought down the wrath of the international community upon South Africa, led to the cutting of links with the United Kingdom and the British Commonwealth, and provoked the hitherto-peaceful AFRICAN NATIONAL CONGRESS (ANC) to form UMKONTO WE SIZWE (Spear of the Nation), a military organisation dedicated to subversion and sabotage.

**SHERUT HABITACHON (SHIN BET)**. (Security Department). The Israeli government's internal security apparatus, responsible for Israel itself and the "occupied territories" (West Bank, Gaza, Golan Heights etc). Like the British SECURITY SERVICE, Shin Bet likes to operate through the civilian or military police wherever possible, making no arrests and remaining deep in the background. But Shin Bet's anti-terrorist unit plunged the organisation (and the Israeli government) into crisis following the GAZA BUS HIJACKING of 1984 after which two captured Arab gunmen were found beaten to death. Israel's Attorney General, Yitzhak Zamir, tried to force Avraham Shalom, head of Shin Bet to resign but Shalom refused. Zamir himself resigned in February 1986, but continued to press for a full police inquiry into the killings.

**SHIELD SOCIETY**. Right-wing Japanese quasi-military society founded in 1967 by the poet and author YUKIO MISHIMA.

Consisting of about 100 members (many of them junior military men) the Shield Society's aim was to restore the ideals of the Samurai, and to overturn the democratic "Peace Constitution" imposed on Japan by the Allies after World War II. A powerful vein of Japanese mysticism ran through the Shield Society which tried to restore the cult of the God-Emperor. The obscure organisation became world news on November 25th 1970 when Yukio Mishima committed ritual suicide at an army barracks in Tokyo.

**SHIN BET**. See SHERUT HABITACHON.

**SINGH, BEANT**. One of the two Sikh policemen who assassinated Indian Prime Minister INDIRA GANDHI in the garden of her house in New Delhi on October 31st 1984. The murder was an act of revenge for the GOLDEN TEMPLE OF AMRITSAR ASSAULT, earlier in the year. A sub-inspector of police, and one of Mrs Gandhi's own bodyguard, Beant Singh shot the prime minister with his service revolver while his accomplice SATWANT SINGH emptied his submachine-gun into the fallen prime minister. Beant Singh then raised his hands in surrender saying, "I have done what I had to do. Now you do what you have to do." The two Sikh assassins were taken to a police post where Beant Singh was shot dead and Satwant Singh seriously wounded during an altercation with the Indo-Tibetan Border Police. In June 1986 Beant Singh's widow, Bimla Khalska, led a violent demonstration into the Gold Temple complex during which one of the temple guards was stabbed to death.

**SINGH, SATWANT**. The younger of the two Sikh policemen who assassinated Indian Prime Minister INDIRA GANDHI on October 31st 1984. Satwant Singh was seriously wounded by the Indo-Tibetan Border Police after the killing but survived to stand trial in New Delhi along with conspirators Kehar Singh (54) and Balbir Singh (45). After a lengthy trial the 22-year-old ex-policeman was sentenced to death for his part in the killing of Mrs Gandhi. The judge described the case as "the rarest of rare instances" for which the three accused "deserve the extreme penalty".

**SINGH, SHAHBEG**. Sikh leader and retired Major-General of the Indian Army who organised the defences of the GOLDEN TEMPLE OF AMRITSAR which Indian troops stormed on June 5th-6th 1984. A man of considerable military talent, Shahbeg Singh served with the Indian Army for many years and helped to train the Mukhti Bahini guerrillas of Bangladesh in their struggle for independence against the Pakistani government. Dismissed from the Indian Army without a pension, Shahbeg Singh became a bitter enemy of the Hindu-dominated regime and a passionate advocate of an independent Sikh homeland, Khalistan. Shahbeg Singh used his experience to train the Sikh terrorists who were (and still are) operating in the Punjab. The skill with which the retired Major-General fortified the Golden Temple of Amritsar with sandbags cost the attacking forces many lives, and forced them to use tanks and artillery. Shahbeg Singh died along with his spiritual mentor JARNAIL SINGH BHINDRANWALE during the attack on the Golden Temple. He was found clutching the walky-talkie radio with which he directed the stubborn defence.

**SIRHAN, SIRHAN**. The 24-year-old Jordanian-born Arab who assassinated Senator ROBERT KENNEDY in The Ambassador Hotel, Los Angeles, on June 5th 1968. Various attempts to prove that Sirhan acted as part of a conspiracy have come to nothing, although there is some medical evidence that he may have been acting under hypnosis. But the young Arab made it plain to his interrogators that he bitterly resented Kennedy's support for the state of Israel and hostility to the Arab cause which, Sirhan reasoned, would suffer grievously if Robert Kennedy was elected President of the USA in 1968. Sirhan was convicted of Kennedy's murder and sentenced to death, but after a plea for leniency by the dead man's brother Senator Edward Kennedy, the sentence was reduced to life imprisonment. The Sirhan family had emigrated to the USA from Jerusalem (via Beirut) in 1957, settling in Pasadena near Los Angeles. Ironically the young Sirhan had grown up admiring the Kennedys as champions of the world's underdogs, and saw Kennedy's espousal of the Israeli/Jewish cause as a betrayal. In his diary for May 18th 1968 Sirhan wrote, "My determination to eliminate R.F.K. is becoming more the more of an unshakeable obsession . . . R.F.K. must die – R.F.K. must be killed."

**SKYMARSHALL**. The popular name for the armed security guards who travel incognito on many airline routes in the more troubled parts of the world. The system was first instigated by the Israeli state airline El Al after the hijacking of one of their passenger liners to Algeria by the POPULAR FRONT FOR THE LIBERATION OF PALESTINE (PFLP) in July 1968. In February 1979 an El Al Skymarshall, Mordechai Rachamim, killed one of three Arab gunmen during the ZURICH AIRPORT ATTACK in Switzerland. He was later tried by the Swiss authorities and acquitted. In September 1970 another El Al Skymarshall shot dead an American-born hijacker (also a member of the PFLP) who tried to take over an El Al flight over southeast England.

After the DAWSON'S FIELD HIJACKINGS of September 1970 when three Western airliners were forced to a remote airstrip in Jordan and blown up, President Nixon of the United States ordered a force of "specially trained armed US government personnel" to be carried on American commercial flights. Although worried about hijacking, the US airlines were not happy with the prospect of shoot-outs at high altitude and asked for the American Skymarshall scheme to be shelved. The airlines' security experts argued that it would be infinitely safer to tighten up airport security to the point that potential hijackers could not get aboard commercial flights.

But other countries – Israel and Egypt for example – insist on at least one Skymarshall, and usually two, travelling on every flight. An Egyptian Skymarshall shot and killed one hijacker during the EGYPTAIR HIJACKING TO LUQA AIRPORT, MALTA in November 1985. The danger of bullets from firearms piercing the skin of pressurised aircraft is very real (as happened on the flight hijacked to Luqa) so El Al Skymarshalls carry small-calibre handguns (0.22 Berettas) armed with low-velocity cartridges to avoid bullets damaging the aircraft, should they ever be fired.

**SOLIDARITE**. (Solidarity). Paris-based terrorist/guerrilla "support" organisation set up and run by HENRI CURIEL until his assassination in May 1978. Solidarité was set up by Curiel in 1963 and operated on two levels. One provided assistance and support for refugees and exiles from various Third World tyrannies and totalitarian regimes like South Africa. On the sub-rosa level Solidarité organised "safe houses", forged passports, bogus identity papers, and occasionally weapons for terrorist organisations such as FATAH, the PROVISIONAL IRISH REPUBLICAN ARMY (PIRA), the Italian BRIGATE ROSSE and an assortment of Latin-American groups. The notorious ILLICH RAMIREZ SANCHEZ ("Carlos the Jackal") is believed to have used Solidarité's back-up facilities.

After exposure in the French magazine *Le Point* in 1976 Solidarité was officially disbanded, but emerged under the new title of Aide et Amitie (Aid and Friendship) which in turn was accused by the German magazine *Der Spiegel* of providing assistance for the West German ROTE ARMEE FRAKTION (RAF). After Curiel's death French police raided various people associated with Solidarité (and a later organisation known as Les Amis d'Henri Curiel) and in one case uncovered thousands of false passports, together with instructions for making explosive charges.

**SOMOZA, ANASTASIO**. One-time dictator of Nicaragua who was toppled by the left-wing FRENTE SANDINISTA DE LIBERACION NACIONAL (FSLN) in July 1979 and fled into exile in the USA and Paraguay. Dictator of Nicaragua from 1967-1979 (a position he inherited from his brother who had succeeded his father) Somoza ran one of Latin America's most corrupt and brutal regimes until he was overthrown. He was shot dead in the centre of Asunción in Paraguay on September 9th 1980 while driving with his bodyguard and financial adviser. Somoza's body was flown to the USA and buried in the Cuban quarter of Miami. On October 1st 1980 the Paraguayan government broke off diplomatic relations with Nicaragua, accusing the Sandinista regime of complicity in Somoza's death. The Paraguayan police, however, blamed Somoza's assassination on the Argentinian Trotskyist movement EJERCITO REVOLUCIONARIO DEL PUEBLO (ERP).

**SOUTH AFRICAN AIR FORCE HQ BOMBING, PRETORIA. (May 20th 1983)**. A car-bomb attack by UMKONTO WE SIZWE on the Pretoria headquarters of the South African Air Force. The bombing killed 19 people (most of them black) and injured more than 200. Although the attack did little or no damage to South Africa's military establishment, it was seen as a significant escalation of Umkonto's campaign of sabotage and terrorism, and a blow at the heart of Afrikanerdom. The propaganda value to the black movement was considerable.

**SPECIAL AIR SERVICE REGIMENT (SAS)**. Elite, highly-trained British Army unit which specialises in undercover operations, Counter Revolutionary Warfare (CRW) and anti-terrorist tactics. Although not without its critics (political and military) the SAS is regarded by many commentators as one of the best units of its kind and one on which many of the others are modelled. The American special operations DELTA FORCE, in particular, is based on the British SAS, and SAS units have been set up in Australia, New Zealand, and in pre-independence Rhodesia. SAS officers and troopers have been involved in most of Britain's post-war campaigns including the Malaya Emergency, Borneo, Oman, Aden, Northern Ireland and the Falklands campaign. Two SAS officers were involved in the West German police operation after the LUFTHANSA HIJACKING TO MOGADISHU AIRPORT,

SOMALIA, and the SAS advised the Dutch authorities during the ASSEN TRAIN SIEGE. It was an SAS CRW team which ended the IRANIAN EMBASSY SIEGE, LONDON, in June 1980. An SAS anti-terrorist unit is now constantly on call to be used at the discretion of the British civil authorities.

Founded in July 1941 by Lieutenant Colonel DAVID STIRLING of the Scots Guards, the early SAS specialised in raiding behind German and Italian lines in the North African desert, and destroying aircraft on the ground. By the end of World War II the SAS were a fully-fledged Brigade, consisting of six "squadrons" (three British, two French and one Belgian), having fought all over Western and Eastern Europe. By 1952 the SAS had been reduced to one regular unit, 22 SAS, supplemented by two volunteer units, 21 and 23 SAS. The regular battalion is divided into four "squadrons" of 72 men and six officers. In the post-war period SAS squadrons have served in Malaya (where they developed the shotgun as a jungle-fighting weapon), Kenya, Borneo, the Yemen, Aden (where they learned to fight urban terrorists), Oman (where they served as mercenaries to the Sultanate), and Northern Ireland (their most politically sensitive posting).

Since 1960 the 22 SAS have been based at Hereford near the border with Wales, where the regiment do most of their training. SAS troopers are carefully selected from other British units (to which many of them return) and are trained to work in 16-man "troops" each divided into four-man sub-units. Each man must acquire a specialist skill (medic, signaller etc.) and at least one man in four must be fluent in the language of the area in which the troop are operating. The SAS specialise in Close Quarters Battle (CQB), the handling of explosives, and in the use of all kinds of firearms (Eastern Bloc as well as Western). After the MUNICH OLYMPICS ATTACK in 1972 the SAS were given the resources to set up a full-time Counter Revolutionary Warfare (CRW) team to specialise in combatting urban terrorism.

Although the SAS passed into national (and international) folklore during the widely televised storming of the Iranian Embassy in London in 1980, the British public's attitude to the regiment has been ambivalent. Their operations in Northern Ireland (some of which have gone badly wrong) have brought down some heavy left-wing, liberal criticism, and many Irish Republicans (not only the terrorists) view the SAS as a ruthless instrument of British oppression. In the late 1960s, before it was officially acknowledged that the SAS were operating in the province, the Northern Ireland Civil Rights Association published a pamphlet entitled *What To Do If You Are Shot By The SAS*, which suggests that the regiment's intelligence-gathering and undercover role was widely known.

In January 1976 the British (Labour) government announced that they were sending a unit of the SAS to operate in the "bandit country" of South Armagh against the PROVISIONAL IRISH REPUBLICAN ARMY (PIRA) and other terrorist groups. But the political/military delicacy of the Northern Ireland situation has led the SAS into a number of grave difficulties, if only because the need for undercover operators outran the number of highly-trained men available. In 1978, for example, two SAS troopers, Allan Bohan and Ronald Temperley, were charged with the murder of 16-year-old John Boyle in County Antrim. Both were acquitted when the Crown accepted that they had mistaken Boyle for a terrorist, but the trial did some damage to the regiment's reputation.

**SPECIAL BOAT SQUADRON (SBS)**. A special-forces unit of combat swimmers, free-fall parachutists and canoeists which forms part of the British Royal Marines. To an extent the SBS is the maritime equivalent of the SPECIAL AIR SERVICE (SAS) and like the SAS was created in the early years of World War II. SBS "sections" were used mainly for coastal reconnaissance and for raiding German, Italian and Japanese coastal installations. Most of the craft used by the SBS were small boats, canoes and even surfboards, often launched from British submarines. Since 1954 the SBS have been based at Poole in Dorset in the south of England.

**"SPETSNAZ"**. The Soviet special forces, roughly the equivalent of the British SPECIAL AIR SERVICE (SAS) or the US Special Forces. Reputed to number around 30,000 (although some sources say 15,000) the Spetsnaz soldiers are specially trained in infiltration, sabotage, assassination and other "behind the lines" operations. They are reputed to have spearheaded the invasions of Czechoslovakia (1968) and Afghanistan (1979) and to have been heavily involved in the campaign against the Polish trade union movement. Spetsnaz troops also have a counter-insurgency role, and are reported to have been used to some effect against the Muslim rebels in Afghanistan. They are controlled by the GLAVNOYE RAZVEDYVATELNOYE UPRAVLENIVE (GRU) Soviet military intelligence.

According to GRU defector Viktor Suvorov, Spetsnaz units have been briefed to infiltrate the United Kingdom in periods of increased tension from where, if war comes, they will try to assassinate the

Royal Family, politicians and key members of the military and police hierarchies. Operating in units of between three and 10 their role is to sabotage important military and industrial installations such as power stations, missile bases, airfields, communication centres, gas and oil pipelines, and gas processing plants. Western military commentators point out that this is precisely the role of Western special forces.

**SPEZIALEINSATZKOMMANDOS (SEK).** West German Lander (state) police special units which are modelled closely on Federal government's GRENZSCHUTZGRUPPE 9 (GSG-9) force. Most SEKs contain 40-60 members who are specially equipped and trained to cope with terrorists, violent criminals, and occasional riots. SEK officers are volunteers from other branches of the police, to which they return after a relatively short term of special-forces duty. SEK units have found a wider acceptance among the German public than the GSG-9 who are seen (and often resented) as a powerful arm of central government. Advocates of the West German SEK teams say that far from acting as "killer teams" they reduce the level of violence. They cite the example of the West Berlin SEK team which in 12 years has arrested 35 terrorists, many armed criminals, confiscated 300 firearms and solved 14 hostage-taking situations without harming anyone, and by firing only two warning shots.

**SPRETI, KARL VON.** West Germany's ambassador to Guatemala who was kidnapped and then killed by terrorists from the FUERZAS ARMADAS DE REVOLUCIONARO (FAR) in 1970. Count Von Spreti was kidnapped on March 31st 1970 and in exchange for his safety his captors demanded the release of 22 of their colleagues being held in Guatemalan jails, plus $700,000 in cash. The West German government of Chancellor Brandt put heavy pressure on the Guatemalans to negotiate with the FAR, and a special envoy was despatched to Guatemala with an offer to pay the ransom money. But the Guatemalan government refused to concede to the demands of the terrorists, and on April 5th Von Spreti's body was discovered. The West Germans accused the Guatemalans of failing dismally to provide proper protection for their diplomats.

**SQUADRE AZIONE MUSSOLINI.** (Mussolini Action Squads). Italian Fascist group which takes its name from the Fascist "Squadrismo" of the 1920s. The Squadre are one of a number of right-wing "Black Terror" groups suspected of planting bombs throughout Europe.

**STETHEM, ROBERT DEAN**. The 22-year-old American naval diver who was shot dead during the TRANSWORLD AIRLINES HIJACKING TO BEIRUT in June 1985. Stethem was the only fatality of the hijacking by Shi'ite Muslims. He was given a full military funeral by the US Navy, and eulogised by President Ronald Reagan.

**STIRLING, DAVID**. Scots-born British Army officer who convinced the military authorities during World War II to set up the British special-forces unit that developed into the SPECIAL AIR SERVICE (SAS) Regiment. An officer of the Scots Guards and an early volunteer for the Army Commando, Stirling devised the idea of highly-trained teams of specialists to operate behind enemy lines while in a Cairo hospital recovering from a parachute accident. Given the number of special-forces units which have been closely modelled on the British SAS, Stirling's influence as a military theorist has been considerable. In the 1970s Stirling became something of a demon figure to the British left when he advocated the setting up of a para-military civilian force to prevent Britain collapsing in a welter of strikes, go-slows and industrial action.

**STOCKHOLM SYNDROME**. Also known as protective affiliation and traumatic bonding. The tendency of hijack victims or hostages to gradually identify with, and even support, their captors. The phenomenon is so called after a hostage-taking incident at the Stockholm Kreditbank in August 1973 where three women and a man were held by raiders inside the bank for six days. The hostages eventually identified with their captors to such an extent that they began to negotiate with the Swedish police on behalf of the robbers. When the criminals surrendered the hostages insisted on providing a human screen so the police would not shoot. One woman hostage later divorced her husband and married one of the men who had held her captive. Even when the negotiating procedures break down and violence is resorted to, the "Stockholm Syndrome" can come into play; it was observed during the IRANIAN EMBASSY SIEGE in London in 1980 when the hostages pleaded with the SPECIAL AIR SERVICE (SAS) troopers not to shoot one of the young Arabs who had been holding them captive.

The Australian psychologist L. Mann claims that the Stockholm Syndrome tends to develop in three stages: firstly, an initial shock and panic often followed by apathy and despair; secondly, an ambivalence to the captor followed by an emotional dependency (particularly in the case of women); thirdly, an acceptance of the hostage-takers' point of view, even, as in the case of PATRICIA HEARST, to the point of joining their captors in their illegal activities. Most psychologists regard the Stockholm Syndrome as an instinctive survival reaction, a way of engaging the emotional sympathy of the captor in the knowledge that it is harder for the hostage-taker to kill or injure someone for whom he has some feeling. When the crisis is over, many people who have been hijacked or held hostage develop a passionate interest in the political or religious causes of the people who put them through the terror.

One of the best accounts of the syndrome is by Special Agent Thomas Strentz of the FEDERAL BUREAU OF INVESTIGATION (FBI) Academy who wrote *The Stockholm Syndrome: Law Enforcement Policy and Ego Defenses of the Hostage* first published in the *New York Annals of Science* in 1980. Strentz described the bond between aggressor and victim as being, "Like the automatic reflex of the knee ... beyond the control of the victim and the subject". But many hostage victims show severe after effects. Although physically unharmed, they may suffer powerful feelings of guilt, anxiety and have recurring nightmares for years after the event. Some recent medical research suggests that the severe stress of a hostage-taking situation produces chemical opiates in the brain of the victim which induce feelings akin to affection for the aggressor (similar to the "addiction" with which some women reputedly respond to physical and sexual abuse).

**STOKE NEWINGTON EIGHT**. See ANGRY BRIGADE.

**SYMBIONESE LIBERATION ARMY (SLA)**. Bizarre left-wing California-based group which achieved notoriety after kidnapping newspaper heiress PATRICIA HEARST in February 1974 and then converting her to their cause. The SLA were responsible for a number of bombing attacks and armed robberies in and around Los Angeles and San Francisco. The group were dedicated to the overthrow of Western capitalism, had peculiar sexual ideas, firmly believed that the non-white and oriental population of the USA was about to join them, and gave themselves "revolutionary" names such as Cinque, Cujo, Zoya, Fahizah and Teko. Hearst was known to the group as Tania. Six members of the SLA, including the group's leader Donald De Frieze (Cinque), died on May 17th

1974 in a spectacular shoot-out with the Los Angeles police during which thousands of rounds of ammunition were fired, and their "safe house" in a Los Angeles suburb caught fire. The SLA broke up shortly after, and the remaining members were rounded up by the police. In September 1975 Patricia Hearst was arrested by the FEDERAL BUREAU OF INVESTIGATION (FBI) and charged with the armed robbery of the Hibernia Bank in San Francisco in April 1974.

# T

**TAFOYA, EUGENE.** American ex-Special Forces soldier who was jailed in Colorado in 1981 for the attempted assassination of exiled Libyan FAISAL ZAGALLAI in September 1980. Tafoya had been hired by EDMUND P. WILSON to assassinate Zagallai who was an active opponent of MUMMUAR QADDAFI. A Vietnam veteran who had served with distinction, it seems likely that Tafoya was deceived by Wilson into believing that he was acting for the CENTRAL INTELLIGENCE AGENCY (CIA). After Libyan radio gloated over the shooting of Zagallai "as a lesson to all traitors and running dogs living abroad" the US broke off diplomatic relations with the Qaddafi regime. Within a few months of the crime Tafoya was arrested and tried for the attempted murder of the Libyan. He was jailed for two years (plus six years for tax offences).

**TAMBO, OLIVER (born 1917).** Black South African political leader currently President of the banned AFRICAN NATIONAL CONGRESS (ANC). Tambo has presided over the ANC's movement away from civil disobedience and industrial sabotage to outright violence against the white South African regime and its black supporters. Educated at Anglican mission schools and at University College of Fort Hare, Tambo became a secondary-school teacher and then a lawyer. In 1955 he set up practice in Johannesburg with NELSON MANDELA, and was arrested on treason charges in 1956 (charges which were later dropped). Tambo became Deputy President of the ANC in 1958, and escaped to London in 1960, and in the same year attended the 15th Session of the United Nations General Assembly. In 1967 he was appointed Acting President of the ANC, and then President in 1977. He now operates from ANC headquarters in Dar es Salaam, Tanzania.

**TAMIL TIGERS.** See LIBERATION TIGERS OF TAMIL EELAM.

**TAMIL UNITED LIBERATION FRONT (TULF).** The most moderate and constitutional of the Tamil separatist organisations in Sri Lanka. Two of their senior members – V. Dharmalimgam and

A. Alaslasundram – were shot dead by the LIBERATION TIGERS OF TAMIL EELAM in September 1985 after being kidnapped from their homes. Both men were former members of the Sri Lankan Parliament but were dismissed in 1983 when they refused to take an oath of allegiance to Sri Lanka. The two men were killed in an attempt by Tamil Tigers to prevent them signing a devolution pact with the Sri Lanka government.

**TAMMUZ NUCLEAR REACTORS ATTACK. (June 7th 1981).** Bombing raid by Israeli warplanes on the Iraqi government's French-built nuclear reactors at Tammuz, south of Baghdad. The reactors were completely destroyed, ensuring that the Iraqis and their allies could not develop an atomic bomb with which to threaten Israel. Although carried out as an overt low-level raid by Israeli aircraft, the operation (codenamed "BABYLON") was the result of years of sub rosa preparation by the Israeli MOSSAD. Two years previously Mossad had destroyed the two reactor cores at La Seyne sur Mer in the south of France, and almost certainly assassinated YAHYA EL MASHAD, an Egyptian nuclear scientist at a hotel in Paris.

The Tammuz nuclear reactors were destroyed in a devastating two-minute raid by eight Israeli F-16s which started at 17.33 on Sunday June 7th 1981. The Israeli aircraft – which had flown hundreds of miles at very low levels across the deserts of Saudi Arabia and Iraq – were armed with conventional MK.84 2,000lb iron bombs. All 16 bombs struck within 30 feet of the centre of their target. So accurate were the Israeli pilots that many observers assumed that the nuclear plant had been destroyed by explosives planted inside the reactor by Israeli saboteurs. One French technician was killed in the raid. The F-16 bombers were given "cover" by a flight of eight F-15 fighters, and all aircraft returned safely to Israel.

The destruction of the Tammuz reactors was justified by the Israeli government as a defence "against the construction of an atomic bomb in Iraq which itself would not have hesitated to use against Israel and its population centres". The Israelis also claimed that they had struck before the reactors became operational, otherwise Baghdad would have been saturated with radioactivity. The raid was denounced by the Iraqis as a "treacherous operation" and "blatant aggression" by the "Zionist entity".

**TAROC, LUIS (born 1913).** Philippino leader of the Communist-led HUKBALAHAP (HUK) movement from 1942 to 1954. Taroc formed the HUK army in 1942 following the Japanese invasion of the the Philippines and fought brilliantly against the Japanese occupation until the liberation of the Philippines. At the end of the war, at American instigation, Taroc was ordered to disarm and disband the HUK army. In 1946 he was elected to the House of Representatives, but barred from taking his seat on the grounds that he was a "terrorist". Taroc then took his organisation underground to wage war against the Philippines government, a campaign which began in 1948, and was abetted by the incompetence and corruption of the government and the army. By 1950 Taroc and his HUK guerrillas controlled most of central Luzon (the "rice basket" of the Philippines), but were eventually defeated by the reforming Secretary of National Defence RAMON MAGSASAY. Taroc surrendered to the government in 1954, was tried for terrorism and sentenced to life imprisonment. He was released in 1968. His book *Born of the People* (1953) was followed by *He Who Rides the Tiger* (1967).

**TELL, WASFI.** Prime Minister of Jordan who was assassinated in Cairo by BLACK SEPTEMBER gunmen on November 28th 1971. Tell was attacked on his way into the Sheraton Hotel in Cairo shortly after a lunch with the heads of government of the Arab League. As he stepped into the hotel foyer he was hit by five shots fired by four gunmen. A close associate of King Hussein, and a man known to be antagonistic to the Palestinian presence in Jordan, Wasfi Tell was regarded by Black September as being responsible for King Hussein's decision to drive the PALESTINE LIBERATION ORGANISATION (PLO) out of Jordan in September 1970. He was also held responsible for the torture and death of ABU ALI IYAD, one of the leaders of FATAH, the military wing of the PLO, and a close associate of PLO chairman YASIR ARAFAT.

**TIEDEMANN, GABRIELLE.** Left-wing West German terrorist and one of those who were released by the government in February 1975 in exchange for the safety of Christian Democrat politician PETER LORENZ who had been kidnapped by the Second of June Movement. Born in East Germany to a Nazi family, "Gaby", as she was usually known, immersed herself in radical politics as a student at the Free University of Berlin and married left-winger Norbert Krocher in 1971. In 1972 she was jailed for shooting a West Berlin policeman, served two years of her eight-year sentence, and then was released to the Middle East where she spent some time training with the POPULAR FRONT FOR THE LIBERATION OF PALESTINE (PFLP). Tiedemann was one of the group of terrorists which staged the OPEC ATTACK in Vienna in December 1975 (where she is alleged to have killed an Austrian security guard in cold blood). In December 1977 she was arrested in Switzerland after shooting at a Swiss customs officer. She was tried, convicted, and is now serving a long jail sentence in Switzerland.

**TOKYO AIRPORT BOMBING, JAPAN. (June 23rd 1985).** Luggage-bomb explosion in the terminal of Narita Airport, Tokyo, which killed two Japanese baggage handlers (Kodo Ideharu and Asano Hideo) and seriously injured four others. The bomb had been planted on a Canadian Pacific flight from Vancouver to Tokyo which had landed shortly before the bomb exploded at 15.20. The device was probably timed to go off while Flight CP 003 was in mid-air, but the aircraft arrived early due to favourable winds over the Pacific. Japanese and Canadian security believe that the bombing was connected with the AIR INDIA BOMBING of the same day, and that both devices were planted by Sikh extremists. The bomb which exploded in Tokyo had been planted in a Japanese-made Sanyo stereo tuner which was traced to an F. W. Woolworth store in the little town of Duncan on Vancouver Island, Canada. The tuner had been sold to two  Sikhs whom the Canadian and Japanese authorities are still trying to find.

**TOWFIGH, SALIM.** Also known as Oan. The 27-year-old leader of the six Arab terrorists during the IRANIAN EMBASSY SIEGE, LONDON, in May-June 1980 which ended when the British Army's SPECIAL AIR SERVICE (SAS) stormed the building. Born in Khuzistan and educated at Teheran University where he became active in radical politics and was arrested and tortured by the Shah's secret police, Towfigh was well educated, sophisticated, and fluent in four languages (Farsi, Arabic, German and English). In a remarkable interview with one of the hostages who happened to be a journalist, Towfigh said that he wanted to resist the "Farsi-isation" of the Arab part of Iran, and struggle for autonomy for the state of "Arabistan". Towfigh claimed that the decisive influence in his political life was an alleged massacre of more than 200 Iranian Arabs in the city of Al-Muhammara on May 29th 1979 by Revolutionary Guards. He went on to assure his interviewer that "we wish this operation should end peacefully". But on May 5th 1980 Towfigh was killed by an SAS trooper after being cornered in a first-floor office.

TRANSWORLD AIRLINES HIJACKING TO BEIRUT, LEBANON. (June 14th-30th 1985). The hijacking of a TWA airliner with 153 passengers and crew by a group of Shi'ite Muslims calling themselves ISLAMIC JIHAD who demanded the release of more than 600 Shi'ite Muslims held in Israel. The aircraft was hijacked after leaving Athens airport and then flown to Beirut, Algiers, and then back to Beirut where, after 17 days of negotiations, the passengers and crew were released. One passenger, ROBERT DEAN STETHEM, an American navy diver was killed. The hijacking was widely regarded as a publicity coup for the Shi'ite cause, and the international media were fiercely criticised by Western governments for playing into the hands of the hijackers.

The hijacking of Flight 847 from Cairo to Rome began at 09.10 on Friday June 14 1985 shortly after the jet left Áthens airport. Two men travelling on (bogus) Moroccan passports and named Ahmed Karbia and Ali Yunes produced 9mm machine pistols and hand grenades and ordered the pilot, Captain John Trestrake, to fly to Beirut, where the aircraft landed at 11.55 and where 17 women and two children were allowed to leave. After demanding the release of all Shi'ites held in Israel the hijackers ordered the aircraft to Algiers where another 18 women, a child and two men (a Syrian and a Sudanese) were released. After refuelling the 727 returned to Beirut. Shortly after landing, the hijackers beat up and shot to death Robert Stethem, and dumped his body onto the runway warning the Beirut control tower that they intended to "finish off" the remaining Americans. President Reagan later described the killing of Robert Stethem as "an attack on all Western civilization by uncivilised barbarians".

After 17 days of intense negotiations which were closely watched by the world's media, the 39 American hostages were released unharmed. Many of them declared some sympathy for the Shi'ite cause.

TRANSWORLD AIRLINES HIJACKING TO PARIS, FRANCE. (September 10th-11th 1976). The hijacking of a TWA Boeing 727 by Croatian nationalists seeking an independent Croatia (now part of Yugoslavia). The hijacked aircraft was flown from New York to Montreal, to Gander, to Iceland and finally landed on September 11th 1976 at Paris where the hijackers surrendered to the French authorities. But a bomb the Croatians had planted in New York blew up while it was being defused by the police, killing one police officer and injuring three others. The five Croatians were later tried and convicted in New York City of second-degree murder, air piracy and kidnapping and given long jail sentences.

TWA Flight 355 from New York to Chicago with 93 passengers and crew aboard was taken over by five Croatians (four men and a woman) at 20.19 on September 10th 1976 when the aircraft was 95 minutes into its flight. The terrorists, all American-born Yugoslavs, claimed to be from the Croatian National Liberation Forces and threatened to blow the aircraft up unless their demands were met. They immediately ordered the aircraft north to Montreal where the 727 landed and was refuelled.

The hijackers then warned the American authorities that a bomb had been placed in a coin-operated luggage locker in Grand Central Station in Manhattan, along with an "appeal to the American people" and a "declaration of Croatian independence". The Croatians said that unless these documents were published in full on the front pages of prominent American newspapers, then another bomb planted in a "highly busy location" in the USA would be detonated. The newspapers agreed to carry the Croatians' message. The bomb in the Grand Central Station was successfully removed by the New York Police, but when they were trying to defuse the device at the police firing range in the Bronx, it exploded, killing officer Brian Murray and severely injuring three other policemen.

The tragedy in New York forced the authorities to take the Croatians seriously, and late in the evening of September 10th 1976 the hijacked jet was allowed to take off for Gander in Newfoundland (where 35 passengers were released) and then to Keflavik Air Base in Iceland where it was refuelled again. Another TWA jet (a Boeing 707) which had been despatched to accompany the hijacked 727 was loaded up with leaflets which were to be dropped over Europe. After dropping leaflets over London and Paris demanding Croatian independence, the TWA 727 landed at Charles de Gaulle Airport at 13.00 on September 11th 1976. When told that the French would not allow the aircraft to leave under any circumstances, the hijackers surrendered peacefully to the French police. They were identified as Zvonko Busic, his wife Julienne, Petar Matavick, Franc Pesut and Mark Vlasic. They were immediately flown back to the USA to stand trial. The Busics were sentenced to life imprisonment, Pesut and Matavick were sentenced to 30 years each, and Vlasic six years.

**TRI-CONTINENTAL CONFERENCE. (January 1966).** Often described as the first "terror summit", the Tri-Continental

Conference was staged in Havana, Cuba, to formulate a "global strategy to counteract the strategy of American imperialism". Regarded by many experts as a turning point in the history of international terrorism, the conference was attended by more than 500 delegates from all over Latin America, Africa and Western Europe. Shortly after the first guerrilla training camps were set up in Cuba in which many European and Latin American terrorists were trained (including the notorious ILLICH RAMIREZ SANCHEZ also known as "Carlos the Jackal").

**TUPAMAROS.** See MOVIMIENTO DE LIBERACION NACIONAL (MLN).

**TURK HALK KURTULUS ORDUSU (THKO.).** (Turkish People's Liberation Army). Left-wing Turkish group which emerged in the late 1960s under the leadership of one Deniz Gezmis, who was executed in 1971 for his part in the kidnapping of four American servicemen and attacks on American military bases in Turkey. The THKO resurfaced in 1975 and began attacking police stations, banks, right-wing newspapers, and the offices of Turkey's conservative poltical parties. The THKO played a large part in the political violence which destabilised Turkish society in the late 1970s and which forced the military to take over the country in 1980 to restore order. Like left-wing European groups, THKO activists were overwhelmingly young, middle-class intellectuals from the cities of Istanbul, Ankara and Izmir. Some historians claim that the THKO were supported by Soviet and East European intelligence agencies using the PALESTINE LIBERATION ORGANISATION (PLO) as a conduit for arms and cash.

**TURKISH EMBASSY ATTACK, LISBON, PORTUGAL. (July 27th 1983).** A violent attack on the Turkish Embassy in Portugal by a group of Armenian terrorists from the Revolutionary Armenian Army (RAA) in which five terrorists, a Portuguese policeman and the wife of the Turkish chargé d'affaires were killed. Most of the fatalities occurred when explosives the terrorists had planted exploded prematurely. The attack on the Turkish Embassy in Portugal was one of a series of raids on Turkish institutions by Armenian extremists seeking to set up an independent Armenian state and revenge the Armenian massacres of 1915.

Located in a quiet Lisbon suburb, the Turkish Embassy was attacked by a group of five armed Armenians at 11.30 on July 27th 1983. After wounding a Portuguese policeman, one of the terrorists was shot dead by a Turkish security officer. The four other Armenians broke into the Ambassador's residence where they took hostage Cahide Michloglu (42), wife of the Turkish chargé d'affairs, and her son Atasay (17). For almost an hour the Armenians held the Turks hostage in a room in which they had planted a large quantity of plastic explosive. As the Portuguese police were cordoning off the area the charges ignited and when police moved into the wrecked building they found the bodies of the four terrorists and a Portuguese policeman, and the badly injured Cahide Michloglu. She died on her way to hospital. Her son Atasay was injured but escaped.

**TYRIE, ANDY (born 1940).** Commander of the Protestant paramilitary ULSTER DEFENCE ASSOCIATION (UDA) and one-time member of the banned ULSTER VOLUNTEER FORCE (UVF). An astute politician and a good organiser, Tyrie has been in command of the UDA since 1973, and is credited with doing much to drive out the criminal elements which plagued the UDA in the mid-1970s. Although steeped in the Loyalist (Protestant) tradition of Northern Ireland, in recent years Tyrie has championed the idea of an Ulster independent of both the United Kingdom and the Republic of Ireland. In 1981 Tyrie raised a storm of controversy when he warned that unless the PROVISIONAL IRISH REPUBLICAN ARMY (PIRA) were more effectively dealt with, then the UDA might have to cross the border to "terrorise the terrorists".

# U

**ULSTER ARMY COUNCIL (UAC).** A co-ordinating body of Northern Ireland's "Loyalist" para-military groups which was set up at the end of 1973 to help organise Protestant resistance to British government policy. The UAC was instrumental in the Ulster workers' strike of 1974 which brought down the power-sharing Stormont assembly. The UAC consisted of the ULSTER DEFENCE ASSOCIATION (UDA), ULSTER VOLUNTEER FORCE (UVF), Ulster Special Constabulary Association, Loyalist Defence Volunteers, and the RED HAND COMMANDOS. Shortly before the Ulster workers' strike in 1974, the UAC threatened a coup d'état in the province if democracy was not observed in Northern Ireland.

**ULSTER DEFENCE ASSOCIATION (UDA).** The largest and most powerful of the many "Loyalist" (Protestant) para-military groups which have been operating in Northern Ireland since the troubles began. Rooted firmly in the Protestant working class, the UDA probably reached a peak in 1972 when it had an estimated 40,000 members and the power to bring whole areas of Belfast to a halt. Although the UDA leadership has always deplored criminal activity, the organisation's reputation has suffered badly from the jailing of its criminal members. Northern Ireland's Roman Catholics believe that UDA members were behind many of the sectarian killings which disfigured the province in the 1970s.

Like the PROVISIONAL IRISH REPUBLICAN ARMY (PIRA) and the ULSTER VOLUNTEER FORCE (UVF) the UDA raise most of their money in Northern Ireland itself by running (often legitimate) taxi companies, security firms, drinking clubs and slot machines. One of the UDA's problems has been its propensity to attract working-class gangsters more interested in the cash they can extract from the Protestant communities than in any political stance. From time to time the undesirable elements have been "purged" with varying degrees of success. Founded in 1971 as a coalition of local "defence associations" the UDA's first leader was Charles Harding Smith who was tried (and acquitted) in London in 1972 on gun-running charges. Harding Smith was succeeded by the more charistmatic ANDY TYRIE who was heavily involved in the Ulster Workers Council and the strike which brought down the power-sharing Stormont Executive in 1974. A number of prominent UDA men – TOMMY HERRON, Hugh McVeigh, Donald Douglas, Billy McCullough – have been assassinated, either by Republican gunmen or by rival Protestant groups.

In 1974 a UDA delegation travelled to Libya to meet President MUAMMAR QADDAFI (who was reputedly very impressed by the way the Protestant para-military organisations had brought the government of Ulster to a halt). According to UDA leader Glen Barr, the delegation told Qaddafi that the PROVISIONAL IRISH REPUBLICAN ARMY (PIRA) were sectarian killers and not "freedom fighters" and that Qaddafi was "interested in our proposal for an independent Northern Ireland . . .". In the late 1970s the UDA leadership became heavily involved in the idea of setting up an independent Ulster, linked neither to the Republic of Ireland nor to the United Kingdom. The idea was promoted in the USA in February 1979 when a UDA delegation had talks with a number of American politicians. In recent years the UDA has been considerably less active (both politically and on the streets) and membership is far below what it was in the early 1970s.

The UDA's links with Scotland have always been strong, and in June 1979 11 Scottish UDA men were given heavy sentences for "furthering the aims of an illegal organisation" and for illegally acquiring arms and ammunition. The convicted men included James Hamilton, the UDA's "supreme commander" in Scotland who was sentenced to 15 years in jail. In 1981 a UDA man claimed on television that the organisation had 2,000 members in Scotland, plus a chain of "safe houses" and a network of arms caches. The Scottish police, however, said the claims were greatly exaggerated.

**ULSTER DEFENCE REGIMENT (UDR)**. The mainly part-time military force raised in Northern Ireland following the disbanding of the Ulster Special Constabulary (USC) in 1970. Part of the British Army, although restricted to Northern Ireland, the UDR has over 7,000 members, 2,500 of whom are full-time soldiers. There are also 700-800 women UDR members (known as "Greenfinches"). In the early days of the UDR about 18% of their complement were Roman Catholics, a percentage which has dwindled steadily under threats and attacks from the PROVISIONAL IRISH REPUBLICAN ARMY (PIRA) and the IRISH NATIONAL LIBERATION ARMY (INLA).

Most Republicans now regard the UDR as a replacement for the detested "B Specials" of the USC.

**ULSTER FREEDOM FIGHTERS (UFF).** Particularly violent Protestant para-military group responsible for the assassination of a large number of Catholics in Northern Ireland in the 1970s and early 1980s. An offshoot of the ULSTER DEFENCE ASSOCIATION (UDA), the UFF emerged in 1973 and claimed responsibility for bombing attacks on Catholic schools, pubs, churches and clubs. Denounced by the UDA in 1977 for its excessive violence, the UFF claimed the right to "strike back" at Republican targets. At one stage the PROVISIONAL IRISH REPUBLICAN ARMY (PIRA) claimed that the UFF was, in fact, an undercover death squad of the British Army. The UFF is believed by the police to have been responsible for a number of purely sectarian murders in and around Belfast.

**ULSTER VOLUNTEER FORCE (UVF).** One of the best organised and most dangerous of the illegal Protestant/Loyalist para-military organisations which have flourished in Northern Ireland. Responsible for the death of many Roman Catholics (not all of whom were active Republicans), the UVF was proscribed in 1966 by the liberal Stormont regime of Captain Terence O'Neill. The proscription was lifted in 1974 in a (vain) attempt to get the UVF to confine its energies to the political process. In 1975 the ban on the UVF was re-applied. Like the ULSTER DEFENCE ASSOCIATION (UDA) the UVF has strong links with the Protestant community in the west of Scotland.

The oldest of the Protestant para-military organisations, the UVF was formed in 1912 to counter the growing clamour for Irish independence. Dubbed "Carson's Army", the UVF smuggled German guns into Ulster to fight the Republicans (and the British if necessary). When World War I broke out in 1914 the UVF (many of them armed with German weapons) formed the basis of the 36th (Ulster) Division of the British Army and suffered grievously on the Somme in 1916. The UVF re-emerged as a force to be reckoned with in the late 1960s. Its commander Augustus "Gusty" Spence was sentenced to life imprisonment for the murder of a Catholic barman in Belfast. Spence later rejected violent political nostrums, and since his release from jail has become involved in community and local politics.

At the height of the troubles in 1972 the UVF was claiming a force of around 1,500 men, mainly ex-soldiers, and well-armed with many automatic weapons (some of which were obtained from a raid on a military arsenal in Lurgan, County Armagh, in 1972). In October 1975 the British security forces struck against the UVF, arresting dozens of UVF men including much of the Belfast leadership. In May 1977, 26 of them were given long prison sentences after one of the most expensive trials in Ulster legal history. In 1979 a 60-strong unit of the UVF in Scotland was broken up by Scottish police, and nine ring-leaders sentenced to lengthy prison sentences for the bombing of two pubs in Glasgow, Scotland.

In the 1980s the UVF continued to fall prey to the British security forces, and its leadership was all but destroyed by a long series of trials. In 1983 one of the UVF's "battalion commanders", Joseph Bennet, turned informer in exchange for immunity from prosecution, and his evidence led to the jailing of 14 of the UVF's senior organisers (including "brigadier-general" John Graham). The UVF's power base has always been in the working-class areas of Belfast, where it still maintains an efficient organisation. One of its roles is to provide a welfare service for the families of UVF men jailed by the authorities.

**UMBRELLA MURDER**. See MARKOV, GEORGI.

**UMKONTO WE SIZWE**. (The Spear of the Nation). The military arm of the AFRICAN NATIONAL CONGRESS (ANC) which is now mounting a serious guerrilla/terrorist challenge on the white regime in South Africa. Umkonto's declared aim is to destroy the Afrikaner-dominated apartheid regime by political agitation, sabotage and terrorism. In recent years Umkonto has developed a four-pronged strategy; rural terrorism against white farmers, industrial sabotage, attacks on African policemen and politicians in the black "townships", and urban terrorism in South African cities. In 1985 Umkonto declared that white farmers were "legitimate" targets, since when a number have been killed by landmines in the areas near the borders with Angola and Mozambique.

Umkonto We Sizwe was set up in 1961 by NELSON MANDELA who said at his trial that the military operation was necessary because the white regime had closed off all lawful means of change and protest. Mandela claimed that Umkonto's aim was industrial and commercial sabotage and not terrorism which he thought "would produce an intensity of bitterness and hostility between the various races of this country which is not produced even by war". For the first 15 or so years of its existence Umkonto tried to avoid terrorism and confine itself to a (largely ineffective) campaign of sabotage as devised by Mandela and the other founders.

But in 1976, following the bitter violence in the townships such as Soweto in which hundreds of blacks were killed by the South African Defence Forces (SADF) and police, the "second Umkonto campaign" began. This was carried out from bases in Mozambique by some of the thousands of young Africans who had fled South Africa in 1976 and been trained in terrorist camps in Libya, Angola and Tanzania. Between 1977 and 1983 Umkonto activists staged more than 200 terrorist incidents, including industrial sabotage, assassinations and attempted assassinations, bombings in city-centres, shooting incidents at police stations and a variety of pamphlet bombings. In 1980 Umkonto pulled off a series of publicity coups when it blew up the huge oil tanks at Sasolburg, infilitrated bombs into South Africa's Koeberg nuclear power-station, and mounted a rocket attack on the Voortrekkerhoogte military academy near Pretoria.

Umkonto gunmen armed with KALASHNIKOV AK-47 assault rifles have attacked police stations in Soweto, Orlando, Soekmekaar and Booysens in Johannesburg. They were also responsible for the SOUTH AFRICAN AIR FORCE HQ BOMBING, PRETORIA, in May 1983, the department of Internal Affairs bombing in Durban in April 1984, and the Amanzimtoti shopping centre bombing in Durban in December 1985 which killed five people, injured more than 60, and brought the terror campaign into the heart of South Africa's most affluent white community.

**UNITED RED ARMY OF JAPAN (URAJ).** Also known as the Japanese Red Army (JRA). Small but fanatical and often brutal left-wing Japanese group active in the early 1970s. The URAJ had extensive contacts with the PALESTINE LIBERATION ORGANISATION (PLO) and a number of West European terrorist groups. The URAJ were responsible for the LOD AIRPORT MASSACRE in May 1972. The URAJ grew out of the Japanese student unrest of the 1960s and its first significant act of terrorism was the hijacking, armed with Samurai swords and ritual daggers, in March 1970 of a Japanese aircraft. URAJ ideology was an odd mélange of Marxism and traditional Japanese militarism which occasionally manifested itself in extreme cruelty. In February 1972 a URAJ hideout was discovered at Kuruizawa containing 14 badly mangled bodies, some of which had been buried alive. They had been killed by other members of the URAJ for lack of revolutionary zeal. In the course of 1974 URAJ terrorists attacked a Shell oil refinery in Singapore, the Japanese Embassy in Kuwait and the FRENCH EMBASSY, THE HAGUE, HOLLAND.

**USTASHA**. Right-wing Croatian independence movement which formed powerful links with the Fascist regimes in Italy and Hungary and acquired a reputation in the 1920s and 1930s (and in World War II) for extreme ruthlessness. Ustasha were responsible for the assassination of King ALEXANDER I OF YUGOSLAVIA in October 1934 in Marseilles. Ustasha's aim of an independent Croatia (carved out of Yugoslavia) was briefly achieved when the German Nazis invaded the Balkans during World War II. Ustasha leader Ante Pavelic was declared "Fuehrer" of the short-lived Croatian regime. The Ustasha regime in Croatia was so appalling that after the war Pavelic became one of the most wanted war criminals in Europe. The Serbians of Yugoslavia claim that more than 700,000 of their number died under the pro-Nazi Ustasha government. Pavelic and some of the Ustasha leadership fled to Argentina where they maintained a shadowy existence. In recent years Ustasha has been eclipsed by newer Croatian groupings such as the Croatian Revolutionary Brotherhood.

**UZI**. Efficient, Israeli-manufactured 9mm submachine-gun heavily used by Israeli and other security forces, and occasionally by terrorist groups. Designed in the late 1940s by Major Uziel Gal of the Israeli Army as a reliable, cheaply built infantry weapon, the Uzi is just over 25 inches long, weighs 7.7 lb, and can fire 600 rounds per minute. It can be used to shoot single rounds, bursts or fully automatic. The UZI magazine (which can contain 25, 32, or 45 rounds) fits into the pistol grip. Used without the wooden shoulder stock the UZI is short, easy to conceal, and therefore popular with both security forces and terrorists. For many years the UZI has been made under licence in Holland, and sold to many countries around the world. In the past five years Israeli Military Industries (IMI) have produced a longer and heavier single-shot semi-automatic carbine for sale on the world market (mainly in the USA). They have also produced the so-called "Mini Uzi" which has a folding metal stock, and which can be used as a machine pistol or as a compact submachine-gun. With the stock folded the Mini Uzi measures only 14.5 inches.

# V

**VALPREDA, PIETRO**. Italian anarchist wrongly and cynically jailed for the BANCA DEL AGRICULTURA BOMBING in Milan in December 1969. A well-known and vociferous anarchist (and former ballet dancer) Valpreda was one of at least 100 Italian anarchists and left-wingers rounded up by the Italian police after the Milan bomb outrage which killed 16 people. Although the Italian secret service, the Servizio Informazione Difesa (SID) had proof that the bombing was the work of the notorious Italian fascist STEFANO DELLE CHIAIE, the Italian authorities insisted on prosecuting Pietro Valpreda. Valpreda languished in jail for 13 years before the Italian courts admitted their mistake and issued a warrant for the arrest of Delle Chiaie (who had long since fled to South America).

**VERWOERD, HENDRICK (1901-1966)**. The right-wing Prime Minster of the Republic of South Africa who was assassinated in the Chamber of the House of Assembly on September 6th 1966. Verwoerd was stabbed to death by a Parliamentary Messenger, a coloured man called Dimitri Tsafendas, the son of a coloured woman and a Greek engineer. Tsafendas was found to be insane but was incarcerated in a high-security prison until he regained his sanity after which he would be tried for the murder of Verwoerd. Hendrick Verwoerd was one of the architects of South Africa's "apartheid" policies and any hope of change was crushed when he was succeeded by the equally hard-line Balthazar Voster.

Born in Amsterdam, Hendrick Frensch Verwoerd was educated in South Africa and Germany, and held a teaching post in Berlin before returning to Stellensbosch University in 1927. He resigned his professorship when South Africa allowed in Jewish refugees from Nazi Germany, and as editor of the Nationalist newspaper he was bitterly opposed to South Africa's participation in World War II. Verwoerd became Prime Minister in 1958 and survived an earlier assassination attempt in Johannesburg in April 1960, following the SHARPEVILLE MASSACRE.

**VIENNA AIRPORT ATTACK, AUSTRIA. (December 27th 1985)**. Two people were killed and 45 wounded when three Arab terrorists threw grenades and opened fire with KALASHNIKOV AK-47 assault rifles at the El Al ticket desk in the passenger terminal of Vienna's Schwecat Airport. The attack was timed to coincide with a similar assault at ROME AIRPORT in which the casualties were much heavier. In January 1986 the Austrian government warned that if they were convinced that Libya – or any other government – was behind the attack Austria would "autonomously" impose diplomatic and economic sanctions "and maybe other actions".

After the attack on the El Al desk at Schwecat the three terrorists shot their way out of the airport buildings and commandeered a car. But they were pursued by Austrian police and trapped six miles from the airport. In the ensuing gunbattle one of the terrorists was killed by the police, and the other two surrendered. The man who died was named as Mongi Ben Abdollah Saadaoui, and the two who were captured as Abdul Aziz Merzough and Ben Ahmed Chaoval. One of the terrorists, 25-year-old Merzough, later told an American TV reporter that he had been acting on behalf of FATAH, the military arm of the PALESTINE LIBERATION ORGANISATION (PLO), but this was discounted as either a muddled response to the questions or an attempt to discredit the PLO and its leader YASIR ARAFAT. The three men are thought to belong to one of the Palestinian groups operated by ABU NIDAL, a sworn enemy of Arafat and the PLO. Austrian doctors say that the men were under the influence of drugs when they attacked Schwecat Airport.

**VIET CONG**. South Vietnamese government shorthand for "Vietnamese Communist". Also known as the National Liberation Front (NLF). The Communist-led guerrilla/terrorists of South Vietnam who were active between 1956 and 1975. Most of the original Viet Cong were southern members of the VIET MINH who had pushed the French colonial regime out of Vietnam. Although the Viet Cong acquired a fearsome reputation in the West, they generally avoided attacking well-equipped American forces, preferring "softer" targets such as government officials, police and the demoralised Army of the Republic of Vietnam (ARVN). Most serious attacks on the Americans were carried out by units of the North Vietnamese Army (NVA) which regularly infiltrated South Vietnam.

As early as 1960 the South Vietnamese government was claiming that anything from 5,000 to 10,000 Viet Cong guerrillas were operating in South Vietnam. The Viet Cong's strategy of terror was ruthless and the assassination of village headmen the booby-trapping of roads and paddy fields, and the bombing of towns and cities became routine. And while the Viet Cong were unable to topple the American-backed regime their terrorism proved impossible to halt (or even seriously curb). Probably the most effective anti-Viet Cong measure was the "PHOENIX PROGRAMME" devised by the CENTRAL INTELLIGENCE AGENCY (CIA) which was widely condemned for its ruthlessness. The Viet Cong insurgency reached a climax in February 1968 when, together with elements of the North Vietnamese Army (NVA), they mounted the "Tet Offensive" which took the war into the heart of Saigon and into the American Embassy itself. The Vietcong and the NVA lost hundreds of men, but the offensive dominated the world headlines, and did much to create the impression that the Vietnam war was unwinnable.

**VIET MINH**. Viet Nam Doc-Lap Dong-Minh Hoi. (The League for the Independence of Vietnam). Communist-led coalition of Vietnamese nationalist groups which, after 10 years of bitter guerrilla war and terrorism, drove the French colonial regime out of Indo China. Formed in 1941 in Southern China, the Viet Minh began as a Vietnamese nationalist coalition, of which the most effective component was the Communist Party led by Nguyen Ai Quoc (better known as Ho Chi Minh).

Ironically, the Viet Minh first learned their terrorist/guerrilla skills from the American Office of Strategic Services (OSS), the forerunners of the CENTRAL INTELLIGENCE AGENCY (CIA) who parachuted teams into the northern half of Vietnam to train the Viet Minh to fight the Japanese. When the Japanese collapsed in August 1945 the Viet Minh and the nationalists took control of both north and south Vietnam until they were driven out of Saigon at the end of 1945 by the British who reinstalled the French. From 1946 until the French collapsed after the débâcle of Dien Bien Phu in 1954, the Viet Minh fought an unrelenting war against the French colonialists, partly in the countryside, but also in the cities of Hanoi, Saigon and Hué.

**VLAAMSE MILITANTE ORDE (VMO)**. (Flemish Militant Order). Right-wing, neo-Nazi Belgian group which hosts an annual international gathering of para-military neo-Fascist groups at Diksmuide, Belgium. This ceremonial event culminates in a march through the town to lay wreathes on the graves of SS soldiers. VMO members are known to attend para-military "manoeuvres" with West German Fascist groups, and in 1981, VMO leader Bert

Erikson and 106 VMO members were tried in Antwerp on charges of attempting to establish an illegal private army. The VMO men were eventually acquitted on appeal.

**VOLANTE ROSSE**. (Red Volunteers). Italian Communist organisation which was formed as an ant-Nazi "partisan" group during World War II, but which continued its guerrilla/terrorist activities well into 1949 in an attempt to establish a "Soviet Republic of Italy". The Volante Rosse was used by the Italian Communist Party as a kind of Praetorian Guard to keep order in the Communist ranks, and to act as escorts and bodyguards for visiting East European officials (although the party liked to distance itself from Volante Rosse whenever members fell foul of the Italian authorities). The organisation was led by Pietro Secchia, a close friend of the left-wing publisher and terrorist financier GIANGIACOMO FELTRINELLI.

*VORI* **HIJACKING. (February 2nd-3rd 1974)**. One of the few maritime hijackings on record. Three gunmen claiming (falsely) to be from BLACK SEPTEMBER took over the Greek-registered freighter *Vori* in Karachi Harbour, Pakistan, and threatened to blow up the ship and two officers unless the Greek government released two Black September gunmen who had been sentenced to death following the ATHENS AIRPORT ATTACK in August 1973. After hasty negotiations involving Pakistan, Egypt, Syria, Greece and the PALESTINE LIBERATION ORGANISATION (PLO) the Greek government agreed to commute the sentences to life imprisonment, after which the hijackers were allowed to leave Pakistan for Libya.

# W

**WARREN POINT BOMBING, NORTHERN IRELAND. (August 27th 1979).** Bombing attack by the PROVISIONAL IRISH REPUBLICAN ARMY (PIRA) on a motorised column of British paratroopers. Eighteen soldiers died in the blast at Warren Point in County Down near the border with the Irish Republic. Two bombs were used, one which devastated the rear of the convoy, and another which was exploded when the shocked soldiers rushed back to try to help their comrades. The Warren Point bombing was one of the worst incidents in the peace-time history of the British Army. A few hours earlier a PIRA bomb attack had killed Lord MOUNTBATTEN off the coast of County Sligo in the Irish Republic.

**WASHINGTON MONUMENT HOSTAGE CRISIS, WASHINGTON. (December 8th 1982).** Extraordinary incident in which an apparently deranged anti-nuclear protestor named Norman Mayer held eight visitors hostage for eight hours and disrupted much of central Washington by threatening to explode 1,000 lbs of high-explosive packed in a van at the Washington Monument. Mayer parked his van at the entrance to the Washington Monument at 09.20 on December 8th 1982, and threatened to destroy the building unless the USA immediately banned all nuclear weapons. Seven national museums and eight major office buildings around the monument were evacuated and thousands of government employees sent home in the course of the 10-hour siege. Eight visitors were trapped inside the monument, although they were released in the middle of the afternoon. When Mayer tried to move his van at 19.30 he was shot dead by police, who discovered that the van contained no explosives or weapons. Mayer was, in fact, a solitary crank, obsessed with the idea of an imminent "doomsday", who had been cold-shouldered by most of the anti-nuclear groups in the USA. A six-week-long investigation into Mayer's death cleared the police officers involved in the shooting.

**WAZIR, KHALIL.** Also known as Abu Jihad. One of the founders of the guerrilla/terrorist organisation FATAH, the most important component of the PALESTINE LIBERATION ORGANISATION (PLO). Wazir has remained a powerful force in Fatah, and in 1980 was voted "Deputy Commander-in-Chief" and a member of the Fatah Central Committee.

**WEAPONS TECHNOLOGY AND TERRORISM**. The striking power of modern terrorists has been hugely enhanced by the advances in weapons technology, particularly in the production of small, easily-concealed machine pistols many of which are capable of firing from 800 to 1,000 rounds per minute. Many of these weapons, such as the Czech-made "SCORPION" and the Israeli UZI and the American Ingram MAC-10 have found their way into the hands of various European, American and Middle Eastern terrorist groups. Terrorists have also been able to obtain larger weapons such as Soviet-built rocket-propelled grenades (RPG-7s), Soviet surface-to-air missiles (SA-7s) and the enormously powerful American-made M-60 machine-guns, all of which have been used in attacks on security forces, airliners and other civilian targets.

One recent development which is causing considerable anxiety to Western security forces is the advent of hand-guns made largely from plastic which are virtually undetectable by standard airport baggage-screening equipment. Some American congressmen are demanding that international action be taken to proscribe such undetectable hand-guns, or to greatly improve the security screening systems. Western security forces are even more alarmed by the ease with which terrorists can obtain sophisticated explosive materials which can be formed into very thin layers and used to line suitcases. One such suitcase bomb uncovered by a Western security force was virtually undetectable; the case was lined with thin sheets of explosive and the metal detonators were concealed behind the locks making them almost impossible to spot on the x-ray screen. The suitcase bomb was easily smuggled on to a flight from Tel Aviv to London, but the barometrically-primed detonators failed to work.

The use of advanced weapons and explosives by terrorists and the need by security forces to counter them has had a considerable effect on weapons design and manufacture. Industry sources say that the submachine-gun was in the process of being phased out and replaced by assault rifles such as the KALASHNIKOV AK-47 and the American ARMALITE AR-15 until submachine-guns were taken up by terrorist groups. This in turn created a demand for the weapons by military and police units. Now both "sides" make extensive use of small, rapid-fire weapons such as the West

German HECKLER & KOCH MP5, the Czech "Scorpion", or the Israeli Uzi. Following the attacks at ROME and VIENNA airports in December 1985 police patrolling British airports were equipped with Heckler & Koch MP5's (which some security experts described as totally unsuitable for the job).

Many civilian police forces are now equipped with a variety of sophisticated, high-performance weapons (with night-sights, image intensifiers, lasers etc.) for use against terrorists. The West German police are now equipped with the Heckler & Koch HK81 rifle which has been designed for anti-terrorist use in a civilian population, and which can be converted from a sniper's rifle with laser-sights, to a belt-fed machine-gun or a tear-gas grenade launcher. The HK81 is described by one expert writer as "a depressing example of the lengths to which European police forces are being driven by political extremists".

Terrorist activity has also created a big demand for personal bodyguards among the world's political, diplomatic and commercial VIP's, which in turn has created a market for easily concealed but powerful hand-guns. This growing (and lucrative) market has prompted a great deal of research among Western armament companies in pursuit of a small, high-performance weapon which will "stop" an attacker. The Israeli SKYMARSHALLS who ride in most El Al aircraft, carry special low-velocity hand-guns (usually 0.22 calibre Italian Berettas) which will not pass through targets to injure innocent passengers and/or pierce the skin of the aircraft.

**WEATHER UNDERGROUND**. Vociferous left-wing American group which emerged in the late 1960s out of the Students for a Democratic Society (SDS). Dedicated to the "overthrow of US Imperialism" the Weather Underground were led by Bernadine Dohrn and Mark Rudd who announced their strategy in a famous pamphlet entitled *You Don't Need a Weatherman To Know Which Way The Wind Blows*. After the "days of rage" in Chicago when the Weather Underground and many others attacked police, government agents and government buildings, Bernadine Dohrn declared "war" on the American establishment. In July 1970 Dohrn and the other Weather Underground leaders were charged (in their absence) with conspiring to commit bombings, and eventually gave up their clandestine existence in the late 1970s. Whether the Weather Underground actually committed the 17 bombings they claimed in their book *Prairie Fire* (published in 1974) remains a matter of some doubt. They also claimed responsibility for a bombing attack on the US State Department on January 29th

1975 (which caused more than $300,000 worth of damage but no casualties).

**WEGENER, ULRICH (born 1931).** West German police official and commander of the GRENZSCHUTZGRUPPE-9 (GSG-9) anti-terrorist force which was set up following the Bavarian police débâcle during the MUNICH OLYMPICS GAMES ATTACK in October 1972. Wegener led the GSG-9 team which staged the successful hostage rescue operation following the LUFTHANSA HIJACKING TO MOGADISHU AIRPORT, SOMALIA, in October 1977.

Wegener's GSG-9 force, which has been described as "the best anti-terrorist force in the world", owes much to its commanding officer's skill in overcoming bureaucratic resistance to the idea of a specialised police force. Wegener's ingenuity and readiness to accept techniques and equipment devised by other anti-terrorist units such as the British Army's SPECIAL AIR SERVICE (SAS) and the American FEDERAL BUREAU OF INVESTIGATION (FBI) outraged many of his more conservative colleagues. In 1976 Wegener was invited by the Israelis (with whom he had trained) to act as an "observer" on Operation "JONATHAN" the Israeli rescue mission following the AIR FRANCE HIJACKING TO ENTEBBE AIRPORT, UGANDA. Wegener is reported to have suffered a minor wound in the operation.

Despite the success of the GSG-9 officers in storming the Lufthansa jet at Mogadishu airport, the idea of a centrally controlled federal police force is still resented by many of the West German state governments. Wegener is reported to have been on the point of resigning several times because of this hostility, and his enthusiasm for the anti-terrorist methods developed by GSG-9 has jeopardised his career.

**WELCH, RICHARD.** Head of the American CENTRAL INTELLIGENCE AGENCY (CIA) in Greece who was shot dead outside his Athens home on December 23rd 1975 by unknown gunmen. Although a variety of left-wing and right-wing groups claimed responsibility for Welch's murder, none were convincing. Welch had been identified as a CIA agent by an Athens newspaper a few weeks before his murder, a disclosure which almost certainly put his life in danger.

**WILSON, EDWIN PAUL (born 1928).** American intelligence agent, business man and arms dealer who specialised in supplying arms, training, high-grade American explosives and electronics to the Libyan regime of MUAMMAR QADDAFI. A one-time "contract agent" for the American CENTRAL INTELLIGENCE AGENCY (CIA) and the Office of Naval Intelligence (ONI) Wilson's intelligence/criminal career became a source of grave embarrassment to the US government and helped bring about the purge of the CIA by Admiral Stansfield Turner in October 1977. Wilson was lured back to the USA and tried by the US Federal authorities for arms smuggling, conspiracy to murder, and currency dealing and is now serving a 25-year sentence in Federal prison.

Born in Idaho, Wilson studied at the University of Portland, joined the Marine Corps in the early 1950s and then became a "contract agent" of the CIA in 1955. He specialised in setting up and running "proprietary" (i.e. "front") companies for CIA operations. In 1971, after using a CIA company to set up a money-spinning property deal, Wilson was sacked from the agency. Within days he was signed up by Task Force 157 (TF157), a clandestine section of the ONI. Wilson worked for TF157 for five years until 1976 when he was ousted by Admiral Bobby Inman, the newly-appointed head of ONI.

Using his contacts in the intelligence community and his reputation as an intelligence officer, Wilson's company Consultants International (set up as a vehicle for TF157) flourished and made huge profits mainly from the oil-rich Libyan government. Together with another ex-CIA man, Frank Terpil, Wilson forged high-level links with the Libyan regime and supplied them with a wide variety of military and strategic equipment, including large quantities of C-4 explosive. Wilson also supplied American military advisors, instructors and helicopter pilots for the Libyan regime. In one attempt (in 1977) to ingratiate himself with the Libyans, Wilson is reputed to have tried to recruit anti-Castro Cubans to assassinate Umar Muhayshi, one of Quaddafi's opponents. In October 1980 one of Wilson's associates, EUGENE TAFOYA, tried to assassinate Libyan exile FAISAL ZAGALLAI in Colorado.

Edmund Wilson's dangerous career came to an end in June 1982 when he was lured by the US Justice department into the Dominican Republic where the authorities immediately deported him to the USA. Wilson was arrested by the FBI at New York airport, and was later tried in Federal courts in Alexandria, Houston, Washington and New York on a variety of arms and explosives smuggling charges. He was also charged with trying to arrange the assassination of lawyers and witnesses involved in his trials. He is almost certain to spend the rest of his life in jail.

**WINGATE, ORDE. (1903-1944)**. Brilliant and unconventional British Army officer who sympathised with the Jewish cause in 1930s Palestine, and organised the Jewish HAGANAH into night-patrolling, anti-terrorist squads to thwart Arab attacks. Wingate's enthusiasm for the Jewish cause ran counter to the pro-Arab policy of the British Army, but was much appreciated by the hard-pressed Jewish communities. Described by Israeli general Moshe Dayan as "a genius, an innovator, a non-conformist", Wingate eventually became a Major General, formed the British Army jungle-fighting unit known as "The Chindits", and was killed in an aircraft crash in Assam in March 1944. Wingate is still regarded in Israel as a hero and an important figure in the long struggle to establish a Jewish state.

Born in India into a deeply religious family, Wingate proved to be a guerrilla soldier and counter-terrorist tactician of great talent. Deeply impressed by the Jewish settlers in Palestine (where he arrived in 1936) Wingate was given a free hand by General Sir Archibald Wavell to help the Jews. One of Wingate's Haganah subordinates was the young Moshe Dayan who never forgot Wingate's lesson that offence is the best form of defence. Wingate's aggressive night patrols did much to check the activities of Arab raiders. Wingate's passion for Zionism was almost mystical. "I found a whole people who had been looked down upon and made to feel unwanted for centuries," he wrote, "yet they were undefeated and building their country anew. I felt I belonged to such a people."

When World War II broke out Wingate led a successful guerrilla group known as "Gideon's Force" which wrought havoc with the Italian Army and took thousands of prisoners. Wingate then was despatched to the Burma Front where he developed the long-range irregular force known as "The Chindits" which harassed the Japanese supply lines, and rear columns. Wingate died when his aircraft crashed in Assam on March 24th 1944.

**WORLD ANTI-COMMUNIST LEAGUE (WACL)**. Right-wing organisation founded in Taiwan in 1967, and with close links to the Unification Church (known as the "Moonies"). Based in the USA, and run by retired US general John K. Singlaub, the League specialises in raising large sums of money for anti-Communist groups operating round the world, mainly in Latin America, Africa and South-East Asia. In recent years Singlaub and the WACL have found more than $20 million dollars to help CONTRA guerrillas in their battles against the SANDINISTA government of Nicaragua, a contribution which was gratefully acknowledged by the Contra leaders Adolfo Calero and Enrique Bermudez. A WACL conference in Dallas, Texas, in September 1985 was attended by delegates from 74 countries, including Nicaragua, Paraguay, Angola, South Korea and the United States. The conference agreed to support anti-government rebels operating in Angola, Afghanistan, Mozambique, and Indo China. WACL support is thought to have been given to the right-wing death squads which operated in Argentina, Uruguay, El Salvador and Chile.

**"WRATH OF GOD" TEAMS**. Name given to the assassination squads set up by the Israeli MOSSAD following the MUNICH OLYMPICS ATTACK in October 1972. Between October 1972 and November 1974 Mossad WOG teams are believed to have killed at least 12 Arabs (most of them Palestinians) believed by the Israelis to have been involved in the terror campiagn against Israel. But the Mossad strategy backfired in the LILLEHAMMER DEBACLE of July 1973 when a Mossad team shot dead an innocent man. Six members of the Lillehammer "Wrath of God" team were tried and jailed by the Norwegian authorities.

# Y

**YACEF, SAADI.** One of the leaders of the FRONT DE LIBERATION NATIONALE (FLN) during the Algerian war of independence with the French. Yacef ran the FLN terrorist network in Algiers between 1956 and 1957 with instructions to "kill any European between the ages of 18 and 54. But no women, no children, no old people . . . ". At the end of June 1957 Yacef's killer squads roamed Algiers killing 49 Europeans in a few days and triggering a process of terror and counter-terror which lasted until the French left Algeria in 1962. Yacef later co-produced a remarkable semi-documentary film of the period called "The Battle of Algiers" in which he played himself.

The seventh son of an Algiers baker, the 29-year-old Yacef proved a resourceful terrorist leader with an intimate knowledge of the Algiers Casbah (Arab quarter) which packed more than 100,000 people into a few square kilometres. With the help of Arab carpenters, bricklayers and plasterers, Yacef created a labyrinth of hidden passages, secret hiding places and clandestine bomb factories inside the Casbah which the French found almost impossible to penetrate, but which Yacef's 1400 or so activists used with ease. One of Yacef's most notorious terror techniques was to deploy a team of attractive, European-looking girls to plant bombs in cafés and bars in the European part of Algiers.

Yacef's campaign of terror in Algiers was so effective that in January 1957 the French authorities called in the 10th Parachute Division of General JACQUES MASSU, whose right-hand man YVES GODARD supervised an anti-terrorist operation which became known as the BATTLE OF ALGIERS which cost Yacef and his FLN network dear. In August 1957 Yacef was finally hunted down by the French to one of his hiding holes in the Casbah, and was persuaded to surrender by Godard himself. In 1958 Yacef was condemned to death three times by French military tribunals, but was eventually pardoned by General Charles de Gaulle when he became President of France. He was released from prison in 1962.

**YAMADA, YOSHIAKA.** Japanese terrorist and member of the UNITED RED ARMY OF JAPAN (URAJ) arrested at Orly

Airport, Paris, in September 1974 carrying $10,000 worth of forged banknotes. Yamada was on a mission to set up the kidnapping for ransom of Japanese industrialists in Europe. His incarceration in France did not last long; on September 13th 1974 three URAJ gunmen attacked and took over the FRENCH EMBASSY, THE HAGUE, and demanded Yamada's release. After five days of negotiation the French succumbed to the Japanese terrorists' demands, and released Yamada. He was given $300,000, set free, and flown to safety in Syria. The attack on the French Embassy in The Hague and the release of Yamada was contrived by ILLICH RAMIREZ SANCHEZ ("Carlos The Jackal") then operating in Paris.


**YOUSSEF, ABBU**. Real name Mohammed Youssef al-Najjar. High-ranking Palestinian leader and believed by the Israelis to have been intelligence chief of the guerrilla organisation FATAH and one of those responsible for planning the MUNICH OLYMPICS ATTACK in October 1972. Abu Youssef was serving as "Foreign Minister" of the PALESTINE LIBERATION ORGANISATION (PLO) when he was shot dead during the BEIRUT RAID in April 1973 by an assassination squad from the Israeli SAYARET MATKAL. Youssef was killed in his Beirut apartment along with his wife, his bodyguards and an elderly Italian woman.

# Z

**ZAGALLAI, FAISAL.** Libyan exile and anti-Quaddafi activist who was shot and seriously injured on October 14th 1980 in Fort Collins, Colorado, USA. After Libyan radio exulted at the "shooting of the traitor Zagallai" the USA broke off diplomatic relations with the Libyan regime of MUAMMAR QADDAFI. Zagallai's assailant was an American, EUGENE TAFOYA, an ex-soldier hired by EDWIN P. WILSON to carry out the killing on behalf of the Qaddafi regime. Although Tafoya shot the Libyan twice in the head (with a 0.22 Magnum pistol) Zagallai survived, but was blinded in one eye and suffered some brain damage.

**ZIMBABWE NATIONAL LIBERATION ARMY (ZANLA).** The military arm of the Zimbabwe African National Union (ZANU) led by Robert Mugabe who later became President of Zimbabwe. Operating out of bases in Mozambique, ZANLA waged a long and tenacious guerrilla/terrorist campaign against the illegal white-dominated regime of Iain Smith. The bigger and more powerful of the two nationalist armies ZANLA was recruited mainly from the Shona tribe of Zimbabwe, and received considerable support from the African "front-line" states of Mozambique and Tanzania. ZANLA terrorists were reasonably well-equipped with Soviet and Chinese weapons, and their training camps in Mozambique and Tanzania were occasionally raided by Rhodesian forces on cross-border "search and destroy" missions.

ZANLA suffered one particularly ferocious raid by white Rhodesians when one of their camps at Chimoio in Mozambique was struck at 07.30 on November 23rd 1977. More than 1200 Zimbabwean men, women and children were killed when a helicopter-borne assault led by the RHODESIAN SPECIAL AIR SERVICE (RSAS) attacked the camp and its hospital. One white trooper was killed. White reporters claimed that hundreds of children had been killed in the massacre at Chimoio, something the Rhodesian regime denied.

Although ZANLA never mounted an effective military challenge to the Rhodesian regime, ZANU's political appeal was irresistible to most of Zimbabwe's blacks. When the British-supervised elections were held in December 1979 ZANU and its Marxist leader Robert Mugabe emerged the clear winners. Since Zimbabwean independence in April 1980 tensions between the two communities (Shona and Ndebele) have been growing, and there have been a number of armed clashes, and rumours of massacres of Ndebele civilians by Shona soldiers.

**ZIMBABWE PEOPLES REVOLUTIONARY ARMY (ZIPRA).** The military arm of the Zimbabwe African People's Union (ZAPU), the mainly Ndebele party of Joshua Nkomo. Like ZANLA, ZIPRA spent many years waging a hit-and-run terrorist war against the powerful and efficient forces of the Rhodesian regime. Much of the organisation's effort was spent attacking white farmers and intimidating non-combatant blacks who appeared to "sympathise" with the white regime.

**ZUMR, ABBOUD ABDEL-LATIF HASSAN.** Military head of the Muslim fundamentalist cell of conspirators which assassinated ANWAR SADAT, President of Egypt, in Cairo in October 1981. A lieutenant-colonel in Egyptian military intelligence, Zumr went underground a few months before the attack on Sadat. When the assassination was being plotted Zumr argued against it, but was overruled by the other members of the conspiracy. The conspirators believed that when Sadat was killed the Egyptian population would rebel against the pro-Western government and install a much more radical Muslim form of government. Zumr helped organise the only uprising which took place, at the University of Assuit, a stronghold of the MUSLIM BROTHERHOOD. Although the revolt was quickly put down, casualties were heavy and more than 100 people were killed. Zumr was captured on October 8th at Giza, tried and jailed. The four gunmen who assassinated Sadat were executed.

**ZURICH AIRPORT ATTACK, SWITZERLAND. (February 18th 1969).** An armed attack by four Arab terrorists from the Palestine Liberation Army (PLA) on an El Al jetliner about to take off from Zurich airport. In the course of the attack one Israeli trainee pilot was mortally wounded and one of the terrorists was shot dead by an Israeli SKYMARSHALL. The three remaining terrorists and the Israeli were all tried by the Swiss courts. The Israeli was acquitted, and while the three Arabs were given long prison sentences they were released within a few months in exchange for the safety of a Swissair jet. The Zurich incident was an early example of terrorist action against a civil airliner, although the PLA apologised to the Swiss people for violating Swiss neutrality.

The shooting began at 17.32 on February 18th 1969 when El Al Flight 432 to Tel Aviv was taxiing to take off from Zurich airport. Four young Palestinian Arabs – Amena Dahbour, Mohammed Abu El-Helga, Ibrahim Youssef and Abdul Mohsin Hassan – opened fire with Russian-made machine guns on the aircraft. More than 200 shots were fired of which 138 struck the aircraft, fatally injuring a student pilot. The El Al Skymarshall Mordechai Rachamim left the aircraft and sprinted across the tarmac to the perimeter where he shot dead Abdul Mohsin Hassan. The Swiss police later claimed that Rachamim shot Hassan after the Arab had laid down his weapon.

After a month-long trial in Zurich at the end of 1969, the three surviving Arabs (one of whom was a young woman) were given sentences of 12 years in prison while the Israeli security man was discharged. The Swiss court did not accept the police evidence that Rachamim had killed Hassan after he had surrendered. A few months after being jailed the three Arab terrorists were released after a Swissair jet had been hijacked and flown to a desert airfield. One of the Arabs – Mohammed Abu El-Helga – was later to train the three Japanese of the UNITED RED ARMY OF JAPAN (URAJ) who carried out the LOD AIRPORT MASSACRE in May 1972.

# SELECT BIBLIOGRAPHY

Akbar, A.J. INDIA: THE SIEGE WITHIN. Penguin Books, 1985.

Ali, Tariq. 1968 AND AFTER: INSIDE THE REVOLUTION. Blond & Briggs, 1978.

Arendt, Hannah. ON REVOLUTION. Penguin Books, 1985.

Asprey, Robert B. WAR IN THE SHADOWS: THE GUERRILLA IN HISTORY. Doubleday, 1975.

Becker, Jillian. HITLER'S CHILDREN. Panther, 1977.

Beckwith, Charlie. DELTA FORCE. Fontana/Collins, 1983.

Berryman, Phillip. INSIDE CENTRAL AMERICA. Pluto Press, 1985.

Bittman, Ladislav. THE KGB AND SOVIET DISINFORMATION. Pergamon-Brassey's, 1985.

Burton, Anthony. URBAN TERRORISM. Leo Cooper, 1975.

Callinicos, Alex. SOUTHERN AFRICA AFTER ZIMBABWE. Pluto Press, 1981.

Camus, Albert. THE REBEL. Peregrine Books, 1979.

Caute, David. UNDER THE SKIN. THE DEATH OF WHITE RHODESIA. Penguin Books, 1985.

Cleaver, Eldridge. SOUL ON ICE. Panther Books, 1971.

Cleaver, Eldridge. POST PRISON WRITINGS AND SPEECHES. Panther Books, 1971.

Clutterbuck, Richard. LIVING WITH TERRORISM. Faber & Faber, 1975.

Clutterbuck, Richard. GUERRILLAS AND TERRORISTS. Faber & Faber, 1975.

Cobban, Helena. THE PALESTINIAN LIBERATION ORGANISATION. Cambridge University Press, 1985.

Coogan, Tim Pat. THE IRA. Fontana/Collins, 1971.

Cornwell, Rupert. GOD'S BANKER: THE LIFE AND DEATH OF ROBERT CALVI. Counterpoint, 1984.

Crankshaw, Edward. THE SHADOW OF THE WINTER PALACE. Penguin Books, 1985.

Davis, John H. THE KENNEDY CLAN. Sidgwick & Jackson, 1985.

Deacon, Richard. A BIOGRAPHY OF SIR MAURICE OLDFIELD HEAD OF MI6. Futura Publications, 1985.

Deacon, Richard. THE ISRAELI SECRET SERVICE. Sphere Books, 1980.

Dempster, Chris & Tomkins, Dave. FIREPOWER. Corgi, 1978.

Dillon, Martin & Lehane, Denis. POLITICAL MURDER IN NORTHERN IRELAND. Penguin Books, 1973.

Dobson, Christopher. BLACK SEPTEMBER. Robert Hale, 1974.

Dobson, Christopher & Payne, Ronald. THE DICTIONARY OF ESPIONAGE. Harrap, 1984.

Eisenberg, Dan & Landau. THE MOSSAD. Corgi Books, 1979.

Emerson, Gloria. WINNERS AND LOSERS. Penguin Books, 1985.

Fanon, Frantz. THE WRETCHED OF THE EARTH. Pelican Books, 1983.

Flackes, W.D. NORTHERN IRELAND; A POLITICAL DIREC-TORY. Ariel Books, 1983.

Fitzgibbon, Constantine. SECRET INTELLIGENCE IN THE 20TH CENTURY. Panther, 1978.

Forester, Margery. MICHAEL COLLINS. Sphere Books, 1972.

Freemantle, Brian. KGB. Futura Books, 1984.

Geraghty, Tony. WHO DARES WINS. THE STORY OF THE SAS 1950-1982. Fontana/Collins, 1983.

Gilmour, David. LEBANON, THE FRACTURED COUNTRY. Sphere Books, 1984.

Glover, Jonathan. CAUSING DEATH AND SAVING LIVES. Pelican Books, 1984.

Goren, Roberta. THE SOVIET UNION AND TERRORISM. George Allen & Unwin, 1984.

Goulden, Joseph with Raffio, Alexander. THE DEATH MER-CHANT. Sidgwick & Jackson, 1984.

Hacker, F.J. CRUSADERS, CRIMINALS, CRAZIES: TERROR AND TERRORISM IN OUR TIME. W.W. Norton & Co (New York), 1977.

Hanlon, Joseph. APARTHEID'S SECOND FRONT. Penguin Books, 1986.

Hearst, Patricia. EVERY SECRET THING. Arrow Books, 1983.

Heikal, Mohamed. AUTUMN OF FURY. THE ASSASSINATION OF SADAT. Corgi Books, 1984.

Henissart, Paul. WOLVES IN THE CITY. Paladin, 1973.

Hoare, Mike. MERCENARY. Corgi, 1978.

Hobsbawm, E.J. BANDITS. Pelican Books, 1972.

Hooper, John. THE SPANIARDS. Viking, 1986.

Horne, Alistair. A SAVAGE WAR OF PEACE. ALGERIA 1954-1962. Penguin Books, 1985.

Jackson, George. SOLEDAD BROTHER. Penguin Books, 1971.

Jansen, G.H. MILITANT ISLAM, Pan Books, 1981.

Jiwa, Salim. THE DEATH OF AIR INDIA FLIGHT 182. Star Books, 1986.

Jonas, George. VENGEANCE. Pan Books, 1985.

Kitson, Frank. LOW INTENSITY OPERATIONS. Faber & Faber, 1971.

Koch, Peter & Hermann, Kai. ASSAULT AT MOGADISHU. Corgi, 1977.

Ladd, James D. SBS THE INVISIBLE RAIDERS. Fontana/Collins, 1984.

Laqueur, Walter & Rubin, Barry. THE ISRAEL-ARAB READER. Pelican Books, 1984.

Laqueur, Walter. TERRORISM. Abacus/Sphere Books, 1978.

Linklater, Magnus, Hilton, Isobel & Ascherson, Neal. KLAUS BARBIE. Coronet Books, 1985.

Malcolm X. THE AUTOBIOGRAPHY OF MALCOLM X. Penguin Books, 1968.

Malik, Michael Abdul. FROM MICHAEL DEFREITAS TO MICHAEL X. Sphere Books, 1968.

Marighela, Carlos. THE MINIMANUAL OF THE URBAN GUERRILLA. Pulp Press (Vancouver), 1974.

McGuire, Maria. TO TAKE ARMS. A YEAR IN THE PROVISIONAL IRA. Quartet Books, 1973.

Meredith, Martin. THE FIRST DANCE OF FREEDOM. Abacus, 1985.

Mockler, Anthony. THE NEW MERCENARIES. Sidgwick & Jackson, 1985.

Palmer, Alan. DICTIONARY OF TWENTIETH-CENTURY HISTORY. Penguin Books, 1985.

Perlmutter, Amos, Handel, Michael & Bar-Joseph, Uri. TWO MINUTES OVER BAGHDAD. Corgi Books, 1982.

Pimlott, John. GUERRILLA WARFARE. Hamlyn/Bison, 1985.

Plate, Thomas & Darvi, Andrea. SECRET POLICE. Abacus, 1983.

Quarrie, Bruce. THE WORLD'S ELITE FORCES. Octopus Books, 1985.

Randal, Jonathan. THE TRAGEDY OF LEBANON. Chatto & Windus, 1983.

Reed, John. INSURGENT MEXICO. Penguin Books, 1983.

Rodinson, Maxime. ISRAEL AND THE ARABS. Penguin Books, 1982.

Saikal, Amin. THE RISE AND FALL OF THE SHAH. Angus & Robertson Publishers, 1980.

Schiff, Ze'ev & Ya'ari, Ehud. ISRAEL'S LEBANON WAR. Counterpoint, 1986.

Scruton, Roger. A DICTIONARY OF POLITICAL THOUGHT. Pan Books, 1983.

Shears, Richard & Gidley, Isobelle. THE RAINBOW WARRIOR AFFAIR. Counterpoint, 1985.

Sterling, Claire. THE TERROR NETWORK. Holt, Rinehart & Wilson (New York), 1981.

Summers, Anthony. CONSPIRACY. WHO KILLED PRESIDENT KENNEDY? Fontana Paperbacks, 1980.

Sunday Times Insight. RAINBOW WARRIOR. Arrow Books, 1986.

Sunday Times Insight. SIEGE! Hamlyn Paperbacks, 1980.

Suvorov, Viktor. SOVIET MILITARY INTELLIGENCE. Grafton Books, 1986.

Sweetman, Rosita. ON OUR KNEES. Pan Books, 1972.

Taber, Robert. THE WAR OF THE FLEA. Paladin, 1974.

Tinnin, David. HIT TEAM. Futura Publications, 1977.

Tully, Mark & Jacob, Satish. AMRITSAR. MRS GANDHI'S LAST BATTLE. Jonathan Cape, 1986.

Vallieres, Pierre. WHITE NIGGERS OF AMERICA. Monthly Review Press, 1971.

Wardlaw, Grant. POLITICAL TERRORISM. Cambridge University Press, 1985.

Warner, Phillip. THE SAS. Sphere Books, 1983.

Wilkinson, Paul. TERRORISM AND THE LIBERAL STATE. Macmillan, 1977.

Wilkinson, Paul. THE NEW FASCISTS. Pan Books, 1983.

Wilson, Colin & Seaman, Donald. ENCYCLOPAEDIA OF MODERN MURDER. Pan Books, 1986.

Winter, Gordon. INSIDE BOSS: SOUTH AFRICA'S SECRET POLICE. Penguin Books, 1981.

Woods, Donald. BIKO. Penguin Books, 1984.

Wright, Robin. SACRED RAGE: THE WRATH OF MILITANT ISLAM. Andre Deutsch, 1985.

Yergin, Daniel & Hillenbrand, Martin. GLOBAL INSECURITY. Penguin Books, 1983.